The British Army in and the 1948 War

Containment, Withdrawal Evacuation

CW01498439

Alon Kadish

Routledge
Taylor & Francis Group

LONDON AND NEW YORK

First published 2020
by Routledge
2 Park Square, Milton Park, Abingdon, Oxon OX14 4RN

and by Routledge
52 Vanderbilt Avenue, New York, NY 10017

Routledge is an imprint of the Taylor & Francis Group, an informa business

First issued in paperback 2021

British Library Cataloguing-in-Publication Data
A catalogue record for this book is available from the British Library

Library of Congress Cataloging-in-Publication Data
Names: Kadish, Alon, 1950– author.
Title: The British Army in Palestine and the 1948 War :
Containment, Withdrawal and Evacuation / Alon Kadish.
Description: London ; New York, NY : Routledge/Taylor & Francis
Group, 2019. |
Series: Israeli history, politics and society | Includes bibliographical
references and index.
Identifiers: LCCN 2019030480 | ISBN 9781138319981 (hardcover) |
ISBN 9780429453649 (ebook) | ISBN 9780429843334 (adobe pdf) |
ISBN 9780429843327 (epub) | ISBN 9780429843310 (mobi)
Subjects: LCSH: Great Britain. Army—History—20th century. |
Mandates—Palestine—History—20th century. | Palestine—
History—1929–1948. | Great Britain—Foreign relations—Palestine.
| Palestine—Foreign relations—Great Britain.
Classification: LCC DS126.4 .K216 2019 | DDC 956.04/2341—dc23
LC record available at https://lccn.loc.gov/2019030480

ISBN: 978-1-138-31998-1 (hbk)
ISBN: 978-1-03-208607-1 (pbk)
ISBN: 978-0-429-45364-9 (ebk)

Typeset in Times New Roman
by codeMantra

For Tamar

Apple of my eye

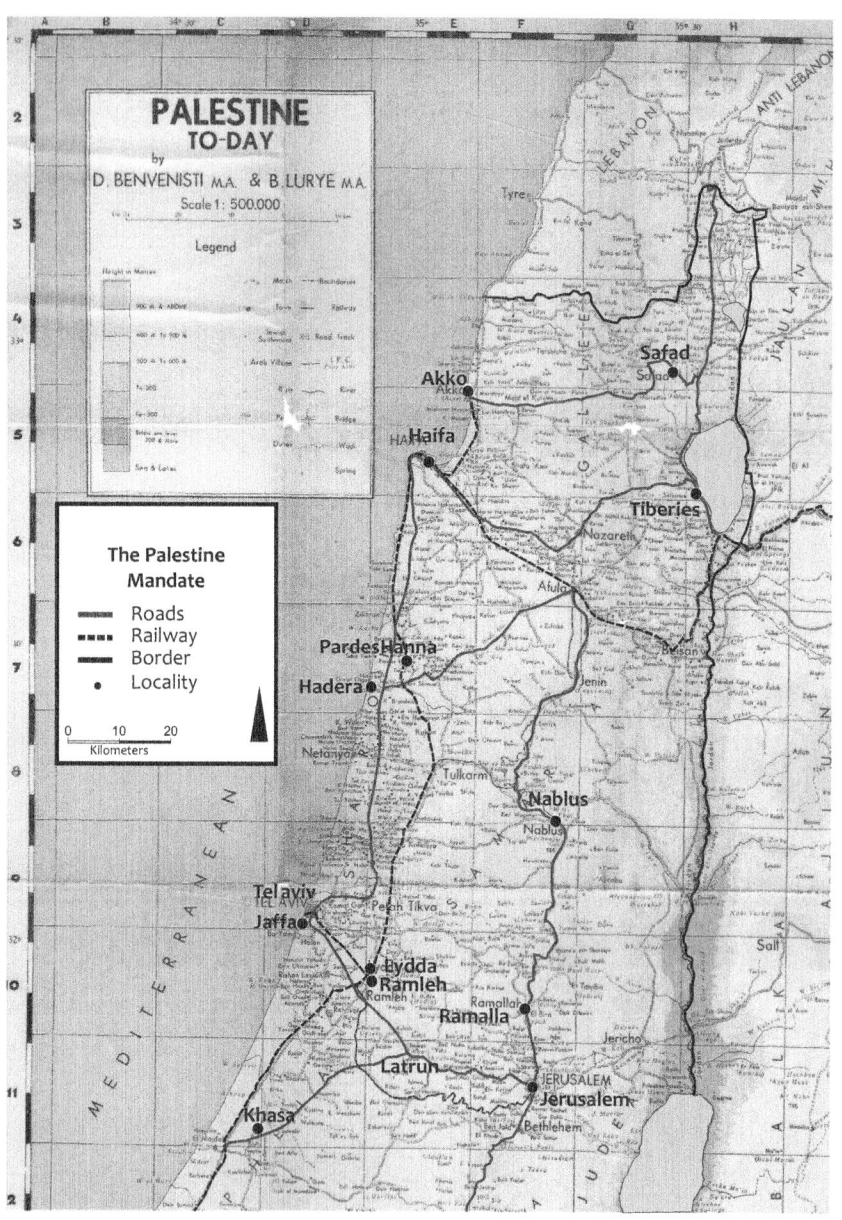

Map 1 The Palestine Mandate.
Source: Benvenisti and B. Lurye.

Contents

Figures

Postcards

Maps

Acknowledgements

As a work of scholarship, which this book purports to be, it is not much of a collective effort. It was written in relative, partly self-inflicted, academic isolation. Most of the factual details are new and there are no specialists on the post Second World War British Army in Palestine. Fortunately, some close friends agreed to serve as sounding boards as to whether the text made any sense to them. They are Nili Daniel, Philip Waller and Avraham Sela, to all of whom I am greatly indebted.

The search for material, spread over many years, was made possible, and indeed enjoyable, by the professional help and courtesy of the staffs of the Imperial War Museum and the National Army Museum as well as the volunteer workers of numerous regimental and corps' associations, custodians of rich traditions and invaluable records. Some of the trips to regimental archives were conducted as part of an effort by the Israeli Army's unit responsible for tracing the remains of soldiers missing in action, to try to uncover new information on cases from 1948. In this, I accompanied my friend Lt.-Col. (res.) Nery Ereli on two trips co-ordinated by the staff of the British military attaché in Israel and the Israeli attaché in London. Their involvement ensured, with rare exceptions, access to a variety of military archives.

In preparing the manuscript for publication, I received vital technical help from many friends, Irit, Nir, Shai and Sari in Yad Itzhak Ben Zvi in Jerusalem, Efrat in the IDF Archive, who helped to secure permission to reproduce some of the archive's photographs and Dafna who edited the maps.

Finally, I decided a book on the subject was both feasible and worthwhile, while on a term's sabbatical, the guest of the Warden, Dame Jessica Rawson, and the Fellows of Merton College, Oxford. Their warm hospitality and generosity contributed greatly to the optimism essential for launching a long-term expedition in uncharted waters. Towards the end of the project, I was awarded the Hecht Prize by the University of Haifa at a time when energy began to flag.

Introduction

The main mission of the British Army in Palestine during the last years of the Second World War and until the end of 1947 was fighting Jewish insurgency, mainly the Irgun Zvai Leumi (IZL) and Lehi (the "Stern Gang") and for a short while the Haganah – the Jewish community's main militia. The Army's role was to assist the civil authorities and primarily the Palestine Police to maintain law and order by means of what were known as Internal Security (IS) duties.[1] The mission changed following the United Nations (UN) General Assembly Resolution 181 of 29th November 1947 to accept its Special Committee on Palestine's (UNSCOP) recommendation that the British Mandate on Palestine be terminated and the country partitioned into two states – Jewish and Arab. The Army was to remain in Palestine until the end of the Mandate and until then maintain, with the Police, law and order in general and the territorial integrity of all communities in particular.

At the time, Britain's armed forces were undergoing an ongoing process of contraction and redeployment, and it was initially assumed that the means employed to subdue the Arab Revolt (1936–1939) and the recent Jewish challenges to British authority would suffice to deal with the anticipated unrest that was bound to follow the partition resolution. And that local outbreaks of Arab violence and Jewish retaliation could be contained allowing the civilian authority to maintain their hold on the country until the official end of the Mandate despite diminishing resources. Instead, the inter-communal fighting only intensified and spread beyond the anticipated flashpoints and the Army soon ran into considerable difficulties in its attempts to fulfil its mission without unduly endangering the troops, and while ensuring a clean and bloodless evacuation.

This book is a study of the British Army's last year in Palestine ending with the final withdrawal of troops on 30th June 1948, a month and a half after the official end of the Mandate on 15th May. It began too many years ago in an effort to glean new facts and gain a different perspective on the 1st stage of the 1948 War, Israel's War of Independence, by searching British military sources. Gradually, two categories of material emerged which had alluded historians of the War – regimental journals[2] and unit files in the National Archive (TNA).

The regimental journals were mainly found in the Imperial War Museum and the National Army Museum (supplemented by regimental archives). Many had been used in the past in producing post-1945 regimental histories. Indeed, some of these were not much more than cut-and-paste jobs of passages from the journals while others, written by more enterprising and professional authors, some with relevant military experience, offer additional material.[3] The journals proved invaluable in providing detailed accounts of units' daily life and details of minor operational activity.

Veterans with experience of low intensity operations, such as IS, are probably aware of the often-decentralized nature of their course, due to varieties of local conditions, circumstances, commanders' temperament, unit characteristics, etc. In such instances, the official hierarchy of the army is only partly evident in its operational demeanour. Given their operational boundaries and discretion, different commanders of different units chose different courses of action in dealing with local challenges. In Palestine, this has often resulted in confusion on the Jewish and Arab sides in trying to discern army policy based on units' behaviour, which, in the instance of Jerusalem was different from one part of the city to the other. This has led to a realization that the history of the British Army in Palestine December 1947–June 1948 could and should be written 'from below', from the battalions' perspective, not simply as a nod to the current fashion of 'voices from the ranks' but as the best means of explaining its record. While battalion life is interesting for its own sake, its importance as a key to operational history should become clearer from Chapter 2 onwards. Additional material of an eclectic nature was found in various regimental archives such as the bound volumes of battalion orders of the Coldstream Guards, the daily newsletter, the *Ocean Shamrock*, of the 1st Battalion the Irish Guards, produced while aboard the R.M.S. *Cameronia* on its voyage to Palestine via Port Said and various memoirs, diaries and manuscripts deposited by veterans.

A unique feature of the journals is their style, and contents – a combination of public school reporting and Boys Own adventures.[4] The journals abound with reports sent from the companies and, typically, the Non Commissioned Officer (NCO) mess on their affairs and exploits (mainly sports) since the latest issue. The style is usually light and humorous and apart from keeping the record, was clearly meant to entertain and uphold moral (with some one-upmanship thrown in). This is one of the reasons for preferring quotations, sometimes extensive, to paraphrases, in as much as the language and style are in themselves primary sources on soldiers' state of mind, used 'to convey their spirit as accurately as possible by letting them speak for themselves', as argued by Robert G.L. Waite in the preface to his work on the German Free Corps after the First World War.[5]

Other reasons are, when discussing unknown aspects and incidents of the 1948 War (Waite again), 'I have done it in simple self-defense. Had I relied on paraphrase, it seems probable that I would not have been believed'.[6] Quotations are also meant to safeguard against my possible misinterpretation of the meaning and the spirit of the text. Finally, in the context of 'history from below', multiple quotations are an obvious device to preserve the plurality of voices and bring out their uniqueness as well as their similarities.[7]

The other category of underused sources of great importance for the operational history side of this work are the battalions' files in the TNA. Historians of the period have, as a matter of course, sought the TNA files with 'Palestine' in their titles and, as a rule, made do with whichever files came up in the catalogue, long since computerized. These mostly cover the formation of general policies, containing official correspondence, intelligence reports, minutes of meetings, memoranda and reports by civil servants and senior commanders. They, however, do not provide sufficient information on events 'on the ground'. Israeli scholars have also relied extensively on the raw intelligence on the Army gathered by the Haganah and deposited in the Haganah and Israel Defence Force (IDF) archives, which is usually fragmentary, biased and inaccurate. But there is in TNA a large number of unit files whose titles, for obvious reasons, are the name of the unit and the period it covers, with no mention of "Palestine". These contain the units' quarterly historical reports signed by the commanding officer (CO) and usually written by a senior staff officer. Appended material can include reports of particular engagements and activity, copies of orders – operational, instructional, etc.

There are also the usual memoirs, mostly chapters in biographies of senior officers based, at best, on letters, diaries and interviews. One exception is a detailed divisional chronology of the 6th Airborne by (then) Major R.D. Wilson, *Cordon and Search*,[8] which, while detailed, is biased and occasionally inaccurate.[9] Memoirs by mid-ranking officers which are more detailed and of greater interest are by Andrew Gibson-Watt and Philip Brutton.[10]

To date, there is no detailed study of the role of the British Army in the fighting in Palestine in the months up to the end of the Mandate and particularly on its impact on the course of events and their outcome. It has been commonly assumed that the course of the 1st phase of the 1948 War had been determined by senior policy-makers as, for instance, on the issue of the responsibility for the creation of the Palestinian Arabs refugee problem which has largely evolved on the question of culpability of the Jewish leadership although the majority of Arab refugees left their homes while the British Mandate was still in place and the British Army still ostensibly in charge of law and order. The change of perspective suggested in this book goes hand-in-hand with the change of choice of primary sources.

The background to this book and leading up to it are a few decades of research, publishing, teaching and supervision of graduate work on the Israeli War of Independence with an attendant acquaintance with the Israeli research on the subject and many of the primary sources. Much remains to be done especially on the Palestinian side using family, local and other Arab archives which are not normally open to Jewish scholars. Presumably future research along such lines will serve to further elaborate and correct the picture offered in this study.

There is also the matter of personal military experience. Many excellent studies in military history have been written by scholars with no military background. The quality of research reflects first and foremost the quality of the researcher. Nevertheless, when it comes to the behaviour of soldiers and their immediate commanders in camp life, in routine policing assignments and in pitched battles, insights derived from personal soldiering experiences can be useful. These should not be magnified out of proportion, nor should they be dismissed. Military units, living and operating as a collective in analogous situations and under comparable conditions often act in similar ways.

Having had similar experiences helps in detecting and describing patterns of military behaviour, for instance, the gathering instinct of "nomadic" units which is at best alluded to in passing, but effects such units' logistical train until forced to abandon it, where upon they start supplementing their equipment over again. The same may be said of the large variety of aids to units' moral recorded herein, such as the incredible variety and intensity of sporting activities including various unusual competitions, "carnivals", pets, initiated adventures, and traditions., which the uninitiated might overlook or dismiss as trivial. The richness of detail is not merely for the sake of the readers' (and author's) amusement. It is an integral part of the soldier's life and a characteristic aspect of his profession.

Notes

1 On the period, see Bruce Hoffman, *Anonymous Soldiers: The Struggle for Israel, 1917–1947* (New York: Alfred A. Knopf, 2015) and [Hebrew] Yigal Eyal, *From Intifada to Revolt* (n.p: Efi Meltzer, 2007).

2 On the origins of the journals, see David French, *Military Identifies: The Regimental System, the British Army, & the British People c.1870–2000* (Oxford: Oxford University Press, 2005, 2008), 81–82.

3 For instance, Hector Bolitho, *The Galloping Third the Story of the 3rd The King's Own Hussars* (London: John Murray, 1963), or Robin Neillands, *By Sea and Land: The Story of the Royal Marine Commandos* [1987] (Barnsley, S. Yorkshire: Pen and Sword Military Classics, 2004).

4 An example of a Boys Own book set in the Middle East, shortly after the 1948 War is Douglas V. Duff, *East of Suez* (London: Herbert Jenkins, 1950), in 'the newest most romantic borderland in the world – where the new State of Israel marches with the Arab Kingdoms' (from the dust jacket). Duff had been an early recruit to the Palestine Police, having previously served with the Black and Tans.

5 Robert G.L. Waite, *Vanguard of Nazism: The Free Corps Movement in Postwar Germany 1918–1923* [1952] (New York: W.W. Norton, 1969).

6 Ibid.

7 The only example I am aware of, of an attempt to describe the life of a British Army battalion in similar operations, is Alan Judd's suspense novel *Breed of Heroes* [1981] (London: Simon & Schuster U.K., 2011), set in Belfast.

8 R.D. Wilson, *Cordon and Search: With 6th Airborne Division in Palestine* (Aldershot: Gale & Polden, 1949).

9 For clearer statements of Wilson's anti-Jewish bias, see his letters from the period in *Tempting the Fates: A Memoir of Service in Second World War, Palestine, Korea, Kenya and Aden* (Barnsley, S. Yorkshire. Pen and Sword, 2006).

10 Andrew Gibson-Watt, *An Undistinguished Life* (Sussex: The Book Guild, 1990); Philip Brutton, *A Captain's Mandate Palestine 1946–1948* (London: Leo Cooper, 1996).

1   Soldiering in Palestine 1947–1948

Arrival

In January 1947, the 1st battalion of the Irish Guards ended its tour of public duties in London and left for Pirbright prior to its departure to Palestine.[1] Following 'a fairly lengthy spell of embarkation leave', and having shed some 200 men to bring it down to the required strength of 815 men,[2] the battalion embarked on the evening of 26th February at Farnborough on two trains arriving in Glasgow around lunchtime the following day. According to the battalion's news sheet,

> It was with considerable anticipation that the Bn left Pirbright. The steely conditions of an unusually severe British winter made the prospect of Palestine, with the saving qualities of warmth and sunshine, more alluring than it would otherwise have been. ... Pirbright, frozen and without fuel, Pirbright of ice-bound baths and solid shaving water, had no power to hold us. So we left in good heart.[3]

The battalion boarded the H.M. Transport *Cameronia*, originally of the Anchor Line. Requisitioned as a transport ship in 1940, it had carried throughout the war and after some 4,000 troops.[4] After a send-off dinner and accompanied by the regimental band, the *Cameronia* weighed anchor in the early hours of 28th February, the same date and the same port from which the battalion had left with the 1st Division in 1943 for North Africa and the battle of Tunisia. 'Later on in the voyage, as we steamed along the North Africa coast, many were to recollect their experiencies [sic] and the memories of the campaign'.[5]

All told, the *Cameronia* carried some 1,800 passengers including families of servicemen bound for India, the ship's final destination, troops' reinforcements and soldiers returning from leave. Initial fears of seasickness proved exaggerated and soon the battalion settled down to the pleasures of a leisurely cruise in the sunny Mediterranean.[6]

> After Boat Stations in the morning, we were free to laze away the hours of daylight, or dispose ourselves, as we wished. The Ships' activity or

inactivity was centered round the deck tennis court, where some slumbered incognito behind enormous sun glasses, and others, elegant in white flannels, played their sets. Except for the prevailing khaki on the promenade decks, and our rather crowded quarters, the voyage bore the aspect of any pleasure cruise before the war; and it was no less lazy or pleasant.

At night there were cinema shows for everyone, and the traditional Tombola [raffle] patter could be heard through wide open ports and windows. Every day, too, the Pipes and Drums played in the afternoon, on the after part of the promenade deck.[7]

Entertainment of some form or another was provided to all ranks, and on the whole the impression recorded by the battalion newspaper was of a relaxed, organized holiday atmosphere.

On the Poop Deck, deck tennis is in full swing, and passengers of the fair sex are to be seen in contest with senior representatives of the Church and the Army. Further aft we are confronted with the agreeable spectacle of the Regimental Sergeant Major and other Warrant Officers trying their skill at that deadly game of deck quoits, attended by an admiring group of small children.[8]

On the lower promenade deck, 'the time honoured game of Housey-Housey' could be found in progress, 'in an atmosphere of tense expectation and dense tobacco smoke. Outside those who prefer the peace of a Mediterranean cruise, bask in the sun in perfect containment'.[9]

The voyage served to strengthen the battalion's cohesion. At the time, the 1st Irish Guards consisted of a mixture of veterans and fresh conscripts as well as reinforcements from the disbanded 3rd battalion and the soon-to-be suspended 2nd battalion.

We have found that life in a ship is impossible without a willing contribution from everybody to the good of the whole. The communal life of the troop-deck, with the crowded floor space and its sultry atmosphere demand a great deal of give and take from each one of us, and it is in such circumstances that the spirit of companionship and co-operation is fostered. The freedom to laze on the deck when the day's task is done has given us additional chances to get to know each other, and knowledge breeds reliance. The voyage is to be welcomed if only for the confidence and understanding that has built up between all ranks, and which will stand us in good stead when we embark on our job in Palestine.[10]

The battalion's voyage daily newsletter, en route, *The Ocean Shamrock*, produced by the Orderly Room staff, made sure to remind its readers of the dire conditions they had left behind: 'Freezing weather continues. North and South are cut off by road, many villages isolated completely, supplies of fuel are difficult, many miners can't get to their work'.[11] In Britain, 'cold and discomfort loom large, and affection proportionately diminishes'. At the same time, it did not ignore the situation in Palestine where Jewish underground groups were waging a deadly and vicious campaign against the British authorities: the newsletter reported the bombing of the Goldsmith Officers' Club in Jerusalem which resulted in twelve dead. But these brief items seem to have had no effect on moral and its commanders were confident that the battalion would surely prevail as it had during the war, in dealing with what seemed a far lesser challenge.

> The same qualities are expected of us now, as when we fought to preserve our livelihoods, the same devotion to the problem on hand, the same conduct. The War may be over, Britain may no longer depend for existence on us and others like us. But it is a principle, that all things must be done well. There is a problem, less urgent, less exciting, less exacting but none the less a problem. We should lend to its solution, as in more urgent times, our unfailing energies.[12]

An indication of what the battalion expected to encounter in Palestine may be seen in *the Ocean Shamrock*'s column 'Easy Arabic' which was jokingly introduced as likely to prove "a popular feature with those far sighted men, who would wish to be on intimate terms with those dusky women, famous for their exotic beauty".[13] Halfway through the voyage, the newsletter noted: 'Yesterday we found an impromptu class, in what we supposed to be Arabic, taking place in the officers lounge. We sincerely hope that the same interest is exhibited daily below the decks'.[14] Apart from standard phrases, questions, numbers, etc., lesson seven included the exclamations "Shut up you rascal!" and the ever useful and relatively mild "May God curse your father!" (yenal abuk).[15]

The voyage ended with an open-deck concert introducing available talent with some help from other units, the ship's company, and a children's party. The main star proved to be Sergeant Gillespie of No 2 Company 'who amongst his other qualities, appears to be the only English man in a company of Irishmen, Scotsmen, and Welshmen'. Gillespie doubled as 'Compere, conductor and comedian'. Choirs of the Irish Guards and the South Wales Borderers sang, soldiers of the Argyll and Sutherland Highlanders performed 'a sword dance and Highland Fling', reciprocated with an Irish jig by the Pipe Major and a Guardsman. Members of the ship's company 'produced some amusing skits and an admirable imitation of a saxophone'. The entertainment concluded with 'a hilarious song about King Cole and the boys of the 1st I.G. which received prolonged applause'.[16] Although the ship was officially dry, 'those of us who had bottles retired either to our cabins, or up to the boat deck to drink, and talk, and gaze, and chase away the stars'.[17]

The *Cameronia* docked in Port Said on the evening of 9th March and the 1st Irish Guards began to disembark the next morning, proceeding to

Qassassin some forty miles away. The trip which lasted four hours served as an introduction to the soldiers' Egypt.

> On the way we stopped at innumerable small stations along the line, and each time the train arrived at the platform our coaches were inundated by a wave of vendors of every kind, selling knives and watches, oranges, eggs, coshes, the inevitable bogus Turkish Delight and dried dates. Often the train started with a dozen of them still aboard. These were pushed off by irate Company Quartermaster Sergeants, as the train gathered speed. Several hung on until it reached its maximum [speed] of 25 m.p.h. before they could be dislodged, with hoots of triumph.[18]

On the 13th of March, the battalion left Egypt by train for Palestine. It arrived at its designated camp Atlit, south of Haifa, late in the evening of the next day having had to switch to lorries in Lydda where the line had recently been blown.[19]

Haifa was the other main gateway to Palestine for British troops travelling by sea. The 42nd Commando arrived in Haifa in April 1948 in order to cover the army's withdrawal. The troops first caught sight of the Palestine coast in evening light.

> There was something clean and refreshing in the sight of the crowd of white houses, set in a climb from the waterside town up the broad flank of Mount Carmel: and in the line of the hill top, pointed by the Carmelite nunnery and monastery. This was a welcome landfall indeed, because it was so entirely the end of our voyage, of the time waiting; and the beginning of whatever we had come to do.[20]

Attitudes and perceptions

'What does the average English boy know of Jews? As Jews, nothing', wrote Ronald Storrs in his *Orientations*.[21] 'My wife', he added, 'had never met a Jew until she reached Jerusalem after our marriage in 1923'.[22]

> Being neither Jew … nor Arab, but English, I am not wholly for either, but for both. Two hours of Arab grievances drive me into the Synagogue, while after an intense course of Zionist propaganda I am prepared to embrace Islam.[23]

Having, in his view, done all he could to serve the best interests of both communities in Palestine, Storrs' memoirs reveal a sense of exasperation with both sides and their persistent practice of 'stupid provocations and disgusting retaliations'. There were members of the British administration who, in their frustration, 'would cry, with Mercutio, "A plague on both your houses!"'.[24]

By many accounts, most British soldiers who were stationed in Palestine arrived largely ignorant of the complexities of the Arab-Jewish conflict. Following the Second World War, many were vaguely sympathetic of the Jews.[25] But direct contact with the Jewish community and the tactics of its struggle against the Mandate government and the White Paper policy often changed that. According to Peter Boucher Cavendish of the 3rd King's Own Hussars and, towards the end of the Mandate (3 January 1948), General Hugh Stockwell's ADC,

> It took about six weeks from arrival to change the British Army's attitude from pro-Jew, in sympathy with what they had suffered under the Germans, to very much anti. They were devious, arrogant people with no sense of humour. The Arabs were also devious, but were courteous and had an immense sense of humour.[26]

Likewise, an article in *The Tank*, published in January 1947, argued that soldiers' antipathy towards the local Jews had been formed in Palestine, by encounters with militant Zionism.

> Until he comes to Palestine, the average Englishman has never met a Jew. Or, if he has, he looks on him just as another sort of "Britisher," but not as a member of a separate race with a different language, a different way of life, and different ideals. In Palestine he finds Jews as a definite homogenous nation. A nation, moreover, which has been responsible for the death of many of his comrades; a nation which he deemed to be responsible for his being stationed in the country, and for the uncomfortable conditions in which he lives; and a nation whose members have, in his opinion, but one objective, and that is to fleece him as much as they possibly can.
>
> Small wonder, therefore, that the British soldier does not like the Jews. ... it is natural and inevitable under the circumstances.[27]

British soldiers typically expressed dismay at the Jewish disregard of the norms of fair play. General Richard 'Windy' Gale, who commanded the 1st Infantry Division in Palestine 1946–1947, wrote:

> I was not a Jew and never a Zionist. I was, however, impressed by two facts. The Jews were in Palestine and they were there under our mandate. Likes and dislikes must not blur judgement; but this was not always easy as it sounds, for the acts of terrorists were such that feeling was bound to run high.[28]

General Horatius 'Nap' Murray, who succeeded Gale in command of the 1st Division (1947–1948), recalled:

> Most of us arrived in Palestine with considerable sympathy for the Jews and their ambitions, after the terrible experiences so many of them had had during the War at the hands of Hitler. Nevertheless it became

increasingly apparent that, in their desperation, they were utterly ruth-less in the matter of creating the Jewish state and their methods ap-proximated to those from which they had themselves fled. They had no mercy on the Arabs and brushed aside their claims to equal rights contemptuously. From the end of the War onwards, whether we were holding the Mandate, or in the process of giving it up, their policy was based on the use of terrorism as a political weapon.[29]

In his memoirs, Murray reveals a relatively commonplace superficial grasp of the situation. Many British soldiers appear to have been unpleasantly surprised by the kind of Jews they encountered in Palestine and their demeanour. Nigel Bromage, who served with the Grenadier Guards in Palestine before transfer-ring to the Arab Legion with whom he fought against the Israeli army in 1948, recalled that he had first met the "new Jew" in the course of searches for illegal immigrants who had landed in Nahariya, north of Haifa. 'I was astonished by the Israeli [i.e. Jewish] settlers. The only Israelis I had met, before then, where distinguished by their gentle manners and religious bearing'.[30] Years earlier, Storrs noted that the 'British officer, work as he might, felt himself surrounded, almost opposed, by an atmosphere always critical, frequently hostile, some-times bitterly vindictive and even menacing'.[31] Colin Mitchell, who served in Palestine towards the end of the Mandate, explained that the Jews' 'hatred of us and continued actions of terrorism had made us anti-Jewish – but not, I think, anti-Semitic in the broadest sense'.[32] Upon reflection, however, he modified his views, possibly influenced by his professional appreciation of the Israeli Army and his experience of dealing with insurgents in Yemen.

> With time on my hands to read, I found the Jews fascinating. One of our most intelligent officers, senior to me, was openly pro-Jewish and saw their struggle against us and their future struggle against the Arabs as a splendid example of courage and resolution and the refusal of the human spirit to accept defeat.[33]

A more charitable yet critical view of the behaviour of the Jews was that of Andrew Gibson-Watt of the Guards Brigade, a descendant on his moth-er's side of the Classical Economist David Ricardo (1771–1823) and conse-quently of Sephardic Jewish lineage. Gibson-Watt was neither Jewish nor pro-Zionist. He professed to have 'always had the greatest admiration for the courage and resourcefulness of the Jewish settlers in Palestine, and for the marvellous way in which they developed the country'. In retrospect, he recalled,

> an infinite number of acts of politeness, and indeed kindness, from peo-ple in whose eyes I was probably just another arrogant young British officer who was presumed to prefer old-fashioned subservient Arabs to clean, progressive Jews. But the trouble with them was, and is, that they are totally single-minded, and totally incapable of seeing any point of view other than their own,

whereas the British were forever burdened with their 'upsetting ability to see the justice inherent in each of the opposite points of view'.[34]

Some attempts to explain the situation to the troops that were published in unit journals were likewise fairly superficial and occasionally heavily biased. A case in point was a lengthy article by Brigadier A.J. Knott, published in *The Royal Engineers Journal* in 1947 and again in *The Tank* in its March and April 1948 issues.[35] Knott, who had served during the war in the Sudan and retired in 1946 with the honorary rank of Brigadier,[36] maintained that as a matter of principle 'the only valid right which a people can establish to part of the earth's surface is that of long occupation and ... all other considerations should give way to this one'.[37] Since following the Roman repression of the Jews' Great Revolt in 70 A.D., 'the Jews were dispersed over the face of the earth and ceased to be an effective race',[38] while the Arabs 'had lived in the disputed territory for 12 centuries',[39] it was clear who had the most valid claim to Palestine. Otherwise, the issue was one of fairness, and the Mandate 'was unsound in its terms and unfair to the Arab race'.[40]

Knott's solution was a form of cantonization which in 1947 was quite unrealistic. He envisioned local Jewish and Arab authorities under a 'central authority on which both Arabs and Jews are represented' and a High Commissioner appointed by the United Nations. He did not believe that Palestine was 'strong enough economically, militarily or financially, to be divided into two separate states'. However, the issue at hand was not simply one of fairness to the 'peaceloving but determined Arabs', or to the 'powerful and unscrupulous Jews'. Underneath it all there lay weightier strategic questions.

> To the defeatists who would advocate evacuation of Palestine and leaving the Jews and Arabs to shoot it out on their own, it should be pointed out that when France fell in 1940, we might well have lost the Middle East as well had it not been for the use that could be made of the port of Haifa and the availability of oil there from the fields of Iraq, and that the possession of Palestine and its coast and harbours by an enemy actual or potential, might seriously embarrass any power as dependent as we are on the Suez Canal.

Beyond the grievance caused by Jewish intransigence and ruthlessness, there lay a sense of a failed mission which did not sit well with the self-image of British heroic and selfless sacrifices that resulted in victory over Nazi Germany. Hugh Foot, who had begun his civil service career in the 1930s in Palestine, summed up in his memoirs the sense of guilt resulting from the way the Mandate ended:

> By trying to please both Arabs and Jews we lost respect and friendship of both and eventually earned the contempt of the world by an ignominious withdrawal. We left those who had relied on our promises to fight it among themselves.[41]

Andrew Gibson-Watt thought that the whole region would have fared much better if the British had remained in Palestine. Unlike Knott, he thought (at least in retrospect) that the British government had been too pro-Arab. But like Knott, he believed that a stable and peaceful solution could be found under British rule.

> It seems to us now [1990] that only quite a small shift in the British Government's policy might have produced a pronounced change in Jewish attitudes, and that such a shift would probably not have precipitated an Arab crisis. A really skilled and experienced diplomatist at the Foreign Office most surely have [sic] been able to negotiate some American support in exchange for a relaxation of our unyielding attitudes towards Jewish immigration. Ernest Bevin ... was not such a man.[42]

The fault then lay with government incompetence, a common enough sentiment within the armed forces regarding a wide range and often conflicting critical views of the situation. Bevin, according to Gibson-Watt, had proved unable 'to overcome the ingrained pro-Arab tendencies in the military and Foreign Office establishments'.[43]

While the Jewish community generally assumed the British Army to be predominantly pro-Arab, its actual attitude was often confused. Roy Fullick, the biographer of Shan Hackett, the last commander of the Transjordanian Frontier Force (TJFF), described the effect on young Hackett of reading T.E. Lawrence, *Revolt in the Desert*, 'the first book he read straight through twice'.[44]

> It had never been difficult for the educated Englishman to develop positive feelings of Arabism and, despite the Arab awakening in the post-1945 world and the development with it of an increasing Muslim fundamentalism, it is something that for a long time existed in the English character and consciousness .... There are those who would say that anyone who had endured the English public school system might have found himself sympathetically drawn to the way of life of the desert Arab and the parallels with his schooldays that could be drawn from it.[45]

The romantic image of the noble Arab applied, accordingly, only to the desert Arab or the Bedouin. Hugh Foot had arrived in the summer of 1929 in Palestine straight from Cambridge and the Presidency of the Union, to begin his career with the civil service as a junior officer, in the Jerusalem Secretariat. There followed appointments as a District Administrator in Haifa and, from 1933, Assistant District Commissioner in charge of Samaria, in the centre of the country.[46] The District of Samaria extended from the Arab town of Ramallah, north of Jerusalem to the plain of Jezreel, and from the Jordan River to the sea. 'In my district', he wrote in his memoirs, 'there were three hundred Arab villages and a handful of Jewish settlements in the coastal plain soon to expand and multiply'.[47] According to the 1931 census, the district's population numbered 156,445, mainly rural Arabs.[48] Once a week Foot travelled by car to Jerusalem to prepare for his civil service examination in Arabic, but most of his time was spent touring the villages accompanied by one of his three Arab District Officers and an Agricultural Officer.[49] Foot thought the system was exemplary. After five years' service as an Assistant District Commissioner, 'one got to know the people and work with and for them and learn their language and share their difficulties and disappointments and their aims and hopes ... he becomes wholly devoted to the people of his District'.[50]

Foot left Palestine in 1938, in the midst of the Arab Revolt. In 1939, he was stationed in Amman as an Assistant British Resident in Transjordan, leaving at the end of 1942 to join the Army, serving in the Military Administration of Cyrenaica. Despite having spent his formative years as an imperial administrator responsible for rural and urban Arab communities, when he came to discuss in his memoirs 'Working with Arabs',[51] he described them as 'children of the desert'.

> Deserts have taught them their distinctive qualities, and the purest Arab characteristics are the result of the influence of the remotest desert. ... their endurance and their generosity and their courage and their dignity.
>
> The humblest bedu ... will gladly die for his religion or his tribe and will carry himself in adversity or danger with a dignity which I have seen in no other race.
>
> He will speak to a king as an equal, respect learning and old age, observe to the letter the exacting rules of desert hospitality and hold the honour of himself and his family above all else.[52]

Admittedly, these qualities had been 'blurred and half-forgotten in the towns', but they remained pure in the desert.[53]

In Palestine, the British troops had little contact with the Bedouin and only in particular areas. An article in *The Tank*, January 1947, argued that while the Arabs formed the majority of the population,

> The ordinary British soldier comes little into contact with them, for they are an oriental people with a way of life different from ours. To the soldier the Arab is just a "wog," an "oozlebat," or a "klifty," and is dismissed as such with a little cheerful banter. In any case, the Arabs mostly live in villages, or in towns remote from the Army camps, and relatively few are found in the big towns.[54]

While serving in Transjordan, Foot and his fellow British administrators and Arab Legion officers 'became Arab enthusiasts. We didn't drink or smoke. We carried the string of Arab beads[55] which we would run through our fingers as we talked of an evening'.[56] He often spent four or five hours studying Arabic grammar during the night. 'I have never ceased to rejoice', he wrote, 'that I had the privilege of spending my early years in overseas service with the Arabs'.[57]

> At their best, their manners are superb, their endurance almost super-human, their hospitality spectacular, their courage romantic and their dignity unequalled. One day, if God wills, they will again combine these qualities with an ability to work together and determination to make a new, positive, creative contribution to the world.[58]

In retrospect, Colin Mitchell of the 1st Argyll and Sutherland observed,

> we had absurdly romantic ideas about the Arabs passed on to us by my boyhood hero Lawrence of Arabia and the desert explorers of the nineteenth century and the illusion that because we liked the Arabs we thought that the Arabs liked us.[59]

The Jews, predominantly urban East and Central European, had little chance of competing with such powerful romantic images which in the case of Foot were not affected by the violence of the 1929 riots or the murderous fratricide of the Arab Revolt (1936–1939). The best that could be said of the Jews was that they brought the country into the twentieth century, for example, in designing the coastal town of Netanya as a British Garden City, or in making life in the southern end of the Dead Sea toler-able.[60] But as a people, there was nothing romantic about them; indeed, their own romantic notions of national revival were derived from East European traditions which were alien to the British, and "making the de-sert blossom" could not have appealed much to those enchanted with the wilderness and its nomadic inhabitants. They had not emerged from the purifying desert and their conduct could not be excused by the corrupting influence of modernity.

   The extent to which British soldiers sometimes completely misinterpreted the nature of Jewish "irrational" nationalism and its leadership's single-mindedness can be evinced from a letter by Dare Wilson, then G2 (Operations) in the Headquarters of the 6th Airborne Division on Mt. Carmel south of Haifa town, to his mother, dated 2nd December 1947. Commenting on the escalation of inter-communal violence following the UN decision in favour of partition on 29th November, he wrote:

> The Arabs are taking great umbrage and I don't altogether blame them. It is amusing to note also that there are already signs of the Jews wishing we weren't going after all they are quite ready to forget what they have been saying all along about us clearing out as soon as possible.[61]

The army camps

During the Second World War, Palestine became one of the British Army's main depots in the Middle East. One hundred and thirteen army camps of various sizes were built, mainly (53) in southern Palestine and the northern coast of Sinai, alongside the railroad west to the Canal Zone.[62] Twenty-three camps were built in the centre of the country in the coastal plain and usually adjacent to railway lines forming clusters of transit camps, training centres' equipment depots, stores and workshops. They were situated around the port of Haifa, the central coastal plain near the main concentration of the Jewish population in and around Tel Aviv, and the southern plain including Gaza and, west of the Sinai border, Rafah, El Arish and, leading to El Auja, in central Sinai.[63] The larger clusters provided the troops with a variety of services and amenities including built accommodation. However, most soldiers had to make do with tents. All in all there were some 1,000 military installations in Palestine.[64]

Following the escalation in Jewish attacks on British administration and military personal and installations and in anticipation of a possible need to evacuate Egypt and especially the Canal Zone should the negotiations on a new treaty with Egypt following the World War break down, it was decided to upgrade the infrastructure of the Palestine camps. At the time, Palestine had been the first choice as Britain's strategic base in the Middle East, providing the justification for a major investment in the construction of standard size camps suitable for an infantry brigade and its support arms.[65]

Each camp was

> To be endowed with peace-time scale of amenity buildings, hospitals, messes, institutes, cinemas, churches, etc., and provided with water, electric light and power, waterborne sewerage, etc. … The main buildings were in most cases let out to contract, but smaller buildings, roads and hard standings were constructed by direct engineer labour. The latter consisted of unskilled Arab labour, pioneers from Mauritius and Seychelles, Egyptian artisans, with British supervision.[66]

Work on the camps following the end of the War began at the end of 1945 and was scheduled for completion by the end of 1947. The dependence on local semi-skilled labourers was a constant source of frustration to their British supervisors: 'in most work done in Palestine the detail finish is not good. Really good work seems unattainable in Palestine, where cement plaster is held to be the sovereign remedy for shoddy work'.[67] However, due to political developments, work on the camps was gradually wound down from July 1947, while the Royal Engineers (RE) began to ship out stores, mainly to Kenya. Instead,

> Owing to the danger of looting by Arabs, camps and depots had to be guarded till the last stores had been cleared and the lorries, carrying

the salvaged RE stores to ports, had to move in escorted convoys, otherwise lorries and stores disappeared *en route*. By the end of 1947 as many stores as could be collected had been removed and within hours of their evacuation by British guards each camp was completely gutted by swarms of looters.[68]

Despite the initial preparations for the evacuation, some maintenance work, for example, improvement of surface draining before winter, continued.[69]

The problem of pilfering and looting by civilians went beyond recently evacuated camps and was exacerbated by the steady reduction of the military establishment in Palestine as well as throughout the Empire. According to a report from the Gaza sub-district,

> The steam injector apparatus for cooking and water heating is not really suited to a country where thieving is so prevalent. It has been found necessary to remove all removable parts of the system whenever a unit leaves a camp and to restore them when the next unit arrives, otherwise they are stolen ... the old fashioned drip feeds are more practical in an uncivilized country.[70]

In towns and cities, wherever there were no camps, army units were stationed in civilian buildings, often the police stations known as the Tegart forts built in the early 1940s recommended by Sir Charles Tegart as a means of strengthening internal security.[71] Fifty-two new stations had been built in commanding sites, overlooking important junctions, in the centre of towns and in the countryside. The walled forts included barracks for the garrison and living quarters for government officials and, where appropriate, their families.

Living conditions in the tented camps could vary greatly, according to season, the immediate surroundings and the local state of security. For instance, the proximity of beaches was considered a great advantage, but their enjoyment depended on the security of the troops in that particular region. Consequently, the relative dreariness of a remote camp in the arid south could be seen as a welcome respite from exhausting guard duty and the tension of serving in a hostile urban centre.

The 3rd Coldstream Guards were stationed during the summer of 1947 in Tel Aviv, the largest Jewish city, situated on the coast. Two companies of Guardsmen and the HQ company were stationed in Citrus House (Beit Hadar) near the train station, Tel Aviv's first office building. Two more companies and the support company were in Sarona, originally a German Templar colony, about a mile north of Citrus House, in a compound that included a police station (previously of the Palestine Mobile Police), 'a very pleasant spot, the billets being surrounded by beautiful gardens and trees of all descriptions'.[72] The battalion's operational role was to support the Palestine Police throughout the Tel Aviv area.[73] With the increase in the spring and summer of 1947 of Jewish anti-British activity, Guardsmen were largely confined to barracks, or else allowed to go into town armed and in parties of at least four, constantly expecting 'some outrage to be attempted!'[74] Upon arrival at Citrus House, the Guardsmen were informed by the police 'that we were due to be blown up within forty-eight hours'.[75] Guard duty proved heavy, reaching at one point twenty Non Commissioned Officers (NCOs) and ninety-one Guardsmen nightly.[76] Additionally, two platoons of twenty-four Guardsmen each were on constant alert with another platoon at an hour's notice. Otherwise, the battalion was busy mounting patrols, roadblocks and search parties.[77]

> Men are getting one night in bed between guards, but there are plenty of incidents all the time to keep men alert. Flashing of lamps, suspicious loiterers, pamphlet posting parties, observers, mysterious cars and so on. While visiting sentries one night, Lieut. Kelly was fired on by a man with a rifle at about 50-yards range. He returned the fire and the sniper withdrew. And also, one of the sentries having challenged a Jew on a cycle three times and fired a warning shot, shot him dead.[78]

On the night of 8th March 1947, during three weeks of martial law imposed on Tel Aviv and Jerusalem following an escalation in Jewish violence,[79] both bases of the 3rd and a position between Citrus House and Sarona, manned by an anti-tank platoon, were attacked. A sentry in Sarona was killed and two police constables were wounded.

The fire on Citrus House, from surrounding buildings, opened up at 9 p.m. Alerted by the earlier attack on Sarona, the guard had been reinforced and it immediately returned fire.

> A civilian lorry loaded with Butagas cylinders, parked nearby, was hit and set on fire: it burned for an hour and the noise of the exploding cylinders sounded like mortar fire: jagged pieces of metal flew in all directions and it was fortunate that the Battalion's Colours had been removed from the wall of the officers' Mess, as a large piece of metal came through the wall immediately behind where the Regimental Colour had been hanging only a few minutes before.[80]

Following the attack, a six pounder (57 mm) anti-tank gun was mounted on the roof of Citrus House,[81] but it was never fired from that position.

With the end of martial law, there ensued a short lull in Jewish attacks in Tel Aviv.

> The main street of Tel Aviv was put "in bounds" for the troops by day only, for the first time for ten months. This was a very welcome relaxation from being confined in the British "Ghetto", as our cantonment is called by the local terrorists! The shops are full of wonderful goods, no coupons required, and the general population seem most friendly.[82]

On the whole, the battalion sensed that despite the acts of Jewish violence against British troops, the local Jewish population was friendly.

> There seems no doubt from all reports that the people are genuinely impressed by the bearing, behavior and discipline of the Guardsmen. The daily guard mounting, forty-eight strong, with the Drums in attendance whenever possible, never fails to attract a large admiring crowd.[83]

On 25th April, Sarona camp was attacked once again. This time a post office telephone van carrying a bomb was allowed to enter the compound by the Sergeant of the Guard, overruling a suspicious corporal. The explosion demolished two buildings including the police telephone exchange, killing four members of the Palestine Police.[84] A greater disaster was avoided when the Haganah uncovered an Irgun Zvai Leumi (IZL) tunnel dug from the basement of a neighbouring building in the direction of Citrus House, intended to blow it up. A Haganah unit was sent on the 18th June to block the tunnel with concrete. However, its entrance had been booby-trapped and a member of the Haganah was killed. Apparently a rumour of the tunnel had reached Brigade HQ, but was not passed on to the 3rd, perhaps because it was deemed technically impossible in the sandy soil. A search carried out a day later (19th June) revealed in a neighbouring building a subterranean Haganah workshop (code named "The Shop") producing parts for the Haganah copy of the Sten submachine gun.[85] That may partly explain the Haganah initiative to stop the tunnelling which was bound to draw British attention to nearby buildings. It would seem that at least the troops were unaware of a subsequent Haganah operation, overlooked by a policeman who had been bribed, whereby the workshop was broken into from an adjacent building and weapon parts, explosives and some of the machinery were removed.[86]

On 1st July 1947, the Guards Brigade, including the 3rd Coldstream, moved north to Netanya, about halfway between Tel Aviv and Haifa. A farewell party by the battalion's officers was thrown to 'both military and civilian notabilities and friends, British, Jewish and Arab' in a Ramat Gan (east of Sarona) restaurant. It was secured by a strong military guard and an additional Haganah force, thereby to prevent any attempt to disrupt the party.[87]

The Irish Guards spent their first months in Palestine in Atlit, south of Haifa, where the main attractions were the beach, the proximity of the holy sites in the Galilee and access to Haifa when not out of bounds. On 6th May 1947, the battalion moved south to Khassa camp, north of Gaza, which was to serve as their permanent base as part of the 61st Lorried Infantry Brigade of the 1st Armoured Division. Khassa, certainly compared to Tel Aviv or Atlit, was a dull arid place 'stuck in the middle of a featureless plain … like being in the bogs without the snipe'.[88] The beach was now about five miles away and could be reached only with transport, 'no more upon the sudden impulse can we rush down to bathe before breakfast or go for a moonlight dip'.[89]

In Khassa, as in similar camps, all ranks were under canvas, which in it-self was not too bad provided that some improvements had been made such as concrete floors and electric lights installed in the tents.[90] The prospect of some permanence was in itself a source of comfort.

> The countryside is flat and sandy, but things grow easily and quickly if you take the trouble to cultivate them and ply them with water. The permanent buildings of the camp are very good, i.e. the Officers' and the Sergeants' Messes, the Cookhouses. N.A.A.F.I. etc. They are white and built of concrete. Their only possible disadvantage is that they are ex-actly the same as everyone elses, being of a standard type. ... It is worth while beautifying and cultivating it as much as possible.

Horticulture proved the special passion of the regimental sergeant major (RSM). The

> garden in front of the Orderly Room is a monument to his energy and his capacity to get the maximum work out of his labourers. The two orange trees on either side of the path are the crowning glory. Unfortu-nately they look a little sickly this morning.[91]

The RSM's concern for the camp's appearance caught on. Lt. Whidborne of No. 1 Company began, as soon as he had arrived in camp, to paint

> The railings blue and the barbed wire red![92] In company lines intricate fences have sprung up around fantastic gardens. The officers' lines have begun to acquire an "Acacia Avenue" aspect .... Both the officers' and Ser-geants' Messes are planning a landscape garden, and every afternoon bull-dozers and various Leviathan monsters trundle about in the sand, building up the foundations of what will one day be lawns and Tennis courts.[93]

A couple of months passed,

> The dun brown earth of May had by July been transformed into neat gay gardens, nurtured carefully by Guardsmen, one company vying with another in friendly rivalry to produce the fairest blooms, always in face of swirling dust which scarcely settled on the main road through the camp.[94]

North east of Khassa, and in a similar terrain and climate, the 1st Argyll and Sutherland occupied a camp in Qastina. Their main mission was to secure an Royal Air Force (RAF) station nearby (today the Israel Air Force base Chat-zor), which had been attacked by the IZL in February 1946. The NCO in charge of stores in C Company had planted a garden which became 'the envy of the battalion', with an assistant who was put in charge of keeping 'the ever increas-ing number of dogs from digging up plants and seeds'. 'We are now hoping', reported the company's correspondent to the regimental magazine, 'for a Battalion garden competition, knowing full well that we will sweep all before us'.[95]

This and similar leisure activity of the Irish Guards was largely made possible by a period of relative calm. Routine duties consisted mainly of guarding the camps, which often extended well beyond the battalion's parameter, from 'thieving Arabs'.[96] There was also a roadblock 'which became a monotonous and unfruitful duty, ... directed as much against [Bedouin] smugglers of Hashish as against the [Jewish] kidnappers of British soldiers'.[97]

The Life Guards joined the Irish Guards in Khassa on 25th May 1947. They found the move from the drab scenery of the Canal Zone 'very refreshing'. However, operational duties were felt to be relatively heavy. They included, in addition to guard duty, escorts for the Divisional Commander and small convoys carrying ammunition and cash, manning roadblocks and mounting patrols on the lookout for smugglers, one of which succeeded in intercepting a large haul of drugs.[98]

In addition to some training, the Life Guards passed the time with 'a limited amount of bathing and an occasional trip to Jerusalem', and a film in the dining hall, three nights a week.[99] The battalion started a magazine, formed an archaeological society with members of all ranks as well as a photography club, did some gardening in the tent lines, rode cross-country motorcycling and started a dance band. The Warrant Officers and NCOs' mess activities were reduced to a few social evenings attended by 'friends from neighbouring messes'. They also brought to Khassa a NAAFI (navy, army and air force institutes) shop.[100]

Perceptions of life in camp were partly influenced by a unit's previous posting. The 1st Battalion of the 71st Highland Light Infantry (HLI) found life in Camp 87 near Pardes Chana in the centre of the coastal plain, 'very boring. It is only kept going by our own comedians and plenty of football matches'.[101] The battalion had lately served in Fayid,

> Egypt, the so-called mystic land of the East, [which] is now a lingering memory of swimming pools, cinemas and if your camp was well "sighted" an occasional dance. 'tis true that memories are built up with the sweet things of life, but Palestine, our new station, does not promise any such pleasant recollections.[102]

Another factor was the local level of threat to the soldiers. Camp 87 was surrounded by orange groves, and it was felt that its 'delightful rural surroundings' could had been 'thoroughly enjoyed were it not for "these people",[103] that is, IZL and Lechi who were particularly strong in that area. The mortar platoon reported that although the area was like a 'tropical paradise',

> it's been no picnic since our return to the "Promised Land." It's only now we can see how well off we were back in Egypt. All we can do now is keep smiling and hope for a speedy return to Civvy Street.[104]

But above all else there were always sports to fall back on, internal and regional, summer cricket and winter football. The regimental magazines were full of detailed accounts of matches, mainly football, beginning with company competitions and ending with major matches such as for the 1947 Third Division League Championship Shield, played at Qastina and won by the 1st HLI against the 2nd Lincolnshire Regiment. The HLI Chronicle proudly reported:

> Among those present was the Div. Commander, who presented the Shield after the game. In a short speech he said, "I am glad the H.L.I. won, as they have been a big name in Army football since I became a soldier."[105]

Another match played at the time was against the Life Guards who

> Came to the M.E. with the title of "Champions of Berlin." As they became accustomed to the heat and sand, etc., of Egypt it looked as though they would have soon another title until they met 1st Bn. H.L.I. After a keen game a great goal by [C.S.M.] Niblo brought us victory. It was the only goal, but the fact that we beat these sel[f]styled champions, was very gratifying.[106]

Part of the 8th Royal Tank Regiment (RTR) spent the winter of 1946–1947 in Rafah. Its "A" Squadron had been sent after six weeks of gunnery training to Transjordan to join units of the 1st Division training there. "B" Squadron had been left in Palestine for demonstrations at the Middle East School of Infantry in Acre leaving the HQ Squadron with some of the 'old stalwarts' of "C" Squadron who had been kept as training cadre while the rest of the squadron reinforced the other squadrons so as to bring them up to strength.[107] While HQ and some of C squadrons were left in Rafah on their own,

> Sport has continued to flourish extremely well and so far we have only been defeated once on the football field.
> We were very fortunate in being able to borrow a bulldozer which has greatly improved our soccer pitch. It is still, however, rather soft in places and participants are often seen battling ankle deep in a sea of undulating sand whilst the ball is practically out of sight.
> … Our only defeat has been by the Gaza Sports Club which proved to be a fast, well-trained team which has obviously played together a great while. The game was played at Gaza on a Sunday afternoon and watched by a large gathering of "wog" children who persisted in throwing stones at our goalie whenever the ball came in his direction.
> … Other forms of sport such as volleyball, hockey and rugger practice take place in odd corners of the camp wherever an open piece of ground can be found.

We are looking forward to the day when we are together again and proper Regimental teams in all sports can be formed under favourable conditions.[108]

The continuous demobilization of veteran soldiers and the relative dearth and slow pace of reinforcements, who required additional training, undermined sports teams and often necessitated the contraction of battalions as noted above in the case of the 8th RTR. Similarly, the Life Guards were forced to disband "B" Squadron in order to keep the other two squadrons up to strength,[109] and the 1st Irish Guards in mid-July 1947 temporarily disbanded its No. 4 Company.[110]

The tedium of life in Khassa was temporarily alleviated for the Irish Guards by their move to Jerusalem in late July 1947, which 'was greeted with the delight of all ranks'.[111]

There are no illusions as to the severity of the Jerusalem commitments, but duties had been heavy at Khassa, and the added interest, together with the recreational facilities of a capital city, was held to outweigh any additional loss of sleep.[112]

The return to Khassa on 1st October was likened to 'moving from Wellington Barracks to the Bog'.[113] The battalion had enjoyed its time in Jerusalem. 'We had all worked very hard, but it had been interesting, active and sometimes exciting'.[114] On the 15th of January, the 1st Irish Guards moved to Rosh Pina, north of Lake Hula.

The best quarters were in the large, purpose-built, camps which constituted parts of army "cities". The 3rd Coldstream Guards spent October 1947 in the Sarafand cantonment west of the Arab town of Ramla on the main road to Jaffa and Tel Aviv. 'Everybody lived in huts and enjoyed the amenities available within the cantonment, which included a swimming pool, shopping centre, cinema clubs and so on'.[115] Although the battalion was assigned numerous operational duties including convoy escorts, minesweeping along the main roads and the railways, and roadblocks, for 'almost the first time since being in Palestine the Battalion could enjoy some social life'.[116] The Sergeants' mess 'started off with a dance, but as it was not a great success owing to lack of ladies in the garrison, we resorted to social evenings which were extremely popular'.[117]

Similarly, the King's Own Scottish Borderers described their quarters in the ex-R.A.F. transit camp in Lydda where they relieved the 3rd Grenadier Guards on 30th June 1947, 'as by far the best' since their arrival in the Middle East in 1945.[118] All ranks were accommodated in stone buildings as well as the offices, and the stores. The cookhouse and the dining halls were pronounced good.

The N.A.A.F.I. is very good and the services are dispensed by a female N.A.A.F.I. staff. This in itself proved a nine days wonder on arrival,

since our previous N.A.A.F.I. have always been operated by dark gentlemen, in nightgowns, whose doubtful appearance and cleanliness is
only equalled by their conspicuous lack of honesty and interest.

The NAAFI shops were dependent on local produce as well as on local
labour. During the war, in view of the paucity of shipping in the Mediterranean, the Army's demand for local goods, including processed food
adapted to British taste, transformed the Jewish food industry. One of the
best known and liked local products was the "Gold Star" dark lager which
has remained one of the most popular beer brands in Israel.[119] Its popularity
may be adduced from the comment in the 1st HLI journal: 'The Jocks will
have their football as they will have other things, but nothing more is important than their football, not even their "Gold Star"'.[120] In addition, the
NAAFI operated, where demand was particularly large, its own plants. Its
bakery in Sarafand, for instance, produced about 300,000 loaves, rolls and
cakes weekly.[121] With supplies disrupted by the escalation of violence towards the end of 1947, NAAFI managers were forced to improvise by using
brewer's yeast in the Sarafand bakery.[122]

A good NAAFI could make a considerable difference in camp amenities
especially in isolated rural locations where facilities were at best basic. In
the Rosh Pina camp on the north-south road through the eastern Galilee,
home of No. 3 Company, the Welsh Guards, in 1946,

> The camp was mainly tented, with some basic buildings (such as the
> cookhouse-cum-mess hall) in corrugated iron. There was a small
> N.A.A.F.I. shop run by two young Arab boys. They produced eggs-and
> chips for the soldiers in the evening, and they already stocked some very
> good South African white wines … which we drank in our small [officers']
> mess. Soon, we were to be astonished by the appearance on their shelves
> of Lanson Black Label the first post war champagne to be available.[123]

Early one morning in November 1946, the cookhouse/mess burnt down while
breakfast was being prepared. An immediate crisis was averted when the
NAAFI stepped in and provided tea, bread and eggs for the company. Only
by noon was the camp reached by the Battalion Quartermaster with a mar-
quee, cooking equipment and products, swearing at the cooks, 'and telling
them that if they started any more fires he would have their guts for garters'.[124]

To return to the KOSB in Lydda, while the camp did not have sports
grounds, a makeshift pitch was dug. The battalion ran its own cinema with
films and a projector provided by a private contractor. Also,

> We had a very successful and popular Concert Party, but after a few
> first class performances it was taken over by Divisional Headquarters
> as the basis of a Divisional Concert Party, and has remained in these
> exalted altitudes ever since. However, we are hoping we will see them

in the near future and once again enjoy the excellent and topical gags, music and dancing which made the previous show such a success.[125]

In summary,

> The improved conditions have been greatly appreciated by all and the whole standard is being raised. It is obvious that after being in tents lit up by oil lamps, in conditions closely resembling of the original inhabitants of the country, the sudden move into a decent camp where the electric light works, where there are electric fans and where there is even street lighting, take a bit of living up to and consequently everyone is a little happier than they were before.[126]

The variety and the intensity of non-operational organized activity helped the battalions maintain a semblance of normality and order in an alien, unstable and often lethal environment. Regimental commemorations, ceremonies, parades and etiquette helped to preserve a sense of identity and purpose. Seen out of context, the occasional insistence on regimental customs and formalities may seem ludicrous, but their continuity and survival clearly vindicate their usefulness.

In early 1947, the 1st Division moved from the Galilee to the centre of the country trading places with the 6th Airborne Division. The Guards Brigade HQ was stationed in Kfar Sirkin, east of the Jewish town of Petah Tikva, home to an air-ground, ex-RAF, co-operation squadron of Gunners, equipped with Auster light aeroplanes. The officers of the Guards Brigade joined the Gunners' mess where, to their horror, they discovered a bar.

> This is strictly "not" in Brigade of Guards messes: one sits in a chair and rings for a waiter … After impassioned discussion the Brigadier was apprised of the situation and asked to arbitrate. With his usual good sense he said, "The bar is here and those who want to will use it."[127]

Where bars were allowed, they sometimes became an especially cherished possession, which accompanied a unit on its wanderings. When, in the autumn of 1946, C Squadron of the 4th/7th Royal Dragoon Guards moved a distance of three miles from one camp to another on Mt. Carmel, they took with them the bar, a gift from the Royal Navy. Its removal required 'four strong men and a three-tonner to itself'.[128]

At times conditions proved a match for regimental culture. Major James F. Gresham, CO of the 1st Battalion Welsh Guards, arrived in Palestine, where he had served before, as second-in-command of 3rd Battalion Welsh Guards.

> On arrival … he concluded that in the scattered company messes in the Galilee things were getting a bit too informal. He therefore circulated

an order 'Officers must invariably dress for dinner.' ... motoring around Galilee on a wet and windy winter Saturday night, found his jeep in trouble and put in to No. 2 Co's camp up in Safed. He asked for the officers' mess and encountered dismayed obstruction. On finally gaining entry he found the company officers ... sitting stark naked round a roaring stove, their wet shooting clothes drying on a line above them, eating dinner on their knees. He sat down and had some dinner.[129]

The situation was explained by Colin Mitchell of the 1st Argyll and Sutherland:

The pre-war regular officers who had arrived taught us the mysteries of the Regiment. This was perhaps frustrating to the large number of officers who held temporary commissions from the war and who eagerly awaited release to civilian life. To be awakened at dawn and ordered to the roof of the Syrian Orphanage [in Jerusalem] where we were all instructed in Highland Dancing by the Pipe Major was bad enough for some of them, but to be threatened with seven days extra Orderly Officer for referring to the Regimental Colours as 'those flags' added insult to injury.[130]

Manpower

The types of manpower problems of the 8th RTR or the Life Guards were commonplace throughout the Army. Veterans of the war were demobilized and reinforcements from disbanded units and of fresh recruits (still in keeping with the wartime call-up system)[131] did not always keep pace[132] and in any event required additional training. Those who had served away from the United Kingdom for three years or more were transferred to a home posting (PYTHON) with a period of leave (LIAP, leave in addition to Python). Others were sent on leave at around the eighteen months mark of a three-year service or, for those who chose to sign up, on LILAP, leave in lieu of Python. Veteran NCOs were given commissions and junior officers earmarked for promotion were sent on courses. Consequently, the differences between actual and official establishments were often dramatic and necessitated the temporary suspension of subunits.

A further complication was the conversion of battalions from their wartime designation to traditional Empire policing roles. This was the case of the 2nd Battalion Middlesex Regiment, originally an infantry battalion, which had been converted during the war into a machine gun battalion, and was to return to its original designation. A training directive issued by its commander Lt.-Col. F. Welden on 20th February 1948 explained:

Though this unit started to convert from MG to an Inf Bn at the end of Nov. [1947] and this conversion was supposed to be completed on

15 Dec [19]47, little real progress has yet been made. I realize that this has largely been due to circumstances beyond our control namely:-

a   Shortage of Inf Bn eqpt.
b   Moves of the unit, and of coys on det[achment].
c   The fact that the Bn is over 220 oa [over all] underpoted.[133]
d   Lack of trained inf WT [Weapons Training] instructors.[134]

The reinforcements from the breaking up of units formed during the war and now unnecessary often constituted a welcome addition of seasoned troops. The 1st Argyll and Sutherland absorbed early in 1947 drafts from the 93rd Anti-Tank Regiment RA, formed in 1941 from the remnants of the 6th Argylls after Dunkirk, and from the 8th Argylls. It was noted at times 'that these are the two smartest drafts we have received since we have been in Palestine. The change can be seen in the ... lists of Officers, W.O.s, and N.C.O's'.[135] Other reinforcements from the Infantry Training Centre were some thirty Danish volunteers who enlisted for three years in the British Army and some veteran NCOs who decided that they preferred army life to 'Civvy Street'.[136] In the words of Colin Mitchell, the army 'offered a life of travel, adventure and excitement in the old Colonial Empire'.[137] Nevertheless, the battalion was forced to amalgamate "C" Company with its training wing.

In the summer of 1947, Brigadier J.G. Bedford, then the commanding officer of the army forces in Jerusalem, suggested to the Palestine Broadcasting Service (PBS) a programme of interviews with soldiers 'of famous regiments in Palestine', in an effort to promote better understanding between the armed forces and the civilian population.[138] Private Daniel Clark of the regimental band of the Lincolnshires, a veteran of twenty-two years, stated that given the chance he 'wouldn't mind serving my 22 years over again'. Sergeant Patrick Dowling, a sniper twice wounded in Europe, had signed up for nine years. Whether he extended his service depended on where the battalion was stationed.

Some of the soldiers interviewed had clear plans for their future. Sergeant William Sims, a shop assistant from Chesterfield, was called up in March 1943. He had deferred his release for six months and hoped to go on a vocational course before his discharge. On the other hand, Private Christian Paulson, a Danish volunteer, was more vague about his future. 'Perhaps I go back to farming in Denmark'. 'Perhaps I go with coalminers in England. I do not know'.[139]

Faced with an increase of operational needs, the infantry battalions in Palestine were supposed to be reinforced to the level of 85% of their war establishment.[140] But even so reinforcements never succeeded in closing the gap entirely despite the deterioration in public security following the UN partition resolution on 29th November 1947, and reorganization directives often proved unrealistic.[141] For example, the aforementioned 2nd Middlesex formed its new "A" Company in the beginning of 1948, consisting of one officer, one sergeant, three corporals and eleven other ranks.[142] This at a time when the battalion was gradually assuming sole responsibility for the sub-district of Acre which included the whole western Galilee, in support of the 6th Airborne Division which was in the process of disbandment.

Consequently, unit commanders were constantly forced to review their ability to fulfil their missions. Maj.-General Horatius 'Nap' Murray who commanded the 1st Infantry Division instructed his unit commanders that when

> Trying to carry out, say, three tasks with sufficient men for only two of them. No attempt will be made in such circumstances to employ inadequate forces for all three. It becomes purely a question of balancing the risks which a temporary abandonment of one or other of the tasks will entail. Only in exceptional circumstances will it be possible to provide reinforcements from elsewhere to enable all three tasks to be carried out. ...
>
> Equally, if a situation such as [this] ... is likely to obtain for a prolonged period the best solution may well be to ring the changes between the tasks to be carried out, abandoning one or other in succession.
>
> Only the local commander can properly appreciate the best way to handle this problem. His object must be to make the best possible use of the resources at his disposal.[143]

Murray's instructions entrusted 'lower commanders' with the responsibility for constant evaluation, in the face of changing circumstances, of the adequacy of the means available to fill their tasks and, where found wanting, to change their tasks or their priorities.

In this Murray was acting in accordance with general policy as enunciated by CIGS Chief of Imperial General Staff Field-Marshal Bernard Law Montgomery. Before taking up his position as CIGS (26 June 1946), Montgomery embarked on a tour of the Mediterranean and the Middle East in order to gain impressions of the situation in a region he considered vital to British interests and in view of impending drastic cuts in the size of the armed forces planned by the Labour government.[144] Intent on preventing the armed forces from drifting 'aimlessly without a policy or doctrine', as it had, he believed, after the First World War,[145] Montgomery was determined to set his commanders a clear path, reducing their main problems to their 'simplest forms' and avoiding 'all complications'.[146] Following a visit to Egypt, Montgomery stopped in Palestine. His view was that the Army was responsible to maintain law and order while the politicians worked out a political solution, following which the Army and the Police could expect 'a firm and very clear directive'.[147] However, he also felt strongly that Palestine's High Commissioner Sir Alan Cunningham was 'incapable of the moral and military firmness necessary to restore order in the country'.[148] And order, he maintained, should be restored by means of

> war against the Jews: a war against a fanatical and cunning enemy who would use the weapons of kidnap, murder and sabotage: women would

fight against us as well as men: no one would know who was friend and who was foe.[149]

Before leaving Montgomery addressed a large gathering of officers in Sarafand and reassured them that he 'would insist that the Police and the Army be given a firm and very clear directive', and that he 'would give the troops the fullest support in their difficult job'.[150]

Montgomery went on to Transjordan, Iraq and India, but he appears to have felt uneasy about the relations between the High Commissioner and the commander of the British forces in Palestine, General Evelyn Hugh Barker who had served as divisional and corps commander under him in Europe. So he stopped on the way back in Lydda airport for a short conference with Barker and General Bernard Paget C. in C. Middle East in an attempt to strengthen Barker's resolve to execute Jewish terrorists despite 'a lack of support by Government authorities'.[151]

Montgomery returned to Palestine later in the year on 29th November 1946.[152] To his thinking the main problem had remained unchanged. The High Commissioner Cunningham had ordered the Army to remain on the defensive whereas the Army argued that the only way to deal effectively with lawlessness was to go on the offensive.[153] Even after the British government gave up in February 1947 and decided to refer the Palestine problem to the UN Security Council, Montgomery, on yet another visit to Palestine in June, instructed his commanders that 'there must be no talk of withdrawal yet … and commanders must not look over their shoulders'.[154]

Montgomery totally rejected Cunningham's policy of "appeasement" towards the Jews, which was followed by the decision to withdraw from Palestine while refusing to help implement partition. At the same time, he kept reassuring his commanders that they had his full support, should they conclude that the civilian authorities had adopted an unrealistic policy without providing the means for its implementation. General Murray's instructions then were a reasonable interpretation of CIGS' policy including the avoidance of mounting casualties.[155]

In June 1947, a Chief of Staff Committee calculated the size of the garrison required for Palestine as one infantry division in the north of the country, one armoured brigade in the south, one infantry brigade in the centre and various ancillary units.[156] This would soon prove inadequate for the task of fully maintaining law and order throughout the country up to the end of the Mandate. On the other hand, the Army was to contract to four divisions, which in the case of Palestine would mean the disbandment of the 6th Airborne in the beginning of 1948. Eventually, during the most violent months of inter-communal strife towards the official end of the Mandate (15th May), the Palestine garrison, as estimated by GOC Palestine, Lt.-General C.H.A. Macmillan, numbered about 70,000 British service personnel,[157] compared with a total of 94,235 in the Palestine garrison in 31st May 1947 of whom 82,180 were British servicemen and policemen.[158]

Discipline

In his introduction to the volume on the HLI in the *Famous Regiments Series*, Lt.-General Brian Horrocks quoted a past commander's explanation of the fighting qualities of the regiment's soldiers.

> You must remember, General, that they come from Glasgow and are mainly of both Scots and Irish descent. They are prepared to fight anyone, anywhere and at anytime so when the fighting is legalized, so to speak, as in war, they are in their element and you could not wish for better troops; but in peacetime or in some boring foreign station, they need first class leaders, or you really are in for trouble.[159]

"Trouble" could take the form of criminal enterprises of a type described in the memoirs of Major-General Sir John Nelson of the Grenadier Guards, who in November 1946 arrived in Palestine to take command of the 1st Guards Parachute Battalion, an airborne battalion which was to be transferred to the Guards Brigade. Nelson, who had served as commanding officer of the 3rd Grenadiers in Italy, anticipated disciplinary problems from the paratroopers who 'had enjoyed the freedom of the current liberal type of discipline and did not wish to alter it'.[160] Nelson described the six weeks of the battalion in Sarona in 1946 as 'the nearest thing to permanent nightmare I had ever experienced'.

The battalion had gone for two months without a commanding officer and a regimental sergeant major, and there seemed to be no one in control. The battalion proved highly efficient in cordon-and-search operations.

> But often, when not on duty, small parties would use this expertise to organize their own private cordon and search operation, taking a block of flats in Tel-a-Viv [sic] as a target. Unfortunately, they did not search for weapons but for money; they were not after terrorists but loot.
>
> These enterprising but ill-disciplined groups would on returning to camp, present the sergeant of the guard with a suitable reward in return for a blind eye to their return.[161]

Consequently, following cordon-and-search operations, soldiers were searched by their officers in an attempt to pre-empt civilian charges of theft,[162] although looters were not necessarily disciplined.

> [T]wo parachutists were caught out late by the Military Police in the vicinity of a flat which had been looted a few minutes previously. The following morning I [Nelson] organized an identification parade consisting of the minimum number of eight including the two suspects. The lady who had been robbed was asked to identify the culprits. Just before her arrival at Sarona Camp, twelve 3-ton lorries drove in and no

less than 200 parachutists, sent by the Brigade Headquarters, joined the parade. Of course the poor lady had no chance of recognizing the two burglars among so many men identically dressed.[163]

'No wonder', Nelson concluded, 'the 6th Airborne Division's reputation had sunk to an all-time low,'[164] to be revived briefly before its liquidation with the arrival of General Hugh Stockwell as CO.

Major John Waddy of the 9th Parachute Battalion (and later Director of the SAS) felt that the Jews were largely to blame for intentionally and deliberately provoking the British troops. Concurrently,

> It must be admitted that the Airborne Division perhaps took stronger action than other formations in dealing with incidents or with activities of the Jewish terrorists or 'defence' [the Hebrew meaning of "haganah"] organizations, and I think that is partly due to the rugged manner in which our troops were trained for the more violent actions of airborne warfare. We were called the 'Kalionots' [Kalaniyot], a Jewish word for a poppy [actually anemone]a red flower with a black heart. Our soldiers, in jest of course, reacted sometimes to this by singing the 'Horst Wessel' [anthem of the Nazi Party], with other suitable words.[165]

Not quite the restraint, understanding and good humour which, rather than the use of force, is supposed to have won the day.[166]

More conventional disciplinary matters were dealt with by the offender's CO or, if he so chose, a Field General Court Martial. Andrew Gibson-Watt of the Guards Brigade HQ was in charge of the administration of courts-martial which he pronounced great fun. The Army Act in the form of the Manual of Military Law covered most crimes, although occasionally he had to resort to Section 40, 'the specimen charge' in the Manual given as:

> Private X (is charged with) conduct contrary to good order and military discipline in that he at Blank on the Blank day of Blank 19-, threw down his rifle, saying to Sergeant Y "You may do as you please: I will soldier no more" or words to that effect.[167]

Standard offences were 'men striking Sergeants or going absent for a week',[168] but the army's main headache was pilfering, mainly of weapons and motor vehicles.

With the army spread thin on the ground, violence escalating and with the civil administration disintegrating, a common feature of growing anarchy was the spiralling out of control of theft of British government and military equipment and stores. Theft of military stores and weapons had been endemic in the past and constituted a large part of pre-independence lore of the various Jewish-armed organizations. The "appropriation" ["re-chesh"], especially of small arms, by whatever means was considered a national mission.[169] During the Second World War, there evolved a large network consisting of many Jewish Palestinian volunteers serving in the British Army who stole, bought and smuggled arms into Palestine while the illegal arms trade in Palestine, largely run by Arab merchants, flourished. But now both Arabs and Jews showed themselves prepared, more than in the past, to use force to obtain arms while British troops and government employees became increasingly reluctant to endanger their lives in foiling theft. An early example of an Arab raid on a Police depot in the Arab town of Ramle demonstrates some of the characteristics of a common form of organized theft.

> A British Military officer, a BOR [British Other Rank], and a Palestine Police Inspector who were the only British personnel present were powerless in the face of the large number of raiders. Certain Arab NCOs who were on guard duty at the time of the raid assisted the thieves and are now absent. On seeing that their own people were responsible for the attack a number of Arab sentries made no attempt to resist them. One of the lorries used to remove the arms and ammunition was halted at a road block manned by Coldstream Guards. A quantity of the loot was recovered. One British Officer was wounded and one Arab killed and one wounded in the firing that followed.[170]

The arms remained missing from this raid included 232 rifles, 46 Sten sub-machine guns, magazines and 85,467 rounds of 303 SAA (small arms ammunition). The disappearance of large amounts of small arms was also the result of theft by deserting Arab policemen. A report from HQ East Palestine [Jerusalem] sub-district for the first quarter of 1948 stated that 'all that remains is for sanction to write off 72 rifles, taken by deserters'.[171]

   Jewish attempts partly followed a commonplace pattern of buying from, or bribing, British personnel.

> Sgt. Anderson, 1st Div. Pro. Coy [Provost Company], was on duty on the Lydds Haifa road when he was approached by a civilian contractor whom he later came to know as Mr. G. Packer. The civilian asked the NCO if he would arrange to collect some ammunition from a British Officer and deliver it to a certain address. The sergeant who was to receive L.30 for the service said he would arrange to transport the ammunition, but on his return to camp reported the matter to the Brigade Major. Sgt. Anderton pretended to carry out the request of the civilian and proceeded to a Jewish gift shop in camp 21 where he saw NO 369672 Lieut. Harcourt, 40/42 Coy RASC, who requested the NCO to follow him to his vehicle. They arrived at the armoury in the line of 40/42 Coy, RASC where a fatigue party loaded a number of boxes of ammunition on the RMP vehicle.

Lt. Harcourt was arrested on the spot by the Intelligence Officer of the 4th/7th Dragoon Guards, was tried and sentenced to three years penal servitude.[172]

Andrew Gibson-Watt was mainly occupied during the final weeks of the garrison in Haifa port following the end of the Mandate, dealing with

> Cases concerning officers and N.C.O.s of the Ordnance Corps and other technical corps; who had sought to enrich themselves by selling out of their huge ordnance depots (the evacuation of which was the chief reason for our lingering presence in Haifa) the arms and equipment which the Jews needed so badly, and for which they were prepared to pay high prices. I organized the sending down of a lieutenant-colonel, a captain and several quartermaster-sergeants, but the convictions were a drop in the ocean.[173]

Figures provided by the Royal Military Police for the value of War Department Stores and of cash stolen and recovered show a sharp rise from the end of 1947.[174]

According to the Adjutant General Branch, there was no diminution in crime figures throughout the Middle East Land Forces despite the constant contraction in the size of the army. The most prevalent offences in Palestine were sleeping on post and loss of arms by neglect[175] for which unit commanders tended to hand out relatively harsh punishment, for example, in the North Palestine District [Galilee] during the last months of 1947 and the beginning of 1948, six months detention for sleeping on post and eighteen months detention for losing arms by neglect. In comparison, a common punishment for 'insubordinate language and wilful destruction of public property' was twenty-eight days detention, ninety days detention for 'disobeying a lawful command; neglecting to obey Camp Orders (four charges), no means of identification, improperly wearing Supernumerary Police uniform' and twenty-eight days detention for 'striking a DAPM and out of bounds'.[176]

In discussing the military significance to the Jewish side of pilfering British stores, it is important to differentiate between the national effort and local initiatives. Nationally, the main effort beginning in 1947 and directed by Ben-Gurion to obtain arms was to stockpile military equipment abroad, mainly in Europe and the USA until such time as it would become possible to transfer it to the Jewish armed forces. At the same time, local Jewish units used local contacts to solve their immediate and anticipated needs to an extent that might prove vital locally even if relatively insignificant nationally.[177] For example, the Haganah brigade formed in Haifa took advantage of the proximity of large British stores and contacts with Jewish army employees in purchasing at discount military equipment, some of which was usefully declared scrap.[178] A particularly dramatic example from the Haifa area was the theft of two Cromwell tanks[179] of the 3rd Troop, B Squadron,

4th/7th Dragoon Guards, attached at the time to King's Company of the 1st Battalion Grenadier Guards, assigned the defence of Haifa Airport during the very last days of the Army in Palestine, following the official end of the Mandate.[180] Two servicemen, a mechanic and a tank commander, were initially paid between L. 3,000 and 5,000 each, to drive, with the help of two Haganah members, four tanks to Kibbutz Yagur nearby. There they would be loaded on tank transporters and moved south to the Tel Aviv area, that is, within the new State of Israel. It was assumed that the date, 30th June, being the final date for the evacuation of the last British troops, efforts, to locate the tanks by whatever means, could not last long.

The mechanic, Mike Flanagan, born in Ireland in 1926, had joined the Army at age sixteen. He had served in Normandy, had been present during the liberation of Bergen-Belsen and had served with the allied occupation force in Berlin. By 1948, he had served in Palestine for three years and appears to have had little prospects awaiting him back in Britain. The tank commander, Harry McDonald, a Scot, had a reputation of a troublemaker with a drinking problem. The two were supposed to arrange to be on guard duty at the camp's gate at 01:00 hours and open it for the tanks to be driven out without raising the alarm. The two Israeli designated tank drivers had no experience and the oral instructions they received proved useless. One tank failed to start and its assigned driver escaped on foot. Furthermore, the two British soldiers were not stationed at the gate so that the three remaining tanks smashed their way out. The tank driven by the second Israeli got stuck in sand and was abandoned. The two remaining tanks driven by Flanagan and McDonald made their way as fast as they could to Yagur. When no transporters arrived, the two tanks led by a jeep continued to Tel Aviv where they were hidden for about a week before joining the newly formed armoured 8th Brigade. Both deserters continued to serve in the IDF for the duration of the war. McDonald eventually migrated, to Canada. Flanagan stayed in Israel, converted to Judaism, raised a family and lived for some thirty years in a kibbutz.

Upon discovery of the tanks' disappearance, the Guards' company commander and his CSM tried to chase them. A platoon on carriers surrounded the area and the next morning a RAF Typhoon was dispatched to locate the tanks and destroy them, but to no avail.[181] The tanks constituted an invaluable addition to the fledgling IDF and were its first, and for some time its only medium tanks. The Cromwell features on the badge of the IDF Armoured Corps and is displayed on top of a disused water tower in the Armoured Corps memorial and tank museum in Latrun.

British soldiers and policemen deserted to both sides, some seeking a (remunerative) adventure, some for ideological reasons. Overall figures are not available although some cases are documented, but in any event desertions do not necessarily reflect low troop morale. As a rule, the units' quarterly reports recorded good troop morale, especially when active. R.D. Wilson of the 6th Airborne stated:

In spite of the conditions, morale was … consistently high … such danger as there was, appeared in no way to influence the troops. The reverse was the case, as without this spark of uncertainty, the effects of an otherwise monotonous existence would have become a matter of far greater consequence. Many units recorded that the effect of a forthcoming operation (in which there was usually some slight chance of opposition) had the most beneficial effect on morale.[182]

This, he believed, was especially true of the junior ranks who had missed the war.

Here they found themselves for the first time on active service, and they were determined to acquit themselves well. As a result there was never any shortage of volunteers for any operational duties, and few tasks were more popular than road escorts. By day or night, near or far, men vied with each other for the job, and the farther it took them the more they liked it.[183]

In contrast, the worst assignments were endless and monotonous shifts of sentry duty, its frequency reflecting the chronic shortage in manpower. Consider, for example, the effect of a short spell of operational duty on the 4th RTR, stationed in the Canal Zone, covering the evacuation.

In Apr, prior to the Regiment's departure for PALESTINE, moral was at a rather low ebb. In May, when the Regiment moved to PALESTINE, it rose to a high pitch, and has remained high since the return to SHANDUR [Egypt]. There has, however, been some reaction in the form of numerous applicants to join the Colonial Forces, Police and Glider Pilot Regiment.[184]

Another factor affecting moral was the nature of the threats to the troops particularly in urban areas. According to Major R.R.W. Norman, Head of Military Intelligence in Palestine,

The great difficulty which always confronted the British soldier was that he could seldom recognize his enemy. The person who was about to murder him might appear in the guise of an Arab, a bearded rabbi, a brother in arms or a pretty girl. The soldier is a kindly person and is usually inclined to trust anyone until he has been shot in the back. Furthermore, there was also the language complication. Hebrew is very difficult, and the number of soldiers who understood more than two words of it was infinitesimal. Hebrew was being spoken all round him, but for all the soldier knew, the speakers might be discussing the circumcision ceremony of their newborn son; or, in what manner that particular British sentry should be liquidated.[185]

Understandably discipline occasionally was strained following fatal attacks on British soldiers. In October 1946, a plastic charge set off by a time device, made to fit the soldiers' routine, killed a soldier, fatally wounded a corporal and further wounded a young officer and six other ranks (ORs) of the 1st Argyll and Sutherlands keeping curfew in Jerusalem.[186]

> The Battalion was deeply shocked by this incident and the curfew was enforced in an even more determined manner from this time on. The Jews came to dislike "Argyll Curfews" intensely. We constantly patrolled the city during the hours of darkness in vehicles. These patrols came to be known as "Milk Rounds", but there was nothing "milky" in the way in which curfew breakers were dealt with.[187]

The account reflects a fairly common sequence of events which had been repeated throughout 1946 and especially remembered in association with the Lechi attack on a car park, close to the beach, on the municipal boundary between Tel Aviv and Jaffa during the evening of 25th April 1946. The car park 'used largely by recreational transport from all formations and units which came into the town on certain afternoons and most evenings'[188] was guarded by eight soldiers including a NCO from the 5th Parachute Battalion of the 6th Airborne. The Lechi had no interest in the precise purpose of the car park, their mission, according to the commander of the operation, was to kill British soldiers 'without hesitation and without restrictions' in what they regarded as a military operation.[189] Seven British soldiers were killed in what Major-General A.J.H. Cassels GOC 6th Airborne described in a statement to the Mayor of Tel Aviv as an 'outrage' in which British soldiers 'were wilfully and brutally murdered'.[190] The attack took place outside a police station, but the Lechi unit managed to escape by laying fake mines which delayed the pursuing forces and found refuge in the Yemenite neighbourhood Kerem Ha Teimanim.[191] In the absence of intelligence on the identity of the attackers or their location, the army resorted to a road curfew, closing places of entertainment including restaurants and cafes, neighbourhood house-to-house searches, rounding up all the local residents for questioning[192] collective punishment, which Cassels explained, was chosen 'because I hold the community to blame. There is no doubt whatsoever in my mind that many members [of the community] either knew or could have given some warning before it happened'.[193] Other harsher measures were rejected as politically inadvisable (Figure 1.1).[194] According to Cassels, he told the High Commissioner

> that I was commanding a very high spirited division of parachutists, that if I did nothing they could very easily mutiny. I wanted to take really strong action, but got no support whatever. He said that if they mutinied he would find them a new divisional commander.[195]

Figure 1.1 Graffiti on a destroyed truck's cab. In Hebrew: 'The beast and its deed'. The 2nd Battalion, the Cheshire Regiment were stationed in Palestine in 1946.
Source: Springman; Courtesy of the I.D.F Archive (file 0–113819), Ministry of Defense, Israel.

It was C.R.W. Norman's assessment that 'those who are given the task of administering successfully a country in which terrorism thrives should not have their actions restricted either by outside political influence, or by the conventions of government and war'.[196]

According to Wilson, the soldiers and their commanders suffered 'a very considerable sense of frustration'.[197] Some 200–300 soldiers from the 3rd Brigade, 6th Airborne stationed in Qastina, a considerable distance from Tel Aviv, stormed the Jewish village of Be'er Tuvia, attacked passers-by, and entered houses and cafes, breaking windows and smashing furniture. An alarm was raised, but before things got out of control the Military Police arrived followed by staff officers from the Division and made the soldiers leave.[198] 'A lieutenant of the Airborne Division who reprimanded a party of soldiers returning from Be'er Tuvia was reported to have been heckled by the men, and saved from [an] assault only by the arrival of Military Police'.[199] Two Jews were attacked and seriously injured.

> Apologies were made to representatives of the settlement ... by the military authorities, who said that three alleged ringleaders had been apprehended and would be punished. They also promised compensation for damage, and reinforced guards.
>
> The O.C. of the neighboring camp said that he would like to visit the settlement and to speak personally to the children, who had been upset by the attack.[200]

In Netanya, a town north of Tel Aviv, a number of paratroopers broke shop windows, stole merchandise on display and were gone by the time the Military Police arrived. Three Jews were reported seriously injured. Similar incidents took place in Givatayim near Tel Aviv and Rehovot south of Tel Aviv.[201] Consequently, discipline was tightened with the result that soldiers' frustration at being targeted was channelled to approved operational activity which might be more harsh than usual but still within bounds, as in the instance of the "Argyll Curfews".

Understandably, open skirmishes with armed Jews, even when minor affairs, were met with enthusiasm. The support company of the Argylls had the good luck of such a skirmish described as the 'event of the month', on St. Andrews Day 30th November 1946.

> The minor battle which broke out about 7 p.m., surprised us either learning the "Ode to the Haggis" or firing a couple of warmers into the bank at the bar of the Officers' or the Sergeants' Mess. The sirens went and out went "Redshank" (this name was the code-word for an operation which entailed half the carriers going out to road blocks and the other half on patrols). As the written order, "as fast as possible," was interpreted by the drivers [of the Bren carriers] to make speed of not less than 30 m.p.h. round corners, the moral effect on the civilian population was not inconsiderable. On this occasion the battle in David Yellin Street [in the Makor Baruch neighborhood of west, i.e. Jewish, Jerusalem] gave rise to a series of quick, subsidiary engagements and there was hardly a carrier whose crew had not touched off. In the early stages a brilliant rearguard action was fought by the Coy Commander and the C.S.M. in a jeep, during which an opposition bullet found its way through the windscreen; then all speed records for jeeps in reverse were shattered and several magazines were dispatched from a borrowed police armoured car into hostile houses. The ensuing search disclosed a miniature battlefield, and several bottles were found which were confiscated in the traditional manner.[202]

Apparently, it was a relatively minor affair that grew out of proportion, perhaps reflecting unusual nervousness due to Field Marshal Montgomery's visit to Jerusalem. What had begun as a fire attack on the police station in the Machane Yehuda neighbourhood escalated into heavy firing throughout the city, probably the result of army and police patrols shooting at each other. The Jewish newspaper *Palestine Post* quoted a police officer as having explained: "Anyone can make a mistake on a night like this".[203] Heavy damage was reported to residential buildings in the area, reflecting possibly a common enough reaction by frustrated soldiers who let go with all weapons available. In any event, the Argylls appear to have had little interest in the identity of the enemy or the results of their action. The mere action without any casualties was all that mattered.

During their eight months in Jerusalem, the Argylls slept on average one in every two nights in bed, and the strain was beginning to tell. On 6th December 1946, the battalion was relieved by the Royal Irish Fusiliers and moved to Egypt, only to return to Qastina, Palestine, on 20th January 1947. Qastina was inaccurately regarded as a 'predominantly Arab Country' for which the battalion expressed gratitude.[204] In 16th February, they were visited by G.O.C. Palestine and Transjordan Lt.-General G.H.A. MacMillan who was also the Regiment's Colonel and told that they 'were to cease calling the "terrorists" by that name as it glamourized them and made them appear what they were not. This pleased us and now we call them by their proper names thugs, criminals, or murderers'.[205] Otherwise, the orders governing the limits of military reactions remained unchanged.

Bands

Late in 1947, three regimental bands arrived in Palestine.[206] Their regiments, the Royal Irish Fusiliers, the Argyll and Sutherland and the King's Own Scottish Borderers, had recently been reduced to one regular battalion each,[207] and the bands were sent out to entertain, and at times to reinforce them. Arriving by train from Egypt, the Royal Irish Fusiliers' band was stationed in the ex-RAF camp in Kfar Sirkin east of Petah Tikva. Life in the camp, considered one of the best in the country, was regarded by the band as grim and boring.[208] Soon it began performing. At first for the battalion.

> Band concerts in the cinema proved very popular, the programmes consisting entirely of items chosen by the audience and in passing it must be mentioned that the high standard of music chosen has been remarkable and we have been hard pressed on occasions to perform some of them. Community singing from the Irish Brigade song book[209] has also proved very popular.[210]

In February 1948, the band toured units of the 2nd Brigade in Jerusalem, staying with the 1st Battalion Suffolk Regiment in the Allenby and El Alamein camps in southern Jerusalem.

> The weather was at its worst and the camp under inches of water. A terrific gale, which raged for three days, tore most of the tents to ribbons and rum issues were appreciated by all. With an Arab village [Beit Safafa] on the one side of the camp and the Haganah H.Q. on the other the place was under constant fire both day and night.[211]

Indeed, one member of the band was lightly wounded on the way back from a concert.

February and March 1948 saw the escalation of the inter-communal violence which led the British Army to stop using the Jerusalem-Jaffa road for which the 2nd Brigade was partly responsible. The tense situation is reflected in the bands' account:

> Judging by the enthusiastic audiences our efforts were well appreciated and every one was very hospitable ... In spite of all this, however, we were not sorry to turn our backs on the Holy City. ... We are looking forward to the evacuation and a more peaceful life.[212]

The Irish Guards' band also went on tour early in 1948. It stayed with the 1st Welsh Guards in Netanya where it played for the troops and provided a dance band for the sergeants' mess.[213] Upon the bands return from a sight-seeing trip to Bethlehem with a party from the 3rd Coldstream Guards who were about to leave Palestine, its lorries were stopped by a roadblock and they were fired upon by Arabs from commanding positions, a standard tactic at the time. One of the bandsmen was fatally wounded and three other and a Guardsman suffered minor injuries.[214]

The rest of the band's tour was spent with the 1st Irish Guards in Rosh Pina, Safad and Zemach, where from mid-January 1948, they played concerts up and down the Jordan Valley. They then left Palestine from Haifa aboard a coaster to Port Said. The highlight of this part of their tour was their participation in St. Patrick's Day parade on the Rosh Pina airstrip (today Machanayim) in the presence of GOC British Troops in Palestine General Macmillan who flew in to present the *Shamrock* on behalf of H.R.H. The Princess Royal, the Regiment's Colonel.[215] As the battalion was drawn up on the airstrip,

> ... a mere picture will not convey the queer feeling of expectancy when the plane appeared, the waiting moment and then the sudden rigidity before the General Salute was sounded by the Band. Possibly some long-forgotten Roman legion had formed up in the same place.[216]

Each battalion of the Scottish infantry regiments and of most of the Irish regiments had a band, as did most of the Irish depots. The bandsmen were trained as soldiers and were used when called upon as stretcher bearers and as general reinforcements. At one point during the winter of 1947–1948 in consequence of a shortage in men in the companies of the 1st Argyll and Sutherland, the Pipes and Drums[217] 'have done a grand job, filing in buckshee [extra] guards and performing a heavy programme'.[218] But their primary function was as an essential component in the pageantry and ceremonial parades of the battalion. While training in Transjordan in the autumn of 1947, the 3rd Brigade held a Royal Searchlight Tattoo in honour of H.M. King Abdullah.

> The Pipes and Drums [of the KOSB], massed with the Drums and Pipes of the Royal Irish Fusiliers, gave a notable performance. They marched on together in darkness playing "The Skye Boat Song," breaking into

quick time as the lights were switched on, then played a selection of Scots and Irish pipe tunes. Dancing teams from each Battalion then performed our Battalion [1st KOSB] performed the "The Argyle Broadswords," and the Fusiliers performed a foursome jig. ... The Pipes and Drums then performed separately later joining up and marching off together.[219]

In the Scots battalions, Pipes and Drums were essential for Highland dancing which were regarded as an important part of their heritage and the excellence of their performance a source of pride, requiring continuous practice and the induction of new officers. The sergeants' mess of the 1st KOSB reported in the late summer of 1947:

Highland dancing classes are now in full swing (or should we say fling) under the able instruction of Pipe Major De Luspee. Even Englishmen try so hard that they tie themselves in knots.

It must not be assumed that a Mess member, doing "Paddy Bars" on his way back from the Mess, is under the influence of "Gold Star." He is merely taking Highland dancing to heart.[220]

Similarly, in the 1st Argyll and Sutherland,

Strange things happen in the Officers' Mess every evening during the week, or so it seems to our next door neighbours [in Sarafand], the Coldstream Guards. But it isn't really so very odd, the officers are merely trying to learn Highland dancing. There are three classes good, average and beginners. It seems to be popular, and we all are keen and work hard even our excellent doctor, who is from south of the Border.[221]

Highland dancing formed a vital part of the battalion's official entertainment of dignitaries. During the last week of March 1948, at the height of the crisis on the Jewish side, soon forcing it to go on the offensive, the Moderator of the General Assembly of the Church of Scotland and his Chaplain visited the Scots units in Palestine. They spent a day with the 1st Argyll and Sutherland and were entertained that evening in the officers' mess which held a Guest Night in their honour. One of the Moderator's 'most vivid memories' were,

The playing by Pipe-Major and pipers of the traditional marches and strathspeys, reels and pibroch, and the Highland dancing which followed. He himself, an old soldier of 1914 and 1939 campaigns, was not a little pleased to be able to compete (and on a concrete floor at that) with those of a much younger generation, by taking part in a vigorous eightsome, followed in quick succession by a violent foursome, and a strenuous Strip the Willow.[222]

Otherwise, few battalions then in Palestine were fortunate enough to have their own bands. Consequently, bands were readily shared for a variety of occasions and functions. While in Khassa, the Pipes and Drums of the 1st Irish Guards played at the battalion's various sports' meetings as well as at other battalions' events including the 1st Guards Para Battalion and 'some Mauration [Mauratian Pioneers] troops' north of Acre in the western Galilee.[223]

Carnivals and organized silliness

The capacity of all soldiers for acts of collective, organized and creative silliness is virtually unlimited. Depending on traditions, norms and forms of discipline and regimental culture, units invested prodigious efforts in extremely foolish endeavours in which they would take great pride. A superb example is that of the 1st Battalion the King's Own Scottish Borderers decision to arrange a dogs' race while on training in Transjordan in September–October 1947. The regimental magazine's proud account is worth quoting in full.

> The Battalion has always been noted for its population of weird and wonderful specimens of the canine world, and the results of the dog racing proved that for variety of size, speed, breed, and temperament we certainly had all the trophies. Of course, as soon as the subject was raised and it was proposed to actually hold dog races, the dog population increased beyond recognition and every dog for miles around that even looked as if it had been bitten by a whippet was quickly "snatched up". This was often followed by recriminations on the part of the rightful owner, who could usually be seen at first light, conveying his dog back to its proper sphere and usually fighting a rear-guard action on the way. The Pioneers made some excellent starting traps, the ground was laid out by the R.S.M., the tote was presided over by the P.R.I. and all C/ Sergeants, a bugler invented a "saddling" call, and altogether the thing was highly organized as Goodwood.[224] Prizes were always awarded for various categories, and as the Brigadier wanted to give a prize for the dog with the longest tail, we had to invent supporting categories. Eventually we had the dog with the longest tail, the dog with the shortest tail, the shaggiest dog and the smoothest dog, the most mysterious dog and the most obvious dog, and so on, until we almost ran out of comparisons. Other units in the Brigade sent their challengers, and some of them were quite good, but on the whole, it was felt that by getting in first, our chaps had picked up all possible prize-winners at the start, and even though the cost of a dog must have been quite high around these parts at this time, we retained the advantage.[225]

The detailed account in the *Chronicle*, the enthusiasm and support shown by all concerned including the Brigadier and neighbouring units, all while undergoing training in the desert, indicate that this ambitious display of collective silliness was widely perceived as a worthy endeavour.

The standard venue for similar outbursts of creative frivolity were the traditional celebrations of Christmas (or Hogmanay, in the Scots regiments) and the Regiment's day. The standard components were a grand meal with prodigious amounts of food and drink, especially noteworthy while Britain was still suffering considerable shortages, with variations on sports in which eccentricity and inventiveness, bolstered by acute inebriation of both players and spectators, were regarded as paramount. A Squad of the 4th/7th Royal Dragoon Guards, then on an airstrip near Afula, celebrated Christmas 1946, with the 'strangest football match of all times … [played] on the asphalt hockey pitch: one side resorted to the use of military tactics in laying a smokescreen to baffle their opponents'.[226] In B Squad the main sports' event took the form of

> a really hard fought soccer match which required the use of soccer, rugger and medicine balls as well as a strategic use of smoke. Fancy dress was worn, which proved very simple for one officer who turned up in pyjamas.[227]

The tradition of the Coldstream Guards' Christmas celebrations includes the hanging of the brick, originally removed from the Hougoumont Farm during the battle of Waterloo. The brick is carried by the sergeants to their mess while the lance corporals and the Coldstreamers try to divert it to their mess, in which case the sergeants have to provide beer for all. In Christmas 1946 the sergeants' mess of the 3rd Coldstream Guards,

> Hired two camels, and with "Pop" Lamps Electric Lucas as a Bedouin and C.S.M. "Tug" Wilson as his "bint" riding them, the brick was carried around the neck of the camel to the Sergeants' Mess. Someone dressed a goat as a Cold streamer and he led the procession. Our Commanding Officer was greatly mystified with all this ceremony, saying he had never heard of it before. We enlightened him in the Sergeants' Mess to which he replied: "I've discovered another method of fooling the Commanding Officer into keeping the bar open!"[228]

The deterioration of internal security towards the end of 1947, following the partition decision, may have affected the scope and the elaborateness of the celebrations of Christmas 1947 but not their spirit. HQ Squadron of the 3rd King's Own Hussars, then in Sarafand, marked the occasion with 'several amusing games of football. Fancy dress, hockey sticks, thunder flashes and "Gold Star" held more attraction than the ball. Half-time was a celebration more than the interval'.[229] The 'Sergeants' Mess Notes', referring to Christmas in Ramat David, east of Haifa, where the rest of the 3rd were stationed, posed the questions: 'Why did the R.S.M. kick a lead-filled ball and then proceed to score for the officers … Who fired the smoke bombs on to the field, necessitating the revival of players with whiskey and beer from the Officers' Mess'.[230]

Hogmanay 1948 celebrated by the KOSB was a minor affair compared to the dog races a few months earlier, but the tradition of general, drink-induced chaos was maintained. After dinner in the sergeants' mess, they

> Settled down to an evening of songs, stories and a "drop" to drink. During the course of the evening a "woman" in purdah' flitted through the Mess carrying a Water Jug on her head, everyone held their drinks by the hand until she got out. C.S.M. Wells made a later appearance with black lipstick on his face. At midnight the Mess resembled Waterloo Station on a Saturday morning in as much as the whole Battalion passed thro' the Mess, including the Pipe Band, and strange to relate we are still trying to recover our glasses. The members dwindled and "passed" away in the early hours of January 1st, to feel awfully sorry for themselves and say "was it worth it".[231]

There followed the customary fancy dress football match between officers and sergeants.

> The costumes on this occasion were intended for hard wear instead of beauty ... the honour, we feel, must go to C.S.M. Wells who was by far the best and beyond all doubt when the dogs chased him. ... The funniest incident was when the referee was about to strike his gong when the ball struck him and it is doubtful as whether he has yet overcome the dizziness.[232]

Another opportunity to let off steam were regimental days although some of them were celebrated with relative decorum. Néry Day celebration on 1st September 1947, commemorating the battle in 1914 during the retreat from Mons and the fighting of "L" Battery of the Royal Horse Artillery, began at 0540 'when the Battery flag was lowered to half-mast and raised again as the trumpeter sounded the Regimental Call, Last Post and Reveille'.[233] There followed some sports in Sarafand, 'an excellent dinner' and a show produced by the Battery Concert Party which consisted of 'fourteen turns ranging from the sublime to the ridiculous', with costumes and make up provided by the Field Entertainment Unit in Jerusalem. Finally, 'the audience joined hands and sang Auld Lang Syne before going to bed'.[234] The 2nd Royal Irish Fusiliers managed to infuse their celebration of St. Patrick's Day on March 1948 with some energetic lunacy. Their Brigadier had agreed to relieve the battalion's companies of duty so as to enable them to participate. The day began with a morning Mass. In the afternoon, once the weather cleared, the Officers vs. Sergeants football match started.

> The ground was a sea of mud and practically under water. The game commenced as rugger and then developed into a mud fight, which the

members of the teams of both sides succeeded in rubbing each other's hair and faces in the dirt. This was very amusing for the spectators until both teams thought that they should also be rolled into the mud. A dash was made for them and in the subsequent scramble the game came to an end with no score on either side, but a good time having been had by all.[235]

Regardless of the occasion, matches between officers and sergeants seem to have been a favourite format for a "carnival" in which most public and typical characteristics of army hierarchy, discipline and gender were suspended as in the match between the Officers' and the Sergeants' Mess of the KOSB on Minden Day, 1st August 1947 as reported by the correspondent for the sergeants, the main guardians of these traditions.

> The score was so great that only approximate figures can be given. I think it was Officers, 2; Sergeants 9. The dresses were many and varied, viz., C.S.M. Cameron made an excellent sheik, whilst C.S.M. Wells, done up as a N.A.A.F.I. girl certainly took the trick ... C.S.M. Cockburn a fairy queen ... Major G.W. Stavert dressed as a Ballet Girl, and the Intelligence Officer as a Sophisticated Pin Up. Against all rules our opponents [the officers] kidnapped the R.S.M. prior to the game but released him just in time for the kick off. The support was great and many fainted in the crowds. The game ended with the ball "deflated" due to a mishap in which it became part of the painted star of the fairy queen's wand.[236]

Dogs and other pets

The first mention of the dog racing project of the KOSR in its *Chronicle* was in its March 1947 number, while the battalion was in camp 22 in Beit Lid, east of Netanya: 'we hope to start dog racing shortly, as the starting traps have at last been made. There is a good assortment of dogs in the Battalion so that we expect good sport'.[237] In keeping with the above claim, dogs are mentioned several times in the *Chronicle*; for example, the 'most recent new discovery' in the sergeants' mess of a '"full blooded Lydda Terrier" which somehow or other has the name "Flannelette"', or 'the C.S.M. who walks the floor every night to get his dog to sleep'.[238] A hard-working officer of the H.Q. Company was 'i/c Wogs and Dogs', and the Intelligence Section reported that they 'kept busy in our doings with the "Wogs and Dogs"'.[239]

The practice of adopting dogs as pets was fairly commonplace, albeit in varying numbers, in other battalions, for example, the 1st HLI. In notes from the support company HQ, 'Our Company Commander, Capt. Fender, went on leave, and left his dog, Ziki, to help the new Company Commander, Lt. Fletcher, with his job'. Or, 'at Latrun a Dog Census was taken. Was it a coincidence that there was a slight shortage of grub a little before it?'[240]

This despite a serious problem of rabies spread by packs of jackals and feral dogs which led the Police to periodically raid open markets at night and put down stray dogs.[241]

As soon as the Irish Guards arrived in Palestine,

> Several of the officers have acquired pets of one sort or another, most of which are dogs, all of which are entirely lacking in charm, look rather fierce and are almost certainly rabid. There is however, one notable exception. Her name is Cap Star [the cap badge of the Irish Guards}, she shines very slightly, and is a donkey. She stands about six hands and has a great turn of speed, but not much stamina. She is extremely well behaved and has the freedom of the Officers' quarters neither of which remarks apply to the dogs. She has had a rather nasty cold during the past few days, and her proud owner [Lt. W.B. Churchill] ... has been issuing frequent bulletins for the information of her many friends and admirers.

It was knowingly pointed out that

> Four weeks old is said to be a tricky age for donkeys. One great pity is that her owner won't allow Cap Star to walk down to the beach, which she would obviously enjoy very much. The reason for this is that her mother lives in a field on the way, and it's just possible that she might start pining to go home to Mum.[242]

Following the battalion's move from Atlit, near Haifa, to Khassa, in the south, it was reported that Lt. Churchill had acquired another donkey 'a smaller edition of "Capstar." It has been christened "Chinstrap." Officers have been heard to utter the most dreadful threats against this pair if any of their geranium heads disappear during the night'.[243]

The custom of adopting stray animals as pets could reach surprising proportions. The 4th/7th Royal Dragoon Guards stationed in December, 1946 in Rosh Pina, had two horses kept by the Colonel in a corner of the camp,

> Major Barraclough has two hound puppies of doubtful breeding and is known to have kept at various times an owl, a tortoise and a chameleon, all of which have in their turn proved very elusive. There are various other dogs in the camp which are kept to a strict minimum because of the fear of rabies. Two are permanent members of the guard picked on account of their fearsome appearance.[244]

Andrew Gibson-Watt, in recounting the history of his own dog, described the dog population of the 1st Guards Brigade in Kfar Sirkin. Gibson-Watt had adopted 'a mongrel fox-hound bitch called Sue ... the illegitimate offspring' of hound bitches brought to Palestine by the Welsh Guards.

Admittedly, she was not 'a very satisfactory dog'. He 'allowed her to be impregnated by one of the pi-dogs which infested all our camps'. In due course Sue disappeared, gave birth to seven puppies and was eventually found. Gibson-Watt drowned four of the puppies. The remaining three 'bedded down with her in a big basket in my hut, but were no trouble at all until they could walk, when at once they became the most impossible trouble'. He took them in his car on the Brigade's months' long training in Transjordan. Throughout 'Sue and the puppies remained quite imperturbable'. Some time later Sue ate some poison and died.[245] The extent of the emotional attachment to such pets is further revealed by the events following the arrival of a new camp commandant, Tony Samuelson, from the Irish Guards,

> accompanied by a huge and very fierce boxer dog. Within two hours this animal had killed three cats and two smaller dogs, and had itself been shot dead with a rifle by an infuriated guardsman who had owned one of the victims. Tony was at first inclined to press for disciplinary measures against the guardsman, but the overwhelming opinion was that he had done a good job.[246]

The presence of a multitude of unruly dogs in a camp could soon become a disciplinary problem as evident from the Battalion Orders of the 1st Coldstream Guards, recently arrived from England, during the final months of the Mandate.

1 April 1948. 'All dogs must be registered'.[247]

Shortly afterwards the battalion moved to Haifa with its HQ in Peninsular Barracks on the western edge of the harbour.[248]

27 April 1948. 'all owners of dogs must ... tie them between 1000 and 16 hrs. 1 May 1948. ... Dogs will NOT be taken into the Mess-Room'.[249]

2 June 1948. 'During Drill Parade all dogs will be kept tied up. Any dogs on the square during Drill Parades will be destroyed'.[250]

Some pet dogs had it better than others. The top dogs in Palestine must have been the High Commissioner's dachshunds, described in a letter by their owner from 22nd July 1947 as flourishing.

> One flourishing too much and although only just over a year old enormously fat. I fear he has found his way to the soldiers of the guard cook house as he seldom eats what I give him. The other, Max, is still very young and rather nervous, but is a sweet little dog.[251]

At the end of the Mandate, the dogs accompanied the High Commissioner leaving Palestine, on the cruiser H.M.S. *Euryalus*. A witness reported:

> I regret to say [that one of the dogs] disgraced himself by doing what he should not as soon as he stepped on board. "So that's what he thinks of our ship!" I overheard one of the sailors say.[252]

By the beginning of February 1948, the 1st KOSB were made responsible for securing the Sarafand camps which required 260 men on guard duty around the clock with some additional responsibilities outside Sarafand and some escorts. On 15th May, the battalion formed the advance guard of the 3rd Brigade as it left Palestine for Egypt. It was reported in the regiment's *Chronicle* that "A" Company's mascot dog Blackie 'died a soldier's death as all dogs had to be put down before leaving Palestine'.[253]

Mascots

In some battalions, the love of animals took the official form of regimental mascots.[254] A good example is the 2nd Royal Warwickshires whose war in 1945 ended outside Bremen. The battalion was soon moved south to the village of Petershagen near Minden where 'it acquired an antelope mascot "Bobby" from Hamburg Zoo'.[255] An antelope featured on the regiments' original badge and was first adopted as a mascot in 1871 in India[256] always to be named "Bobby".

While in Patershagen, the battalion was visited by Field Marshall Montgomery, there to present decorations. Montgomery, who had joined the regiment in 1908, addressed the battalion and stated that he 'was particularly pleased to see the battalion had an Antelope once more'.[257] "Bobby" also took part in the Army's parade in Brussels, commemorating the city's liberation, led by the 2nd Warwickshire with Bobby 'who was in excellent form... had his photograph taken at least 300 times'.[258]

In October 1945, the 2nd Warwickshires were stationed in Jerusalem, where Bobby was on parade when the battalion formed in December 1945 the Guard of Honour for the Emir Abdullah of Transjordan when visiting the High Commissioner. Sadly Bobby was not at his best form.

> Poor "Bobby" struck a bad spell shortly after arriving in Jerusalem, and was not at all well. He was evacuated to the veterinary hospital in Ramle, where after about a month he recovered, but was left quite blind.
>
> After some deliberation it was decided to keep him, and we are now[259] very glad that we did so, as he is extremely fit, and really very little inconvenienced by his blindness. His other senses are so well developed that he has no trouble at all in his pen, which is a very big one.[260]

After a few months in Jerusalem, the 2nd Warwickshires left at the end of April 1946 for Egypt where "Bobby", who is reported to have suffered from the climate, died and was replaced in October 1946 by "Bobby II" from the Cairo Zoo,[261] who proved a 'most lively customer'.

In April 1947, after a year in Egypt, the 2nd Warwickshires were back in Palestine, initially in Pardes Hanna. On 11th June, the battalion provided the Guard of Honour for Montgomery during a few hours' stopover in Aqir on his way to the Far East, according to the regimental magazine.

It had been intended that Bobby II should have been present as well, but very unfortunately he met with an accident while being taken off the truck which had brought him from Pardes Hanna to Aqir, and his leg was cut rather badly. He was unable to be present on the parade as a result, 'but since then he has recovered, and his leg has now healed satisfactorily'.[262] Otherwise, the parade was pronounced a success. Its account in the regimental magazine is not much longer than the above report on Bobby II's accident.

Hunting, shooting and riding

The traditional pursuits of hunting, shooting and riding as the preferred forms of officers' recreation survived the war, mechanization of cavalry units' and social change. In June 1947, the 4th/7th Royal Dragoon Guards held the Regiment Shoot.

> There was no lack of guns in the Regiment for this year's shooting season, since several officers brought out their own, and four more were supplied by the Sporting Fund. Cartridges were plentiful too, though many were clay-load; some guns were not used to these and became known as "the gentleman wot fire blanks."[263]

The whole of Palestine was described as 'in fact a paradise for the shooting sportsman',[264] and the battalion enjoyed plenty of hunting grounds within easy reach in northern and central Palestine 'for a day's or even an afternoon's shooting'.[265]

> At Rosh Pinna [Lake Hula] before the duck season opened, doves would come to roost in the evenings to a long line of trees near the camp, and provided some good sport though the bag was never large. In the Haifa area there was good duck shooting on Acre mud flats and some inland ponds nearby, and on the Carmel Ridge itself a few "Chukor" [Chukar partridge] could be put up, though entailing very long walks over the hillside.[266]

Lake Hula, north of the Sea of Galilee, formed a major staging point for the annual migration of duck, snipe and other birds, and consequently was the most popular bird shoot in the country. Gibson-Watt, when with 3 Company of the Welsh Guards in Rosh Pina, recalled enjoying 'shooting beyond the dreams of most men, at an age when it was most ready to enjoy it'.[267]

> We would set out before dawn ...Reaching the Huleh area, we would find a throng of young Arabs, all anxious to carry cartridge bags, waiting in the darkness at the roadside villages. The day would start with an early-morning duck flight. ...Nobody had any waders or boots.

We simply walked, in thin khaki-drill trousers, into the very cold water to a point well above the knees. This was fairly agonizing. Dawn
broke ... and we sloshed painfully out of the marsh to the dry point
where our drivers had organized a simple, warming breakfast.

There followed a day's shooting of snipe and duck, with a break for lunch a
'slightly expanded version of breakfast'. In the evening back to Rosh Pina
'to a hot bath, a drink, a quiet dinner, and bed'. 'It was a marvelous life', he
concluded, 'for young and fit men'.[268]
During 'the halcyon days' of 1946 of the 1st Welsh Guards in the upper-
eastern Galilee, with battalion HQ in Tiberias, and the Guards Brigade HQ
in Nazareth, the Guardsmen enjoyed a free run of Lake Hula. The only
neighbouring battalions were of the 6th Airborne who fortunately 'were
keener on soldiering than shootin'.[269] Early in 1947, the Guards Brigade
changed places with the 6th Airborne Division. Now it was the Guardsmen
'who had to make the long, dark journey northwards in the early morning, and fit in to any unoccupied bit of marsh'.[270] Competition over the use
of Lake Hula for shooting began to get out of hand requiring the direct
involvement of HQ Palestine in Jerusalem. A committee was appointed,
chaired by G.O.C. Lt.-General MacMillan, 'to give all players as fair a crack
possible of the whip'.[271]
An alternative site for shooting water fowl were the fish ponds of the Jewish kibbutzim in the south-eastern Galilee in the Beisan Valley. The rushes
on the banks of the ponds offered good cover and where the ponds were
drained for maintenance snipe came to feed. Guardsmen of the 4th/7th Dragoons found that on the whole, the number and variety of 'bird life round
the ponds is not unlike some places in England'. It 'would have taken an
ornithologist to remember them all'.[272] Unfortunately, weekends were often
taken up by operational duties where 'Jewish gentlemen do mining operations, and illegal emigrant ships arrive', allowing the ducks to enjoy some
peace and quiet.[273]
In the matter of shooting, some battalions were more keen than others.
In October 1947, the King's Own Hussars, equipped with Staghound armoured cars, moved from Atlit to Ramat David airport, east of Haifa, in
support of the 6th Airborne.[274] The move was considered 'most suitable
from the shooting aspect for it put us thirty miles nearer to our main shooting haunts'.[275] As security deteriorated strict precautions were required,
and all travelling was in at least two vehicles with at least two men in each.
But despite the escalating violence between Jews, Arabs and the subsequent
curfew in the Haifa area imposed with the help of half of the regiment's
armoured cars, and the worsening manpower situation necessitating the
amalgamation of A and C squadrons, 'we had many enjoyable [shooting]
days'.[276] These included 'a very amusing' day and a half's shooting in Lake
Hula which 'proved to be very difficult to visit on account of the Arab-Jew
contest', and otherwise, on weekends and most Wednesdays, from October

1947 to February 1948, in the ponds and streams of the Beisan Valley. The total bag came to about seven hundred birds, mostly duck, snipe and the occasional woodcock.

The worsening war between Jews and Arabs seems to have been regarded as an irritant, occasionally worthy of comment indicating almost total detachment. An example is the impression left by the attack by the 1st Yarmouk Battalion of the Arab Liberation Army (ALA) on kibbutz Tirat Zvi on 16th February 1948, the first attempt by the ALA to occupy and destroy a Jewish community in a set battle, on a couple of shooters from the 3rd Hussars.

> One day two guns shot near a Jewish settlement called Terat Tsevi, and did extremely well against the duck. At dawn the next morning the Arabs had launched a full-scale attack against it. This was repulsed with somewhat heavy losses to the Arabs, and on our next visit to the area grenades and many rounds of ammunition were seen lying around.

The Arab-Jewish war soon interfered with the shooting to an annoying extent.

> Following the season for waterfowl, the quail season began. Unfortunately, the Arab-Jew tension was very high and we considered, armed with shotguns, we would not exactly be welcomed wandering around the fields by either side. For this reason, and for the fact that the season was a very early one and the crops were very high [due to an exceptionally wet winter] before the birds really arrived, very few quail were shot.[277]

In 1939, the First Cavalry Division arrived in Palestine with 8,000 horses. The Division was mechanized in 1941 and the horses were retained for other tasks. By the end of 1942, the army kept in the area 6,500 horses, 10,000 mules and 1,700 camels.[278] Horses of the mechanized cavalry units no longer needed were cared for by the Royal Army Veterinary Corps in Jerusalem. The Veterinary Corps people were happy to allow anyone to exercise the horses for them, while officers could hire a "government horse" for L. 4.10.0 a month, up from the pre-war rate of 15 s.[279] By 1947, the youngest ex-cavalry horse was sixteen years old.[280]

When the 2nd Irish Fusiliers moved to Jerusalem in 1947, the CO bought three horses, two of which, probably ex-battery leaders, were destined for the use of the mess. They were kept in the stables of the Jerusalem Riding Club in Allenby Barracks in southern Jerusalem, where the Club owned a manage with show jumps and a small handy-hunter course which was used when the security situation deteriorated. Meanwhile, though 'the Judean Hills do not compare favourably with Meath or Galway as a fair hunting country there are some good rides to be had in the valleys with plenty of stone walls to jump'.[281] As security in and around Jerusalem deteriorated, riding as well as all other activities outside the security zones was restricted. At first it was limited to armed pairs, then to armed parties of four, and finally riding was confined to the manage, 'which was patrolled by four mounted military policemen armed with sabres!'[282]

Polo in Palestine was largely limited to the TJFF which at the time was part of the army, and to the Sarafand Polo Club. In the autumn of 1947, the TJFF was under the command of the 6th Airborne, following the latter's move to the Galilee. One of the TJFF's regiments [battalions], stationed in Samakh, at the southern tip of the Sea of Galilee, was cavalry, consisting of four squadrons.[283] On the 27th and 29th of June 1947, it held in Sarafand the Open Horse Show and Display in aid of the Jerusalem Babies Home and the TJFF Benevolent Fund.

> A colourful touch was provided by the Cavalry Regiment of the T.-J.F.F. With lances and pennants, 16 men on greys and another 16 on bays maintained perfect formation as they gave a display of precision riding, circling, wheeling and forming intricate figures without the slightest hitch.[284]

All were for the benefit of a crowd consisting mainly of military, police and TJFF personnel. Music was provided by the band of the 1st Welsh Guards, and the trophies were presented by the High Commissioner.[285]

Most of the ponies in Sarafand belonged to the Horse Transport Company and were ex-cavalry, sixteen to twenty years old, used in the winter for hunting. By late 1947, those 'wanting to play [Polo] far exceeded the availability of ponies and, consequently, no one can play more than once a week'.[286] The Irish Fusiliers' CO 'played for a team called the Jackhunters; the combined ages of the players totalled about 200, and with the ages of the ponies added it must have been nearer 400!'[287] By then the cost of ponies and their maintenance was perceived as too expensive.

The best known hunt in Palestine was the Ramleh Vale Hunt (RVH), originally founded by Brigadier Angus McNeil, Commandant of the British Gendarmerie (1922–1926), as early as 1923.[288] McNeil brought over from England several couples of foxhounds which he installed in Sarafand near his headquarters. When the Gendarmerie was disbanded and replaced by the Palestine Police, the hunt kennels were moved to Mt. Scopus in Jerusalem and later back to Ramleh near the police station.[289] By late 1947, they returned to Sarafand, to the Horse Transport Company. Due to the scarcity of foxes in the area, most of the hunting was of jackals (*Canis aureus*) of which there were plenty.

> Although not fox hunting it is extremely good fun. There are two types of country hunted over the open and the close country. The open country is not unlike bits of Salisbury Plain, very little cover and nothing to jump. The jack is found in wadis, and can be viewed for miles, when he

goes away. On poor scenting days, the Master had some difficulty in restraining the unruly field, who should have known better, from riding the jack and leaving the hounds behind. The close country consists of miles of olive and orange groves. The former are like riding through a close woodland country, with cactus [Opuntia Ficus-Indica] fences to jump. Orange groves are invariably wired off, but produce excellent refreshment to a thirsty field. It is unusual form of hunting to be able to pick oranges from the trees while hounds are drawing.[290]

The author of the above, written towards the end of 1947 and the outbreak of hostilities, expressed hope that the next hunting season would find the Irish Fusiliers stationed closer to the Ramleh Vale so as to be able 'to take advantage of this very good sport!'

Gibson-Watt's impression was that usually the jackal got away.

I once saw a beautiful saluki dog … embark on a jackal-chase over a moderately easy stretch of North Palestine country. The saluki is the fastest thing on four legs after the cheetah and this one quickly caught up. The jackal turned at bay and showed his teeth, whereupon the saluki immediately pretended that he had just been jogging, or looking for wild flowers.[291]

Apart from the RVH, keen battalions usually managed to gather a few horses and some hounds to form an improvised hunt or at least organize some regular riding, as did the Irish Fusiliers when in Beit Lid, near Netanya, although the horses 'had to have a [Bren] carrier escort when going to and from the farrier'.[292] In 1946, the 15th/19th the King's Royal Hussars organized a hunt in the Plain of Esdraelon. Some of the officers borrowed horses from the Base Remount Depot near Beit Lid and stabled them in the Jenin police station. Hounds were provided by the 1st Welsh Guards whose CO had served with the Hussars. The officers of both battalions set off from Jenin and by the end of the day 'had accounted for one jackal'.[293]

For especially keen battalions, desperate times meant desperate measures. By the summer of 1947, the Remount Depot near Beit Lid was nearly cleared of horses, only mules remaining. So on Saturday, 14th June, the Irish Fusiliers held mule races.

There was a tote and paddock, and the judges sat in a wagon in traditional point-to-point style. There were ten races, two confined to officers, the rest open to all ranks. Mules were drawn for by jockeys and were ridden without saddles. The Battalion produced a majority of jockeys, not all of whom stayed the course; especially in the hurdle races. It was a very successful afternoon for riders, spectators and backers alike.[294]

While in Beit Lid, in between its return from training in Transjordan and its move in December 1947 to Kfar Sirkin, the Fusiliers managed a further use of the available horses by incorporating them in a ceremonial parade with the Colours. Probably 'the last time the C.O., Second-in-Command and Adjutant were all mounted on parade'.[295]

The last mounted army unit in Palestine was a squadron (four horses) of the Royal Military Police which formed part of the Sarafand garrison, used for patrolling the parameter wire. When the army prepared to leave the country, and since the horses could not be evacuated, they had to be shot.[296] According to the Hebrew newspaper *Ha'aretz* a non-kosher sausage factory in Tel Aviv bought from the army earlier in the year, some horse carcasses from a camp near Netanya. The horses reportedly were killed in accordance with army custom, when the camp was transferred to the Netanya municipality.[297]

Sightseeing

One of the main attractions of serving in Palestine were the opportunities for sightseeing including, but by no means exclusively, the holy places associated with the life of Jesus. 'It is amazing', wrote a correspondent to *The Tank*, 'how much history has been made in this tiny country biblical, medieval and modern. Nearly every name on the map conjures up some historical association'.[298] Major the Hon. N.I. Forbes arrived at HQ Palestine in spring 1947 as GSO Training Duties. 'It was not long', he wrote in a memoir, 'before the charm of Palestine fell on me. Palestine seemed a Biblical land with its terraces of ancient olive trees and [Arab] peasants tilling the land with wooden ploughs pulled by camels and donkeys'.[299] Andrew Gibson-Watt of the Welsh Guards, and from the autumn of 1946 at HQ 1st Guards Brigade in Nazareth recalled,

> walking in the hills overlooking the town, on the afternoon of Christmas Eve. There were shepherd-boys and flop-eared sheep. It grew dark, and the stars came out. All the bells of Nazareth began to ring, one after the other, and the New Testament story seemed very near and very real.[300]

Whenever feasible, training was combined with sightseeing in Palestine and Transjordan so as to include as many troops as possible.[301] The 1st Irish Guards upon their arrival in Palestine and while in Atlit, just south of Haifa, made sure that

> All ranks had numerous opportunities of seeing the north of Palestine. Even the truck drive round Haifa Bay, past the mysterious forbidden domes of Acre to the ranges, where zeroing of rifles and Bren guns was carried out, provided a pleasant change of atmosphere. But

emphatically the best opportunity occurred with Company Marches of Support Company, who journeyed far afield up to the plateau of Transjordan ..., of No. 1 Company in the mountains of the north, marching south to Capernaum and by transport to Nazareth; and of No. 4 Company who started at Nazareth, marched across country to the Sea of Galilee, and thence north to Safad.[302]

In the course of the battalion's seven weeks in Atlit, before their move to Khassa, 'there was hardly an individual who did not see something of north Palestine'.[303] The Intelligence Section of the 1st HLI reported that during the battalion's short stay in Latrun, guarding the detention camp, before travelling to Transjordan for training: 'the Section has been seeing the sights ... and ...we are getting lost quite regularly in Transjordan'.[304]

It was also common for officers to combine sightseeing with hunting. Philip Brutton, on the staff of the 1st Guards Brigade, used the opportunity of the brigade's training in Transjordan to drive to Qasr El Hallabut, twenty-five miles north east of Amman,

> To shoot dove or wild pigeon. It was an ancient site, an outpost of the Roman and Ottoman empires, beyond which was the desert and Bedouin tribes. One observed walls and a deep well, inside which the birds roosted. A stone thrown inside brought them out and brought them down. This reduced the pecking order and provided a change of food for dinner. I pondered as I glanced around the place: "Go to Hallabut!" must have been a terrible phrase to hear. It was certain death, not least from boredom.[305]

Apart from the Galilee, Jerusalem was especially fascinating with biblical associations unaffected by current troubles. The 42nd Commando was stationed, in April 1948, on Mt. Scopus, on the ridge overlooking the old city from the north. Its mission was to cover the withdrawal of the army in an area that had seen some intensive fighting including the Arab massacre of the Hadassah convoy and the Palmach attempt to occupy the Sheich Jarach neighbourhood. By then the Jews had gone on the offensive. Most of Jerusalem, including the walled Old City, was off limits for the Commandos and they were confined to their static positions overlooking the evacuation road north, and to the view from other army positions closer to the walls. Yet the proximity and sight of Jerusalem excited biblical and romantic associations which had nothing to do with the current desperate struggle between Jews and Arabs.

> Jerusalem had still a pleasant air about it as we saw it from dawn to dusk each day. From the roof of the Hospice Notre Dame de France [overlooking the north western corner of the wall of the Old City], and from the [1st] Suffolk's positions in a [north western] corner of the Old City, some

of us saw the walls and domes of the Holy Places church and minaret, synagogue and mosque, the Dome of the Rock and the Wailing Wall. We could not visit them, not the Mount of Olives and the dark cypresses of Gethsemane, the road to Bethany, nor the steep valley where the road goes down to Jericho. To these last the eye travelled with mere longing, for they had a place in History: the buildings belonged to what [R.W.] Emerson calls "the caricature of institutions." What a small place the great city of Jerusalem must have been, built of small stones on a stony hillside; and how fine to walk on the Mount of Olives in the evening, so near at hand, and to look back on it and be right away from it.[306]

A similar sense of detachment can be found in an article published after the evacuation in the Suffolk Regimental *Gazette*, which seems oblivious of the nature of the conflict:

Is it too much to hope that whatever else the outcome, there may be a re-surgence of true Christian charity and cooperation in preserving these sacred spots or that the jarring notes of jealousy and discord between sects in the past will fade before a common crisis into an acknowledge-ment of the universal Christian responsibility for these scenes of such great moment in the life of Christ?[307]

Another source of fascination was the desert and the exotic East in general. The more adventurous officers toured Transjordan, Syria and Lebanon com-bining sightseeing with hunting. The Damascus Bazaar was recommended for 'its opportunities to buy, at a reasonable price, luxuries at present un-obtainable in Europe or Western Asia'.[308] Similarly, Lebanon was recom-mended for its scenery which 'is even more lovely than it is in Palestine, the life is gay and the food luxurious. The lovely mountains offer opportunities for climbing and, in winter, excellent ski-ing'.[309] The only drawback were the prices: 'practically nothing costs less than a pound'. Similarly, currency regulations were a deterrent to travelling on leave to Egypt.

When the state of internal security permitted, especially during the war, Palestine was similarly attractive.

British, Dominion and Allied soldiers filled the cabarets and cinemas, the cafes and bathing beaches. They explored orange groves, and in-spected Jewish communal farms. They danced with Jewish girls, visited Jewish homes; some of them took Jewish wives. They visited Arab vil-lages, drank Turkish coffee with Mukhtars, ate roast mutton and kebab in their fingers and rode races on Arab donkeys.[310]

There was also shopping. With the population in Britain still struggling with the economic consequences of the war, including severe shortages in con-sumer goods, soldiers 'spent their pay on things to send home, orange-juice, locally made beer and liquers, on razorblades that would not cut, on matches that would not strike, on soap that would not lather'.[311] Apart from the poor quality of some of the locally produced goods, prices were high, and there was a feeling that the Jewish shopkeeper was taking advantage of the soldiers' 'misfortune to line his own pocket', by setting different prices to soldiers and to civilians.[312]

With the deterioration of internal security, the army developed Cyprus as an alternative destination for the recreation of troops. Cyprus had the advantage of belonging to the Sterling area so that vacationing there was not subject to foreign exchange restrictions. A number of vacation camps, both near the sea and in the mountains, were opened in the summer of 1947, and a ski resort in the Troodos Mountains in the following winter. Vacations there could be applied for through unit HQs or the Army Welfare Service. Passage was provided (free for officers with booked accommodation) on board the HMS *Tripolitania* (capacity 500) originally an Italian steamer scuttled in Massawa in 1941, salvaged and put to use as a troop ship. Troops boarded about tea time and arrived in Famagusta in time for breakfast.[313]

One of the main attractions for troops in Cyprus was the freedom from barbed wire and from the constant threat, of attack, when outside camp. Soldiers left their rifles and Sten guns with the Military Police until returning to Palestine.[314] They were allowed to wander without an armed escort, and buses were available for travel around the island. The nature of some of the unofficial local attractions may be deduced from an official statistic of the 1st Division's Medical Services according to which the majority of reported cases of venereal diseases were contracted in Cyprus.[315]

In the autumn of 1947, the 1st Irish Guards left Jerusalem and after a fortnight (3th–17th October) near Hadera, between Haifa and Netanya, as Divisional Reserve to the 6th Airborne, it returned to Khassa. Having missed the excitement of training in Transjordan with other units of the Palestine garrison, the CO Lt.-Colonel D.M. Gordon-Watson initiated 'a steady stream of Platoon training drives' through the Negev desert in the south of Palestine to Aqaba on the northern tip of the Red Sea, 'where Section and Platoon training are the order of the day. Then to Petra, followed by the fleshpots of Amman and so back to the Allenby Bridge [over the Jordan], through Jericho and Jerusalem, to home Khassa!'[316] The CO's turn came in mid-November. With two other officers, three officers' servants, three drivers and 'Hassan the cook', they embarked on a 'ten day reconnaissance of the Negev and Transjordan'.[317] The party travelled in two jeeps and a three ton truck for provisions, staying in police posts along the way. They made an early stop in the Beersheba market in order to purchase 'an Arab head-dress-keffyr [kaffiya] and argal [akal]. With an Irish Guards cap-star inserted in the front, we felt quite the part, and why anyone wore any other type of head-dress in the war in the desert I cannot think'.[318]

Gordon-Watson was mainly interested in shooting grouse, pigeons, ibex, wild pig and gazelle, dining at the end of the day on whatever the party or their hosts shot. They fished in the Red Sea and went sightseeing in the footsteps of Lawrence, whose memory was frequently evoked, including the boils he suffered from. The party went on to Petra and to the Saudi Arabian border, 'over the same mud-flats as Lawrence had travelled to attack the railway at Mudawara'.[319] It continued down the Wadi, in a scenery, 'Lawrence himself was deeply moved by'.[320] Finally, returning to their first stop, the police post, Gordon-Watson experienced by his own account, 'a day I shall not forget for a long time' following which 'I was miserable ... for two days and kept on asking myself how many people had missed two ibexes in one morning in Palestine'.[321]

During the final day of the trip, they heard over the radio that the UN General Assembly had voted in favour of the partition of Palestine.

> We passed through Beer Sheeba in the afternoon the tension of unrest was already in the air. We felt after our ten days with these charming, hospitable and perfect-mannered Bedouins that our Negev had been given away. The justice of it all was not easy to understand.[322]

Notes

1 *The Household Brigade Magazine* (Spring, 1947), 89.
2 Ibid., 89–90.
3 Wellington Barracks, London, Irish Guards Archives, News Sheet No. 1 [n.d.].
4 Irish Guards Archives, *Ocean Shamrock*, 1st Irish Guards H.M.T. Cameronia, No. 5, 5th March 1947.
5 *News Sheet* No. 1.
6 The Irish Guards were fortunate in their assigned transport and the weather. For an account of some worse voyages, see Tom Hickman, *The Call-up, A History of National Service* (London: Headline Book Publishing, 2004, 2005), 63–68. For an earlier example of the excitement of the sea voyage from England, see Robin H. Martin, *Palestine Betrayed: A British Palestine Policeman's Memoirs (1936–1948)* (Ringwood: Seglaw Press, 2007), 21–22.
7 *News Sheet* No. 1.
8 *Ocean Shamrock* No. 6, 6th March 1947.
9 Ibid.
10 Ibid No.8, 8th March.
11 Ibid.
12 Ibid No.7, 7th March.
13 Ibid No. 1, 1st March.
14 Ibid No.5, 5th March.
15 Ibid No. 8, 8th March.
16 Ibid Final Edition, No. 9, 9th March 1947.
17 *News Sheet* No. 1.
18 Ibid.
19 Ibid.
20 P. Le and S. Harris, 'Journey to Jerusalem', in *The Globe and Laurel*, vol. LVI, No. 10 (October, 1948), 302.
21 Ronald Storrs, *Orientations* [first published in 1937] Definitive Edition (London: Nicholson and Watson, 1945), 338. Chapters IX and XVIII (On T.E. Lawrence), and Chapter XV (On Zionism) were issued by Penguin as Sir Ronald Storrs, *Lawrence of Arabia Zionism and Palestine*, 1940.

22 *Orientations*, 339.

23 Ibid., 340.

24 Ibid., 371.

25 For example, Lt.-Colonel Colin Mitchell, *Having Been a Soldier* (London: Hamish Hamilton, 1969), or William Whitelaw, *The Whitelaw Memoirs [1989]* (London: Headline, 1990), 24.

26 Quoted in J.P. Riley, *The Life and Campaigns of General Hughie Stockwell: From Norway, through Burma, to Suez* (Barnsley, South Yorkshire: Pen & Sword Military, 2006), 167. See also Cavendish's obituary in *The Bugle* [Alport, Middleton and Youlgrave, Derbyshire], no. 141 (December, 2011), where he was quoted as saying "wryly", 'As we set off, they told us the Israelis were the good guys and the Palestinians the bad. I found the opposite was the truth'.

27 R.E.S.S., 'A Letter from Palestine', in *The Tank*, vol. 29, No. 333 (January, 1947), 143.

28 General Sir Richard Gale, *Call to Arms an autobiography* (London: Hutchinson, 1968), 164.

29 John Donovan [ed.], 'A Very Fine Commander': The Memoirs of General Sir Horatius Murray* (Barnsley, South Yorkshire: Pen & Sword, 2010), 220–221.

30 Nigel Bromage, *A Soldier in Arabia: A British Military Memoir from Jerusalem to Saudi Arabia* (London and New York: The Radcliffe Press, 2012), 6.

31 *Orientations*, 363. For example, in A.J. Sherman, *Mandate Days: British Lives in Palestine 1918–1948* (New York: Thames and Hudson, 1998), 87.

32 *Having Been a Soldier*, 58. See also David Cesarani, *Major Farran's Hat, The Untold Story of the struggle to Establish the Jewish State* (Cambridge, MA: Da Cape Press, 2009), Chapter 1. Some latent anti-Semitism occasionally emerged in response to particular deadly Jewish violence as in the case of Lt.-Col. Richard H.L. Webb, CO 1st Argyll and Sutherland, Mitchell's unit, whose anti-Semitic outburst following the death of one of his soldiers and the wounding of an officer and six ORs in October 1946, cost him his post. Bruce Hoffman, *Anonymous Soldiers the Struggle for Israel 1917–1947* (New York: Alfred A. Knop, 2015), 334–335.

33 *Having Been a Soldier*, 58.

34 Andrew Gibson-Watt, *An Undistinguished Life* (Lewes, Sussex: The Book Guild, 1990), 241–242.

35 Brigadier A.J. Knott, 'Background to the Palestine Problem', in *The Royal Engineers Journal*, vol. LXI (December, 1947), 332–340, and *The Tank* No. 347, vol. 30 (March, 1948), 190, 199–201 and No. 348 (April, 1948), 232–233.

36 Second supplement to the *London Gazette*, 7th May 1946.

37 *The Tank* (March, 1948), 199.

38 Ibid., 200.

39 Ibid., 201.

40 Ibid., *The Royal Engineers Journal* published in its March 1948 issue a lengthy response by R.S. Dougan, who had served in Palestine and in Transjordan during the War, refuting Knott's historical account of the Mandate and arguing that the Arabs, in fact, 'have had a very fair deal from Great Britain'. *The Royal Engineers Journal*, vol. LXII (March, 1948), 88.

41 Hugh Foot, *A Start in Freedom* (New York and Evanston: Harper & Row, 1964), 36.

42 *An Undistinguished Life*, 240–241.

43 Ibid., 241.

44 Roy Fullick, *Shan Hakett: The Pursuit of Exactitude* (Barnsley, North Yorkshire: Lee Cooper, 2003), 15. Fullick had served in the Middle East. His last appointment in the Army was instructor in the Army Staff College.

45 Ibid.

46 *A Start*, 42.

47 Ibid.
48 *Statistical Abstract of Palestine 1944–1945* (Department of Statistics Government Printer, Jerusalem [no year]), 23.
49 *A Start*, 43.
50 Ibid., 46.
51 The title of Chapter VI in ibid., 86.
52 Ibid.
53 Ibid.
54 R.E.S.S., 'A Letter from Palestine,' in *The Tank* (January, 1947), 143.
55 Prayer beads used for reciting the ninety-nine names of Allah.
56 Ibid., 77.
57 Ibid., 87.
58 Ibid.
59 Lt.-Colonel Colin Mitchell, *Having Been a Soldier* (London: Hamish Hamilton, 1969), 54.
60 Ibid., 47, 98.
61 Major General Dare Wilson, *Tempting the Fates* (Barnsley, South Yorkshire: Pen & Sword, 2006), 145.
62 [Hebrew] A. Biletsky and M. Amster (Editors), *In the Years of Emergency (The "Camps" Period 1937–1947)* (Published by the Union of Construction Workers, 1956), 287–288, and map, 297.
63 [Hebrew] Amiram Oren, *"Drafted Territories" The Creation of Israeli Army Hegemony Over the State's Land and Its Expanses during Its Early Years (1948–1956)* (Givataim: Madaf, 2009), 21–24.
64 Ibid., 20.
65 These consisted by the end of the War of three battalions of 36 officers and 809 other ranks (OR) in three rifle companies, one support company and a headquarters company, each. George Forty, *British Army Handbook 1939–1945* (Thrupp, Stroud, Gloucestershire: Sutton Publishing, 2002), 165.
66 Major General R.P. Packenham-Walsh, *History of Royal Engineers*, vol. IX, 1938–1948 (Chalteham: The Institute of Royal Engineers, 1958), 559–560. See also Royal Engineers Archive, CE Monthly Narrative Report. Palestine Works Services September 1946–1947, Serial No. 12 Chief Engineers Narrative Report for Period 16 August–15 September '47, 29 September, '47, A directive was received from 'E' Branch GHQ on 14 September giving the RE rundown from 1 July 47 to 31 December 47'.
67 Royal Engineers Archive, Serial No. 13, East Palestine Sub District, 16 September–15 October 1947.
68 *History of the Royal Corps of Engineers*, 561.
69 C.E. Monthly Narrative Report No. 12, op. cit.
70 Ibid., No. 13, 16 September–15 October, 1947, 29 October, 1947.
71 [Hebrew] Gad Kroizer, *The Tegarts The Construction of the British Police Forts in the Land of Israel* (Mikve Israel: The Yehuda Dekel Library, The Council for Heritage Preservation in Israel, 2011).
72 *The Household Brigade Magazine* (Spring, 1947), 37.
73 Ibid. (Summer, 1947), 86. Richard Crichton, *The Coldstream Guards 1946–1970* (The Coldstream Guards, 1972), 7. The PMP base in Sarona had been attacked unsuccessfully by the Hagana's Palmach in February 1946.
74 *The Household Magazine* (Summer, 1947), 7.
75 Ibid. (Spring, 1947), 36.
76 Crichton, 7.
77 Ibid.
78 *Household Magazine* (Spring, 1947), 36.

79 Norman Rose, *A 'Senseless Squalid War': Voices from Palestine 1890s–1948* (London: Pimlico, 2009), 145. [Hebrew] Yigal Eyal, *From Intifada to Revolt* (Efi Meltzer, 2007), 410–412, [Hebrew] Ya'akov Banai (Mazal), *Anonymous Soldiers the Book of Lechi Operations* (Tel Aviv: Hotsa'at Chug Yedidim, 1958), 670–671.

80 Crichton, 9–10.

81 *The Household Magazine* (Spring, 1947), 37.

82 Ibid.

83 Ibid.

84 Crichton, 10–11, *The Household Magazine* (Summer, 1947), 86.

85 Crichton, 12, [Hebrew] Yehuda Slutsky, *History of the Hagana*, vol. 3, part 2 (Tel Aviv: Am Oved, 1973), 956. On the political background, see Bruce Hoffman, *Anonymous Soldiers: The Struggle for Israel, 1917–1947* (New York: Alfred A. Knopf, 2015), 443–444.

86 [Hebrew] *History of the Hagana*, 1232–1233, [Hebrew] Avraham Vineberg, *Chapters of Ta'as Hagana Underground Weapon Smiths* (Ma'arachot, "Alilot" Library, 1951), 167–178.

87 Crichton, 12.

88 Peter Verney, *The Micks the Story of the Irish Guards* (London: Peter Dawes, 1970), 169.

89 IG archive, 1st Battalion Irish Guards *News Letter* No. 3, 17th April 1947.

90 See 4th/7th *Royal Dragoon Guards Regimental Magazine* (June, 1947), 82 on camp 21.

91 IG *News Letter* No. 3.

92 The facing colours of the Guards.

93 Ibid.

94 *The Household Magazine* (Autumn, 1947), 183.

95 *The Thin Red Line*, vol. 1, No. 2 (May, 1947), 42.

96 *Verney*, 183.

97 *The Household Magazine* (Autumn, 1947), 183.

98 Ibid. (Summer, 1947), 88; (Autumn, 1947), 128.

99 Ibid. (Summer, 1947), 80.

100 *The Household Magazine* (Summer, 1947), 90.

101 *The Highland Light Infantry Chronicle*, vol. XLIII, No. 3, July 1947.

102 Ibid., 'Intelligence section notes', 128.

103 Ibid., '"C" Company notes', 127.

104 Ibid., 'Mortar platoon Notes', 130.

105 *Chronicle* No. 3, 132.

106 Ibid., 132–133. Niblo had apparently, 'taken part in every game' since joining the battalion before it left Cairo, 'and more than one outside left has felt like packing in after playing against him'.

107 *The Tank*, vol. 29, No. 333 (January, 1947), 'The Eighth', 169–171.

108 Ibid., 170.

109 *The Household Magazine* (Summer, 1947), 80.

110 Ibid., Autumn, 1947, 139.

111 Ibid.

112 Ibid.

113 Ibid. (Winter, 1947–1948), 193.

114 Ibid., Verney, 170.

115 *The Household Magazine* (Winter, 1947–1948), 188.

116 Ibid.

117 Ibid., 189.

118 *The Borderers' Chronicle* (September, 1947), 118.

119 Other beers produced at the time were given Hebrew names.
120 *The Highland Light Infantry Chronicle*, vol. XLIII, No. 4 (October, 1947), 172.
121 'Beer to the rescue', in *Soldier The British Army Magazine*, vol. 4, No. 1 (March, 1948), 33.
122 Ibid.
123 *An Undistinguished Life*, 201–202.
124 Ibid., 211.
125 *The Borderers' Chronicle*.
126 Ibid.
127 *An Undistinguished Life*, 221.
128 4th/7th *Royal Dragoon Guards Magazine* (June, 1947), 89.
129 *An Undistinguished Life*, 209.
130 Lt.-Colonel Colin Mitchell, *Having Been a Soldier* (London: Hamish Hamilton, 1969), 57, see also 55.
131 See Charles Messenger, *For Love of Regiment: A History of the British Infantry*, Volume Two 1915–1994 (London: Leo Cooper, 1996), 155. It was not until 1st January 1949 that the National Service came into effect.
132 For example, the support company of the 1st Argyll and Sutherland Highlanders had an establishment of 200 in 1945 and of 40 in early 1947 at a time when the regiment was reduced to one battalion.
133 'Pot', short for potential.
134 National Army Museum *[NAM]* 1999-11-190-23 Dept. EPFS, '2nd Bn The Middlesex Regt (DCO) [Duke of Cambridge's Own] Trg. Directive No. 1, 20 Feb. 48'.
135 *The Thin Red Line*, vol. 1, No. 2, 40.
136 Ibid., 43.
137 *Having Been a Soldier*, 60.
138 Lincolnshire County Archives, 2nd Battalion Royal Lincolnshire Regiment, Digest of Services 1 Appendices, REG-1/Box 2/375 Robert Finigan to CO 2nd Lincolns 11 June 1947.
139 Ibid.
140 *TNA* WO 261/81 AG Branch and Services, GHQ MELF Fayid, Quarter ending 14 June 1948.
141 *TNA* WO 261/654 Quarterly Historical Report Headquarters 1st Infantry Division for period ending 10 March, 1948, Appx. U 20 January, 48.
142 *The Die Hards*, vol. VIII, No. 5 (March, 1948), 152.
143 *TNA*, WO261/654 Appx., U.
144 Nigel Hamilton, *Monty Final Years of the Field-Marshal* (New York, etc.: McGraw-Hill, 1986), 633–634.
145 *The Memoirs of Field-Marshal the Viscount Montgomery* (Cleveland and New York: The World Publishing Company, 1958), 373.
146 Ibid., 393.
147 Ibid., 379.
148 Hamilton, 636.
149 Ibid., 637.
150 *Memoirs*, 379.
151 Ibid., 381.
152 Hamilton, 665.
153 Ibid., 666.
154 Ibid., 684.
155 *Memoirs*, 418–419.
156 King's College, London, Liddel Hart Centre, 7/1/6 Minutes, 6 June 1947.
157 Lt.-General G.H.A. MacMillan, 'The Evacuation of Palestine', in *Journal of Royal United Services Institute* (November, 1948), 609.

158 The rest were soldiers, mainly Arab, serving with the Arab Legion and the Transjordan Frontier Force. [Hebrew] Yona Bandman, 'Planning the British Withdrawal from Eretz Israel' in Alon Kadish (editor), *Israel's War of Independence 1948–1949*, vol. 2 (Tel Aviv: The Ministry of Defence Publishing House, 2004), 644.

159 Lt.-General Sir Brian Horrocks, 'The Highland Light Infantry, A Special Introduction', in L.B. Oatts, *The Highland Light Infantry* (London: Leo Cooper, 1969), n.p.

160 Major-General John Nelson, *Always a Grenadier*, printed without publishing details, 60.

161 Ibid.

162 Oliver Lindsay, *Once a Grenadier: The Grenadier Guards 1945–1995* (London: Leo Cooper, 1995), 21.

163 Nelson, *Always*, op. cit.

164 Ibid.

165 Arthur Max, *Men of the Red Beret: Airborne Forces 1940–1990 (1990)* (London: Warner Books, 1992), 441. See also Nicholas Bethell, *The Palestine Triangle: The Struggle between the British, the Jews and the Arabs 1935–48* (London: Andre Deutsch, 1979), 241.

166 Major R.D. Wilson, *Cordon and Search: With 6th Airborne Division in Palestine* (Aldershot: Gale & Polden, 1949).

167 *An Undistinguished Life*, 217.

168 Ibid., 218.

169 The subject has its own heroic literature, for example, [Hebrew] Meir (Munya) Mardor, *Secret Mission* (IDF Ma'arachot, 1957), [Hebrew] Pinchas (Pinik) Vaze, *Mission Rechesh* (IDF Ma'arachot, 1966).

170 *TNA* WO 261/758 Special Investigation Branch Royal Military Police MELF, Quarter ending 31 March 1948.

171 *TNA* WO 261/644 HQ East Palestine Sub District, Quarter ending 31 March 1948.

172 Ibid., Quarter ending 30 June 1948.

173 *An Undistinguished Life*, 218. See also Maurice Tugwell, *Herzl Street* (Princeton, NJ: Xlibris, 1997), a crime novel set in Haifa during the last days of the Mandate, in which a syndicate operating within the army sells 1,200 weapons. Tugwell served in 1947 with the 6th Airborne.

174 *TNA* WO 261/758 Reports of the Special Investigations Branch of the Royal Military Police, MELF for the last quarter of 1947 and the first two quarters of 1948.

175 *TNA* WO 261/81 AG Branch of Service, GHQ MELF Fayid, Quarter ending 14 June 1948.

176 *TNA* WO 261/645 Appendix 'B' Historical Report North Palestine District, copy of NPD/4261/a dated 16 February, 48.

177 On the national policy in the matter, see summary in [Hebrew] Yoav Gelber, *The Emergence of a Jewish Army* (Jerusalem: Yad Ben-Zvi Institute, 1986), 54.

178 [Hebrew] Zadok Eshel, *The "Carmeli" Brigade in the War of Independence* (IDF Ma'arachot and Ministry of Defence, 1973), 24.

179 A previous attempt to steal tanks, while on the move from Ramat David to Haifa, had failed.

180 4th/7th *Royal Dragoon Guards Regimental Magazine*, December, 1948, 47, 49. Lindsay, *Once a Grenadier*, 28–29, and [Hebrew] Amiad Brezner, *Origins of Israeli Armour* (IDF and Ministry of Defence, 1995), 132–134. See also article in [Hebrew] *Armour*, no. 45, June 2014, 97, posted 4 February 2014 in *www.Yadlashiryon.com*.

181 Lindsay, 28–29.
182 Wilson, *Cordon and Search*, 202–203.
183 Ibid., 203.
184 *TNA* WO 261/579 Quarterly Historical Report for the 4 R Tks, Quarter ending 30 June 48.
185 Imperial War Museum 87/57/2 C.R.W. Norman, 'Terrorism in Palestine', 17 November 1948.
186 Mitchell, *Having Been a Soldier*, 58–59. At the time, Mitchell was OC of the battalion training wing. The police and army carried out house-to-house searches while the population was concentrated in makeshift detention centres for questioning. The main complaints in the Jewish newspaper *Davar*, representative of the Jewish leadership, were the looting and vandalism of private, commercial and industrial property in the Givat Shaul neighbourhood.
187 *The Thin Red Line*, vol. 1, No. 2 (May, 1947), 36.
188 Wilson, *Cordon and Search*, 46.
189 [Hebrew] Ya'acov Banai, *Unknown Soldiers: The book of Lechi operations* (Tel Aviv: Hotsa'at Chug Yedidim, 1958), 402–402.
190 *Palestine Post* 28 April 1946. Wilson, *Cordon and Search*, 47n.
191 Banai, 405. Wilson did not realize that the mines were fake.
192 According to the *Palestine Post* 28 April 1946, 1,500 were questioned and 79 were detained.
193 *Palestine Post*, 28 April, 1946.
194 Hoffman, *Anonymous Soldiers*, 258–259.
195 In Bethell, *Triangle*, p. 233.
196 Imperial War Museum, C.R.W. Norman papers.
197 Wilson, *Cordon and Search*, 48.
198 [Hebrew] *Davar*, 28, 29 April 1946, and *Palestine Post*, 29 April 1946.
199 [Hebrew] *Davar*, 29 April 1946. *Palestine Post*, 29 April 1946.
200 *Palestine Post*, 29 April 1946.
201 Ibid.
202 *The Thin Red Line*, vol. 1, No.2 (May, 1947), 44.
203 *Palestine Post*, 1 December 1946. See also [Hebrew] *Davar*, 1.2.12. 1946.
204 *The Thin Red Line*, May, 1947, 36. In fact, there were nearby a number of Jewish farming communities including Be'er Tuvia and the younger Kfar Warburg, who were as a rule peaceful.
205 Ibid., 40.
206 On regimental bands, see Ian F.W. Beckett, *Discovering British Regimental Traditions* (Princes Risborough, Buckinghamshire: Shire Publications, 1999), 82–85.
207 Due to the reduction in 1947 from 143 battalions to 91, all regiments, except for some of the Foot Guards, were reduced to a single regular battalion. See Messenger, *For Love of Regiment*, 156.
208 *Faugh a Ballagh* (July, 1948), 297, 298.
209 Produced for the 38th (Irish) Brigade, 1944.
210 *Faugh a Ballagh* (July, 1948), 298.
211 Ibid., 299.
212 Ibid.
213 Irish Guards' Archive, 'Band Tour of Palestine1948.'
214 Ibid. and *The Household Brigade Magazine* (Spring, 1948), 36.
215 On the origin of the ceremony, see Peter Verney, *The Micks*, 6.
216 *The Household Magazine* (Spring, 1948), 38. In his forward to Verney, *The Micks*, pp. xii–xiii, Field-Marshal Templer recounted a chance encounter in Tunisia with a company of Irish Guards which, with the help of the company piper formed a small parade with regimental flourishes.

217 *The Thin Red Line*, vol. 1, No. 2 (May, 1947), 43: 'The Pipe Band is now the pride of the Battalion; it has 34 members'.
218 Ibid., vol. 2, No. 1 (January, 1948), 22.
219 *The Borderers' Chronicle* (December, 1947), 156.
220 *The Borderers' Chronicle* (September, 1947), 124.
221 *The Thin Red Line*, vol. 2, No. 1 (January, 1948), 18.
222 The Rev. John A. Fraser, 'The Moderator's Visit to the 1st BN' in ibid., no. 3 (September, 1948), 84.
223 Irish Guards Archive, *News Letter* No. 3 (17 April–17 May, 1947).
224 Probably, a reference to the Goodwood racecourse in Sussex, known also as Glorious Goodwood, reflecting its popularity. I am grateful to Philip Waller, who saved me in this (and other) instances from an embarrassing mistake.
225 *The Borderers' Chronicle* (December, 1947), 155–156.
226 *The 4th/7th Royal Dragoon Guards Regimental Magazine* (June, 1947), 82.
227 Ibid., 86.
228 *The Household Magazine* (Spring, 1947), 37.
229 *3rd The King's Own Hussars Journal*, vol. III, No. 2 (January, 1948), 47–48.
230 Ibid., vol. III, No. 3 (January, 1949), 99.
231 *The Borderers' Chronicle* (March, 1948), 8.
232 Ibid., 9.
233 '"L" Battery, R.H.A. Palestine', in *Gunner*, vol. XXIX, No. 7 (October, 1947), 164.
234 Ibid., 165.
235 *The Faugh-A-Ballagh*, vol. XXXVII, No. 164 (July, 1948), 289.
236 *The Borderes' Chronicle* (December, 1947), 157.
237 *The Borderers' Chronicle* (March, 1947), 46.
238 Ibid., 157, 159.
239 Ibid., 122–123.
240 *The Highland Light Infantry Chronicle*, vol. XLIII, No. 4 (October, 1947), 168, 169.
241 Edward Horne, *A Job Well Done: (Being a History of the Palestine Police Force 1920–1948 [1982])* (Sussex: The Book Guild, 2003), 453.
242 Irish Guards Archive, 1st Battalion Irish Guards *News Sheet* No. 2.
243 Ibid., no. 3 (17 April17 May, 1947).
244 *4th/7th Royal Dragoon Guards Regimental Magazine* (December, 1946), 19.
245 *An Undistinguished Life*, 222–223, 226.
246 Ibid., 226.
247 Wellington Barracks London, Coldstream Guards Archive, Coldstream Guards Orders (January–June, 1948), No. 75 [1] (April, 1948).
248 *TNA* WO 201/297 Quarterly Historical Report for the quarter ending 31 June 1948.
249 Coldstream Guards Battle Orders, No. 86.
250 Ibid., No. 116.
251 National Army Museum, London, 1983-03-104, Cunningham papers, Cunningham to Connie-Mary 22 July [1947].
252 Ibid., Cunningham papers no. 27, 'The End of the Palestine Mandate.'
253 *The Borderers' Chronicle* (June, 1948), 43.
254 On mascots, see Ian F.W. Beckett, *Discovering British Regimental Traditions* (Prines Risborough, Buckinghamshire Shire Publications, 1999), 78–79.
255 Marcus Cunliffe, *History of the Royal Warwickshire Regiment 1919–1955* (London: William Claws, 1956), 173.
256 Beckett, 78.
257 *The Antilope* (May 1947), 33.
258 Ibid. See also photograph in Cunliffe, facing page 180.
259 April 1946.

260 *The Antelpe* (May, 1947), 34.
261 Cunliffe, 179–180.
262 *The Antelope* (November, 1947), 95.
263 *4th/7th Royal Dragoon Guards Regimental Magazine* (June, 1947), 71.
264 *An Undistinguished Life*, 210.
265 *4th/7th Magazine* (June, 1947), 71.
266 Ibid.
267 *An Undistinguished Life*, 200.
268 Ibid., 208.
269 Ibid., 209.
270 Ibid.
271 Ibid., and *4th/7th Magazine* (June, 1947), 72.
272 *4th/7th Magazine*.
273 Ibid.
274 Since 1st February 1946, the Hussars had been officially designated the Armoured Airborne Reconnaissance Regiment. *3rd The King's Own Hussars Journal* vol. III, No. 1 (January, 1947), 2.
275 'Shooting' in ibid vol. III, No. 3 (January, 1949), 106.
276 Ibid., 106.
277 *3rd Hussars Journal* (January, 1949), 107.
278 George Forty, *British Army Handbook 1939–1945* (Thrupp, Stroud, Gloucestershire: Sutton Publishing, 2002), 134.
279 N.A.M. 1999-04-10-1 Memoir of Service by Maj. The Hon. N.I. Forbes, 81.
280 'Riding', in *The Faugh-A Ballagh*, vol. XXXVII, No. 163 (November, 1947), 237.
281 Ibid.
282 Ibid.
283 'The Transjordan Frontier Force' in *4th/7th Magazine* (December, 1946), 17, and Roy Fullick, *Shan Hackett*, 168.
284 *Palestine Post*, 30 June 1947.
285 Ibid. (29 and 30 June 1947).
286 *The Faugh-A-Ballagh*, 237–238.
287 Ibid., 238.
288 Horne, *A Job Well Done*, 352–353. McNeil remained in Palestine as the manager of the Government Stud Farm and as Stock Breeding Officer for Palestine 1927–1931. Upon retirement he settled in an Arab village near Acre where he died in 1949.
289 Horne, 353. See also Thomas Curd, *Rural Thoughts in the Holy Land* (East Sussex: Ukfield Press, n.d.), 71.
290 *The Faugh-A-Balagh*, 237. See also Horne, 352–353, and Philip Brutton, *A Captain's Mandate Palestine: 1946–1948* (London: Leo Cooper), 81.
291 *An Undistinguished Life*, 222.
292 *The Faugh-A-Balagh*.
293 Jeremy Bastin, *The History of the 15th/19th The King's Royal Hussars 1945–1980* (Chichester, West Sussex: Keats House Ltd., 1981), 29.
294 *The Faugh-A-Balagh*, vol. XXXVII, No. 163 (November, 1947), 237.
295 Ibid., no. 164 (July, 1948), 289.
296 *TNA* WO 261/758, GHQ MELF Fayid, Quarterly Report of the Provost Marshall, GHQ Middle East Land Forces, for Quarter ending June 1948.
297 [Hebrew] *Ha'aretz* 2nd February 1948.
298 R.E.S.S., 'A Letter from Palestine', in *The Tank*, vol. 29, No. 333 (January, 1947), 144.
299 NAM 1999-04-10-1 Memoir of service Maj. the Hon. N.J. Forbes.
300 *An Undistinguished Life*, 220–221.

301 E.g. *The Tank*, vol. 29, No. 334 (February, 1947), 218.

302 *Household Magazine* (Summer, 1947), 90.

303 Ibid.

304 *The HLI Chronicle*, vol. XLII, No. 4 (October, 1947), 167.

305 Brutton, *A Captain's Mandate*, 111.

306 P. Le S. Harris, 'Journey to Jerusalem', in *The Globe and Laurel,* vol. LVI, No. 10 (October, 1948), 303. See also G.G.I. Barker R.T.R., 'Bethlehem, Christmas, 1945', in *The Tank* (December, 1946), vol. 30, No. 344, 91.

307 'The Holy Places in Jerusalem', in *The Suffolk Regimental Gazette* (November, December, 1948), 19.

308 R.E.S.S., 'A Letter from Palestine', in *The Tank* (January, 1947), vol. 29, No. 333, 144.

309 Ibid.

310 'Palestine as a Playground', in *Soldier*, vol. 4, No. 6 (August, 1948).

311 Ibid.

312 'A Letter from Palestine', 143.

313 Richard Elley, 'Cyprus Holiday', in *Soldier*, vol. 3, No. 7 (September, 1947), 17 and *TNA* WO 2201/188 Quarterly Historical Report 1st Guards Brigade, Quarter ending 31 December 1947.

314 'Cyprus Holiday'.

315 *TNA* WO 261/466 1st Infantry Division Medical Services. As far as the army was concerned prostitution mainly posed a health threat to the troops. Other aspects such as moral or security were of little interest. See [Hebrew] Deborah Bernstein, *Women at the Margins: Gender and Nationalism in Mandate Tel Aviv* (Jerusalem: Yad Izhak Ben-Zvi, 2008), 235–240, 263–267.

316 *The Household Magazine* (Winter 1947–1948), 193.

317 G.M. Gordon-Watson, 'A Trip to the Negev and Transjordan', in ibid. (Spring, 1948), 15.

318 Ibid.

319 Ibid., 17.

320 Ibid.

321 Ibid., 18.

322 Ibid.

2   The southern sector

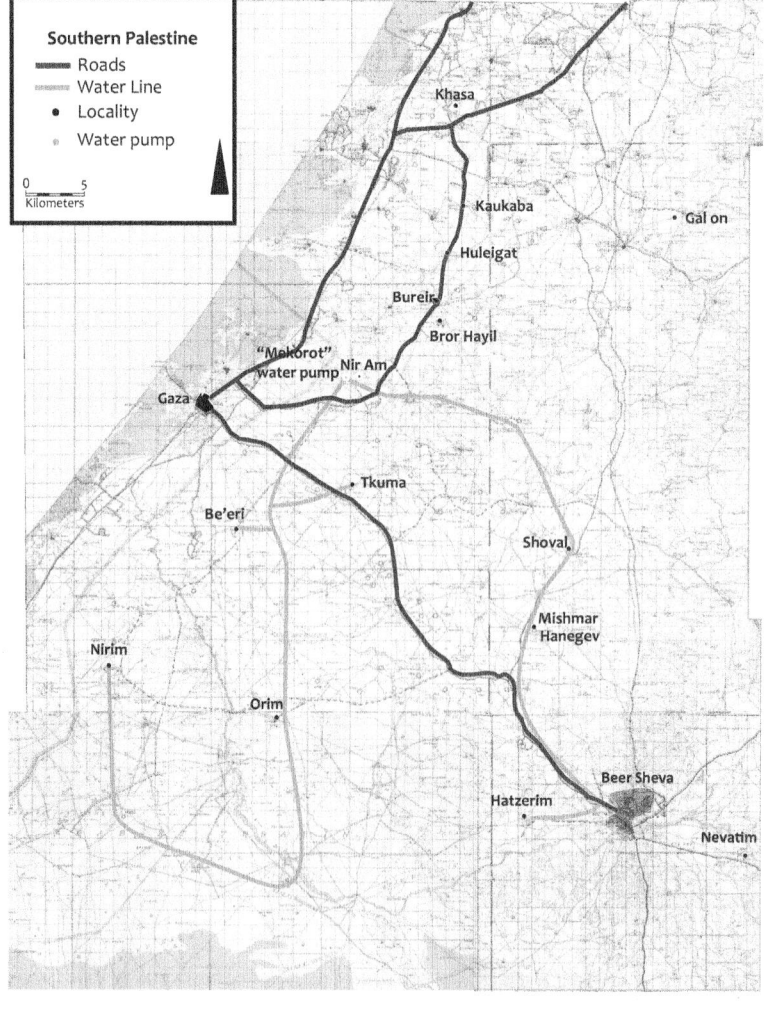

Map 2 Southern Palestine.
Source: Survey of Palestine 1947 and survey of Israel 1955/1956.

Based on the experience of the 1929, and the 1936–1939 outbreaks of inter-communal violence, the Haganah anticipated, at the end 1947,[1] a repetition of the previous patterns:

> Attacks on Jewish neighborhoods in mixed towns, necessitating the construction and manning of static defensive lines.
> Attacks on isolated Jewish rural and urban neighbourhoods.
> Attacks on Jewish traffic on roads connecting Jewish communities, thereby undermining the economic viability of Jewish agriculture by isolating it from its urban markets (whereas Arab villages were primarily economically autarkic).

In the southern military sector of Palestine, consisting of the Gaza civilian district, there were few towns, none of which were mixed. The district was the largest in Palestine – 13,813 square kilometres (5,333 sq. miles) out of a total of 27,009 square kilometres for the whole of Palestine.[2] In 1944, the population of the Gaza District was 190,880 out of a total of 1,764,520 in Palestine: 136,650 resided in the Arab town of Gaza, 11,180 in the town of Khan Yunis, 9,820 in Majdal, all on the coast, and 5,360 inland in Beersheba.[3] In the two sub-districts of Gaza and Beersheba, there were 3,040 Jews.[4] The rest of the residents of the district were nomadic and seminomadic Bedouin and Falaheen-Arab farmers residing in small villages.[5] All the Jews in the district lived in various types of collective farming communities.

In the late 1930s and especially following the Second World War, the south of country, loosely labelled as the "Negev", had become the main focus of Zionist pioneer settlement. Consequently, in 1948 many of the younger Jewish communities were very small. Furthermore, since their location was largely determined by the availability of Jewish-owned land and the political aspirations of the Zionist leadership rather than by economic viability, none of them had reached a stage of economic self-sufficiency and they depended on external support for their survival. In addition, most of the settlements south of the Majdal-Beersheba line were dependent on water pumped from wells dug in NirAm and Dorot in the southern coastal plain. Two pipe lines had been laid in 1947. An eastern line of two 6" pipes to Kibbutz Khatserim, completed in October 1947 and a western line to Kibbutz Nirim of a single pipe, completed on 15th September 1947.[6] Jewish settlements featured, as a distinguishing landmark, a water tower used to collect the water from the pipes.

In view of the geography and demography of the sector, most attacks against the Jewish presence were made by Bedouins on Jewish traffic and on the water lines. Especially problematic to deal with were attacks by villagers on roads which ran through their communities, especially the large village of Burayer.[7] In anticipation, the Haganah reinforced the smaller Jewish settlements with small Palmach units of the 2nd Battalion which was transferred to the Negev, in addition to civilian reinforcements sent by the various settlement movements. Thus, the Palmach, which had been designated a strategic reserve, was in fact sent to fill in gaps in the map of Jewish settlements wherever these were thin on the ground and incapable of defending themselves or their surroundings. Adverse to defensive tactics the Palmach continued to prefer, wherever it was stationed, offensive tactics even when their mission was defensive.

On 21st October 1947, following the disbandment of the 1st Armoured Division, the 61st Lorried Infantry Brigade (commanding officer Brigadier T. Brodie) was given responsibility for the South Sector of Palestine.[8]

Differing from regular infantry, Lorried Infantry were equipped with three-ton lorries, in addition to Bren carriers and American halftracks which were meant to enable them to keep up with tank units to which they were usually attached and provided them with greater firepower.[9] One of the Brigade's battalion's, 2nd King's Royal Rifle Corps, 'The Green Jackets', had seen action during the war in North Africa, Italy and Western European as a Motor Battalion. Following the war, it was stationed in Libya, reverting to a regular infantry battalion. But in 1946, it was redesignated a Motor Battalion and sent to Palestine.[10] At the time, the battalion consisted of three lorried companies, each with three lorried infantry and one reconnaissance platoons, the latter equipped with White scout cars and halftracks. Due to constant manpower changes (500 riflemen left and arrived in 1947),[11] a training company was established and often used in operations.[12]

2nd King's Royal Rifle Corps (KRRC) was placed under the command of Royal Artillery Head Quarters (RAHQ) of 3rd Infantry Division (CO Brigadier D.W. Nielson) responsible for the sub-district of Gaza. The battalion was stationed first in Qastina and later in El Bourej. The other battalions in the brigade were the 1st Royal Sussex based in the ex-RAF camp in Qastina and the 1st Irish Guards in Khassa. The brigade was reinforced by 1st Royal Horse Artillery and "C" Squadron of the Life Guards equipped with five Humber armoured cars. The Brigade's mission was the preservation of law and order in the district against the possibility of '(a) Increased Jewish activity in the Sector. (b) Any aggressive Arab action other than a widespread rising [which presumably would require greater forces]'.[13]

The method and means consisted of a combination of

- static ROAD blocks,
- control of towns,
- snap road checks,
- a cordon on the north and north-east of the Sector, isolating it from the rest of the country, and
- mobile reserve.

With the increase in attacks on traffic, the battalions were further instructed: 'To patrol the main rds in the Gaza area with AFVs [Armoured Fighting Vehicles] during the hours of daylight in order to discourage and isolate attacks on civil or mil. vehicles'.[14] Road patrols between the hours 07:00 and 17:00 were each to consist of two Armoured Fighting Vehicles (AFVs) and accompanied by a member of the Palestine Police. They were instructed to 'stop and examine occasional vehs. during their patrol. Contact with any crowd will be avoided and no attempt will be made to get through any procession or demonstration'.[15]

It was thought that in the case of 2KRRC, operating in 'open, sandy country, where mobility and communication could be used to the full' was ideally suited to the capabilities of a motor battalion.[16] In an attempt to re-establish law and order by a show of force,[17] the battalion organized six columns of mixed arms, including artillery, armoured cars and motor platoons, to tour the local communities, Arab and Jewish, and thereby deter them from further aggravating the situation. According to initial reports, 'Reception was friendly, and it proved most useful later to have got to know both the desert routes and the leading personalities in each village and settlement'.[18]

One of the columns, described by Major E.M. Turnbull, OC of "C" Squadron, the Life Guards, consisted of a troop of his armoured cars, a platoon from 1st Irish Guards, a section of twenty-five pound field guns from 81st Field Regiment, the Colonel's caravan and some Palestine Policemen commanded by an Arab sergeant.[19] Over a ten days period, they visited twenty-one Arab villages and were received, everywhere, 'most cordially'. At first, they were suspected as Jews dressed in British uniforms, but once their credentials were established, a 'few dilapidated chairs would soon be produced for the comfort of myself and the village notables and, as the crowd grew larger, the inevitable cups of mint-flavoured tea and unsweeted coffee... would make their appearance'.[20] Meanwhile,

> To attract the crowd and at the same time to keep them amused, the Irish Guard platoon, complete with piper, staged a platoon march through each village and this proved a great success, even if it did appear somewhat incongruous to the military observer. They would disappear up the narrow mud streets and for the next ten minutes only the pipes could be faintly heard to tell us of their approximate position. Soon they would reappear from a different direction marching with great skill over and round the many obstacles, covered with flies and, not unlike the pied piper, followed by a large crowd of shouting, gesticulating Arabs. They would complete their show with some arms drill, watched by a silent and spellbound audience. The Gunners would then bring their 25 – pounders into action and perform the many complicated maneuvers which, I must confess, are still as much a mystery to me as they were to any of the Arabs watching the performance with such studied concentration and awe.
>
> ... By this time the entire population of the village would have assembled to witness the strange sight and, with armoured cars driving

madly round the village parameter each carrying a cargo of a dozen or so delighted natives clinging precariously to turret and wings, the exhibition would come to an end.[21]

During its ten days on the road, the column visited the troublesome village of Burayr. The British show of arms which included a mock attack by the RAF proved of little effect in deterring the inhabitants from repeatedly blocking the passage of Jewish convoys. Other highlights included a ten-minute visit of GOC Palestine General McMillan while the column was in Al Majdal, and the disappearance of the clinometer (tilt meter) of one of the twenty-five – pounders. 'Under the circumstances', it was pointed out, 'it was lucky no more serious loss was suffered during the proceedings'.[22] In conclusion, Major Turnbull wrote, 'we all learned a great deal about the lives and customs of the average Palestinian Arab and received, first hand, their views on the present crisis in the country'.[23]

Initially, it was felt that the presence of the columns throughout the area was in itself beneficial to the preservation of some order.

When disturbances broke out near the Eastern group of settlements in the Negev, near Asluj two of these columns were diverted and by their prompt arrival were able to prevent the spread of the trouble and to assist in a quick settlement of the disturbance by a considerable show of force.[24]

Some of the columns were supported at times by RAF flights 'so as to show the inhabitants the close link that exists between the ground and air forces and there is no doubt that this increased the steadying effect of these columns'.[25]

Typically, the Jewish account of the above-mentioned incident was quite different and focuses exclusively on an Arab attack on a Jewish vehicle, its failure to obtain some help from the Army near Asluj in evacuating a wounded Jew and the perceived British complicity in allowing an Arab attack on the vehicle leaving the Asluj camp. The local Jewish force in kibbutz Revivim appears to have been unaware of the arrival of the Army column nor to explain why the observed concentration of numerous armed Arabs in Asluj did not develop into an attack on the kibbutz.[26]

A consequence of the rise in inter-communal violence was an increase in Arab attempts to steal arms from the Army and the Palestine Police, fuelled by a surge in the price of small arms. The Brigade observed that in these attacks 'on individuals and small parties with the sole object of stealing arms, no real hostility has been shown'.[27] The main means of dealing with the problem was to tighten the troops' discipline and diligence. During the last quarter of 1947, there had

been an increment in the number of cases tried for loss of arms, most of which have arisen from drivers leaving their weapons unattended in the cab of a vehicle. There have also been several cases of armed soldiers being attacked by a crowd of Arabs. Troops do not seem to realize that they carry arms for a purpose.[28]

The first attack on Jewish vehicles that came to the attention of the 2KRRC took place outside their camp's gate shortly after Christmas. The Army had no local intelligence sources and was mainly dependent on the Police for information. Hence, previous attacks on Jewish vehicles and patrols along the water pipes, from 9th December onwards,[29] either went unnoticed or were dealt with by the Police. Jewish suspicion of British intentions and the common belief that the Army and Police were colluding with the Arabs[30] precluded at first co-ordination of the passage of Jewish supplies with the British authorities. By the end of December, the Jews organized the traffic in convoys of which they were initially reluctant to inform the British. Consequently, the armed forces never knew when a convoy was due, how many vehicles it would consist of, nor when it had finally passed.[31] Neither did the Army's method in securing the passage of convoys they were notified of, infuse much confidence on the Jewish side.

For the sake of impartiality, the British did not provide

> escorts, but standing patrols were put out to cover vulnerable areas; although it was intensely cold in the early hours of the morning these provided excellent training for junior commanders, drivers and wireless operators as well as a form of battle inoculation. Occasionally, as near Beersheba, patrols were forced to fire to break up attempts by Arabs to destroy a convoy, but persuasion was used where possible.[32]

The confidence felt by the 61st Brigade in December that the situation in its sector was largely under control,[33] was shattered when it became aware of a 'sudden deterioration in the IS [Internal Security] situation'[34] towards the beginning of 1948. 'There were several attacks by the Arabs on Jewish convoys but by far the most disturbing element was the increase of attacks on British and Mauritian [pioneers] soldiers usually by irresponsible Arabs who wanted arms'.[35] Previous attempts to ensure some training of the fresh reinforcements had to be abandoned, while their units found themselves fully committed in daily operations.

The 1st Royal Sussex of the 61st Brigade had been stationed at the end of 1947 in the ex-RAF camp in Qastina, where the high standard of their quarters had raised morale 'by leaps and bounds'.[36] Amenities included a camp cinema, run by a local contractor, with two houses nightly and a daily change of program. Guard duties were relatively light allowing four nights in bed in between.

During the early autumn of 1947, the 1st Royal Sussex had spent a month in Jerusalem. It was later sent on short notice to Hebron for a few days as 'a deterrent to rash behavior on the part of the Arabs'.[37] On moving back to Qastina, the battalion left behind in the Arab village of Halhul, two miles north of Hebron, "A" Company with two sections of carriers[38] to secure the Jerusalem-Hebron road which served as the main route for the transfer of supplies to the Arab Legion from the British Army's stores in the Canal Zone. Inter alia it constituted the line of communications of the Arab Legion with its garrison company stationed in Gaza and Rafah.[39]

On 9th January, the battalion's strike platoon with a section of carriers was rushed to the Arab town of Yibna, to break up a battle between Arabs and Jews.[40] Two squads of twenty-five Jewish new recruits of the Givati Brigade, stationed in the Gan Yavne settlement, had set out in the morning on patrol between Gan Yavne and the Arab village of Sukreir, combining basic training with a seemingly light operational mission as was the common practice in transforming of the Haganah militia into an army. As a precaution, in case they ran into a British patrol, the Jewish force was only lightly armed so that when surprised by armed Arabs they were unable to put up much of a resistance and were taken captive. Fourteen managed to escape back to their base while eleven remained missing. A Jewish search party came under Arab fire near the coastal road, east of Sukreir. Both sides were exchanging fire while reorganizing and receiving reinforcements when the strike platoon of the 1st Royal Sussex arrived on the scene.[41] Having travelled by road, the British troops were caught in the crossfire. Fearing the confiscation of their arms, the Jewish force withdrew. The British strike platoon fired some 500 rounds in an effort to suppress the Arab fire. Eight or so Arabs were killed, and over the next two days the Army recovered the severely mutilated bodies of eleven Jewish fighters.[42] It was generally assumed at the time on the Jewish side that all Jews taken captive would be tortured, and executed, and their bodies mutilated. The standing order was to commit suicide rather than risk being captured alive.

A few days later, on 15th January, the battalion's CO Lt.-Col. Oliver was ordered with his remaining companies to Jerusalem where he arrived within ten hours in camp Alamein in the south of Jerusalem. At dawn on the previous day, 14th January, a large Arab force, estimated by the Jews at about 600 strong, attacked the settlements of the Etzion bloc, south of Bethlehem. The Arab force consisted of local villagers, residents of Hebron and recruits of the Jerusalem area Arab militia – the Holy Jihad (al-Jihad al-Mucaddas) led by the commander of its eastern brigade and the Grand Mufti's nephew – Abd al-Qadir al-Hussayni. The Etzion bloc was an isolated cluster of four small Jewish settlements south of Jerusalem and west of the Jerusalem – Hebron road, of which Kfar Etzion was the largest. The mission of the military force in the bloc, as set by the Haganah high command, was to ambush Arab traffic on the road and if possible bring it to a complete stand still.[43] Ambushes were laid on 13th and 14th January, the latter observing on its way back to its quarters in the bloc the concentrations of Arab fighters preparing to attack.[44]

The Arabs failed to overrun the bloc on the 14th and after a day of fierce skirmishing the local Arab fighters, who were unequipped to continue the fight during darkness disengaged and returned to their villages.

According to the standard Israeli account, the battle on the 14th was decided by a local Jewish counter-attack of two squads who surprised a larger Arab force in the field. But the surprised Arab fighters managed to make good their retreat, reorganized and successfully attacked one of the squads who tried to pursue them.[45] In any event, this account, based on the testimonies of the Jewish defenders, makes no mention of the presence of the 1st Royal Sussex.

In Jerusalem, the 1st Royal Sussex were joined by some tanks, armoured cars and artillery, and were given air support, with the mission to stop the Arab attack on the bloc.[46] The task force, commanded by the 2nd [Jerusalem] Brigade, moved south passed Bethlehem on the 16th and remained in the area for three days.

The fighting on the 14th was observed by the commander of Hebron Police Station, John Hamish Dougan, who had maintained friendly relations with the Jewish settlers, as well as some other British observers (possibly from the Battalion's "A" Company) who reported the events to Jerusalem. Dougan told the Jewish Mukhtar of Kfar Etzion that he had heard of the attack on the morning of the 14th and reported it to Police HQ in Jerusalem who reassured him that according to its sources the attack had been contained by the defenders, and advised "A" Company in Halhul to be on the alert should the fighting get out of hand and their help in supressing it would be required. At 16:30 hours, Dougan, accompanied by some local Arab dignitaries, warned the leaders of the Arab attackers that unless the fighting stopped he would have to send for the army with the excuse that a British brigadier was held up on the road by the attacking Arabs while travelling from Hebron to Jerusalem.[47]

Lt.-Col. Oliver arrived in Kfar Etzion on the morning of 15th January with ambulances and military vehicles in order to evacuate the dead from the battlefield.[48] The deterrence created by the military presence along the road was enhanced by flights of the RAF which, at least in its own mind, constituted 'a convincing demonstration [which] was the decisive factor in dispersing the attacks, without British Forces becoming involved'.[49] To add to the deterrent, the 1st Royal Sussex staged on the 17th a demonstration south of Hebron 'as a warning to the local population'. It was received with great excitement by the locals.[50]

> This was an impressive shoot and included Bren guns, 3-in. mortars and 6-pdr. anti-tank guns, and a battery of field artillery, Eagle Troop, 6th R.H.A. [Royal Horse Artillery]. The Arabs were greatly impressed and arrived on the scene in hords, by lorry, camel, donkey and on foot. Instead of being cowered, however, they thoroughly enjoyed the whole affair. A sequel to this was that a deputation from Halhul approached the commander of the detachment there and asked for a repeat performance. To balance the admonition of the Arabs, a flag march through the more restless Jewish suburbs of Jerusalem was carried out the same afternoon by the armoured element of the Force.[51]

While the local and the Jerusalem Jewish command suspected, following a large number of intelligence reports, that the Arabs were preparing to resume their attack on the Etzion bloc, an attack did not materialize.[52] The seriousness with which the Jewish command took the threat of a renewed attack was reflected in the urgency with which a platoon of thirty-five ("Lamed Heh") fighters were sent by foot, carrying ammunition and medical supplies to reinforce the bloc's defenders. After an abortive attempt on the night of the 14–15th, the platoon tried to reach the bloc on the following night. It was discovered by local Arabs in the early hours of the morning of the 16th and were all killed in battle near the Arab village of Surif where the Holy Jihad had a training camp.

Rumours of the battle reached Hebron Police Station on the evening of the 16th and early the next morning (17th) Dougan, an army commander, and an Arab dignitary went in search of the bodies.[53] Most of them were found on a hill where the platoon made its last stand, and some in a nearby Wadi. By evening, with the help of the local Arabs, the thirty-five bodies were all located and were collected in two piles, one on top of the hill which was inaccessible to motor vehicles and the other near the bottom. The corpses 'had been stripped of all their clothing, but no desecration had been made to the bodies'.[54]

Early the next morning (Sunday the 18th), Dougan, with the help of some locals, who were paid 500 mil per body, began moving the corpses to a spot where they could be reached by a lorry. After carrying eight bodies to the loading spot, the locals were summoned back to Surif by a signal of two rifle shots. The rest of the bodies were carried by the soldiers of "D" Company, loaded onto three Army lorries and, escorted by carriers, brought to Kfar Etzion for burial.[55] Carriers also escorted the mourners from Jerusalem and back, as well as the funeral procession.[56] On the 18th, with the situation under control, the 1st Royal Sussex returned to Qastina, leaving behind "D" Company, which replaced "A" Company in keeping the Jerusalem-Hebron road open, under the command of the 1st Suffolk of the 2nd [Jerusalem] Brigade.[57]

Meanwhile in the South Sector units were as a matter of routine, on alert in case the Jews tried to land illegal immigrants on the coast, code named "Operation Taffy". Information to that effect on five different occasions during November–December 1947 proved false. In one instance, on the 3rd of December, the 1st RHA was sent to the beach west of Majdal. It reported that a 'large number Arabs gathered, armed with every type of weapon... and it was obvious that if any landing took place the protection of the immigrants from the Arab population would be a very considerable problem'.[58]

While such alerts became increasingly infrequent, the units in the South Sector were faced with mounting difficulties in both securing road traffic and the repairs of the Jewish water pipes whenever it was decided to pump water to the settlements. While the mobility of the 61st Brigade's units was supposed to prove advantageous in dealing with these missions, and although it had retained "Q" Branch [logistics] and sections of the disbanded 1st Armour Division's Ordnance Field Park, it was unable to cope with all of the Brigade's ordnance problems. These included the loss of stores in transit due to unprofessional staff work and supervision, resulting in shortages which included brake fluid and vehicle batteries.[59] One result of this problem combined with the increase in operational strain was an alarming rise in the number of road accidents.[60]

On 30th December 1947, Brigadier Brodie, CO of the 61st, met at his HQ, with Michael Hanegbi, representative of the Sector's Jewish settlements.[61] Hanegbi complained that the Army's method of securing traffic by taking up positions along the road or running patrols rather than accompanying Jewish convoys failed to prevent Arab attacks once the British position was passed or the patrol was out of sight. Such was the case, according to Hanegbi, when on 27th December a Jewish convoy travelling between NirAm and Gvulot was attacked near Kfar Darom resulting in six wounded passengers and two tenders destroyed.[62] Brodie answered that the Jewish demand that the Army escort convoys was contrary to their instructions. Hanegbi added to his criticism of the Army's method an instance in which a convoy was attacked near Deir al Balach while waiting the return of a tender from Kfar Darom.[63] The Army patrol kept driving back and forth, refusing even to evacuate wounded female passengers from the convoy or members of the Jewish Settlements Police who covered the convoy's withdrawal. Their original understanding had been that the convoy would be escorted by an Army vehicle equipped with a wireless set which would coordinate its security, but the officer on the site informed the convoy that his instructions were to keep a mile's distance from it.

The Brigadier reassured Hanegbi that while he could not provide escorts there would be, in the future, sufficient forces to secure the roads as well as a vehicle with a wireless set nearby to direct the convoy. They agreed on the Army securing the passage of one convoy a week later reducing it to one in ten days. However, he informed Hanegbi, the Army could not secure both the roads and the mending of the water pipes on the same days. And inasmuch as supplying water to the settlements with tankers every few days was likely to prove much more difficult, the Army was keen to facilitate the use of the pipes when required, that is, at about once a month. As for the Jewish complaint that soldiers had confiscating weapons used for the protection of convoys, Hanegbi was told by the Brigadier's Intelligence Officer in a meeting on 21st December that it had been a local initiative rather than the official policy.[64]

On 31st December, Hanegbi met Brigadier Nielson, CD South Sector in his HQ in El Bureij.[65] Despite their attempts to work out some viable arrangement, there appears to have been little the Army could do with its limited means. Nielson suggested that the Army secure the passage of a convoy to the south on one day and its return on the next, while remaining throughout in the area. He undertook to ensure personally that all the security measures promised will be taken beginning with safeguarding the periodic operation of the pipeline, and the passage of a convoy on the next day. Most significantly Hanegbi, who had complained that the Army had not kept previous agreements, was shown a telegram from the Chief Secretariat stating that the government will not object to the Jews using their own armoured vehicles to protect passengers, but will not allow offensive looking cars that might scare the locals when driving through Arab communities.[66]

The committee of Negev settlements, which Hanegbi represented, had demanded from the Haganah high command in mid-December nine armoured vehicles to secure traffic and transport reinforcements in case of an a attack. Local initiatives included armoured platting of vehicles for their protection,[67] making use of the expertise gained during the Arab Revolt. It was generally assumed on the Jewish side that the use of armour, even if improvised, would greatly contribute to the effectiveness of its response to Arab attacks. The local Jewish command used armoured vehicles whenever available arguing that left to their own devices they were capable of solving their own security problems. This was especially true wherever the Army lacked the means to provide an acceptable alternative. A case in point was the problem of convoys passing through Arab Beersheba on the way to the Jewish settlement of Beit Eshel, east of the town. The locals tended to fire on all vehicles, including the Army's, and the bypass commonly used proved impassable during the winter. The Army, for its part, was careful not to provoke Beersheba's population and, therefore, avoided travelling through the town.

Consequently, when the return of a Jewish convoy from Beit Eshel was delayed in early January, the Jews chose to drive through Beersheba (8th January) providing their own security. When the convoy was attacked and one of the cars broke down, another one stayed with it, while the convoy continued on its way, and a Jewish armoured car was sent from Beit Eshel to extract them. In the event, the Jewish side had suffered no casualties and the convoy made it to NirAm.[68]

When the Army failed on 11th January to keep its promise to safeguard the mending of the water pipeline, the Jews sent with the workers four armoured cars which were later forced by the British to leave the area for fear that they may provoke a violent reaction from Beersheba.[69] The problem of securing the operation of the pipeline was effectively solved when the government declared that since it was a private utility its operation was not the government's responsibility. Having begun producing its own improvised armoured vehicles as early as December 1947, the Jewish side operated by the end of January 1948 seventeen armoured cars in the Negev[70] which provided an independent solution to threats to the convoys and the pipeline.

There remained the problem of Arab roadblocks in Arab villages through which the road passed. At first, a standard British peacetime response was employed.

It became a rule that whenever a clash took place a mobile force with Police and reps of the civil government visit the villages concerned soon after the incident as possible to investigate it and impress on the leaders of the community that we were still responsible for law and order and that we were prepared to use force to ensure that normal life of each community could be maintained.[71]

In the case of Beersheba, in order to stop the locals from attacking both Jewish and British vehicles driving through the town, and fearful of the situation getting out of hand, the Army placed a garrison in the town consisting of "B" Company of the 2nd KRRL minus a platoon which was sent to Asluj along the road to central Sinai.[72] It was considered vital to prevent a confrontation whereby the Jews would occupy Beersheba through which passed two of the Army's eventual evacuation routs from Jerusalem to Sinai, through Asluj and through Gaza.[73] The same roads had been in use for the passage of supplies for the Arab Legion and incidentally the illegal supply of arms from Egypt to the al-Jihad al-Mukades and the arms illegal market in general, and the passage of volunteers to join the Arab forces activities of which the Jewish side was fully aware.[74]

The Beersheba garrison was reinforced by the 39th Medium Regiment Royal Artillery equipped with an Observation Post tank (with additional radio equipment) from the 1st Royal Horse Artillery. It was thought that the presence of the tank had 'a very great steadying effect on both communities as they knew that they had no means of dealing with heavy tracked AFVs [Armoured Fighting Vehicles]'.[75]

The Jewish military leadership at first considered Beersheba impassable.[76] Early in 1948, the Arab Legion had sent a team of instructors to train the local residents. Captain C.H. Todbury, "A" Company, the 2nd KRRL observed upon his return to Beersheba at the end of March 1948, when his company replaced "B" Company, that the state of the local defence had greatly improved 'About 100 locals now underwent daily instruction in all arms, including platoon attacks interspersed with occasioned panics when they [the Arab Legion instructors] helped all Beersheba to man strong points, ditches and roof tops'.[77] The British garrison further lent a hand in planning defence positions.

Gradually, Jewish confidence increased as Jewish forces deploying their armoured cars when not securing convoys, attacked Arab traffic, often on the roads leading to Beersheba,[78] including, on 6th April, an Arab Legion lorry en route from Gaza to Beersheba.[79] The British observed that

The Arabs suffered from a lack of co-ordination between Gaza and that town, and would have run out of supplies if not escorted. As the police left [Capt. Tidbury] OC "A" Company became entirely responsible for such order as could be maintained in the area, using road patrols.[80]

According to Captain Tidbury,

> The climax was reached... when [20.4] a Jewish supply convoy for Beit Eshel came up the road from Asluj in broad daylight and its escort sat... for half-an-hour 300 yards from Beersheba town. The whole Beersheba population manned the defenses, fired all their weapons and got out their only armoured car, which started on a right flanking attack and then ran out of petrol!
>
> That afternoon was an unforgettable sight for most of "A" Company who watched from the police station roof after repeated efforts to stop the Arabs firing by signals and after the A.D.C. (Abu Haida), the District Officer (Mohammed Effendi) the Mayor and Joad Effendi had all failed by shouting, the firing was, if anything increased by all these notables going home, getting out their private Brownings, L.M.G.'s [Light Machine Guns] and rifles and going off to add to the chaos. For all their firing the Jews still sat... in their armoured car until the convoy reappeared from Beit Eshel and disappeared southwards... from then on an evergrowing Arab panic started up.[81]

The situation was further exacerbated when fifteen Arabs were killed on the Asluj road by a Jewish patrol.[82] All of Beersheba spent three nights in the town's trenches, convinced that they were facing an imminent attack.[83] Nor was the panic felt by the local Arabs confined to Beersheba. One of the garrison's platoons,

> spent a night at Imara Police Post to give the Arab police and irregulars confidence. The Jews, meanwhile, drove their armoured cars round Arab strong points most of the night, especially at Imara and Huzayel Police Posts and Beersheba. The Arabs lost a lot of sleep.[84]

By 1st May, Huzayel was abandoned and by 3rd May Imara, both occupied by Jewish forces of the Palmach Negev Brigade.[85] By the end of April, the Jewish forces were in control of the open country around Beersheba. With Jewish vehicles protected by armoured plates, now with the advent of the dry season, convoys could leave the roads and travel across the open desert, accompanied by a light reconnaissance airplane.[86]

Another road junction vital for the transportation of supplies including Army stores evacuated to the Canal Zone and for the Army's final evacuation was Gaza town where the road from Beersheba met the coastal road to Rafah and the Canal. In the beginning of February, the situation in Gaza was described in a KRRC Operations Instruction as 'outwardly peaceful', but liable to 'boil over at any moment'.[87] In order to ensure that Gaza remained peaceful, it was assigned a powerful regular patrol consisting of an officer, eighteen other ranks (ORs) in three halftracks, a police representative and a tank.[88]

The patrol was instructed to drive along main roads thereby bolstering 'the confidence of the local population'. The particulars of the patrol's mission included:

1   These patrols will be carried on a friendly basis with the local population. Pl [Patrol] Comd will stop on the route and speak to Arabs at suitable intervals.
2   Great care will be taken to avoid damage to property, particularity the crops.
3   Fire will be opened only as a last resort and only if this is necessary to extricate the patrol from a dangerous situation.[89]

On 10th February, responsibility for the sub-district of Gaza passed from Commander Royal Artillery (CRA) 3rd Infantry Division to O.C. 2nd KRRC.[90] Patrols continued as before but were reduced in size. Gaza patrol now consisted of one officer, eleven ORs and two trucks.[91]

On 28th January, an armoured car of the Palmach's 2nd Battalion with ten fighters had lost its way and entered Gaza town.[92] According to the 2KRRC's account,

> They had arrived at the police station, located well West of the town, and with no recognized exit except by the route by which they had entered. By some miraculous means they had passed down the main street and through the bazaar before the alarm was raised. On enquiring of the route at the police station they sensibly agreed to be taken in for safe custody before the gates shut on an angry and milling crowd of some two hundred Arabs.[93]

The Army's dilemma was how to safely evacuate the Jews from Gaza without provoking a violent Arab response.

> The Jews confined in the police station could not stay there for ever. They had to be returned in safety to their settlement, even though they had been disobeying the law by carrying arms. Outside were many Arabs, also armed prepared to await the reappearance of their enemies.[94]

The KRRC's account testifies to their preoccupation with seeking an elegant solution, a possible reflection on their level of boredom.

> Various covert plans were... instituted with the object of outwitting the thugs in wait. First, a platoon... was dispatched to live permanently in the police station with orders to reconnoiter alternative routes by way of the coast, either to the North or South. Secondly, a three – ton lorry, clearly marked "Rations, No lifts", was ordered to drive into the town through the municipal road block, at regular

intervals three times a day. And, thirdly, an impressive fire-power demonstration was laid on to take place on the coast West of the town in about one week's time.[95]

The only reference to the end of the affair in the memoirs of the CO of the Palmach's 2nd Battalion was 'our men were released after a week, but alone [i.e. without their arms and without the armoured car]'.[96] The KRRC provides a more satisfactory account. On 8th February, it was decided to employ a double bluff.

> At first light that morning, the Platoon formed up in the police station for its normal reconnaissance patrol, but just as it was leaving the Jews were bundled into the half-tracks, made to lie on the floor and were covered with tarpaulins. The platoon then drove straight through the town and the road blocks without incidents! In many ways a simple operation, but one which caused a great deal of worry, and much excitement.[97]

During February, the units of the 61st Lorried Infantry Brigade gradually withdrew from Palestine leaving 2nd KRRC in charge, supported by "C" Squadron, The Life Guards (Maj. Turnbull), a self-propelled anti-tank battery of 12th A/Tk Regiment RA an Air Observation Post (AOP) detachment of 651st Squadron AOP with five aircraft, and detachments of sappers, signals and medical personnel. All these constituted Southforce under the command of GOC 1st Infantry Division.[98] Its main mission, the 'maintenance of law and order taking the form of protection of all main roads, railway lines and pipe lines (Water)' by means of patrols, had remained unaltered from that of the 61st Brigade.[99]

There were five daily patrols in addition to a patrol sent out of Beersheba by its garrison, with a company on alert. Their orders were 'preventing bands of armed Arabs and Jewish Armoured cars from attacking the other's villages and settlements. And also... the prevention of mine laying on the main roads by the forces of the Arab Liberation Army' (probably meaning any foreign Arab forces in the area, e.g., the Moslem Brotherhood fighters from Egypt).[100] In addition to securing the use of the Sector's main roads the patrols were sent into areas off the main roads and in particular, 'to visit isolated JEWISH settlements', and ordered to 'prevent any organized armed body or vehicle with heavy mil equipment and weapons from passing ASLUJ',[101] meaning Second World War weapons smuggled out of Egypt for the Palestine weapons' market. Any obstacles to traffic such as roadblocks were to be removed and, in general, the patrols were to drive slowly, and stop for ten to fifteen minutes at junctions, crossroads, villages 'and other busy points'.

An additional task was guarding evacuated Army camps. Initially, the policy was to sell camps, their installations and equipment to local contractors. However, the Arabs soon discovered that they could raid with impunity evacuated camps by using women and children as a shield. By February,

> any empty camp was systematically looted by the local villagers who not only removed doors, windows and fittings, but demolished everything including cinema halls constructed of reinforced concrete. It was found that such looting could be prevented by day in most cases by providing a piquet of three men with a Bren [gun] in a commanding place in the camp. Provided this was done as soon as the camp was vacated most looters would clear off when a warning burst was fired in their direction, but in some cases the warning was ignored and casualties were inflicted on tresspassers. If looting had started it was almost impossible to stop it without causing considerable casualties. This looting continued even after the camps had been purchased by ARABS so that finally it became almost impossible to get any offers for camps as the potential purchasers knew that either the material would be looted before they could arrange for their removal or they could have them without payment by organizing looters as soon as the camp was left unguarded.[102]

A solution was to sell the camps before they were evacuated and allow the buyers to occupy them during their evacuation. However, most camps had not been sold by the time their occupants departed which often was with little prior notice and with no troops available to guard them.[103] The 2KRRC observed that within '48 hours of evacuation of a camp there would not be one brick upon another. Even the pipes and cables were uprooted'.[104] By early March, while Southforce was formed, only occupied camps remained standing. The rest had been stripped bare.

Gradually control of the Sector slipped from the Army's hands. It found itself powerless to force the passage of Jewish convoys through the villages of Burayr,[105] Kawkaba and to a lesser extent Hulayqat situated on the road to the southern Jewish communities. The Arab roadblocks in the villages consisted of parallel impassable ditches and, increasingly, of electric anti-tank mines, used also in ambushes along the main roads. On 15th March, a Jewish convoy travelling south succeeded in forcing its way through Burayr. On its way back the next day, this time with an Army escort, it failed to drive through the village and a later attempt using armoured cars was similarly unsuccessful. An attempt to retaliate on the 17th, using a portable bridge, was foiled by a new ditch, while aerial reconnaissance revealed more ditches in Burayr and in Kawkaba.[106]

The only alternative road ran closer to the coast, between the Arab towns of Majdal and Gaza through a populated Arab area. It had been designated part of the Army's eventual evacuation route and as such was to be kept permanently open. The Haganah hoped that although more dangerous, using the road while threatening with retaliation on Arab traffic following any attacks on its convoys, would force the Army to act in order to keep it open.[107]

For ten days (16–25 March), the Haganah used the coastal road until escalating violence forced the Army to close it to Jewish traffic. The Haganah continued to retaliate against Arab traffic while seeking an alternative route for supplying the southern settlements. On 4th April, the Palmach 2nd Battalion reconnoitred, now that the dry season had set in, a passable dirt road through Arab fields east of the troublesome Arab villages.[108] For the Army, this was an ideal solution in as much as it ensured the safe passage of Arab traffic along the coastal road and absolved it of its responsibility for ensuring passage of Jewish convoys through the Arab villages of Burayr and Kawkaba. Consequently, on 19th April, the Army allowed the foundation, on Jewish owned land, of kibbutz Bror-Chail, about one kilometre east of Burayr, which served to secure the passage of Jewish convoys along the alternative road.[109]

Since February, the Jewish forces in the south had been gradually reinforced. Another Palmach battalion (8th) was created and in March the two battalions formed the Negev Brigade. With growing Jewish confidence, and a sense that at least the Bedouins had been largely pacified,[110] the Negev Brigade extended its offensive operations with the aim of establishing its control on the countryside in anticipation of an Egyptian invasion following the end of the Mandate. This was directly challenged by the Moslem Brothers concentrating around Gaza who on 10th April attacked the religious kibbutz of Kfar Darom.[111] The attack had failed but the next day information was received by the Haganah of further reinforcements camping in the Gaza airfield, which in turn was raided on 12th April by a Haganah force using armoured cars.[112] The raiders penetrated the airfield's defences with difficulty. It appears that the intelligence was false, but the operation had established the Jewish capability of using armoured cars in offensive operations.

On 21st April, the Palmach 8th Battalion, responsible for the southernmost Jewish settlements was misinformed that the Army had evacuated "Arundal Castle", its roadblock on the Gaza-Rafah road, a kilometre north of the Rafah camps, on the Palestine-Egyptian border. The local Palmach company commander (and future I.D.F. general) Avraham 'Bren' Adan, acting on his own initiative, as was common for Palmach commanders, decided to seize the opportunity to attack, with two armoured cars, Arab traffic near the border with the intention of capturing Arab vehicles.[113] Accordingly, Adan took with him ten drivers. True to the standard Palmach tactic of choosing the least expected route of approach, Adan closed in on the roadblock from the direction of the border, only to discover that it had remained manned. However, the temptation of easy targets coupled with a misplaced confidence that the Army would not react forcefully, led him to open fire and destroy an Arab truck carrying timber, in plain view of the roadblock. The two armoured cars then returned to their bases – kibbutz Mivtachim and kibbutz Gvulot.[114]

"Arundel Castle" was manned by the 1st Royal Sussex, who, upon leaving Palestine left a detachment in Rafah where it took over guard duties, convoy escorts and formed a strike force of a platoon in case of an emergency. It was equipped with three Staghound (T17E) heavy armoured cars, armed with two machine guns and a 37 mm gun.[115] Following Adan's attack, the strike force with an armoured car, a Bren carrier, and two Comet tanks were sent in pursuit of the Jewish armoured cars.

The tanks came from a composite troop of the 4th Royal Tank Regiment stationed in Rafah (since 23 February 1948) consisting of four Comet tanks, one Daimler Scoutcar and two 3-ton lorries.[116] Normally, there was little to do in Rafah except guard against constant Arab attempts to steal vehicles and equipment. The men were also sent, without their tanks, on escorts. Early in April, in consequence of a series of mechanical breakdowns, all four tanks were sent to the workshop for an overhaul. Following the Jewish attack, 'two recently overhauled tanks hurriedly left the workshops with wet paint and loaded up with ammunition'.[117]

The strike force moved out at about 13:00 hours with three officers and the District Intelligence Officer. It had recently rained and the tyre marks of the Jewish armoured cars were easily followed. 'It was observed that one set of tracks doubled back into... MITVAHEN [kibbutz Mivtachim] – and here one of the so called armoured cars was run to earth'.[118] In fact, the armoured car had previously entered the kibbutz and left. Instead, the Army found a three-ton truck with an armoured cab and towed it back to Rafah.

In Rafah, it was decided that the Mukhtar of Mivtachim the official representative of the kibbutz in its dealings with the authorities should be fetched and warned against similar behaviour (although it is unlikely that he had been consulted by Adan). A force was sent out again with the two Comet tanks of the previous day, a scout car and a platoon of the 1st Royal Sussex in a Staghound and a halftrack.[119] The Jewish settlers were not impressed.

> This settlement was a typical Negev settlement, a cluster of wooden framed buildings with a water-tower and look-out in the midst of them surrounded by a barbed wire fence and a minefield, some thirty yards across. The commander of the platoon parleyed for three-and-a-half hours in all, but the Muk[h]tar refused to leave the settlement or to admit the British even though he had been assured of a safe conduct to and from military headquarters. An effort was made by the "strike Platoon" to break into the settlement and the first gate was in fact breached, but when the Jews opened fire upon this platoon, it withdrew according to orders. After further parleying, an ultimatum was given, at the expiry of which fire was opened with Comet tanks on the settlement. Each tank fired sixteen rounds and material damage was inflicted.[120]

It was the first time that a Jewish settlement in the south had been fired upon by heavy, flat trajectory guns. Consequently, it provided an important lesson on the vulnerability of structures and positions above ground.[121]

In retrospect, Adan confessed that he was surprised by the Army's reaction, but even so he had assumed at the time that it merely tried to intimidate the Jewish forces and would not dare to attack.[122] The soldiers, on their part, were elated. The tanks officially reported firing sixteen rounds whereas in fact they had used twice as many, a common means of relieving tension and frustration especially when crews are given little opportunity to train with live ammunition. From their perspective, 'This minor incident was very popular with the troops and no further outbreaks occurred from the settlement until after the evacuation',[123] not realizing that in fact the Jewish attack had nothing to do with kibbutz Mivtachim. In any event, the Army's deterrence was further eroded due to its self-imposed limits on retaliation against Jewish attackers on Arab traffic.

As the end of the Mandate neared, 'the situation became less under control, but the main roads remained open for the British Forces. Gradually we allowed events to take their natural course in areas away from the main roads'.[124] The initial policy of keeping law and order and maintaining the territorial status quo had been practically abandoned. The Egyptian Moslem Brotherhood's volunteers were allowed to concentrate in the area of Gaza. Their first attack on kibbutz Kfar Darom on the morning of 10th April was investigated by the Gaza patrol after reports of much shooting had been received the previous night. The patrol recorded that it had come across 'a largish battle in progress',[125] whereas in fact the Egyptian attack had petered out by 06:30 hours. All that was left for the patrol was to arrange the evacuation of the bodies of thirteen Arabs and of five wounded, in addition to some eighty casualties removed by the Egyptians.[126]

On 11th May, days before the end of the Mandate, the Moslem Brothers attacked Kfar Darom again. Since this did not interfere with traffic on the main coastal road to Rafah, the Army did not intervene or even try to arrange a truce. The attacks continued throughout the next days during the Army's evacuation and while the Egyptian Army invaded Palestine. The Army's sole concern was that the mines, laid by the Moslem Brothers along the Gaza-Khan Yunis road, 'once removed on our orders, were not replaced'.[127]

Similarly, the Army did not intervene when the Jews tried to isolate Beersheba from Hebron and from Gaza by blowing up bridges, or when attacking and occupying some Arab villages such as Burayr (15th May).[128] Unessential outposts were evacuated leaving small detachments in Asluj, on the road from Beersheba into central Sinai, and in Iraq Suweidan on the main lateral east-west road which served both Arab and Jewish traffic[129] thereby allowing some flexibility in redirecting military traffic from the coastal road to Gaza and Rafah to the road to Beersheba and Sinai.

In summing up its period in Palestine, the KRRC felt that in

> Spite of many unpleasant and sometimes dangerous tasks, most of us enjoyed those days. Everyone was busy and there was a definite task in hand... we were left on our own to see the job through. Although many had been counting the days until we left the two sides to settle their trouble between themselves, there was almost an equal number of those who were sorry to end a most interesting and certainly responsible task.[130]

On 28th August 1948, the 2nd KRRC was disbanded.

Notes

1 For a useful collection of documents in Hebrew on the evaluation of the Haganah in 1947, see Shoshana Stiftel (ed.), *Plan "D": The First Strategic Plan, in the Independence War* (The IDF Archive and the Ministry of Defence, 2008).
2 *Statistical Abstract of Palestine 1944–1945*, Compiled and published by the Department of Statistics (Printed by the Government Printer [n.d.]) 2.
3 Ibid., 12, 23.
4 Ibid., 22.
5 [Hebrew] Ya'acov Shimoni, *The Arabs of Erets Israel* (Tel Aviv: Am Oved, 1947), 6–8.
6 [Hebrew] Amiad Brezner, *The Struggle on [sic] the Negev 1941–1948* (Tel Aviv: The Ministry of Defence and the Galili Center, 1994), 82–91.
7 For details on Burayr, see Walid Khalidi (ed.), *All that Remains: The Palestinian Villages Occupied and Depopulated by Israel in 1948* (Washington, DC: Institute for Palestine Studies, 1992), 91–92.
8 TNA, WO 261/693, Quarterly Historical Report of Headquarters sixty-one Lorried Infantry Brigade. For Quarter ending 31st December 1947.
9 Forthy, *Handbook*, 96.
10 *The King's Royal Rifle Corps Chronicle 1947* (Winchester: Warren and Son, 1948), 49.
11 Overall strength by the end of 1947 was 750. Ibid., 54.
12 Ibid., 51.
13 TNA WO 256/693 sixty-one Lorried Infantry Brigade Op. Instr. No. 13, 20 October 1947.
14 Ibid., Op. Instr. No. 15, 2 December 1947.
15 Ibid.
16 *The Annals of the King's Royal Rifle Corps*, vol. 17 (Celer et Audax Club, Gale and Polden, 1979), 204.
17 *The King's Royal Rifle Corps Chronicle 1948*, 37.
18 Ibid., TNA WO 261/693 Quarterly Historical Report of Headquarters sixty-one Lorried Infantry Brigade for the Quarter ending 31st December 1947, sheet 2.
19 Maj. E.M. Turnbul, 'Palestine Paradox,' in *The Household Magazine*, Spring, 1948, 5.
20 Ibid.
21 Ibid., 5–6.
22 Ibid., 7.
23 Ibid.
24 *TNA* WO 261/693, sheet 3.
25 Ibid.
26 [Hebrew] *The Negev Brigade in the War* (IDF, Ma'arachot [n.d.]), 30–31.
27 *TNA* WO 261/693, Quarterly Historical Record.

28 Ibid.

29 [Hebrew], *Negev Brigade*, 28–30.

30 E.g. [Hebrew] Yigal Alon [commander of the Palmach and later of the Southern Front], *Palmach's Campaigns* (Tel Aviv: Hakibbutzs Hameuchad, 1968), 202–203.

31 *KRRC Chronicle*, 1948, 38.

32 *The Annals of the KRRC*, vol. 7, 204, *KRRC Chronicle*, 1948, 37.

33 *TNA* WO 261/693, Quarterly Historical Record, 5(a).

34 Ibid., 6(b).

35 *TNA* WO 261/643, Gaza Sub District, January 1–March, 1948, Report by CO Col. V.J.L. Napier.

36 *The Roussillon Gazette, Journal of the Royal Sussex Regiment*, vol. 27, No. 3 (December, 1947), 7.

37 *The Roussillon Gazette,* vol. 27, No. 4 (Spring, 1948), 5.

38 *TNA* WO 261/338, Quarterly Historical Record, The 1st Bn.

39 John Bagot Glubb, *A Soldier with the Arabs* (New York: Harper & Brothers, 1957), 77.

40 *TNA* WO 261/336.

41 For a reliable Jewish account see [Hebrew] Avraham Eylon, *The Givati Brigade in the Independence War* (I.D.F. Ma'arachot, 1959), 231–232.

42 Ibid., 232, *The Roussillon Gazette*, vol. 27, No. 4, 5.

43 The best Israeli account of the battles in and around Jerusalem is [Hebrew] Itzhak Levy, *Jerusalem in the War of Independence* (Ministry of Defence, 1986). On the First Battle of Gush Etzion (January 1948), see Yochnan Ben Yaacov, *The Mountain Platoon. The Story of the Thirty-Five* (The Ministry of Defence, 2008).

44 Levy, 84–85.

45 Ibid., 87.

46 *TNA* WO 261/338, Quarterly Historical Record, The 1st Bn The Royal Sussex Regiment, Period 1 January 1948 – 26 February 1948.

47 The Mukhtar's account in [Hebrew] Dov Knoel (ed.), *The Etzion Block's War* (Jerusalem: The Jewish Agency, 1957), 134–135. See also 136.

48 Ibid., 135.

49 TNA AIR 23/8350, Air Vice Marshall W.L. Dawson, Report on the Evacuation of the Royal Air Force from Palestine, 9.

50 *TNA* WO 261/338.

51 *The Roussillon Gazette,* vol. 27, No. 4, 5. According to the Jewish *Palestine Post,* 18 January 1948, citing Arab sources, 'Army units entered Hebron during the week-end (17th)... and took up positions in the main-street. Army and Police officers and the Assistant District Commissioner... called on the local branch of the [Arab] national committee and warned them not to attack Jewish settlements in the neighborhood. It was also announced that searches would be made in houses and vehicles'.

52 Ben-Yaacov, *The Mountain Platoon*, 49–50.

53 History of the Hagana Archive, Tel Aviv, 80/3740/3 9, Dougan's testimony, 21/1/1970, *TNA* WO 261/338 DIVPOL HEBRON to DISCID Jerusalem [17.1].

54 DIVPOL HEBRON.

55 Knohl, 146.

56 Ibid., 146–148.

57 *TNA* WO 261/755 KRRC Operation Instruction no. 31, 14 February 1948.

58 *TNA* WO 261/693 61st Lorried Infantry Brigade.

59 Ibid.

60 *TNA* WO 261/694 Quarterly Historical Report A/Q Branch Headquarters 61st Lorried Infantry Brigade, Quarter ending 31 March 1948.

61 IDF Archive, Tel Hashomer, 64/680, 155, signed 5 January 1947[1948].
62 Ibid., and *The Negev Brigade*, 34.
63 For details of the incident see [Hebrew] Moshe Netser, *A Shoot from Its Roots* (Tel Aviv: Ministry of Defence, 2002), 81.
64 [Hebrew] David Ben-Gurion, *War Diary*, vol. 1, 55, ref. to a telephone conversation in which Henry Gurney, Chief Secretary of the Mandate Government informed Golda Myerson [Meir] of an explicit order not to search for Jewish weapons and not to confiscate them if they are only used defensively.
65 IDF 64/680, 55.
66 Ibid., Netzer, 80.
67 [Hebrew] Amiad Brezner, *Origins of the Israeli Armoured Corps*, Ministry of Defence, 1995, 33.
68 *The Negev Brigade*, 35.
69 IDF 64/680, 155.
70 Brezner, *Armour*, 41.
71 *TNA* WO 261/694 61st Brigade... Quarter ending 31 March 1948.
72 *TNA* WO 261/755 2KRRC Operation Instruction No. 23, January, 48 and No. 25, 31 January 48.
73 *KRRC Chronicle, 1948*, 40.
74 Ben-Gurion, *War Diary*, vol. 1, 104 (2 January 1948).
75 *TNA* WO 261/694.
76 Ben-Gurion, *War Diary*, 48 (15 December 1947).
77 *KRRC Chronicle, 1948*, 49.
78 *The Negev Brigade*, 45 (21 March 1948), 46 (28 March 1948), 50 (17 April 1948), 53 (20 April 1948).
79 Ibid., 57.
80 *The Annals of the KRRC*, vol. 7, 206.
81 *KRRC Chronicle, 1948*, 50.
82 Probably on 16th April, *The Negev Brigade*, 50.
83 *KRRC Chronicle, 1948*, 50.
84 Ibid.
85 *The Negev Brigade*, 54. Huzayel is near kibbutz Shoval and Imara near kibbutz Urim.
86 [Hebrew] Dan Bar-On, *Rebels in the Wilderness, The Story of Beit-Eshel 1943–1948* (Moshav Hayogev [n.y.]), 144–145. On the Haganah airplanes in the Negev, see [Hebrew] Avi Cohen, *The History of the Israeli Air Force in the War of Independence October 1947–July 1948* (Ministry of Defence, 2004), 19–22.
87 *TNA* WO 261/755 2KRRC Ops. Inst. No. 26, 1 February 1948.
88 Ibid.
89 Ibid.
90 *TNA* WO 261/694 61st Brigade, and WO 261/755 2KRRC Ops. Inst. No. 28, 9 February, 1948.
91 *TNA* WO 261/755 Ops. Inst. No. 29, 12 February 1948.
92 Netzer, 82. See also Ben-Gurion, *War Diary*, vol. 1, 193–194. Itzhak Sade reported to Ben-Gurion that the car had not lost its way but had been forced by the Army to drive to Gaza. The incident was a considerable embarrassment to the Jewish side and the facts were altered in the Jewish press. Following a brief trial of the Palmach members for carrying illegal arms, they were each fined twenty Palestine Pounds, *Haboker*, 9 February 1948.
93 *KRRC Chronicle, 1948*, 38.
94 Ibid.
95 Ibid.
96 Netzer, 81.

97 *KRRC Chronicle, 1948*, 39.
98 *Annals of KRRC*, vol. 7, 205.
99 *TNA* WO 261/755 Ops. Quarterly Report of the 2nd Battalion, The King's Royal Rifle Corps For the Quarter ending 31 March 1948, Appendix 'A', and Southforce Ops. Inst. No. 1.
100 These, by their own account, constituted in February 1948 a battalion. [Hebrew, translated from Arabic] Camal Ismail el-Sharif, 'The Moslems Brothers in the Palestine War,' in *In the Enemy's Eyes* (IDF 'Ma'arachot', 1954), 75.
101 Ops. Inst. No. 1.
102 *TNA* WO 261/694 61st Brigade.
103 Ibid., A/Q Brigade.
104 *KRRC Chronicle, 1948*, 40.
105 *TNA* WO 261/755. Southforce Ops. Inst. No. 5, 19 March, '48.
106 Brezner, 175–176; Netzer, 90, *The Negev Brigade*, 45.
107 Brezner, 176; Netzer, 91–92.
108 Netzer, 93–94.
109 For example, conversation between Nachum Sarig, commander of the Palmach Negev Brigade, and Ben-Gurion, 10 March 1948, in Ben-Gurion, *War Diary*, 291.
110 Netzer, 98–99.
111 *The Negev Brigade*, 49, Netzer, 94–95.
112 Brezner, 185, *The Negev Brigade*, 49, Netzer, 95.
113 [Hebrew] Avraham Adan, *The Ink Flag* (Ministry of Defence, 1984), 130.
114 Ibid., 130–132.
115 'Notes from Detachment, 1st Royal Sussex, Rafah, Palestine,' in *The Roussillon Gazette*, vol. 28, No. 1 (Autumn, 1948), 5.
116 'The Rafah Troops 'in History of the 4th royal Tank Regiment September '47–October '49,' 10–11, Ms in The Tank Museum, Bevington.
117 Ibid., 10.
118 Ibid., 11, *The Roussillon Gazette*, vol. 28, No. 1 (Autumn, 1948), 7. *The Negev Brigade*, 53. In Adan's memoirs, the dates are confused.
119 4 RTR, 11.
120 *The Roussillon Gazette*, op. cit.
121 Adan, 139–140; [Hebrew] Alon Kadish, 'Settlements prepare for war,' in Alon Kadish (ed.), *Israel's War of Independence, 1948–1949*, vol. 2 (Ministry of Defence, 2004), 810.
122 Adan, 140.
123 4 RTR, 11.
124 *KRRC Chronicle, 1948*, 46; *Annals KRRC*, vol. 7, 206.
125 Ibid., 45.
126 Ibid., and *The Negev Brigade*, 49.
127 *KRRC Chronicle, 1948*, 46.
128 Ibid., 45; *The Negev Brigade*, 54.
129 *KRRC Chronicle, 1948*, 45–46.
130 Ibid., 46. See also ibid., 52: '"A" Company thoroughly enjoyed its Beersheba detachment'.

3   Railways

Initially railway lines in Palestine were constructed for the use of pilgrims. The first – from Jaffa to Jerusalem, was laid in 1890 by a French company using equipment left over from the digging of the Panama Canal. The second, separate line, completed on the eve of the First World War, joined Haifa with the Pilgrims' Railway from Damascus to Medina, known as the Hedjaz Railway, in Dera'a, east of the Jordan river. The stretch across Palestine through the Jezreel Valley, was known in the Yishuv as the Valley Train and was renowned for its slowness.[1]

The rest of Palestine's railway system consisted mainly of the joining of two military railways, Turkish and British, constructed during the First World War. The Turkish line, which branched from the Haifa-Dera'a line at Afula, was laid inland, out of the range of the guns of the Royal Navy, through Jenin and Tul Karem on to Beersheba and to central Sinai along the route used in 1915 by the Turkish army to attack the Suez Canal. The construction was not completed due to the British advance into Sinai using the northern route. The British Army laid its own railway line, along the coast to El Arish. Following the British breakthrough in the Third Gaza Battle in October 1917, the railway was extended into Palestine as far as Lydda where it met the Turkish military line, thereby establishing Lydda as the country's main railway junction. The line was further extended north to Haifa where in joined the Haifa-Dera'a line. Both military lines were constructed in haste using whatever materials were available often of inferior quality and without any general plan or policy for its use after the war.

In 1920 with the establishment of the British Mandate, the railways came under the authority of Palestine Railways, a department of the Palestine government. For a variety of reasons, the system was not greatly developed during the Mandate. Some minor extensions were laid, mainly for the construction of army camps with one exception the "Jewish" line between Petah Tikva and Ras el Ain, partially financed with Jewish capital for the shipping of citrus fruit for export through Jaffa. During the Second World War with the system used to its full capacity, the Palestine railway was joined to Lebanon's system by an extension of the Haifa-Acre line along the coast to Beirut and Tripoli.

Most of the traffic at the time was in the service of the British Army and the war effort. The civilian passenger service was of relatively minor significance and was used largely by Arabs while the Jewish economy strove to develop self-sufficiency in transportation, investing in road haulage. With the association of the railways with the Mandate government and the Army's needs, it inevitably became a major and frequent target for Arab attacks during the Arab Revolt (1936–1939) and for Jewish sabotage in its violent campaign against the Mandate which intensified following the end of the war and the Labour's government adoption of the 1939 White Paper policy. During the Arab Revolt, the railways were secured by a combination of fixed positions – pillboxes and blockhouses in the stations and beside vulnerable sections of track such as bridges. In time, special patrol vehicles were developed namely Ford tenders fitted with train wheels, protected by armour plates and joined back-to-back so that they could move backwards and forwards with ease.[2] They were manned by a special Jewish auxiliary police – the Palestine Railway Detachment which was partly responsible for the security of the tracks from the summer of 1938.[3] By the end of the war, the number of Jews protecting the lines was reduced and the fixed positions were taken over by Arabs.[4] By the summer of 1947, one hundred Jews remained in the Detachment, down from the initial 800.[5]

During the last quarter of 1946, while the units of the 2nd Infantry Brigade were training in Transjordan, the security of the main Haifa-Lydda railway line was made the responsibility of The Armoured Trolly Squadron, consisting of "C" Squadron of 12th Royal Lancers under the command of the 41st Field Regiment Royal Artillery.[6] The joined tenders from the Arab Revolt were replaced by pairs of joined Marmon-Harrington armoured cars with, in between them, caged platforms for carrying troops. The armoured cars' crews included a commander, a radio-man, a gunner and two drivers.

> The commander, besides carrying out his normal duties, was constantly having to watch his driver, whose only occupation was to 'keep his foot down.' With the remarkable sang-froid of the British soldier, drivers would be up to every trick in the book – reading a comic, a quite cigarette, trying to get a brew going, tuning in to the BBC, or catching up on sleep. After all, it was driving deluxe, with no steering wheel or clutch.[7]

By 1946, the armoured cars were old and unreliable and due for replacement by pairs of new Daimler scout cars ("Dingo") similarly fitted with train wheels but operated separately driving three or four hundred yards apart. 'Great care has to be taken not to run one car into the other car if you happen to develop a little too much momentum'.[8] But the promised new equipment had yet to materialize, whereas, following the breakup of the short lived alliance between the Haganah, the Irgun Zvai Leumi (IZL) and the Lehi ("Stern Gang"), after the bombing of the King David Hotel, the latter had renewed their attacks on the railways. The new campaign included attacks

on stations (Haifa 20 September 1946, Ras el Ein 10 November 1946), police blockhouses and the derailment of trains. Daily armed escorts required
forty men. On 14th November, it was decided that the tracks themselves
would have to be guarded and the Gunners were reinforced by a company
(and later another one) from the 3rd Grenadier Guards and elements from
the 2nd Battalion, the Cheshire Regiment.

Every day, 'every yard of the track was swept at first light with the aid
of Arab gangers who refused to be hurried, despite urgent quacking of
"Qweiss Qweiss" from all sides'.[9] Another similar sweep was made at last
light, and during darkness search lights illuminated the tracks. In one instance, a mine was discovered

> buried some inches below the sleepers. We blew it up "in situ" and it de-
> stroyed 30 yards of track and blew out a nice lot of windows and doors
> in nearby Binyamina. The local Jewish inhabitants then demanded
> compensation out of regimental funds![10]

As a result, Arab engine drivers and firemen went on strike on 19th November
demanding better security.

To stem, the escalation of Jewish attacks on the railways necessitated the
deployment of the whole 6th Airborne Division in operation Earwig. To
begin with, the effort to reassure the railway workers (of whom only a small
minority were Jews) required the constant presence of a large number of
troops, which meant that soldiers 'had to leave camp well before dawn each
day, and return in the dark after a boring and tiring day on the line, during which they watched perhaps half a dozen trains pass'.[11] The hundred
kilometres or so of the Haifa-Lydda line were divided into red, amber, and
green sectors according to the nature of the locality and the level of danger.
Each sector was allocated an appropriate number of troops so that the 'men
knew their stretch of railway so intimately... that they could tell at once if
the ballast had been interfered with'. Once a mine was detected, the Sappers
were brought in to disarm it.[12] In the course of November 1946, two officers
of the Division's Royal Engineers were killed and one officer and two other
ranks (ORs) wounded when handling railway mines, some of which were
booby-trapped.

The situation was relieved early in December with the beginning of the
citrus season (for about a hundred days) since the oranges for export were
mainly shipped by rail to the ports. Shortly afterwards, the 2nd Infantry
Brigade returned from Transjordan and line security operations returned
to normal.[13]

In May 1947, a detachment of about a squadron, made up of soldiers
from each of the squadrons of the 17th/21st Lancers, took over the operation of the railway armoured cars – now both Marmon-Harringtons and
Daimlers.[14] Headquarters were established in Atlit, south of Haifa, with
troops stationed in Jerusalem (5) and Lydda (40), and later Gaza and Jaffa.

The newcomers underwent special instruction by their predecessors, the 12th Lancers, followed by a week's course conducted by Palestine Railways.

Since all the lines were single track only one coupled armoured car (two separate cars if Daimlers) could operate at a time between two stations. While some threat remained, and a Marmon-Harrington on patrol between Lydda and Jaffa was blown up by a pressure mine, the Lancers experienced a relatively calm period. At first, light the Arab platelayers inspected on foot the length of the line between stations.[15] Once the lines were pronounced clear, the armoured cars set off in accordance with a fixed time table, between 05:15 and 07:00 hours.

> The run south from Athlit [Atlit] started with the orderly officer getting the 'baton' from the local stationmaster and opening the points, to allow the patrol, parked for the night on the siding in the camp, on to the main line. Even in the summer months 4 a.m. was cold and there was always an unpleasant feeling in the pit of one's stomach, that some nasty little boy would have put a stone on the line – or worse.[16]

Numerous methods were employed to disrupt trains mines, electric or pressure, were only one of them.

> A sharp lookout must be kept for obstruction on the line. One Daimler rail car on rounding a corner saw a tin on the line. The tin was partly jammed down between two railway lines, and inside it was a stone. The car, being unable to stop, was derailed. Another method... is to place a metal bar in the joint of the two lines. Bricks and stones on the line are a frequent occurrence.[17]

Finally, there was the competition with road traffic for the use of level crossings. 'As a warning has little effect on most drivers, our "bag" was one staff car, one three-tonner and one taxi the engine of which stalled when it was half way across the lines.'[18] There were also animals.

The morning patrol from Atlit ended in the large Arab village of Tul Karem, the southern tip of a traditionally troublesome Arab area known as the Triangle.

> There had been no competition for the line early in the morning, but now the line was clear, it was a matter of waiting one's turn to be allowed on to each section of the line, to work one's way back to base. There was time to exchange news with the other patrol that had come up from the south, from Lydda, or to shout ribald remarks to a friend on the leave train. Probably about 10 a.m. the cars would get back into the Athlit [Atlit] siding, and after maintenance till midday, the crews would spend the afternoon on the squadron's private beach, and then go early to bed.[19]

In August, 'Python' and demobilization had depleted the Armoured Royal Detachment, and it was replaced by the battalion's "B" Squadron. 'It is with regret', the chronicler of the Detachment wrote, 'that we leave the railways – the most unusual commitment that we have ever undertaken'.[20]

By the end of 1947, with the general escalation in violence throughout Palestine, the operation of the railways was once again under serious threat, this time from the Arabs.

The 1st Guards Brigade, part of the 1st Infantry Division, responsible for the centre and (from February 1948) the south of Palestine, was in charge of the Samaria district, which included the Triangle. In its weekly Intelligence Review of 10th February 1948,[21] issued for the first time since October 1947, it observed that the Arab reaction to partition, started 'endless trouble' with attacks beginning on 2nd December on Jewish shops in Jerusalem[22] and in Haifa, and rioting in several Arab capitals. British assessment was that following the initial elation felt by the Jews and their realization that "we must fight or die", the Haganah 'wants to co-operate with the Army, Police and Civil Administration in this area'.[23] Consequently,

> Relations between troops and [Jewish] civilians are good. ...There have been no incidents or clashes since partition was announced, on the contrary a strong will to co-operate and make themselves as friendly as possible with the British has been registered.[24]

Roughly, the boundary between the majority of the Arab and the Jewish communities in the Samaria Sector ran along the railway line from Lydda to Haifa. Appropriately, the first serious Arab violent "outburst" registered by the Guards, 'was that of the first attack on the railway on 19th December where over 20 tons of sugar and rice were looted'.[25] The report associated the timing of the attack with the rejection by the United Nations of the Arab demand for a one state solution in Palestine instead of partition. However, the details of the incident suggest that the attack was mainly for profit. According to an official report published in the *Palestine Post*,

> About 100 armed Arabs held up a goods train on its way from Haifa to Lydda... and stole 35 tons of sugar... The gang halted the train... by exploding a small charge in front of the engine. The crew were held up and the gangsters unloaded the sugar into trucks and rode off.[26]

The newspaper's Kfar Saba correspondent added that the village's watchmen close to the scene did not hear any shots and that no policemen from the Railway Auxiliary Police (who by then were all Arabs), a kilometre away, were sent to the site.[27]

The British report surmised that the raid was intended to dislocate Jewish economic life. However, by February, this new cheap method of obtaining expensive goods soon became nothing less than hooliganism, the idea of dislocating Jewish economic life has long been forgotten since. Four or even five trains have been held up daily and looted by ordinary highway robbers, often accompanied by their wives and children.[28]

The 1st Infantry Division circulated in 1st October 1947 regulations for escorting trains carrying military stores.[29] Normally, railway escorts should be provided only for certain stores, that is, arms, ammunition and explosives, official mail, "A" [combat] vehicles and, bullion, while in transit until their final destination (including Egypt). The ratio of escorts to stores was one Non Commissioned Officer (NCO) and four British soldiers to each car of stores. In cases of large consignments of arms and ammunition 'which are particularly liable for pilferage', an officer would be added. The escort was to travel in a boxtrunk, the 'closest to the load most subject to pilferage, with doors kept open throughout'.

By the beginning of 1948, sensing that it was quickly losing control over the security of trains in its sector, the 1st Infantry Division initiated operation Sparrow Hawk for the provision of armed escorts on trains from Hadera to Rafah and from Tel Aviv to Jerusalem with added patrols along the tracks and spotter airplanes from a flight of 651 Air Observation Post (AOP). Their mission was to 'take all steps to prevent looting of trains and to arrest any Arab looter'.[30] The escorts were organized in *RAIL FORCE* which consisted of a rifle company of 1st King's Own Scottish Borderers (KOSB) which had at the time been employed in keeping the peace between the Jewish and Arab neighbourhoods along the Jaffa-Tel Aviv border, tanks and halftracks from 4th/7th Royal Dragoon Guards, and, in operational command, a composite company from 1st Welsh Guards,[31] commanded by Major D.C.M. Mather, ex-Commando and Special Air Service (SAS) who had rejoined the regiment after the war.[32] The 4th/7th Royal Dragoon Guards were to provide mobile patrols along the Ras-el-Ain-Lydda line (it being the citrus season), with the aid of a mobile force from 3rd Infantry Brigade which was also responsible for the Lydda-Tel Aviv line. In addition, the 4th/7th was responsible for the safety of at least six night trains on the Lydda-Hadera line. The infantry companies of Railforce were to escort all trains on the Lydda-Jerusalem and Lydda-Rafah lines, and whenever possible help with the security of the Lydda-Tel Aviv line.

Railforce was instructed:

If the train is stopped and surrounded by a gang of Arabs, the gd [guard] will attempt to disperse the crowd. Fire will not be directed into the crowd except as a last resort, but the gd will take whatever action is considered necessary to prevent the train from being looted and to enable the train to continue its journey. If fired upon the gd will return fire at the attackers.[33]

The AOP was scheduled to operate daily for four hours between 6 and 11 January. Upon detecting a suspicious 'band of Arabs' on the line or a robbery in progress, it was to alert a mobile patrol. Upon arrival,

> Any Arab crowd on the rly line will be dispersed, and if any looting has already begun, the patrol will prevent further looting and will force the Arabs to abandon any goods taken. Fire will NOT be directed into the gang except as a last resort. Ringleaders will be arrested and the loot will either be returned to the train or guarded until it can be disposed of.[34]

It soon became apparent that the prescribed mode of operation did not provide for instances in which armed thieves chose to fight rather than surrender their loot. Nevertheless, the Guardsmen found their assignment,

> By far the most amusing the Battalion had since its arrival in Palestine. For some days before the Battalion took on this job, armed bands of Arabs on the line from Lydda to Jerusalem had more or less succeeded in preventing any trains getting to their destination. However, on the second day the Battalion was there orders were received that trains must get through at all costs, and the particular train that day succeeded in "fighting" its way through successfully past several Arab blocks to arrive with its load complete at Jerusalem. After this, every train got through but on most journeys the guards were given a good chance of using their weapons against Arab bands in the hills.[35]

Hence, the troops' contentment.

> There were also "flag marches", through Arab villages near the railway line, where they demonstrated with tanks, etc., the sort of fire power the Arabs might expect to have against them if they started any trouble. Needless to say, a large amount of coffee was drunk with the Arabs at nearly every village.[36]

While the Welsh Guardsmen professed to have enjoyed their time with Railforce, their actual impact on the deteriorating state of security was minimal. For instance, according to a press report,[37] trains on the Haifa-Lydda line were attacked twice on 27th January by Arab gangs. In one attack, 200 bags of cement were stolen. Later in the day another, fifty bags were taken. Armed Arabs also broke into a railway wagon in the Haifa Eastern Station Goods Yard, apparently in collusion with the police. At Lydda station, a police patrol fired on armed Arabs looting barley. The Arabs returned fire. A rail was removed from the Jerusalem-Jaffa line and was later located nearby. Finally, the line near Lydda was badly damaged and a bridge destroyed.

On 29th January, the 1st Infantry Division issued a new Operations Instruction replacing the one from 3rd January.[38] Railforce was now left with one company of the Borderers. Yet the Division was aware that 'Arab gangs are continuing to fire on trains, block the rlys with boulders and use other methods to stop the trains. Trains without Brit. Gds. are still being stopped and looted'.

With the ongoing contraction of the 6th Airborne Division and despite the undiminished attacks on the Haifa-Lydda line, the northern boundary of Railforce's sector was extended beyond Hadera to Haifa to include the whole length of the network from Haifa to Rafah, including the lines Lydda-Jerusalem and Lydda-Tel Aviv whenever necessary. The mission remained to 'prevent looting of trains' and the method was unchanged except for the instruction: 'If fired upon the gd. will return fire at the attackers and aim to kill'.[39] This change appears to reflect the evaluation of CO 1st Infantry Division General Horatius 'Nap' Murray from 6th January:

> [The Arabs] are in the first place professional looters. At the same time they are doing all they can to prepare themselves as far as is possible for a conflict with the Jews when we leave the country. Their activities are mainly directed at clamping down on communications as far as they can and seizing all and any arms they find within reach.[40]

More specifically,

> The manner in which the trouble on the railway has tended to increase has led me to consider whether the time has not come for more aggressive measures. For instance for a period of 36 hrs it was impossible for trains to get through to JERUSALEM. This is intolerable. Equally our men are, from time to time, wounded or murdered whilst doing their duty and suitable means of retribution have not always been to hand. This clearly cannot be allowed to go on.[41]

By late January, Railforce was under the command of the 6th Field Regiment Royal Artillery supported by the company of the Borderers who were also made responsible for the road between Ramle and the Judean foothills ("km 23") on the way to Jerusalem, as well as the trains between Lydda and Rafah. Rocket Troop, 6th Field Regiment, provided guards for twelve trains daily between Lydda and Haifa, and Dragon Troop for trains to Jerusalem and some road patrols.[42]

The sum of methods deployed in January to try to contain the situation included

> "flag marches" throughout the district, the destruction of illegal road blocks, the agreement to [sic] local Special Police in certain towns and villages, the shelling of definite areas along the railway line, carrier patrols and road blocks.[43]

But all these were to little avail. The Lancers, operating their armoured cars, noted

> Firing on the cars and derailing them, in attempts to capture the weapons of the crews. One patrol was mined and ambushed near Tel Aviv, and three men shot to pieces while lying unconscious after the explosion.[44]

A summary[45] of violent incidents in the Samaria district for the period of 1 January–6 February 1948 enumerated thirty-six instances of Arab attacks, of which seventeen were on trains, many near the large Arab village of Kakun. In a letter to the press from late February, the General Manager of the Palestine Railways A.F. Kirby stated that since December 1947 the loot from trains amounted to under 70 tons of wheat, about 120 tons of barley, 28 tons of rice, 200 tons of flour and no more than 40 tons of sugar out of a total of 30,000 tons of foodstuffs meant for civilian consumptions.[46] This, he thought, under the circumstances, was not too excessive. The Jews, on the other hand, detected a high degree of organization behind the robberies and complained of the absence of an effective British response which, to conspiracy minded journalists, proved that this was a covert method for supplying the Arab forces.[47]

The sense of prevailing chaos was heightened on 29th February when Lechi, using three electric mines, blew up a troops train on its way back from Egypt, minutes after leaving the Rechovot station. Most of the soldiers aboard[48] were returning from leave whereas Lechi claimed that they were reinforcements for the 'Army of Occupation'.[49] Lechi stated that the attack on the train was in retaliation for the car-bomb exploded in Ben Yehuda street in Jerusalem a week earlier, in which British deserters took part. The presence of the deserters was seen by Lechi as clear proof of British culpability despite British protestations that in fact they were wanted as deserters by the Army.

British loses were reaching unacceptable levels. Following the attack on the Lancers' patrol near Tel Aviv, it was decided 'that the lives of British troops were being risked unnecessarily and the [Lancers'] whole rail commitment [along the Haifa-Lydda line] was therefore ended'.[50] "B" Squadron was moved to Be'er Ya'akov, near Sarafand to help guard the Lydda-Rafah and the Lydda-Jerusalem lines.[51]

Gradually, some of the lines were abandoned. Kirby admitted that

> After several weeks of ding-dong struggle in repairing the line between Lydda and Tel Aviv and Jaffa we have had to relinquish operations. Repair Gangs working day and night and train crews being shot at can keep up no longer.[52]

Late in March, Jewish local units blew up three bridges of the Haifa-Zemach line with the excuse that shots were fired from carriages at Jewish settlers.[53]

The line was abandoned and the Army promised Zemach Arab residents that its units would maintain a daily presence near their village where the attacks on the line had occurred.

With the Lancers terminating mobile patrols along the Haifa-Lydda line, security of the trains remained the concern of armed escorts provided by Railforce which from 20th January to 20th February was the responsibility of 6th Field Regiment Royal Artillery. At first

> on the Haifa run, only down trains were guarded as the up trains, probably because their contents usually consisted of oranges [for export], were not normally attacked. However, by the beginning of February, several attacks had been made and up trains looted by Arabs in broad daylight.[54]

Consequently, the Gunners were made responsible for all the trains, day and night, which forced them to use their own reserve-Eagle troop which had been left in camp 21 near Kfar Yona, and slightly reduce the number of guards on each train.

The Arab village of Kakun had remained a particularly troublesome spot. Every night trains were fired on from the village. Fire was returned but from a moving train it had little, if any, effect. Since the village was within the range of Eagle Troop's guns in camp 21, several targets in the vicinity were registered and a system of very lights was established to enable the train guards to summon artillery support. Railforce believed that the mere threat proved 'sufficient warning to the Arabs' since the fire from Kakun stopped. When, on 20th February, 6th Field Regiment handed over Railforce to the 41st Field Regiment it noted with satisfaction that during its period only one train had been looted, and it had been guarded by the Borderers.[55]

The 41st Field Regiment had spent the weeks since the beginning of 1948 in a training camp in St. Jeans' north of Acre, subjected to 'vile weather and the lessons learnt not the least was how to function in rain and mud'.[56] From Acre, it moved to the ex-RAF camp in Tel Litwinsky where, with KOSB it became Railforce until 27th April when train services in Palestine were terminated. For the period from 20th February, the 41st Field Regiment reported four major incidents: two on the Jerusalem line. An ammunition train from Jerusalem was brought through under fire and on the same day an oil train from Lydda was forced to return. A third incident was the attack by Lechi on the troop train near Rechovot, and the forth a train derailed by Arabs.[57] After months of training, first in Transjordan and then near Acre, the Gunners found train duty heavy going. Having 'to travel up and down the line in converted cattle trucks... an easy prey to a mine or a loosened rail'.[58] Furthermore, 'since 15 or more trains run each day, and the turnround was so erratic that we never knew when the escorts would get back' from Egypt. The force had sustained considerable casualties, seven killed (and another two in the 'Rechovot outrage'), ten seriously wounded, one missing and a number had suffered minor injuries.[59]

And yet there was a noticeable decline in the number of Arab attacks, especially on the Lydda-Haifa line. The reason appears to have been the effect of the increased presences of the Arab Liberation Army (ALA) in the Samarian Sector.[60] Formed by the Arab League, the ALA (Jaysh al-Inqadh) consisted of eight battalions and a number of separately organized companies. Units began entering Palestine from January 1948 with the aim of strengthening the defenses of the local Arab communities and preparing them for the inevitable confrontation with the Jewish army. According to Fauzi al-Qawuqji, the field commander of the ALA in Palestine, he entered the country from Transjordan on 6th March 1948 and was visited in his headquarters in the village of Jaba, some ten kilometres north-west of Nablus, 'by a British military mission headed by an officer with the rank of Colonel'.[61] The Colonel informed him 'on behalf of the British Command in Palestine, that as from that day I was to be held responsible for security in the whole country'. Qawuqji replied that his responsibility as defined by the League's High Command in Damascus was confined to 'the Nablus, Jenin-Tulkarm triangle, and the area of Galilee and Lajjon'.

The presence of the ALA west of Nablus was noted by the local Army command.[62] In the Tulkarm area, the ALA's Hittin Battalion had joined forces with the local National Committee in an attempt to regain control of the area, reduce unauthorized attacks on the British Army and Jewish communities and preserve the status quo while preparing for war.[63] Haganah intelligence learnt that a local instigator of train robberies was arrested by the ALA, sent to Syria and ordered to enlist in it.[64] In doing so, the ALA suppressed the activities of the criminal gangs, politically endorsed by the Mufti's Arab National Committee. The Army reported that the ALA

> are enforcing law and order as much as they can in the whole area [of Samaria]. Petty crime, looting, train robbing and firing in the streets has practically ceased. Their military patrols are active and they have succeeded in recovering some sacks of sugar stolen by train looters ten days ago.[65]

"A" Squadron, 4th/7th Royal Dragoon Guards, now responsible for the Samaria Sector in general, added to its mission

> to keep track of the Arab Liberation Army in our sector and to make sure they understood that we still had an interest in the area they occupied. They always appeared friendly and many people in the Squadron enjoyed their hospitality over beverages of many different varieties.[66]

It would appear that the ALA were seen by the Royal Dragoons as incidental partners in keeping the peace, while both sides were preparing for war. The Royal Dragoons recorded with satisfaction a successful attempt on 25th April to deter kibbutz Ramat Hakovesh ("Ramat le Kovesh"), 'at the southern end of our patrols over Arab Liberation Army territory', from taking 'pot shots at anything that moved around it'.[67] While this was going on an envoy from the commander of the local Arabs [i.e. not the ALA] arrived with a message to the effect that '500 Arabs were at our disposal if we so wished – they too, it seems, were anxious to punch the Kovesh nose'.[68] Unbeknownst to the Royal Dragoons, the supposed indiscriminate shooting was the result of an attack on the morning of 20th April by armed local Arabs from the large village of Kalkilya on a Jewish outpost securing workers in the outlying fields of Ramat Hakovesh. The attackers were apparently led by a leader of a Kalkilya youth organization who was later found dead on the battlefield, dressed in an officer's uniform. His body was taken to the kibbutz and handed over to the police. The Jewish position, manned by Haganah recruits stationed in Ramat Hakovesh, was overwhelmed but a squad managed to withdraw and the position was retaken by the 'quick response section' of the kibbutz at an overall price to the Jewish side of five dead and two wounded.[69]

Further sniping was reported on 25th April.

At the time of the incident in the fields of Ramat Hakovesh senior members of the Haganah intelligence met in the Arab village of Tira, north of the Kiboutz, the CO of the ALA Hittin Battalion, in an effort to avoid provocations (such as the firing from Tira during the attack on the field workers) and unnecessary incidents and punish those responsible.[70] They were instructed by Ben-Gurion to state their preference for a direct Jewish-Arab agreement while preventing war mongering by a 'third party'.[71]

Unlike the first months of 1948, the most devastating attacks on the railways in the weeks leading to the cessation of services were by the Jewish underground organizations. Using electric mines, as it had near Rechovot, Lechi derailed a passenger train near Binyamina on 31st March. According to the *Palestine Post*, forty Arabs were killed and about sixty wounded when three coaches were hit, 'one of them, according to an eye-witness, being flung 10 meters from the line'.[72] At the time, Rocket Troop of the 6th Field Regiment R.A. was stationed in camp 87 near Pardes Hanna, with the responsibility for internal security in the sector between Zichron Ya'akov and Hadera (two other Troops guarded the detention camp in Atlit).

> The inlying picquet was immediately dispatched from the camp... together with another party that was also ready to leave and had been going to a football match in Haifa, and 10 ambulances from a medical unit in the next camp.[73]

Troops travelling in the train's last three coaches were fortunately unharmed and were quickly driven away to Haifa. The injured were taken by ambulances to Haifa, the dead and the surviving Arabs to Tul Karem. The Gunners noted that

> The accident occurred in full view from the main coast road, from which our fairly small rescue parties could be seen at work. Military

and Jewish vehicles passed up and down the road throughout the after-noon, but none turned to see if they could be of any help.[74]

The stretcher bearers, mostly young conscripts, had shown great fortitude 'in carrying the bloody messes that had once been or still were human beings'.[75]

CO of the 1st Guards Brigade, responsible for the sector, immediately ordered roadblocks sealing the closest Jewish communities – Binyamina and Zichron Ya'akov, 'known dissident strongholds'. The roadblocks remained for three days and were deemed effective punishment since the mayors of Tel Aviv and of Haifa appealed for their removal.[76]

The most audacious Jewish attack on a train was by the IZL in the same area – between Binyamina and Hadera, on Saturday 17th April. Whereas the Lechi, which used remote controlled electric mines, with the sole purpose of killing as many passengers – Arabs and British, as possible, the IZL attacked a train carrying ammunition to Egypt (although the official IZL version was that the arms were intended for the ALA)[77] with an eye on its cargo. According to the IZL, the plan to ambush the train had been two weeks in the making.[78] Preparations were mainly logistic, with no attempt made to rehearse the plan with the designated commanders and fighters although most of the IZL rank-and-file, and some of their commanders, had little or no training or combat experience in fighting regular troops.[79] Three assault groups were positioned east of the tracks. Two of them, purposely to isolate the area, one a kilometre to the north and the other to the south. The main group was assigned the detonation of mines under the second and eighth carriages which were known to carry the armed escort from the 41st Field Regiment R.A.[80] It would then storm the train under close cover of automatic fire and silence all resistance. Seventy to eighty lorries (accounts differ) stood by, with about 100 IZL members and supporters, ready to remove the train's contents. They assembled in the ancient Khan and small fort of Shuni between Binyamina and Zichron Ya'akov which had served as an IZL training camp, and were moved forward in anticipation of the train's arrival.

The train was escorted by three sections: One officer and seven soldiers in the front, one warrant officer and eight soldiers in the centre and one sergeant and seven soldiers in the rear, altogether twenty-three.[81]

At around 10:30 hours, the electric mines were detonated as planned and the main IZL force opened fire. The two escorts positioned on the footplate were killed and the engine driver and the fireman wounded. The section in the front immediately dismounted and opened fire with rifle, light machine gun (LMG) and 2" mortar. Although they did not attempt to rush or outflank their attackers, their fire from a slightly elevated position was effective and they held off the IZL for forty minutes.

Fortunately, for the IZL a few British soldiers jumped from the train and tried to escape in the direction from which the train had come. They ran into the northern IZL block and were taken prisoner. The IZL sent a captured soldier with a message to the escort that they would shoot the prisoners un-less the escort surrendered within five minutes.[82] Otherwise, they would be left unharmed. The local IZL commander succeeded in stopping the thirty remaining trucks from leaving the site and with their "stevedores" began to unload the train which carried crates of mortar bombs. In addition, the IZL enlisted the help of eighteen British soldiers. According to IZL accounts, 20,000 3" mortar bombs were removed and hidden in Zichron Ya'akov. The British reported that IZL came away with '3 or 4 ten-ton lorry loads of amn mainly 2 in mortar'.[83]

The unloading was interrupted at 13:30 hours with the arrival of a re-lief train with two sections from the 41st Field Regiment in Haifa, and an-other section from the 6th Field Regiment picked up en route in Atlit. The train was stopped by the explosion of a mine and came under automatic fire from the IZL. It withdrew to the Binyamina station, where the escorts dismounted and began to advance on foot. However, perhaps fearing for the safety of the soldiers taken prisoner, the relief opened fire from a distance. The unloading was abruptly stopped at 13:45 hours and the IZL fighters withdrew leaving the prisoners behind.[84]

By now, some three hours from the detonation of the mines, the 3rd Troop, followed closely by the 5th Troop, of "A" Squadron, 4th/7th Royal Dragoon Guards arrived on the scene, 'on the heels of the retiring Jews who were probably beginning to feel discouraged by the sight of a troop of tanks and so many other vehicles and men'.[85] They spent the rest of the day and the night guarding the train and its remaining contents. The escort lost three soldiers, the IZL three commanders.[86] British arms lost were five Bren LMGs, eight Sten submachine guns, ten rifles, two 2" mortars and one revolver. Neither side covered itself with glory.

Allegedly, after the first Arab attacks on the Lydda-Jerusalem line, Abd al-Qadir al-Hussayni, commander of Eastern Brigade of the Holy Jihad, promised not to attack trains to and from Jerusalem carrying oil or Brit-ish military stores. 'This promise he had always implemented and so trains ran'.[87] However, Abd al-Qadir al-Hussayni was killed in the early hours of 8th April while approaching Jewish positions in the recently occupied village of Qastel on the road to Jerusalem, with the result that 'the Arabs apparently got out of hand'.

A train was prepared in Jerusalem on 11th April loaded with ammuni-tion, for Lydda. The commander of the escort, Captain C.A.F. Babbage decided to reinforce the train with an additional escort which had been on stand by and try to break through. The train, with two locomotives, set out at 08:00 hours.

> As they were approaching Battir, some eight miles west of Jerusalem, he noticed that the windows of such houses as there were packed with Arab spectators, and that the hill sides had their quota as well. The local pop-ulation had turned out in strength to watch the fun.[88]

The ambush was well planned. The railway signal short of Battir was against the train, and the driver obediently stopped. When the train started again a few minutes later, it was discovered that in the meantime its rear carrying the escort, had been uncoupled. Captain Babbage 'jumped down and ran towards the engine. As he did so fire was opened from the surrounding hills on the engine and escort wagon'. BSM Wright, in command of the second escort, forced the driver, at pistol point, to drive backwards enabling Babbage to recouple both parts of the train.

Slowly, the train resumed its journey through Battir while fired upon by the Arabs, and returning fire 'with vigour'.

> Shortly after leaving the [Battir] station, the train again came to a standstill as two large boulders were placed across the line. It took six men to remove them, working the whole time under fire. When they had been cleared the train, with by this time one of the two engines damaged and losing steam, ran down out of range.[89]

Later in the day, at 13:10 hours, the first engine of a goods train from Lydda was derailed a mile west of Battir by a boulder on the line. About forty Arabs opened fire and threw grenades. When the commander of the escort tried to negotiate with the Arabs 'they seized his Sten gun, revolver and very pistol and also took 2 rifles from 2 BORs who came to his assistance'. Meanwhile the second engine managed to pull the first engine back on to the rails and the train withdrew west to Lydda. Two Arab railway men were wounded 'and 1 Arab fireman believed absconded'.[90]

After 11th April, the Jerusalem line closed. No more fuel reached Jerusalem with the result that water could not be pumped through the municipal pipes and had to be distributed by improvised tankers. On 12th April, Palestine Railways announced the cessation of all passenger services in or out of Palestine.[91] A fortnight later, on 27th April, all trains ceased to operate.[92]

Notes

1 On the Palestine railways, see:
   Anthony S. Travis, *On Chariots with Horses of Fire and Iron. The excursionists and the Narrow Gauge Railroad from Jaffa to Jerusalem* (Jerusalem: The Hebrew University Magnes Press, 2009).
   Paul Cotterell, *The Railways of Palestine and Israel* (Abingdon, Oxon: Tourret Publishing, 1984).
   [Hebrew] Ilan Falkov, *Trains in Erets Israel Past, Present, Future* (Haifa: Rakevet Israel, 1982).
2 Falkov, 59.
3 [Hebrew] Gershon Rivlin (ed.), *La'esh Velamagen* (Ministry of Defence, 1964), 259–278.
4 Ibid., 278.
5 Ibid., 267, 464.
6 'Gunners vs. Terrorists,' in *The Gunner*, vol. 29, No. 9 (December, 1947), 217.

7 Lt. Col. R.L.V. French Blake, *A History of the 17th/21st Lancers 1922–1959* (London: Macmillan, 1962), 241.
8 *The White Lancer and the Vedette*, vol. 29 (November, 1947), 52.
9 'Gunners vs. Terrorists.'
10 Ibid.
11 R.D. Wilson, *Cordon and Search. With 6th Airborne Division in Palestine* (Aldershot: Gale and Polden, 1949), 83.
12 Ibid.
13 Ibid., 84
14 Blake, 240, '17th/21st Lancers Armourd Rail Detacment,' in *The White Lancer and the Vadette*, vol. 29 (November, 1947), 51.
15 *The White Lancer and the Vadette*, vol. 29 (November, 1947), 51.
16 Blake, 240–241.
17 *The White Lancer*, vol. 29 (November, 1947), 52.
18 Ibid.
19 Blake, 241. The beach in Atlit is one of the most beautiful in the country.
20 *The White Lancer*, 53, and Blake, 241.
21 TNA W.O. 261/189 1st Guards Brigade Weekly Intelligence Review, 10 February 48.
22 The commercial centre outside Jaffa Gate. Israeli accounts usually date the beginning of the war from 30th November with attacks on Jewish traffic near Petach Tikva.
23 Weekly Intelligence, 5.
24 Ibid.
25 Ibid., 6.
26 *Palestine Post*, 21 December 1947.
27 Ibid.
28 Weekly Intelligence, 6.
29 TNA W.O. 261/182 Quarterly Historical Record of Headquarters, 1 Infantry Division. For Period ending 15 December '47, App. "N" IS Instr. No. 7, 1 October '47.
30 TNA W.O. 261/654 I Inf. Div. Op. Instr. No. 7, Op. SPARROW HAWK 3 January. '48.
31 *The Household Brigade Magazine* (Spring, 1948), 40. By then, the 1st Welsh Guards were reduced to 200 all ranks.
32 Sir David Carol MacDonnell Mather 1919–2004, future Conservatine M.P. and Whip.
33 1 Inf. Dir. Op. Instr. No. 7.
34 Ibid.
35 *The Household Brigade Magazine* (Spring, 1948), 40.
36 Ibid.
37 *Palestine Post*, 28 January 1948.
38 TNA W.O. 261/654 I Inf. Div. Op. Instr. No. 9, Op. Train ends, 29 January, '48.
39 Ibid.
40 TNA W.O. 261/654 I Inf. Div. Op. Instr. No. 8, The Use of Weapons for Internal Security in Palestine, 6 January, '48.
41 Ibid.
42 TNA W.O. 261/233 Quarterly Historical Report of the 6th Field Regiment Royal Artillery for the quarter ending 31 March 1948.
43 TNA W.O. 261/189 1st Guards Brigade Intelligence Review, 10 February, '48, 8.
44 Blake, 242.
45 Appended to TNA W.O. 261/189 1st Intelligence Review, 10 February.
46 *Palestine Post*, 27 February 1948.

47 [Hebrew] Shalom Rosenfeld, '"Between hills and boulders the train speeds" [a popular childrens' song]', *Hamashkif*, 21 January 1948. See also *Davar*, 30 January and 3 February 1948.

48 Including Lt.-Col. F.M.V. Tregar C.O. 1st KOSB returning from a course in England with another officer and three ORs. All unhurt. *The Borderers Chronicle*, June 48, 39–40.

49 [Hebrew] Avraham Vered, *Israel Doeth Valiantly, Fighters for the Freedom of Israel in the War for Independence* (Tel Aviv: Yair Publications, 1998), 198.

50 Blake, 242.

51 'Regimental Notes,' *The White Lancer*, vol. 30 (May, 1948), 4.

52 *Palestine Post*, 27 February 1948.

53 [Hebrew] *Hamashkif*, 26 March 1948, and *Kol Ha'am*, 26 March 1948.

54 TNA W.O. 261/233.

55 Ibid.

56 TNA W.O. 261/237 Quarterly Historical record of 41st Field Regiment, Royal Artillery for Quarter ending 31st March 1948.

57 Ibid.

58 'Last Days in Palestine. The Record of the 41st Field Regiment,' in *The Gunner*, vol. 30, No. 5 (August, 1948), 127.

59 Ibid.

60 See Ben Gurion's *Diary*, vol. 1, entry for 14 February 1948, Fauzi al-Qawuqji, 'Memoirs, 1948, Part 1,' *Institute for Palestine Studies*, 1971/72.

61 Qawuqji, '*Memoirs*'.

62 TNA W.O. 261/189 1st Guards Brigade Intelligence Review, No. 4, 16 February 1948, for the period 10 February 1948 – 16 February 1948. See also District Commissioner's office, Nablus to Chief Secretary, Fortnightly Report 1–15 February, 16 February 1948, in Robert L. Jarman (ed.), *Political Diaries of the Arab World, Palestine and Jordan vol. 10, 1945–1948* (Cambridge Archive Editions, 2001), 229–230.

63 [Hebrew] Shmaryahu Ben-Pazi, 'The Arab criminal gangs in the inter-communal war 1947–1948,' in Alon Kadish (ed.), *1948 and After The Jerusalem School on War, the Military and Society* (Moshav Ben-Shemen: Modan, 2015), 94–171. Based on Ben-Pazi's doctoral dissertation in the Hebrew University.

64 History of the Haganah Archiv 102/105, 22 February 1948.

65 TNA W.O. 261/189. See also *Palestine Post*, 6 February 1948, 'Arab Gangs Rob Trains Again' – on an attack on 5 February on a train in the Kalkilya station in which three wagon loads of sugar were stolen.

66 *4th/7th Royal Dragoon Guards Regimental Magazine* (December, 1948), 42.

67 Ibid., 44.

68 Ibid.

69 [Hebrew] *Davar*, 21 April 1948, *Hamashkif*, 21 April 1948, *Hatsofe*, 21 April 1948, 22 April 1948, *Palestine Post*, 23 April 1948. [Hebrew] Gershon Rivlin (ed.), *Yemei Rama. Pirkei Ramat Hakovesh* (Ma'arachot, 1964), 192. For details of the Jewish fallen, see [Hebrew] *Yizkor In memoriam Comprising Biographies and Photographs of all the fallen in the War of Liberation in Israel* (Ministry of Defense, 1955). Ramat Hakovesh had previously been attacked on 29–30 March and would be attacked again on 10 April.

70 Ben Gurion's *Diary*, vol. 1, entry for 31 March 1948.

71 Ibid.

72 *Palestine Post*, 1 April 1948.

73 '6th Field Regiment, R.A. – Palestine,' *The Gunner*, vol. 30, No. 2 (May, 1948), 44.

74 Ibid.

75 Ibid., and TNA W.O. 261/233 6th Field Regiment, R.A.

76 Ibid., and TNA W.O. 261/233.

77 Menachem Begin, *The Revolt,* Revised Edition (London: W.H. Allen, 1979), 350, and [Hebrew] David Niv, *The Irgun Zvai Leumi Part Six In Open War (1947–1948)* (Tel Aviv: Klausner Institute, 1980), 141–142.

78 The fullest IZL accounts are in [Hebrew] Chaim Lazar (Litai), *The Conquest of Jaffa* (Tel Aviv: Shelach Publishing, [n.y., c. 1951]), 111–113, and [Hebrew] Joseph Evron, *Gidi The Jewish Insurgency Against the British in Palestine* (Ministry of Defense, 2001), 17–40.

79 *Gidi*, 21.

80 TNA W.O. 261/237.

81 Woolwich, Royal Artillery Archive, UR 625 to OC To OCJ TP OB TY A/TK, 18 April. According to Lazar, 112, the escort comprised of 40 soldiers, armed with two 2" mortars, ten Bren LMGs, rifles and submachine guns.

82 URG 625 To OC J Troop.

83 Ibid., and *Gidi*, 35–36.

84 URG 625 and *Gidi*, 38–39.

85 *4th/7th Royal Dragoon Guards Regimental Magazine*, December, 1948, 42. Their arrival on the scene is not mentioned in the IZL accounts.

86 Lazar 113, Niv 142.

87 'Jerusalem Journey. Train Escort Work by the 41st Field Regiment, R.A.' in *The Gunner*, vol. 30, No. 3 (June, 1948), 73.

88 Ibid.

89 Ibid., R.A. Archive, UR 625 To OC J TP U BTY A/TK, 11 April 1948.

90 UR 625, 11 April 1948.

91 'Palestine Railways Notice,' *Palestine Post*, 13 April 1948.

92 TNA W.O. 261/237 41st Field Regiment, Cotterell, 83.

4 The road to Jaffa, the road to Jerusalem

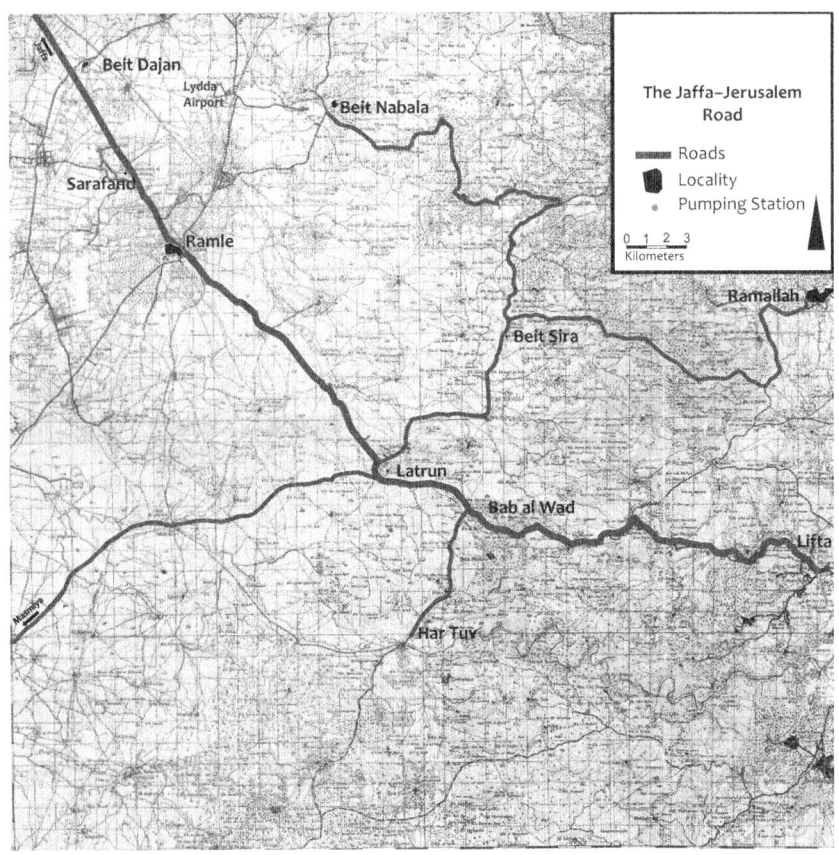

Map 3 The Jaffa–Jerusalem road.
Source: Survey of Palestine maps 1947.

At the outset of hostilities, Arab attacks on Jewish transportation were regarded as highly probable, following a familiar pattern established in previous periods of inter-communal violence. This was the case throughout the country although then, and in retrospect, much of the attention was drawn to the Jaffa-Jerusalem road, most of which was through Arab-controlled countryside and Arab communities. Water was pumped to Jerusalem by a pipe line which on the whole operated throughout most of the period. It was supplemented by the contents of water cisterns which had been surveyed, cleaned and sealed before the outbreak of hostilities and filled with rain water during the exceptionally wet winter of 1947–1948. Fuel was brought to Jerusalem by the government-owned Palestine Railways. But everything else, particularly food, was hauled by road, mainly from the coast. Hence keeping the road to Jerusalem open and secure was a major concern to the Jewish leadership.

On 2nd December 1947, Ben-Gurion discussed the problem of ensuring road security in general and the road to Jerusalem in particular with senior Haganah commanders.[1] On the same day, Jewish traffic from and to Jerusalem was stoned near the western entrance to the Arab town of Ramle, and an official of the Jewish Agency, Max Fine, was killed.[2] The main Jaffa-Jerusalem road ran through Ramle, and the surrounding area, thickly planted with olive and citrus groves did not offer many alternatives.

Following these and similar incidents over the next few days, the Police stopped all Jewish traffic along the road and allowed its resumption only when it organized itself in convoys escorted by police-armoured cars. On 5th December, police-escorted Jewish buses were attacked near Ramle with rifle fire.[3] A convoy from Jerusalem on 7th December was fired upon, near the village of Kubeiba, between Ramle and Latrun, with automatic weapons.[4] The government informed the mayor of Tel Aviv that the Army would take up positions every day until 16:00 hours in Tel Abu Kabir at the eastern entrance to Jaffa and at Ramle in order to secure the passage of Jewish traffic without having to resort to armed escorts.[5] A government spokesman stated at a press conference on 24th December that it would keep the roads open by whatever means necessary.[6]

Meanwhile, the Haganah tried to defend against the Arab attacks by organizing convoys and escorting them with armed Haganah members and whenever possible with patrols of the Jewish Settlements Police (JSP). Permanent positions were established in Jewish-owned buildings along the road between Jaffa and Beit Dajan junction and traffic was directed to alternate roads bypassing the large villages of Abu Kabir and Yazur. In addition, the Palmach began to retaliate with raids on Ramle (12th December) and Beit Dajan (8th December, 18th December).[7]

The partition decision had served to redefine the mission of the British troops in Palestine from fighting Jewish terror to keeping the peace between Jews and Arabs. Escalation was gradual as was the choice of the appropriate means to enforce law and order.

To begin with, the Arabs contended themselves with stoning Jewish vehicles and beating up the occupants if caught. As the tempo increased, Jews and Arabs caught and killed anyone of the opposing side who exposed themselves to holdups, and then full scale armed attacks on each other's villages began.[8]

As violence grew in intensity and frequency, the 1st Kings Own Scottish Borderers (KOSB) became increasingly involved in the fighting in an area which included the westernmost stretch of the Jerusalem-Jaffa road and the Jaffa-Tel Aviv border. Their orders were to impose curfew from 17:00 to 06:00 hours.[9] 'Sniping and attacks by Jews on Arab transport using the Jaffa-Jerusalem road had to be dealt with daily. P.I.A.Ts were used against houses from which our patrols were fired upon'.[10] On 28th January, the KOSB was replaced in the 3rd Brigade by the 1st Battalion Argyll and Sutherland, becoming the garrison battalion of the Sarafand camps. Their new duties, they soon discovered, 'were boring and lacked the interest and excitement that the previous ones affected'.[11]

Along the road east of the turning to the Jewish agricultural school Mikve Israel were two Haganah positions in Jewish-owned workshops facing each other – the spirit factory "Hamashke" and a foundry "Hayotsek". During the initial stages of the conflict, these positions were used against Arab traffic. The Army soon realized that in order to secure the road, it would have to pacify the area along its shoulders.[12] With the redirecting of Jewish traffic away from the main road and in view of the Army assuming responsibility for the safety of all vehicles using it, the main function of the Jewish forces in strongholds along the road was now to defend themselves against the Arabs without unnecessarily provoking the Army. This was not always simple. On 20th January, without any prior coordination, an Irgun Zvai Leumi (IZL) detachment showed up at the foundry, fired for about twenty minutes on Arab vehicles and withdrew.

On 22nd January, seven Jews of the JSP station in Mikve Israel under the command of a Jewish Non Commissioned Officer (NCO) – Eli Shamir,[13] were killed near the village of Yazur. Jewish retaliation against Arab traffic was quick and furious. In return, the Army fired on both the spirit factory and the foundry arguing that the shots on Arab traffic on the 20th were responsible for the events on the 22nd. On the 24th, the Palmach blew a large crater in the road further east. Next came the demolition of the western wing of the spirit factory, by the Royal Engineer (RE) 'as it had been used repeatedly by Haganah forces for attacks on Arab transport'.[14]

On 3rd February, the 1st KOSB were replaced along the road by the 2nd Battalion the Royal Irish Fusiliers which had joined the 3rd Brigade. The Brigade's missions consisted of three groups of assignments:

1   Road patrols along the ten miles stretch between Ramle and Jaffa so as 'to keep it open to all traffic during the hours of daylight'.[15] By then

the Jews had ceased using the road choosing, instead, to direct their convoys from Tel Aviv south through Jewish settlements and then either south to the Negev, or eastwards, bypassing Yazur and Ramle, joining the road to Jerusalem at Latrun. At the same time, the Haganah increased its attacks on Arab traffic in general and on traffic to Jaffa in particular.[16] The situation as seen by the Argyll and Sutherlands was,

> Both Jews and Arabs occupied posts on the road and overlooking it, and the former, since the traffic was entirely British or Arab sniped Arab and sometimes British Army vehicles as opportunity offered. Occasionally, to vary the procedure, they mined the road. The Arabs, for their part, put up road blocks, as a defense against possible Jewish attack, and these, apart from one or two which had a semi-official status were not permitted and had to be removed by their builders under military supervision.[17]

The 3rd Brigade ran two mounted daily patrols, from Ramle to the Police fort commanding the Beit Dajan junction and from the junction to Jaffa.

A particular mission of the patrols was to escort (separately) Arab and Jewish workers to and from Sarafand. Due to the Army's chronic shortage in manpower both in the field and in its various maintenance centres and camps, exacerbated by the preparations for evacuation, including packing and shipping, the employment of large numbers of civilian local labour continued well into 1948. On 1st January 1948, 23,344 labourers, of which the majority were Arabs, were employed by the Army. By 1st April, about half of them remained.[18] Without them it would have been impossible to ensure both an acceptable level of maintenance and ship out the vast quantities of equipment stored in Palestine.[19]

Alexander Ward, a junior officer in the 1st Argylls described the routine of the escorts' detail.

> The escort usually consisted of one Bren Gun carrier and one very worn 15 GWT vehicle occupied by a subaltern and about a dozen soldiers. The Arab workers piled into ancient buses, then with the Bren carrier in front and the 15 GWT vehicle the column then set off in time for the workers to start work first thing in the morning and then the escort had to return for them again in the evening. These convoys frequently ran into some sort of trouble. Often it was just from the odd sniper trying his luck, but sometimes the opposition was more serious, and required a call for assistance from the escort. Several vicious little battles developed from time to time on the convoy routes, resulting in the deaths of a number of the escorting British soldiers.[20]

It was thought that being 'shot over during our convoy escort duties was excellent battle inculcation'.[21]

The Brigade's other two groups of assignments were:

2   Static pickets in important installations including the water pumping stations[22] along the Ras al Ein-Jerusalem line near Latrun and the western entrance to Bab el Wad and in telephone exchanges. 'These, though lacked glamour, were most necessary and were a drain on manpower'.[23]

3   Jaffa. Guarding *Jaffoon* – the offices of the British administration in the 'German Colony', and patrolling 'no man's land' between the Arab and Jewish lines along the Jaffa-Tel Aviv front. The border between the two communities soon became a strip of derelict buildings in neighbourhoods which, to begin with, had been peripheral economically and socially, the largest being Manshiya in northern Jaffa.[24]

The Brigade had two more permanent missions – guarding Lydda airport and the petrol point in Kafr Jinnis east of the airport.[25] Its three battalions – the 1st Argyll and Sutherland Highlanders, the 2nd Royal Lincolnshire and the 2nd Royal Irish Fusiliers – rotated the missions every fortnight. They were supported by the 2nd and 3rd troops of "D" Squadron, 4th/7th Royal Dragoon Guards equipped with heavy-armoured cars.[26]

The relatively rapid turnover of units patrolling the Jaffa-Ramle road meant that their experience and acquaintance with local conditions and local forces was limited. The patrols were frequently fired upon by both sides and one of their main concerns was to prevent local conflagrations from blocking the road, with little regard to the more general issues involved.

The 1st Argyll and Sutherland Highlanders took over road patrols from the 2nd Irish Fusiliers on 20th February. On the same day, the Ramle patrol was fired on while in Ramle. A common Arab explanation of such incidents was that they mistook the patrol for Jews dressed in British uniforms, a frequent Jewish ploy.[27] Consequently, 'orders were issued that at least one member of every operational party would wear the kilt for easy identification'.[28]

Five days later (25th February), the Beit-Dajan-Jaffa patrol was shot at by Jews from an orange grove near the Holon Junction. In the course of searches by the patrol and police, one Jew was killed.[29] On 28th February, the patrol came under heavy Arab fire along the same stretch of road while escorting Jewish electricity workers. 'The patrol was pinned down for about three hours, but eventually extricated itself without suffering any casualties'.[30] At the time, a series of intense short battles were fought in the villages of Salama and Yazur in which Arab forces tried to destroy the Jewish positions along the road. The damage to the Jewish outposts necessitated the dispatch of Jewish workers to repair and strengthen the defenses of Hayotsek foundry and the spirit factory.[31]

Work at Hayotsek continued on 29th February when a Jewish truck nearly ran into an Arab one carrying oranges, followed by a police armoured car. The Arab truck swerved into a ditch and the Police stopped to investigate. They came under Arab fire from the direction of Abu Kabir and the Army patrol came to their assistance. The patrol, which included an armoured car of the 4th/7th Dragoons, returned fire and silenced the Arab positions.

Meanwhile, the soldiers entered Hayotsek and began to search for arms.[32] The Jewish force had been instructed not to resist searches. The telephone line to the nearby Haganah command post in Mikve Israel was down. Three members of the Haganah garrison were allowed to leave and it was probably assumed that they would contact the other local Jewish forces.

The arms found by the soldiers, and the disarmed Jewish garrison, were turned over to the Police. As the soldiers withdrew to resume their patrol, their officer advised the Haganah men to escape the site as soon as they leave. The Jews tried to, but their truck would not start. They were seized by an armed Arab crowd, including fighters from Jaffa, which converged at the entrance while the search took place, and were massacred. Eight mutilated bodies were later removed from the site. A ninth corps, the truck's driver's, was found nearby and a tenth was captured alive, tortured and killed.[33] The next day (1st March), the patrol discovered that the building as well as the spirit factory had been demolished by the Arabs and that the Jews were killed after the Police had removed their arms. On the same day, the 4th/7th Dragoons took over the road patrols.[34]

For a while, the massacre in Hayotsek gained notoriety as an example of Britain's perfidy towards the Jews and its blatant support of the Arabs. Tension between the Army and the Jewish population and forces in Tel Aviv rose and "A" Company of the Argyll and Sutherlands recorded that 'Tel Aviv was said to be plastered with "Wanted-Dead or Alive" notices, prominently featuring a member of the Company'.[35] This was mentioned in a meeting held on 3rd March between Brigadier R.G.C. Poole CO of 3rd Brigade and Amos Ben-Gurion liaison officer for the Haganah in Tel Aviv (and son of David Ben-Gurion). Trust between the Army and the Haganah had been seriously impaired and there was a real danger that Jewish fighters would be instructed (as they had been occasionally) to use force against the Army whenever they felt threatened.[36] Poole promised to instruct his soldiers not to search for Jewish arms except under extreme circumstances, for example, if by disarming Jewish fighters the Army would be allowed by the Arabs to take them to safety (as indeed happened when evacuating the passengers of the Nebi Daniel convoy, 27 March 1948).

Poole confirmed the change in policy in a further meeting on 10th March in the presence of the Chief of Jaffa Police and the CO of the Irish Fusiliers.[37] In addition, military vehicles could enter Tel Aviv from one road only and would have to present a pass issued by the Haganah. A part of the railway line between Tel Aviv and Jaffa was dismantled to ensure that Tel Aviv could not be breached from the south. Poole would not allow the Jews to rebuild the spirit factory and Hayotsek foundry but nor would he allow the sites' occupation by the Arabs, leaving Keren Kayemet house as the sole Jewish outpost along the Jaffa-Ramle road. He would later consent for the Haganah to reoccupy the site of Hayotsek but doing so served no practical purpose and it was abandoned. The Army also returned some of the arms taken from Hayotsek, but it was discovered that they had been rendered useless.[38]

Poole's change of policy concerning weapon searches indicated an important change in the Army's understanding of its problem. Up to then it had
technically adhered to its policy from its war against Jewish terror that all
unlicensed weapons were to be confiscated. This policy was still in force during the initial stages of the war on the roads although its application became
increasingly intermittent and subject to local commanders' discretion, leading the Haganah to dismiss Army policy as inconsistent.[39] Now the Army
had technically admitted that it was unable to force its initial intention of
retaining responsibility for the safety of all road traffic. It had already de
facto allowed the Haganah the use of armoured self-manufactured vehicles
and armed escorts in its convoys. The carrying of weapons for self-defence
was tolerated even if not officially legal. Henceforth, the Army admitted
the Jewish right to self-defence. It would still have to face the problem of
preventing the use of arms for offensive purposes.

The last Haganah outpost on the Ramle-Jaffa road was Beit Hakeren
Hakayemet (the Jewish National Fund house) further east, near the Beit Dajan
junction and the Arab village of that name. The building and its surroundings
were owned by the Jewish National Fund (JNF) and occupied by Haganah
forces – Palmach reservists and then (17th February) the Givati Brigade. Like
the positions in the spirit factory and Hayotsek, it had lost its usefulness once
the British Army demonstrated its determination to ensure the free flow of
traffic along the road during daylight, and the Jewish convoys were redirected
to an alternative road further south. The Haganah fighters manning the position were, as a rule, careful not to fire on Arab traffic which included armed
reinforcements to Jaffa.[40] Its only remaining military significance was as part
of the armed Jewish presence in the vicinity of the alternative "security road"
which had become the main route to Jerusalem and the south.

Nevertheless, the mere presence of an isolated Jewish outpost made it a prime
target for local Arab attacks. The main Arab force in the area was the Western
Brigade of the Holy Jihad led by Hasan Salame, another veteran of the Arab
Revolt of 1936–1939, who spent part of the War in Iraq and in Germany. He par-
achuted back into Palestine, was injured and spent the rest of the war in hiding
near his native village of Qula in the District of Ramle.[41] One of Salame's main
concerns was to establish his authority in Jaffa where some of the local leaders
and their militias refused to recognize his claim to supreme command over the
Arab forces in the area. Hence to some extent, his attacks on Beit Hakeren
Hakayemet were intended to bolster his prestige throughout the district.

The British presence in the Beit Dajan Police fort between the Arab village and the Haganah position, and its policy of keeping the peace along the
road during the day allowed only night attacks on the Haganah position, led
by a German commander whose orders and curses in German were heard
and understood by the Jewish defenders.[42] The favourite Arab technique
was to drive up to the wall of Beit Hakeren Hakayemet with a truck and roll
off its back a metal drum filled with explosives. The gradual destruction of
the front of the building facing the road and the exposure of its defenders led

the Givati command to order its men to dig a defensive position some 50–75 metres behind the building where they could not be reached by exploding drums. Since from the dugouts, it was impossible to keep the road under observation a position in the partly demolished building was maintained.

While the Haganah presence in Beit Hakeren Hakayemet did not constitute a direct threat to the Army, the constant fighting it generated throughout March prevented the pacification of the area. During his meeting with the Haganah representatives in early March, Brigadier Poole suggested that either the building be turned over to the Army and returned to the Haganah at the end of the Mandate or it be completely torn down. Following a major Arab attack on the night of 19th–20th March,[43] the defenders of Beit Hakeren Hakayemet opened fire the next morning on an Arab convoy travelling from the direction of Yazur (west) destroying two lorries. An Arab force from Yazur began to assemble for a retaliatory attack and was stopped only by the presence of British troops.

Over the next few nights, the Haganah tried to blow up neighbouring Arab positions. The Army's solution for preventing the situation from getting out of hand, without endangering its own soldiers or appearing to favour one of the sides, was to station a platoon of the Royal Lincolnshires, who's turn it was to patrol the road, on the ruins of Beit Hakeren Hakayemet thereby positioning itself between the Haganah dugouts and the road in a slightly commanding location. The move had been coordinated with the Haganah command and the remaining Jewish position was allowed to remain among the ruins alongside the British.[44]

As a concession to the Arabs, Brigadier Poole ordered the removal of the Jewish national flag from the top of the building's ruins. As the Haganah fighters complied, some of the Lincolnshires saluted the lowered flag thereby winning the friendship of their Jewish neighbours. According to Aylon, who compiled the official Givati history, the Haganah and the British soldiers held friendly football matches. The Navy, Army and Air Force Institute (NAFFI) supplied the Jews with Players' cigarettes and in return the Jews provided a local brandy. British officers and NCOs were invited to join in the Sabbath and Holiday celebrations and Jewish commanders were entertained with beer and tea. According to an Haganah N CO, a British corporal approached him with an offer to cross over to the Jewish side with three of his friends, their personnel arms, two Bren carriers and four Brens in return for a promise of full pay and reasonable conditions. Everything was arranged but at the last moment the unit was rotated.[45]

By April a general change was noted in the Army's attitude towards the Jews in this sector. The Jewish occupation of the evacuated Tel Litwinsky after a short battle with Arab fighters (15th April) and the sight of thousands of Arabs fleeing the area confirmed that the Arab successes of March had only resulted in determined Jewish counter-attacks and the occupation of areas evacuated by the Army.

Poole's solution had the desired effect. The local Jewish command was careful not to antagonize neighbouring Army units for fear that the

Haganah would be forced to evacuate the site. The threat was made explicit by a British captain when the local Haganah force was ordered to ambush a Miser [Egypt] Airlines car, carrying the Iraqi General Ismail Safwat, appointed supreme commander of the ALA in Palestine, on his way to Jaffa.[46] Aylon suggested to his superiors that the ambush be placed at some distance from Beit Hakeren Hakayemet. While his solution was accepted by the time the ambush had reached its chosen position, the vehicle had already passed.[47] The same happened the next day when Safwat returned from Jaffa. An order to fire on the passing car when it passed by the Beit Hakeren Hakayemet was ignored when it was observed that the car was accompanied by an armed British escort.

A tactic adopted by the British forces in their efforts to pacify the road was, whenever possible, to physically remove objects of friction which in the case of outposts meant demolition with the risk of worsening relations with local forces. Another means, whenever traffic was ambushed from the tree line of orchards was to cut them down. The Lincolnshire had used this punitive method on 22nd January following the killing of the several mounted JSPs near Yazur. The excuse was that the JSPs 'were shot and finally dragged from the car into a nearby orange Grove, where they were found by a the 2 R. Lincolns brutally mutilated'. The company CO interpreted the event as falling within a divisional directive 'that if any violence from either Jew or Arab originated from an orange grove, a portion of it (TO A DEPTH OF AT LEAST 20 YARDS) would be immediately destroyed'.

> A REME detachment was present, complete with petrol-driven saws, to tackle the larger trees, every other man being equipped with either an axe or a hand saw. The task of removing the trees was nobly tackled and enjoyed by all. The idea of becoming woodsmen appealed to every member of the operation and loud and constant shouts of 'timber' could frequently be heard.[48]

Cutting down the citrus orchard had done nothing to pacify the area but that did not prevent the Lincolnshires from cutting down another orange grove of 200 × 250 yards on the Ramle-Gaza road, east of Rechovot. The means were the same. The soldiers were provided with handsaws and axes, aided by power saws operated by the Royal Engineers.[49]

> The Grove was Jewish-owned and, our activity was greeted with cries of approval, cheers and hand-clapping by the delighted groups of Arab civilians... 'Johnny' soldier was quite the hero... the whole affair in their eyes being 'quite quoise.' The removal of the protective wire also pleased immensely the inevitable crowd of young and old from the neighboring villages who sat a little distance away calmly watching the activity and patiently waiting their opportunity to ransack the fruit laden trees when the last of the column left.

This type of operation had remained popular with the troops.

> The men themselves fell to the task with great enthusiasm partly be-
> cause it gave an authoritative opportunity to even off some old scores,
> but mainly because it proved such a pleasant change from normal rou-
> tine duties, a day in the woods appealing to both officers and men and
> in authentic style they set the woods re-echoing with cries of 'TIMBER'
> as one by one the objects of their labor toppled to earth.

The British success in ending the fighting around Beit Hakeren Hakayemet
merely shifted the fighting a small distance away from the main road. The
Arabs of Beit Dajan under the command of Hasan Salame blocked the road
from Rishon Letzion to the Beih Dajan junction, thereby forcing the Jews in
Beit Hakeren Hakayemet to fetch supplies manually through the citrus orchards between their position and the Haganah lines to the south, near the
'security road'. In response, the Haganah raided Arab positions in the area.
The problem for Jewish traffic was resolved when the Haganah occupied the
village of Yazur (30th April) thereby regaining the use of the Jaffa-Ramle
road as far as the Beit Dajan junction.[50]

Once the Jewish convoys finally abandoned the use of the Jaffa-Ramle
road after the Yazur ambush (22th January),[51] their main obstacle on the
way to Jerusalem remained the stretch of road beyond the Latrun fort
through the Judean foothills to Bab el Wad – the gate of the vale, leading up
to the Judean hills. As of 9th December, the reservists of the Palmach were
made responsible for the safety of the convoys to Jerusalem. They provided
armed escorts travelling with the convoys while its 6th Battalion, stationed
in kibbutz Kiryat Anavim, west of Jerusalem, sent out daily pickets to positions overlooking the road.[52] In addition, in the spirit of the Palmach that
believed that the best defence is the offense, the battalion raided Arab villages which were identified as having provided bases for the attackers of the
convoys. The Arabs as a rule used secondary alternative roads.

The Army had designated the Latrun-Jerusalem road as its main supply
route and as the eventual main evacuation road from Jerusalem when the
Mandate ends, and as such to be kept at all times open. In addition, the
Army guarded the pumping stations at the western entrance to Bab el Wad
and just east of its eastern entrance. Along the road, the telephone wires
were often torn during battles or else stolen for their copper. Because of the
inadequacy of the Palestine telephone system, the Army had laid during
the Second World War a double cable, under the road.[53] Maintenance of the
cable was provided by the government postal workers. The rate of repairs
increased with the Arab introduction of electric mines (from 7th February)[54]
and the intensification of fighting on the road (March). The Arab postal
workers insisted that they work only during regular working hours, that
they be picked up from, and returned to the central post office in Jerusalem
by an armed escort and be constantly guarded while fixing the cable.

By February, the Army concluded that securing the road for constant use had become too costly. On 23rd February, Palestine HQ forbade the Army's use of the road except for operational purposes, mainly patrols and supplies for the employees and garrisons of the pumping stations.[55] Army supplies to Jerusalem were to be transported either by rail or by road via Ramallah, or Hebron, that is, through Arab-controlled areas. The road block in Latrun which inspected Jewish convoys was removed and a M10 tank destroyer was positioned there so as to 'engage any Jew convoy', attempting to use the road to Ramallah through the "Northern Loop," that is, through Beit Sira and the Beit Ur villages (which the Jews had no intention of doing). More importantly, the 'Ramallah road was about to be used for the evacuation of the troops in Jerusalem and it was not intended that it would become a battlefield'.[56]

Throughout late January and February, while the Arab Liberation Army (ALA) deployed in Palestine, small units of Iraqis reached the Jerusalem area and reinforced the Holy Jihad forces in the surrounding villages.[57] In 1941, the Mufti of Jerusalem, the exiled leader of the Arab Rebellion (1936–1939), joined forces with Rashid Ali, the Iraqi Prime Minister, who wished to join the Axis against Britain. According to the Mufti's account, his supporters led by his nephew Abd al-Qadir al-Hussayni joined the Iraqi forces fighting the British Army.[58] In 1948, Iraqi officers and soldiers, who had supported Rashid Ali, joined the ALA and entered Palestine to join the Mufti's Holy Jihad forces.

Their military expertise soon became evident in the considerable improvement in Arab tactics including the use of close fire support, electric mines and the planning and execution of ambushes. So long as the Army maintained a high profile along the road, the Iraqi reinforcements seemed to have made little difference but as soon as it had scaled down its presence the Jewish convoys began to sustain greater loses.[59] During February, 102 convoys left to Jerusalem. A total of 1299 trucks made it and two vehicles were destroyed. In March, 42 convoys were dispatched, 559 vehicles had arrived and 23 were destroyed. In February, six Jewish passengers and escorts were killed and twenty-four were wounded. In March, the figures were thirty-six and forty-two, respectively.[60] Considered together with the escalation of fighting in Jerusalem, the HQ of the Jerusalem sub-district concluded that 'This was probably the main turning point of the "Holy War," in that the Jews began to realize that they no longer held the winning hand'.[61]

Beginning 1st March, the Life Guards were responsible for patrols and convoy escorts in the Lydda district, that is, the area of the 3rd Brigade, as well as the road to Jerusalem as far as Bab el Wad. The 2nd Brigade in Jerusalem operated (29 February) a patrol from the 2nd Battalion the Royal Warwickshire Regiment reinforced with "A" Squadron of the Life Guards, from Jerusalem as far as Latrun. A platoon of the Warwickshires with Bren carriers and 3" mortars was stationed in the ("upper") pumping station at Saris,[62] combining stationary pickets and mobile patrols.[63] The Life Guards'

ROADFORCE ran a patrol of "U" Battery 12th Anti-Tank Regiment Royal Artillery from Ramle to Latrun and beyond to the western entrance to Bab el Wad. The two patrols met daily at the Bab el Wad pumping station ("The Lower Pumps") at 09:00 and 15:00 hours. Their orders were to refrain from escorting convoys unless specifically ordered to do so 'or unless the op situation makes it imperative to do so'.[64]

By then,

> The Arabs have developed a "set piece"... in the form of an attack on Jewish convoys. The preliminaries to the attack consist of heavily mining the road and positioning anything up to a thousand armed men in the hills covering the stretch of road which is chosen. As the convoy advances and on a given-signal, the mines, are electronically detonated, the road is blocked with boulders in front and in the rear of the convoy, and the Arab gang then sets to work upon the trapped vehicles. In spite of heavy armour on all vehicles and contingents of the Haganah for local protection, the Arabs usually succeeded in inflicting very heavy loses, and in some cases the destruction of an entire convoy of thirty vehicles or more.[65]

The details, minus some exaggerations, fit that of the convoy of 24th March in which twelve out of thirty trucks and two out of seven Jewish armoured cars were destroyed. The convoy was attacked during the afternoon by some 200 Arabs at the western entrance to Bab el Wad. Some of the trucks and their escorts found shelter with the British garrison in the pumping station and the surviving trucks were escorted by the Army at 01:00 hours to kibbutz Gezer west of Latrun.[66]

The Army had not entirely given up on its efforts to pacify the area. On 22 March, a company of the 2nd Warwickshires with a troop of 75th Field Battery attacked the village of Ishwa, a few kilometres south of the entrance to Bab el Wad on the road to the small Jewish settlements of Har Tuv, from which Arabs had attacked convoys on the way to Jerusalem. Two British soldiers were killed and two were wounded. On the next day, a show of force was made in the area near Har Tuv including tanks, guns and carriers, ending with a fire display.[67] But by now the size of the Arabs forces and the ferocity of the fighting dictated greater caution when dealing with ongoing Arab attacks – 'it has had to be accepted recently that unless a sufficiently large force happens to be on the spot when the attack is being prepared there is little or nothing that can be done to prevent a major disaster'.[68]

The Life Guard Regimental account does not indicate any sense of frustration due to the patrols' inability to influence events.

> Morale in the Regiment remains very high and we are all benefitting from the excellent training which is afforded by the duties we are required to undertake ... The operation of the Regiment is inevitably

at present carried out under almost war-time conditions: echelons are run daily to the detached squadrons and wireless communications are maintained by a Regimental forward and rear link.[69]

On the other hand, the excitement of combat notwithstanding, the need for carrying personal weapons at all times when away from camp and the 'ever present need to be on the alert for possible attack', were novelties that had long since worn off, 'and it will be a great relief to be away from the chaos and strain under these conditions in Palestine'.[70]

"U" Battery's patrol between Ramle and Bab el Wad was carried out in two pairs of White scout cars or halftracks '(bristling with Brens, Brownings, P.I.A.T.'s and a sergeant respectively)'. In reserve, the Battery kept four M10 Tank Destroyers (on the chassis of a Sherman tank and therefore often mistaken for one). Later the number was reduced to two while the other two were sent to reinforce the 2nd KRRC near Gaza.[71]

> The Arabs referred to them as "the tanks which go backwards" and firmly believed a tale told to them by the Battery Captain, to the effect that they could with ease shell Jerusalem from El Qubab [west of Latrun] (a distance of about 22 miles.)[72]

Compared to the Life Guards account, the Gunners operational experience had been less stressful, since their sector, a rural, sparsely populated area of low hills witnessed fewer ambushes.

> The "U" Battery patrol was, on one occasion, dismayed (only slightly, of course) to find that its return passage westwards to Sarafand was very definitely prevented by an electrically-mined road-block, which had been quickly erected during their absence, in a certain ravine, the precipitous sides of which were swarming with semi-friendly Arabs eagerly awaiting the arrival of a Jewish convoy.[73]

The Battery Captain arrived quickly with reinforcements including an M10 'which was waving its gun vaguely in the direction of the Arabs'. There followed a short 'parley' with the Arabs' leader, who soon withdrew with his fighters.

The 2nd Lincolnshires, who provided in March guards for the Latrun and Bab el Wad ("Lower") pumping stations, witnessed the destruction of the 24th March Jewish convoy and helped extricate its surviving vehicles and escorts back west. In their view, 'it was only one of the normal Arab attacks on the daily Jewish convoys'.

> The significance of this and other similar attacks is obvious to everyone in Palestine. The Arabs have the run of almost the whole country as also they possess most of the food stocks. The Jews on the other hand, live in

a number of relatively small settlements most of which are in very isolated positions, with little inter-communication between them, food has
to be ferried especially from Jaffa to Jerusalem. As long as this situation
continues, the Arabs hold a powerful weapon in their fight against the
Jews, a fact which will probably be even more obvious when the Mandate ceases to exist and the responsibility for keeping law and order in
the country no longer rests on the shoulders of the British Army.[74]

March ended with another costly defeat for the Palmach when a convoy of
twenty-six trucks on their way to Jerusalem was ambushed near its assembly area, south of Latrun near the Arab village of Khulda, a considerable distance from Jerusalem. The Arab forces involved had little to do with
the Holy Jihad's exertions to bloc the road in Bab el Wad. It began with a
rogue company of Syrians from Hama, technically volunteers in the ALA,
who were at first sent to Jaffa, but decided to fight their war elsewhere and
moved, without authoritization, to the camp in Wadi Sarar south of Latrun,
recently evacuated by the British Army. Once they joined battle with the
convoy, they were reinforced by Hasan Salame's force travelling by road
from his headquarters between Sarafand and Ramle and the nearby villagers.[75] The battle itself consisted of the Palmach's attempts to extricate the
convoy and return to kibbutz Hulda, but its outcome meant loss of control
over parts of road which until then were considered safe. The convoy was
intended to reinforce the Palmach units fighting to reopen the road in Bab
il Wad with the help of the Haganah's last major available reserve – the Palmach's 4th Battalion. Now it appeared that even if it got through Jerusalem
would still face a real danger of strangulation.

Since the autumn of 1947, the Haganah had been forming an army which
would defend the Jewish partition state once it was established, and the
Mandate ended. Events until March meant that the nascent army had to
fight the local Arab forces and the ALA while forming. This was far from
ideal but was considered manageable until the convoys' crisis of March.
The Arab successes coupled with the British Army's de facto withdrawal
from contested areas where local commanders felt that loses and paucity of
troops meant that they lacked sufficient means to successfully maintain the
territorial status quo without endangering their troops, forced the Haganah
on the offensive lest the situation in Jerusalem deteriorate out of control.

On the night of 5th–6th April, the Haganah launched the Nachshon Operation, which aimed at opening the road to the passage of convoys by occupying the areas immediately adjacent.[76] The focus remained on the road
and the passage of convoys, but in retrospect Nachshon was recognized as
a turning point in the Haganah strategy. Rather than abide by the British
policy of preserving the territorial status quo until the end of the Mandate,
the British Army's withdrawal from the road and the Arab offensive forced
the Haganah to initiate a counter – offensive and enabled the Jews to occupy
areas which were outside the UN agreed boundaries of the partition state.

Nachshon began as two simultaneous but independent efforts, by Palmach and Givati battalions to secure the road at its two endangered stretches – between kibbultz Hulda and Latrun and in Bab el Wad. "U" Battery of 12th Anti-Tank Regiment in Latrun witnessed one of the first battles, the occupation of the Arab village of Der Muheisin on the road from Latrun southwards. The village was taken on 6th April in a dawn attack by two companies from the Givati Brigade, in the face of little resistance.[77] In the course of the afternoon and evening, the Arabs counter attacked from several directions and although they succeeded in gaining a foothold in the village they were eventually repulsed.

During the night, the Jewish force occupying the village was replaced. The next day (7th April) another Arab counter-attack gained initial success before being driven back. The Gunners in nearby Latrun, angered by the news of the IZL attack on the rest of their battalion in which their CO Lt.-Col. Hildebrand was killed, shelled the occupied village with H.E. [High Explosive shells] for half an hour, inter alia silencing or so they believed, a Jewish 3" mortar.[78] Curiously enough the Haganah forces, who had come in the course of the day under Arab fire, did not realize that they were also shelled by the British nor were any of their mortars hit. Meanwhile the situation was discussed between the Army and the Haganah high command and in consideration of the village's proximity to the supply and evacuation route from Latrun south, the Jewish force evacuated the village[79] with the Army's promise that Jewish convoys in the area would be safe.

According to the gunners in Latrun,

> The local Arabs were quite hysterical with delight at our intervention, though furious at the cancellation of the follow-up; nevertheless, the whole affair gave rise to a most satisfactory amount of coffee-drinking, which became a regular, indeed indispensable, part of the patrols.[80]

The Nachshon Operation transformed the security situation along the road to Jerusalem. During the first day (6th April), a convoy of sixty vehicles reached Jerusalem. A week later, on 13th April, a convoy of 200 trucks came through. The Haganah quickly occupied the areas along the road and the fact that more convoys were not immediately sent was probably due to the surprise at the speed with which the mission was accomplished.[81] Generally speaking, from Nachshon onwards, the Haganah was in control of the road from the entrance to Bab el Wad to Jerusalem. Battles over the ridges on both sides of the road continued until mid-May but by now the Arabs were on the defensive while the British troops became mere observers.

Notes

1 Ben Gurion, *Diary*, entry for 2 December 1947.
2 [Hebrew] *Hatsofe*, 3 December 1947, *Hamashkif*, 3 December 1947.

3 [Hebrew] *Hamashkif*, 6 December 1947, *Al Hamishmar*, 6 December 1947.
4 [Hebrew] *Al Hamishmar*, 8 December 1947.
5 [Hebrew] *Hamashkif*, 10 December 1947, Ben Gurion, *Diary*, entry for 12 December 1947.
6 [Hebrew] *Davar*, 25 December 1947.
7 [Hebrew] Avraham Aylon, *The "Givati" Brigade in the War of Independence* ("Ma'arachot, I.D.F., 1959), 314.
8 '1st Battalion', in *The Borderers Chronicle*, June '48, 38.
9 Ibid., March '48, 9.
10 TNA W.O. 261/322 Quarterly Historical Report 1st Bn The King's Own Scottish Borderers, 7 April 1948. PIAT Projector Infantry Anti-Tank. An infantry anti-tank weapon with a limited range but an effective hollow charge shell.
11 *The Borderers Chronic*, June '48, 39.
12 WO. 261/322, [Hebrew] *Hamashkif*, 25 January 1948.
13 Eli's brother, Moshe, was one of the most prominent authors of the 1948 generation. His eulogy of Eli: – *By his own hands – Elik's Chapters*, published in 1951, was extremely popular and is regarded as a classic.
14 [Hebrew] Hamashkif 25 January 1948, [Hebrew] Yosef Olitzki, *From Disturbances to War. Chapters on the history of the defense of Tel Aviv* (IDF Culture Service, n.y.), 331–333.
15 'Battalion Notes,' *The Thin Red Line*, vol. 2, No. 3 (September, 1948), 96.
16 Ayalon, *Givati*, 315.
17 *The Thin Red Line*, vol. 2, No. 3 (September, 1948), 96. See also TNA W.O. 261/388 Quarterly Historical Record of the 1st Battalion The Argyll and Sutherland Highlanders for quarter ending, 31 March 1948.
18 [Hebrew] Alon Kadish, 'The Army Camps' workers and Palestinian Society on the eve of the 1948 War,' in Alon Kadish (ed.), *1948 and after*, 40. See also 'Last unit in Tel Aviv,' in *Soldier*, vol. 4, No. 1, March 1948.
19 [Hebrew] *Hamashkif*, 16 March 1948. According to an official statement the Army had shipped out by mid-March 145,000 tons of equipment.
20 Stirling Castle, Argyll and Sutherland Highlanders Archive, Box 354 Alexander Ward, 'Prologue the road to the city,' 9–10.
21 Ibid., Alexander Ward, 'Convoys will have strong escorts,' deposited 15 May 1988.
22 One platoon for forty eight hours.
23 *The Thin Red Line*, vol. 2, No. 3, September 1948, and W.O. 261/388.
24 Ibid.
25 W.O. 261/388.
26 '"B" Squadron Notes,' *4th/7th Royal Dragoon Guards, Regimental Magazine* (December, 1948), 47.
27 E.g. [Hebrew] Ayalon, *Givati*, 325.
28 W.O. 261/388.
29 Ibid.
30 Ibid.
31 Olitzki, 337–338.
32 [Hebrew] Ibid., 338–339, *Hamashkif*, 2 March 1948, W.O. 261/388. Olitzki mentions officers in Kilts.
33 Olitzki, 340.
34 W.O. 261/388.
35 *The Thin Red Line*, vol. 2, No. 3 (September, 1948), 97. See report in [Hebrew] *Hamashkif*, 1 March 1948, headline 'British abandoned 8 Jews to Arab murderers near T.A.,' 2 March 1948, 'Under British Sponsorship "Hayotsek" attacked again'.
36 Efal, Yad Tabenkin Archive, 15.163.5, document no. 14, 'Meeting between Brigadier Poole and Chanan [Amos Ben Gurion] 3 March 1948'.

37 Yad Tabenkin, document no. 24.

38 [Hebrew] Olitzki, 342.

39 [Hebrew] Levy, 132. See, for instance, 'Jews Would Guard Convoys' in *Palestine Post*, 16 December 1947.

40 [Hebrew] Ayalon, 166–167.

41 For a description of Hasan Salame in 1948 from an unusual perspective of a German P.O.W. who escaped from Egypt and joined the Mufti's forces in Palestine, see Herbert Pritzke, *Bedouin Doctor My Adventurous Years With the Arabs* (trans. By Richard Graves) (New York: E.P. Dutton and Company, 1957), 148–150.

42 E.g. [Hebrew] Ayalon, 177–178, 185, 187, 189, 195.

43 According to Aylon, 186, 188 two Scots, who had deserted from Sarafand on the 15th with an armoured car, participated in the attack.

44 [Hebrew] Aylon, 202. Avraham Aylon had served as a squad leader in Beit Hakeren Hakayemet since the battle of 19–20 March. He would remain in the IDF to become head of the army's History Branch.

45 Ibid., 203–204. [Hebrew] Ya'akov Arnon, 'A Solitary House (diary excerpts),' in *In their Memory*, produced by the Givati Brigade, no details, partly reproduced in [Hebrew] *Yankale Chablan* (Tel Aviv-Paris published with assistance of Front 5, November 1949), 60–64. Arnon was killed later in the war, 17 October 1948.

46 [Hebrew] Aylon, 204.

47 [Hebrew] Aylon, 205.

48 'Operation Orange-Grove,' in *2nd Battalion The Royal Lincoln Regiment Monthly News Letter*, No. 10, January 1948. See also the operation of the 3rd Grenadier Guards in *Household Magazine* (Spring, 1948), 33. And *4th/7th Royal Dragoon Guards Regimental Magazine*, June '49, 'mowing down' an orange grove of 100 × 150 yards alongside the Haifa-Lydda railway.

49 'Operation Orange-Grove,' in *2nd Bn The Royal Lincolnshire Regt. Monthly News Letter*, No. 11, February 1948, 2–3.

50 [Hebrew] Aylon, 206–207.

51 [Hebrew] Levy, 131.

52 Ibid., 129.

53 [Hebrew] Alon Kadish and Moshe Ehrnvald, *The Yevusi Battles* (Ministry of Defense, 2008), Chapter 5.

54 [Hebrew] Levy, 134.

55 IDF History Department Archive [Hebrew] Teodor, 'Teddy' Preuss, 'The War of Independence, The War on the Roads' [c. 1953] 22, One of the studies produced following the War of Independence under the auspices of the IDF History Branch.

56 '"U" Battery on Road Patrol,' in *The Gunner*, vol. 30, No. 7 (October, 1948), 183.

57 [Hebrew] Preuss, 20.

58 [Hebrew] Zvi Elpeleg, *Grand Mufti* (Ministry of Defense, 1989), 64. See in particular [Hebrew] Daniel Rubinstein, *The Battle on the Kastel 24 hours that changed the course of the 1948 War between Palestinians and Israelis*, (Tel Aviv: Aliyat Gag and Miscal, 2017), Chapter 5.

59 [Hebrew] Levy, 137–138.

60 Ibid., 137–138.

61 TNA W.O. 261/644 H.Q. East Palestine Sub District Quarter ending 31 March 1948.

62 Known to the Haganah troops as the "Higher Pumps." '2nd Battalion,' *The Antelope* (November, 1948), 101.

63 Ibid., May 1948, 25.

64 TNA W.O. 261/619 The Life Guards OP INSTR No. 1, 28 February 1948.

65 'The Life Guards,' *The Household Magazine*, Spring 1948, 28 and TNA W.O. 261/619.

66 [Hebrew] Levy, 135, Royal Lincolnshires, ms of the March 1948 Newsletter, 'The Jews sheltering in the pumping station'.

67 TNA W.O. 261/305 Quarterly Historical Report, 2nd Bn The Royal Warwickshire Regiment for the Quarter ending – 31 March 1948.

68 *The Household Magazine*, 28.

69 Ibid.

70 Ibid.

71 '"U" Battery on Road Patrol,' in *The Gunner*, vol. 30, No. 7 (October, 1948), 182.

72 Ibid.

73 Ibid.

74 Lincoln, Lincolnshire Records, Archive of the Royal Lincolnshire Regiment REGI/Box 5/794, ms of 2nd Bn. News Letter March 1948.

75 [Hebrew] Alon Kadish, 'Who attacked the Khulda convoy (31 March 1948) and why is it interesting,' in Haim Nirel, (ed.) *Uzi Narkiss – His Zionist Vision* (Jerusalem, the Zionist Library, 2000).

76 [Hebrew] Levy, 141.

77 [Hebrew] Ibid., 141–143, Aylon, 423–424.

78 *The Gunner*, vol. 30, No. 7 (October, 1948), 182.

79 By then the main battle had moved east, beyond Bab el Wad, to Qastel. The decision to evacuate Deir Muheisin was left by the Haganah HQ to the Nachshon commander's discretion, Tel Hashomer, IDF Archive 922/75,1088, Yadin to Nachshon, 6 April 1948.

80 *The Gunner*, 182–183.

81 [Hebrew] Levy, 160.

5   Jerusalem

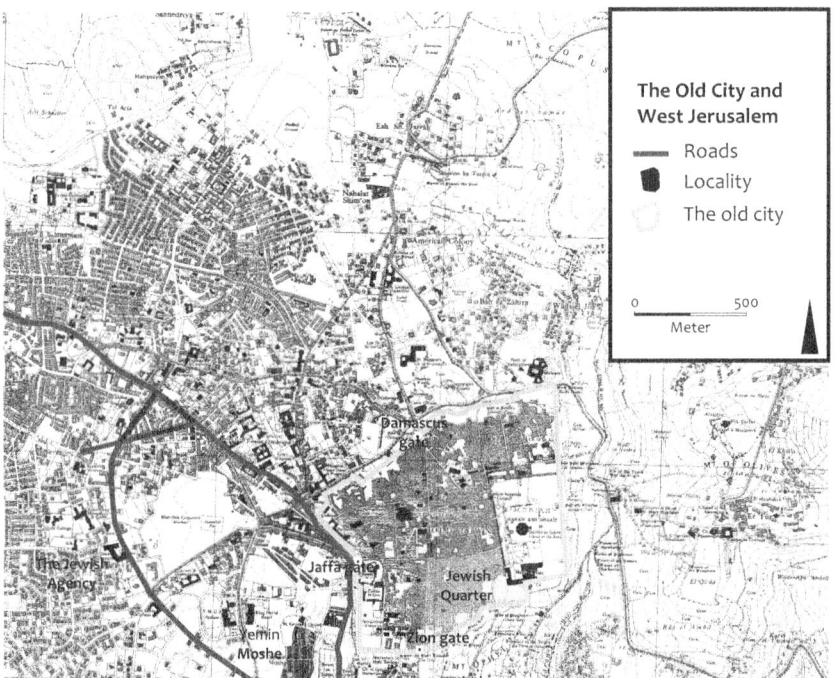

Map 4 The Old City and West Jerusalem.

The process whereby the British Army in Palestine gradually withdrew into its camps and cantonments thereby relinquishing its control of contested areas began in Jerusalem well before the UN's resolution of 29 November 1947 in which Jerusalem was to be given a special international status. In February 1947, the worsening state of security dictated that all the British families of the administration's personnel should leave Palestine (Operation Polly). Concurrently, all civilian personnel were moved into special security zones in Palestine's cities (Operation Cantonment).[1]

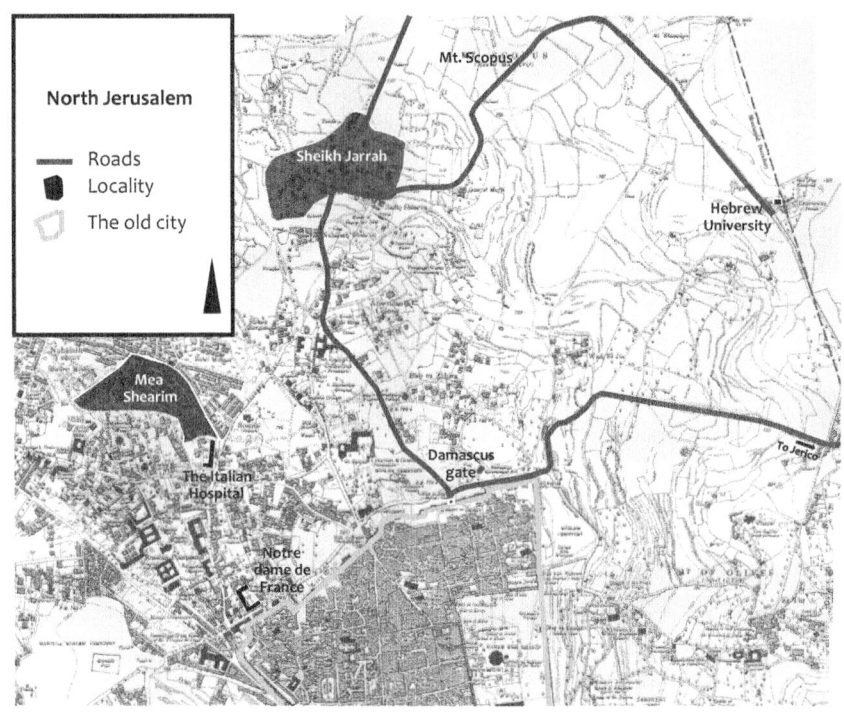

Map 5 North Jerusalem.
Source: Survey of Palestine maps 1926, Govmap.gov.il.

Major government ministries and installations in central western [Jewish] Jerusalem, including the Criminal Investigations Department's (CID) offices, the central prison, the law courts and the central Post Office, designated "the Citadel", had already been surrounded with coils of Dannert wire and fences earning it the popular sobriquet of "Bevingrad". It was now redesignated as Zone C with the addition of the Royal Air Force (RAF) Headquarters opposite Damascus Gate – the main northern entrance to the Old City. The other Jerusalem zones were Zone A – which included the train terminal, the Government Printer and the residential area of the German Colony, Zone B – west and south of Zone C, beginning in the rear of the Jewish Agency buildings, and including Young Men's Christian Association (YMCA) and the King David Hotel opposite it, and Zone D – the Syrian Orphanage (Schneller) – a walled compound, north of the city centre, which served as the 2nd Brigades' HQ.[2]

A number of other isolated installations were occupied by the security forces including the Allenby and El-Alamein camps and the High Commissioner's residence in southern Jerusalem, Augusta Victoria Hospital on the Mt. Scopus – Mount of Olives ridge in the east, overlooking the Old City, and the Italian Hospital and the Police School in the north. The designated security zones A–D were all in west Jerusalem and their Jewish residents were ordered to evacuate them within forty-eight hours. Like the Citadel (Zone C), they were surrounded with belts of Dannert wire, mesh wire fences and concrete Dragon Teeth. Access was through a small number of gates manned by the Army and Police and entry required a special permit.

A 'Fairy Story' which appeared on notice boards on Christmas Eve 1947 opening with 'Once upon a time, there were four zones', described the contribution of the separate zones, each guarded by a different unit, to the general state of confusion in Jerusalem, whereby 'they [the units] used to shoot at each other for hours before they discovered that they were really on the same side. When the zones got together to have a talk they always used to blame it on someone else'.[3] Well before the UN resolution, Jerusalem had gained notoriety as a tough assignment where the guards and duties 'were reckoned to be so arduous that it was thought battalions should be relieved every four months to prevent any undue strain', wrote the correspondent for the 2nd Battalion, Royal Warwickshire Regiment in the Regimental magazine[4] in May 1947. The Battalion was to remain in Jerusalem for a year until the final evacuation in May 1948.

Throughout the Mandate, Jerusalem had become a regular flash point in Jewish-Arab relations. On 2nd December 1947, an Arab mob attacked, looted and burnt Jewish shops in the commercial centre west of the Old City. The next day, a similar mob tried to attack the Jewish neighbourhood of Yemin Moshe south of the commercial centre and west of the walls, and was dispersed by British forces. The security forces prevented the Jews from intervening on 2nd December and similarly dealt with a Jewish attempt to attack Arab shops in the area on 4th December. The Irgun Zvai Leumi (IZL) contributed by attacking British soldiers and bombing Arab markets. Local attacks by one community on the other became routine. They consisted mainly of small arms fire, sniping, blowing up the other's positions and attacks on traffic between neighbourhoods and on the approaches to Jerusalem.

By mid-January, Brigadier George Henry Inglis, Royal Artillery (RA), acting commanding officer (CO) of the 2nd Brigade, responsible for Jerusalem, decided to decentralize the Brigade's operations. Each of the three battalions under his command, based in one of the major zones, was made responsible for its immediate area.[5]

Zone "C" – 1st Battalion Highland Light Infantry Regiment
Zone "A" – 1st Battalion Suffolk Regiment
Zone "B" – 2nd Battalion Royal Warwickshire Regiment.
Zone "D" – The Syrian Orphanage was the 2nd Brigade's H.Q.

The policy of decentralization remained unchanged when Inglis was replaced a few days later by Charles Phibbs "Splosh" Jones, Royal Engineers (RE), his first independent command of an infantry unit. Jones was described as 'a great extrovert... whatever he undertook was carried out with tremendous enthusiasm'.

> Sometimes he landed in trouble with both feet, and a colossal splash – a trait which gave him his nickname, "Splosh" – but more often than not, he was successful. He had all the Irishman's charm, gaiety and wit, but underlying it all was complete dedication to his profession.[6]

The 1st Battalion, the Suffolk Regiment had already served briefly in Jerusalem. On 26th September 1947, it left what had been its permanent camp, camp 87 near Pardes Hanna, following six weeks' training in Transjordan and joined the 2nd Brigade in Jerusalem. Stationed in south Jerusalem in Camp El-Alamein, it was immediately assigned guard duties – two companies in Zone "A", a company in Government House and a company in the 2nd Brigade HQ (Zone "D").[7] The Battalion suffered from an acute shortage in manpower that would only worsen. In July 1947, its strength was 1,131, declining steadily and then dropping to 880 in December, and 650 by the end of March 1948.[8] At the end of 1947, one rifle company ("D") went into suspended animation, and the remaining three rifle companies were reduced to two platoons each. It had been reinforced by the 95th Field Battery 48th Field RA Regiment and a detachment from the 339th Mobile Light Battery, RA, but assignments kept multiplying. They included escorts for Jewish funerals on Mount of Olives, occasional escorts for food convoys to the Jewish Quarter in the Old City, escorts with the Life Guards for convoys of the Palestine Potash Company from its Dead Sea works to the Jerusalem train station and an Immediate Action Platoon. Having been made temporarily responsible for the Arab neighbourhoods of Talbiah and Qatamon (1 April–26 April 1948), it positioned two anti-tank six pounders on a roof of a building overlooking Qatamon, manned by the three remaining members of its anti-tank platoon (Figure 5.1).[9]

The return to Jerusalem was welcomed by the 1st Suffolk with minor reservations.

"A" Company – 'many of the Company are enjoying the coolness of Jerusalem much more than the heat and dust of Transjordan. Everyone seems to be taking advantage of their off duty days to tour the sights of the city and generally to indulge in shop-gazing and bargaining'.

"C" Company – 'After our return from Transjordan we found the green, cultivated fields of Palestine a pleasant change from the bare, desolate stretches of desert. Our present job is that of guarding various vulnerable points in the city, which is quite a change from the monotonous duties in our previous camp'.

"D" Company – 'the place hasn't changed, nor have the guards and duties which go with the "privilege" of being in Jerusalem. We have at least one consolation, we do see life – even if it is from behind barbed wire!'[10]

Figure 5.1 Jerusalem. A 6 pounder anti-tank gun and positions on the roof of a
        building in south Jerusalem.
Source: Yehuda Eisenstark; Courtesy of the I.D.F. Archive (file 0-247), Ministry of Defense,
Israel.

As the situation in Jerusalem changed so did the Battalion's missions.
Although still under threat of attacks by the IZL and Lechi who maintained
that it was up to them to ensure that the British indeed leave, the violence
in Jerusalem became mainly inter-communal with both sides suspicious of
British intentions.

> We live in a camp surrounded by Jew and Arab settlements with the
> former in the minority. Life is made difficult by the enthusiastic ef-
> forts which each side makes to destroy the other. The marksmanship
> of the contestants leaves much to be desired and various buildings,
> including the Officers' Mess, Orderly Room, Q.M.'s office and the
> C.O.'s have been hit from time to time. When our patience becomes
> exhausted we mortar each side with utmost impartiality; this, how-
> ever, is a deterrent rather than a cure. Our experts tell us... that it
> requires 4,592 Arab bullets to kill one Jew; the figure for the opposing
> side is slightly lower.[11]

To make matters worse winter had set in. 'If it isn't raining its hailing, usually accompanied by a gale, and in consequence the mud makes Paschen-
dale [sic] look like a macadam road'.[12]

When spring came the mood improved but not by much.

Palestine at the moment is at its loveliest; the whole countryside is covered in spring flowers and the weather is at its kindest. It is a pity, however, that the

> pleasantries of the elements are not copied by the local inhabitants; the latter's habits becoming increasingly unpleasant and there are few in the Battalion who will not be glad to shake the dust of this land off their shoes.[13]

'As the weather grows warmer so the unpleasantness around here grows worse and duties get heavier'.[14] The prospect of leaving was becoming increasingly attractive; 'it will be a relief to leave Palestine – and how'.[15] After leaving 'I don't think anyone was sorry to see the end of it. It had been everything except pleasant'.[16]

With the situation in Jerusalem rapidly getting out of hand there was hope 'of being in a peace-time station, where there will be opportunities for training, sport and social activities'[17]; that is, normal soldiering. With the endemic manpower shortage, "B" Company had settled into a 'routine of 48 hours on and 24 hours off duty, whilst the men are doing their utmost to dodge bullets which are occasionally whizzing across the camp'.[18] Matters were not helped by the stoppage of trains 'owing to the fanatical stupidity of both sides',[19] with the result that the Battalion had to escort 'vast road convoys' moving stores and equipment which otherwise would have been sent by train.

Yet, in retrospect, some came to miss the action. Brigadier William C. Deller, then recently commissioned, was to recall the last months in Palestine as the nearest thing to 'what I had joined the Army to do'.[20]

The Battalion's most memorable operation was the extraction of the Jews travelling in the Nebi Daniel convoy in Arab-controlled territory. The convoy from Jerusalem to the Etzion Bloc consisted partly of vehicles that had arrived in Jerusalem on 26th March from the coast and whatever armoured vehicles and trucks that were in the city. Its planners had relied largely on the element of surprise, hence, ever suspicious of the British, they did not co-ordinate its passage with the Army. The convoy left Jerusalem just before dawn on Saturday 27th March, the Jewish Sabbath and the weekly market day in Bethlehem. Its unloading in Kfar Etzion was planned and rehearsed to be completed in fifteen minutes while the road back was supposed to be watched from the air by a light Haganah airplane and patrolled by four armoured cars.[21] But the convoy was delayed and although reports came in of the Arabs erecting roadblocks along the way the convoy only left after two hours. The convoy ran aground south of Bethlehem near Nebi Daniel. Eleven vehicles managed to turn around and return to Kfar Etzion. Thirty-nine, including ten armoured, cars came to a standstill.[22] The passengers took shelter in a stone building next to the road where, surrounded and outnumbered by Arab fighters they held out throughout the night and most of the next day (28th March). Powerless to extract the survivors and their vehicles, the

Haganah negotiated with the Army, who in turn contacted the local Arab command. It was agreed that the Army would evacuate the survivors, leaving behind their vehicles and weapons. An unusually large British force was dispatched including 'some 166 Troops of 1/Suffolk with detachments of Life Guards, R.E. and 95 Fd By R.A.... In all, 210 live Jews were extricated, of whom 45 were wounded'.[23] On the following day, Easter Monday, another party of the Suffolks was dispatched to recover Jewish bodies. Eleven out of fifteen were found and brought back to Jerusalem.[24]

Shalom Dror CO of the "Michmash" Battalion, one of the two battalions of the Haganah in Jerusalem, had his main base in the Talpiot neighbourhood in south Jerusalem. By his own account, one morning in February 1948 a Jeep drove up with a British Colonel who, when brought to Dror, saluted and introduced himself as Colonel Harper, commander of the neighbouring Allenby camp. He professed his faith in the Bible, always a useful opening, that he was aware that the British would shortly leave the country and that he saw no reason for fighting the Jews. Harper suggested they establish co-ordination procedures Dror professed disbelief in the purity of his intentions and asked for five boxes of small arms ammunition as proof of good will. Harper replied "You got it!" Dror then appointed a liaison officer, who had served in the British Army.[25]

A few days later the Haganah raided the Arab village of Beit Safafa and demolished four buildings used by the local Arab command. On H hour, the liaison officer informed Harper of the operation. Twenty minutes later, Harper notified him that he was ordered to go to Beit Safafa and help the Arabs. They arranged with the Haganah company commander that he would withdraw within fifteen minutes, and after the British force was reassured that the mines blocking the road were fake the Army entered the village.[26]

Whatever Harper's sentiments were, he had succeeded in improving local relations with the Haganah and creating sufficient good will to minimize the intensity of local fighting and the attendant risk to his soldiers. During its stay in Jerusalem, the Suffolks suffered only two fatalities, one in camp, from a stray bullet, the other, an attachment from Royal Electric and Mechanical Engineer (REME) on 22nd February in IZL retaliation for the Ben Yehuda bombing.[27] Harper had extended his term as CO so as to see through the Battalion's tour in Jerusalem. Upon his leaving the *Regimental Gazette* noted:

> By his cheerfulness and drive Col. Harper has managed most successfully to steer the Battalion though these troubled waters. His tact and diplomacy in dealing with the contesting Jews and Arabs in Jerusalem was one of the main contributory causes to the fact we suffered so few casualties during that period.[28]

The contact and co-ordination with Harper, Dror noted, continued until his leaving the country.[29]

The 2nd Battalion the Royal Warwickshire Regiment had served briefly in Jerusalem from October 1945 to April 1946 mostly on guard duty and internal security assignments. Following a period in Egypt where more time was available for sports and training, it returned in February 1947 to Palestine, first to camp 87 near Pardess Hanna, then a month's training in Transjordan and upon its return it moved to Jerusalem in September 1947 and was assigned "B" Zone.[30] The Battalion welcomed the change especially since its strength at the time allowed soldiers the luxury of three nights in bed a week. Accommodation in Jerusalem also proved an improvement on Pardess Hanna (Figure 5.2).

> More than half the Battalion was living in blocks of [requisitioned] civilian flats, while those in tents enjoyed the mild climate of Jerusalem in October and early November. It is true that there was a barbed wire perimeter, but by this time the battalion had become connoisseurs of barbed wire perimeters, and the size of the Jerusalem one, and the joys to be had so close without, made ridiculous any comparison with Pardess Hanna; so said the older soldiers.[31]

While tension in Jerusalem was already on the rise,

> One was able to get out and about, albeit armed and in parties of not less than four. Jerusalem had much to offer. An expensive but very plentiful shopping center, many cafes purveying excellent foods and wines, cinemas, in fact all those amenities the lack of which made life in Pardess Hanna seem so dull.[32]

Figure 5.2 Jerusalem. Roadblock at the top of Gaza street, at the south-western entrance to security zone B. In the background, Terra Sancta College.

Source: Yehuda Eisenstark; Courtesy of the I.D.F. Archive (file 0-112), Ministry of Defense, Israel.

The effect of the accelerated deterioration of the state of internal security was, as in the case of the Suffolks, further exacerbated by bad weather and the growing manpower shortages due to demobilization. Soon the fighting in the city fell into a pattern which rendered the troops onlookers or else unnecessarily endangered them.

> All through the cold and wet nights of this bitter winter in Jerusalem, it has been the same. Sometimes there are just a few rounds fired by Arab snipers at a Jew or by a Jew at an Arab. Sometimes the shooting flares up between them and the sound resembles more closely a night in Normandy soon after D-Day, than one in the city where our Lord was crucified. When things really get going, there is the sound of Mortars and Light Machine Guns punctuated at intervals by the blowing up of a demolished house. These houses are destroyed either because they are strategic points for observation of offensive action by one side or because they are valuable property and each community wishes to ruin the other,[33]

a curious explanation which reveals the difficulty in understanding the extent and nature of inter-communal hatred which transcends rational behaviour.

Guard duty usually took up three nights out of five, two hours each watch, 'Standing in the dark night only the wire of the perimeter fence separating them from the lighted warm houses of the civilians... It is a strange life in Jerusalem living in a city and not part of it, for no one goes out now'.[34]

This was especially true after a soldier of the Warwickshires was murdered and his friend wounded in Zion Square in the centre of Jerusalem in broad daylight.

Occasionally, the whole city, Arabs, Jews and British, erupted with everyone shooting at each other, while many bullets landed in "B" Zone. One Warwickshire 'had a narrow escape when an un-aimed bullet, while he was on sentry, passed through his greatcoat and smashed the bolt of his rifle'.[35]

The continued targeting of individual soldiers, either by IZL and Lechi who chose to continue their war against Britain regardless of the changing political circumstances, or by Arabs seeking to steal their weapons, contributed to the growing alienation, physical and mental, of the soldiers from their surroundings. The Army's peace-keeping mission became one of self-preservation as its primary objective while awaiting evacuation.

> We used to be allowed out in pairs, always armed, always afraid of having our rifle stolen and getting four months. We even sleep with them tied to our wrists... Nobody is allowed now on foot outside the Zone. We have our own camp cinema and our own canteen. No one would want a stroll outside now.[36]

Initially, the Army was prepared, even keen, to actively intervene in trying to stop the fighting. In February,[37] the Warwickshires had allocated for the purpose an Emergency Section of Bren Carriers and a rotation of reserve companies.

> Sometimes the trouble is over before they arrive on the scene, sometimes they plunge headlong into a battle for both sides have armoured cars, mortars, machine guns, anti-tank weapons and make considerable use of mines. Both sides have erected their own road blocks guarded by their own armed forces at the entrances to their various quarters and villages at which we have to stop and identify ourselves as both sides are fond of stealing British trucks and British uniforms to gain entry into the others territory.[38]

A case in point was the Jewish neighbourhood of Yemin Moshe (named after Moses Montefiori), south of the King David Hotel on the ridge facing the western wall, of the Old City and Mt. Zion. In the valley between the wall and Yemin Moshe ran the main road connecting the Arab neighbourhoods of north Jerusalem and the Old City with Bethlehem and Hebron (the other roads south were blocked to civilian traffic by the security zones). Thus, the Haganah fighters in Yemin Moshe could fire at will on Arab traffic in, for instance, retaliation for Arab fire on Jewish traffic to Mt. Scopus or on the road from the coast to Jerusalem. The Arabs, in return, could quite easily fire back on Yemin Moshe from their positions along the wall of the Old City, Mt. Zion and the nearby neighbourhood of Shamma. The area was the responsibility of the Warwickshires (Figure 5.3)[39] and in an attempt to stop

Figure 5.3 Jerusalem. The Jewish neighbourhoods of Mishkenot Shananim and Yemin Moshe, on the ridge west of the Old City, as seen from the turret of an armoured car on the Hebron-Jerusalem road.

Source: Unknown photographer; Courtesy of the I.D.F. Archive (file 0-43205), Ministry of Defense, Israel.

both sides from shooting at each other the CO Lt.-Col. H.J. Tedder placed an anti-tank six pounder (57 mm) gun in Yemin Moshe facing east and one on Mt. Zion facing west.[40]

Although Yemin Moshe was lower than the wall, its plan, with narrow alleys parallel to the wall and hidden from it, and its proximity made it a useful staging area for Jewish raids (Haganah and IZL) on the Old City and its western entrance – Jaffa Gate. Immediately following the Arab mob attack on the Jewish shops in the commercial centre outside Jaffa Gate, the Haganah began to reinforce Yemin Moshe and continued to do so, as many of its residents left, with its garrison reaching the strength of a company (Figure 5.4).[41]

Following the UN resolution and sporadic exchanges of small arms fire, Yemin Moshe was searched several times by the Army, and weapons were confiscated. Arab fire on the neighbourhood and attempts to assault it reached a climax in an attack from the north on 10th February of, according to the Haganah estimate, some 150 fighters including, as one of its leaders, sheik Yasin al-Bakri from Hebron one of the Arab commanders of the Old City.[42] The Army intervened with reserve companies from all the Brigade's battalions. The battle lasted for five hours and led to the establishment of a permanent Army position in St. George Chapel, a monastery just north of

Figure 5.4 Jerusalem. Haganah positions in Yemin Moshe facing the southern slope of Mt. Zion, the Valley of Hinnom and the Arab Shamma'a neighbourhood.

Source: Yehuda Eisenstark; Courtesy of the I.D.F. Archive (file 0-230), Ministry of Defense, Israel.

Yemin Moshe overlooking both the neighbourhood and the approaches to Jaffa Gate.[43]

On 19th February, an Arab attack from the south was stopped by the Haganah defenders. Meanwhile, 'Troops [were] sent out and, as Jews continued to fire, an armoured car of Life Guards [Squadron "A", attached to the 2nd Brigade] fired 2 2 pdr shells at them. 2 Jews were killed and the firing ceased. Two Haganah positions were destroyed'.[44]

After a calm fortnight sniping was renewed. On 11th and 13th March and again on 21st March, Yemin Moshe came under heavy fire from Arab positions on the wall between Jaffa Gate and Mt. Zion and across the Valley of Hinnom to Deir Abu Tur. The Arabs tried to demolish Haganah positions with the use of car bombs (23 March, 25 March). The Haganah retaliated with a fifteen-minute "barrage" from 3" and 2" mortars and machine guns. By now the Army was content to try and stop the firing with counter-fire from its own fixed positions using a six pounder with a platoon on Mt. Zion and a Projector Infantry Anti Tank (PIAT) fired from St. George's Chapel. The current policy was that whenever the Haganah began sniping 'a 6 pounder shell was hurled at them, which kept things quiet for a while'.[45] The policy worked in as much as the fighting around Yemin Moshe remained static until the Army's final evacuation.[46] Similarly, Arabs, 'mainly Iraqi irregulars' firing from the area of the Palace Hotel on the Mamilah Road which led to Jaffa Gate, were silenced by creating a no man's zone in between with a manned position covering it (Figure 5.5).[47]

Figure 5.5 Jerusalem. A roadblock with dragoon teeth and Dannert wire at the south-eastern entrance to Zone B, Mamilah road.

Source: Yehuda Eisenstark; Courtesy of the I.D.F. Archive (file 0-252), Ministry of Defense, Israel.

While struggling to maintain the territorial status quo in Jerusalem and controlling the volume of fire and at the same time minimizing the risk of casualties, the Warwickshires continued to see action along the Latrun-Jerusalem road and the road to the Jewish settlement of Har-Tuv. The Battalion had set up a force for dealing with Arab ambushes including a section of twenty-five pounders from the 75th Field Battery, RA escorted by four carriers, its fire directed by light aircraft. On 22nd March, a company of the Warwickshires supported by twenty-five pounders attacked in retaliation the Arab village of Ishwa losing two soldiers killed and two wounded. On the following day (23 March), a show of force was made near Har-Tuv ending with a fire display.[48] But soon the need for such measures dissipated with the Haganah's successful offensive along the road in April and May.

The Brigade's third infantry battalion, the 1st Battalion, the Highland Light Infantry, saw the most action during the last months of the Army in Jerusalem which may well have to do with its soldiers' reputation as brawlers of the Glaswegian variety.[49] The 1st HLI arrived in Palestine in April 1947 and were stationed in Jerusalem in 30th September. It had previously served in Jerusalem in 1945, followed by two years in the Canal Zone.[50] In 1947, it had initially spent a few months in Pardess Hanna which it found 'very boring'.[51] 'Instead of the sand and glare of the Canal Zone we have the sand of Camp 87 in delightful rural surroundings which would be thoroughly enjoyable were it not for "these people"'.[52] Sentiment among the Deferred Regulars was that they 'should be able to stick it out [in Pardess Hannah] until "demob"'.[53]

The Battalion moved in July for three weeks to Latrun, where they guarded the detention camp '(better known throughout the Bn. as Belsen)'[54] and in August to Transjordan where it trained with the 2nd Brigade.

The Battalion appears to have cultivated the art of grumbling 'Notes' in the *Chronicle* by the mortar platoon while in Pardess Hannah mourned the demobilization of "Cribber" Mason, 'whose cribs were tonic to listen to', and dedicated to him a 'little poem' recording 'crib-session/Based on cribs and moans in the platoon'.[55] The Transjordan desert had no appeal to the Jocks. In "C" Company, 'Everyone agrees it is the worst place we have ever had the misfortune to come across. (And that is certainly saying something.)'[56]

> Dust is an essential part of our wilderness. It moves around in clouds and spirals. We breathe dust, eat dust, drink dust, and in dust we live and move, and sometimes have our being.
> ...Our future plans? Not so dusty.[57]

The Battalion returned to Pardess Hannah and from there moved to Jerusalem replacing the 1st Battalion, the Irish Guards with a promise that they would be relieved in two months.[58]

The prospect of serving in Jerusalem in the autumn of 1947 was not received with great enthusiasm. 'In more peaceful days the Holy City is probably a beautiful place, but the descriptions voiced by the boys are too blue to be printed'.[59] Jerusalem was referred to as 'Not so Holy City' while England became 'the far-off land of milk and honey',[60] or, more in keeping with the *Chronicle*'s usual style, 'that strange land of little butter and even less sugar'.[61]

In Jerusalem, the Battalion split into two parts. Half of H.Q., "C", "D", and Support Companies were based in the Police School west of Mt. Scopus and in the Notre Dame convent and hospice facing the north-western corner of the Old City wall. The rest-Companies "A" and "B" and Battalion HQ were made responsible for Zone "C". Later the Battalion took over the Hospice of St. Paul, opposite the Damascus Gate, which had previously housed RAF headquarters.[62] The enemy were 'our dear friends the Jews'.[63] "B" Company prided itself that

> There is a rumor that during searches, we do more than our share, and that our "friends" – the "four by two's" [rhyming slang for Jews] – on seeing a green shoulder flash, sometimes regret their hasty exit from the seemingly friendly shores of Europe. This rumor is of course quite unfounded.[64]

It would seem that the Battalion had adopted the harassment of the Jewish population as a legitimate tactic in dealing with its expressions of hostility.

> On one occasion an Officer turned out the occupants of a bus and searched the vehicle, all the time trying to ignore the complaints of a very attractive Jewish girl of obvious position and education. This young lady insisted that she ought to be allowed to sit in the bus out of the sun while the search was taking place. Since she was obviously merely trying to make a nuisance of herself the Officer ignored her nagging, and only when he had satisfied himself regarding the contents of the bus did he allow the passengers to re-embark. As the Jewess was about to re-enter the bus she glared at the officer and said, "Captain, you are a most inconsiderate young man." Quick as a flash the Corporal standing beside the officer retorted, "Aye, an' you're a wee smasher-get on the bus!" This sort of incident helped to lighten our duties and allowed us to give vent to our distaste to those who deliberately made our task more difficult.[65]

On another occasion, the Battalion ran check patrols to try and locate a missing young Jewish girl.

> How many Jocks volunteered for this patrol and what a time they had stopping every presentable female they saw, and questioning her with a thoroughness that somehow suggested an interest in the task not wholly confined to the call of duty![66]

On 5th October 1947, a snap-check patrol of "D" Company shot the driver of a car in Zion Square in the centre of west Jerusalem after failing to stop when twice challenged. The driver died later in hospital from his wounds. On 10th October, an "A" Company platoon, manning a roadblock in a Jewish neighbourhood shot and killed a young motorcycle rider who attempted to avoid the block, and wounded the pillion rider.[67] 'So within a few days of taking over their duties, the Officers and men of the Battalion showed that they intended to do their job thoroughly and efficiently',[68] regardless of whether the Jews killed were found in retrospect to have posed an actual threat (they didn't).

There followed on 13th November the Lechi attack on the Ritz café, a popular bar for the exclusive use of members of the British security forces in a basement on King George V Avenue in the centre of west Jerusalem. The Ritz was attacked with grenades which were hurled from the entrance and a rear window while the street outside was under covering fire allowing the attackers to retreat.[69] Sixteen members of the Battalion were hit, one died of his wounds and one lost a leg.[70] Casualties included members of other battalions as well, but the men of the 1st HLI seem to have reacted with exceptional vehemence in immediately attacking Jewish civilians, in searches of Jewish neighbourhoods during the next days and in enforcing nightly curfews. The Battalion became known as 'the notorious Ritz Regiment'[71] whose soldiers supposedly swore to take revenge of the Jews. We would like, wrote "Bob Spud" of "D" Company, to give the Jews more reasons to call Jerusalem "Holy", 'i.e. bullet holes'.[72] Relations with the civilian population worsened noticeably.

> No longer might we enjoy a pleasant meal in Hess's [a Jewish restaurant near Zone C] or stroll aimlessly along Jaffa road admiring the shops. Hess's was out of bounds, and one was discouraged from wandering too far into any Jewish area even in broad daylight and with escorts.[73]

Following the changing patterns of violence after the UN resolution, a new area was added to the Army's responsibility – the Jewish Quarter in the Old City which was isolated from the rest of Jewish Jerusalem. At the end of 1947, the population of the Jewish Quarter numbered 2,700 most of whom were there because they could not afford to move to west Jerusalem.[74] They formed a small and socially and economically weak minority within the general population, mostly Arabs, of the Old City of about 34,000 (1944 estimate). The population of west, that is, Jewish Jerusalem with some Arab neighbourhoods, was about 100,000 hence the curious situation whereby the residents of the Jewish quarter were a minority, within the Old City. Within the municipal boundaries of Jerusalem, the Jews were a majority and finally the Jewish population of Jerusalem was a minority within the sub-district with a population of 240,880 in 1944 of whom 96,760 were Moslems and 43,770 Christians.[75]

During 3rd and 4th December 1947, an Arab mob tried to storm the Jewish Quarter and was repelled.[76] The physical and imminent threat quickly led to a flight of refugees whereby non-Jews left their homes in the Quarter.[77] Contact with west Jerusalem was maintained by the Jewish bus co-operative Hamekasher through the Zion Gate in the south which entailed driving through Arab areas along a road exposed to Arab fire. Morale in the Quarter was low and there was a serious danger of the whole population leaving to the relative security of west Jerusalem.[78] The escalation of fighting in Jerusalem in general included Arab efforts to prevent supplies from reaching the Quarter thereby forcing the Police and Army to intervene in ensuring the passage of convoys. By the end of January, an agreement was worked out between the Army and the Quarter's leadership on the number of weekly convoys and their contents.[79]

On 14th December 1947, at 06:00 hours, "B" Company (later replaced by "A" Company) of the 1st HLI took up six permanent positions in the Old City facing the Haganah posts defending the Quarter.[80] Company H.Q. were established in the Police Station by the Citadel ("David's Tower") inside Jaffa Gate. The

> Battalion now had the responsibility of escorting Jewish food convoys to the Old City and seeing the food safely delivered at the Zion Gate. This duty was continued during our stay in Jerusalem, and although the Arabs objected to our helping the Jews in any way, they never attacked these convoys.[81]

The Battalion's Intelligence Officer's account of the 1st HLI's time in Jerusalem written shortly after the evacuation attests to the distaste with which members of the Battalion defended the Jews while their sympathies were with the Arabs. The escalation of the violence and the brutality of both sides did not diminish the romantic image of the simple, likable Arab, unlike his opposite, the Jew.

> In the Arab Quarter, the narrow crowded streets, the innumerable little shops with merchants and craftsmen sitting on low stools in the sun, their wares displayed in the little alcove shops behind them presented a scene of lazy contentment which had probably remained unaltered for countless generations.
>
> The gay colours, the swarm of chubby, dark eyed attractive children, the patient donkeys plodding over the slippery cobbles, brushing unceremoniously against one, combined to make a fascinating picture so well known to many a British soldier.
>
> In the Jewish Quarter, the streets were just as narrow, but the people were sullen, unsmiling and furtive. Here was lacking the simple lazy happiness of the Arab Quarter, here were unhappiness, dullness and an undercurrent of sinister scheming.[82]

Apparently, the Battalion's command was quite happy with its main Arab contact in the Old City 'Sheikh Yussein [Husseini], a proud, dignified Arab of some influence, and whose regard for us was sincere'.[83] Their Jewish contact, Mordechai Weingarten 'ex-mayor of the Jewish Old City' (in fact, Mukhtar of the Quarter) was unfortunately hounded for not being 'a member of the Haganah or any other illegal organization. His professions of strong pro-British sentiment were sincere, and on occasion he gave us some very useful information', as he had also done for the Haganah representatives in the Quarter, trying to prove useful to both sides. For Crawford, the Intelligence officer, he 'was a brave old man, for he was already on the Haganah Black List, and his giving information to us made his position even more precarious'.[84] Weingarten had indeed tried to maintain an independent position vis-à-vis the Jewish political and military leadership in west Jerusalem, making full use of his good relations with the British authorities, but he was quite powerless to solve the Quarter's supply problems or to ensure its safety. The Haganah chose to appoint its own commander of the Quarter, assuming overall authority over all aspects of its existence while tolerating Weingarten's attempts to reassert his own authority, largely using his good relations with the British.[85]

The HLI's Jocks soon learnt to find their way in what had seemed like 'hundreds of alleys and streets that looked and smelt exactly the same'. Having settled in, they 'set about making themselves at Home. Spring beds and a reasonable degree of comfort began to creep into the various posts'.[86]

The Battalion also took part in escorting Jewish funerals on Mount of Olives until these became too dangerous and were stopped.

> This was an exceedingly unpleasant duty, owing to Jewish funeral habits whereby the corpses, only lightly covered and often not as "fresh" as they might have been, were brought up in open lorries. The burial parties jammed the corpses into small stone tombs, and one remembers vividly the occasion when, just as the cortege was about to leave, an odd leg was found in the lorry. Confusion reigned and all the graves had to be opened so that the leg might rest with the proper corpse since apparently the Jews consider that at the Resurrection a limbless person would be seriously jeopardised in the race to the Judgment Seat.[87]

One such funeral on Mount of Olives was of four members of the Haganah who on 12th February were arrested by an HLI patrol led by a Sergeant Major. They had at the time manned a position at the edge of the Jewish ultra-orthodox neighbourhood of Mea Shearim, separated from the Arab neighbourhood of Sheikh Jarrach, by St. Stephen's Road, which became Nablus Road, the main route north to Ramallah and to Mt. Scopus. In view of the strategic importance of the road, which also let to Jerusalem's only airport, the Army was firmly committed to keeping it open to all traffic without allowing any side to obstruct it. Consequently, the Army attempted to pacify the neighbourhoods alongside it. On the other hand, both sides, recognizing the road's importance for the other, constantly fought over it. In order to prevent Arab incursions into Jewish neighbourhoods adjoining the road, the Haganah had set up road blocks, at the entrances to the Jewish areas manned by the Civil Guard ("Mishmar Ha'am") which, while organized by the Haganah was allowed by the British.[88] In addition, the Haganah had set up its own positions overlooking the roadblocks manned by its armed members. According to reports in the Jewish press, the Haganah fighters in a house overlooking the entrance to the Jewish neighbourhood west of the road were responding to an Arab attempt to penetrate Jewish territory when at 17:40 hours an Army vehicle (truck or halftrack) carrying an HLI patrol approached their position, searched it, confiscated the weapons of its four defenders and arrested them.[89] Standard procedure would have been to turn the Haganah fighters over to the Police.[90] Accordingly two Jewish witnesses immediately contacted the Mea Shearim Police Station and reported the incident.[91] After about forty-five minutes, the Police passed on to the Haganah an Army message whereby the four were released unharmed in the nearby Jewish neighbourhood of Shimon Ha'tsadiq. After a further thirty minutes, shots were reported from the direction of the Damascus Gate.[92] Apparently, the four were released unarmed near the Gate where they were killed by an Arab mob. Three hours later their bodies, badly mutilated, were retrieved by the Police.[93] The sergeant-Major and his soldiers were arrested and an immediate inquiry was ordered by General Macmillan. It was later reported that the Sergeant-Major and the soldiers would be court-martialed.[94] The HLI's account complained that 'Army and Police Officers had to waste valuable time sifting the case, and a perfectly good W.O. had to be posted to another unit, out of the country'.[95] The city was declared off limits for off-duty soldiers, and Brigadier Jones was advised by the Jewish leadership to keep his men at a safe distance from Jewish neighbourhoods.[96]

This was exceptional even in relation to the existing strained relations between the HLI and the Jews. David Shaltiel, the Haganah commander of Jerusalem, ordered his men to resist forcefully any British attempt to search for weapons or to arrest Jewish fighters unless these were made in the presence of Jewish policemen. Later the order was rescinded by Ben-Gurion and the Haganah High Command.[97]

The incident confirmed Jewish suspicions of the Army's policy and inherent anti-Semitism, but it was by no means typical throughout the 2nd Brigade. A few days earlier the *Palestine Post* carried a story whereby a soldier of the "48th" (probably 41st) Field Regiment, RA encountered a group of Arabs armed with pistols and knives attacking a Jew near the railway station (the Suffolk's zone) and trying to force him into a taxi. The soldier reportedly 'used his fists and the butt of his rifle to shield the Jew who was lying on the ground and being kicked and beaten... The attackers were finally dispersed by reinforcements called by a passing army vehicle and the Jew, who was not badly hurt, was taken to safety. The gunner returned to his post and reported the incident to his unit'.[98] But such incidents were usually reported in the Jewish press as exceptions to the rule.

Keeping the two communities apart along St. Stephen's-Nablus Road proved to be the HLI's most demanding mission. Arab fighters, reinforced by Arab Liberation Army (ALA) volunteers, kept attacking Jewish vehicles on their way to the Hadassah Hospital and the Hebrew University on Mt. Scopus and the Haganah kept retaliating. In addition to snipping and in keeping with the tactics of inter-communal warfare elsewhere in Jerusalem, both sides resorted to blowing up each other's positions thereby clearing fields of fire and observation. The same logic led the HLI to clear an area at the edge of Mea Shearim and to confiscate buildings for permanently manned positions starting with "Robert's Post" (21st January) followed by more positions in Sheikh Jarrach (28st January) which were meant to secure Jewish traffic to Mt. Scopus.[99] This proved futile. Throughout February, the fighting along the road continued, forcing the Haganah to confine the use of the road to convoys of armoured vehicles escorted by armoured cars.

By now, with commitments piling up and with "C" Company in suspended animation due to insufficient reinforcements, the HLI companies followed an exhausting routine of eight days in the Old City, followed by forty eight hours in Sheikh Jarrach, which meant one night in twelve in bed,[100] and no time for other pursuits such as sports or training the new recruits. "B" Company CO helped to organize 'our new quiet room' and provide it with games. He also arranged for his soldiers to use the swimming baths at the YMCA.[101] Another initiative was the Sergeants Mess screening films in Notre Dame on Saturdays and Sundays.[102]

As evident elsewhere, the Army was gradually losing control over security in Jerusalem outside the security zones. On the night of 1st–2nd February at 23:00 hours a bomb placed in a small army lorry exploded outside the offices and the printing shop of the Jewish *Palestine Post* in a small street off Jaffa Road near Zion Square. Four Jews were killed and sixteen wounded. According to information received by the Haganah intelligence, one of the perpetrators was a Police sergeant from the Mea Shearim Station (Figure 5.6).[103]

The Haganah responded by increasing the number of roadblocks. The Army responded by removing new unauthorized Jewish roadblocks, one of them (18th February) by "B" Company of HLI in an operation of a type described as 'good for the Jocks', 'a safety valve for their pent up feelings', and 'an opportunity to show the Jews and the Arabs there was a

Figure 5.6 Jerusalem. The effects of the bombing of the *Palestine Post* offices, 1st–2nd February 1948.

Source: Yehuda Eisenstark; Courtesy of the I.D.F. Archive (file 0-435), Ministry of Defense, Israel.

limit to our patience' (Figures 5.7 and 5.8).[104] The roadblock in question was near the Syrian Orphanage (Zone D), which the Army would soon evacuate, in a purely Jewish neighbourhood.[105] The roadblock in the entrance to a side street was manned by (the legal) Civil Guard and did not impede military traffic. Nevertheless, it was treated as a prime military objective.

> With the Syrian Orphanage as a Start Line "B" Company, under Captain Faulkner, moved into position on either side of the street, using doorways and windows as firing positions. A platoon of Sappers cleared the Road Block and their work was a joy to behold. Trucks, tailboards down, reversed at full speed to the Road Block, the Sappers leapt out, pulled the Road Block apart, and hurled the stones and debris into the backs of the trucks. As the first two trucks sped back to unload their cargo at the Orphanage another two took their place at the Road Block, and so the work went on at an incredible pace. In a very short space of time the Road Block was cleared away and reluctant "Shonks" were made to sweep up the resulting mess.
> "B" Company, besides covering the Sappers, policed a large crowd of frightened and bewildered Jews who gathered in the street, who were

Figure 5.7 Jerusalem. Soldiers and friendly locals at the entrance to the Syrian
Orphanage – Zone D.

Source: Yhehuda Eisenstark; Courtesy of the I.D.F. Archive (file 0-49), Ministry of Defense,
Israel.

Figure 5.8 Jerusalem. A search in an orthodox Jewish neighbourhood.

Source: Courtesy of the I.D.F. Archive (file 0-2205), Ministry of Defense, Israel.

taken completely by surprise by the unexpectedness and speed of the operation. The only shots fired were to open reluctant door locks and no opposition was offered by the Jews.[106]

The relevance of "reluctant door locks" to the dismantling of the road-block may be inferred from the descriptions of the operation in the Jewish press whereby, after taking up positions, and subduing the locals with a few shots in the air, the soldiers surrounded a block of residential buildings and searched civilian flats 'in the style of Farran's men',[107] smashing furniture and utensils, stealing cash, wrist watches, jewellery and silk stockings. They also broke into a synagogue and emptied collection boxes for charity. The soldiers and their commanders wore gas masks to prevent their identification. No gas was used in the operation.[108] In a possible precaution against Haganah, retaliation troops were henceforth ordered to use discretion in confiscating arms and in destroying roadblocks.

Later in February, the Haganah had received intelligence of preparations for another car bomb. On the morning of 22nd February, what appeared as a small military convoy of three Army trucks led by a (recently stolen) police armoured car entered Jerusalem from the west. Having bluffed its way through a Jewish roadblock at the entrance to town, it drove to Ben Yehuda street – connecting Jaffa Road and King George V Avenue, in a mixed commercial and residential area which came to replace the burnt commercial centre near Jaffa Gate.[109] A watchman at the nearby Palestine Discount Bank ran out to investigate the presence of the convoy and was shot and killed.[110] The uniformed drivers of the lorries quickly abandoned their vehicles, mounted the armoured car and drove back west leaving Jerusalem by the main road on which they came. At 06:30 hours, bombs placed in the lorries exploded killing forty-nine and wounding 140.[111] The CO of "B" Company, Captain Faulkner and Crawford the Intelligence Officer rushed to the site where they 'witnessed a scene of the most awful destruction and chaos. It seemed that the top end of the street was completely destroyed and the smoke and rubble brought back memories of the London Blitz' (Figure 5.9).[112]

According to Haganah sources, the bombs were assembled, delivered and detonated by five British Police deserters three of whom were later arrested in the course of an attack on the Jewish settlement of Neve Ya'akov north of Jerusalem. They were reportedly court-martialed on board the S.S. *Ocean Vigor*, otherwise used to deport illegal Jewish immigrants to internment camps in Cyprus. However, three weeks later, the body of one of them was found in the ruins of the Arab village of Qaluniya, west of Jerusalem, when occupied by Palmach forces.[113]

The reactions to the explosion reflected the extent of Jewish-British mutual loathing. Feeding on the observed details of the uniforms worn by the deserters, their use of Army trucks and their success in deceiving the guards

Figure 5.9 Jerusalem. The aftermath of the bombing of Ben Yehuda street, 2nd February 1948.

Source: Yehuda Eisenstark; Courtesy of the I.D.F. Archive (file 0-2698), Ministry of Defense, Israel.

at the roadblock, the security forces were indiscriminately blamed for the attack. According to the hostile account in the HLI magazine,

> The offers of help by Police and Army were violently rejected, and the situation was distinctly ugly. Angry Jews were crowding menacingly around senior Police officers, screaming abuse and threats at them, and there were many cases of British Constables being spat upon by Jews: the restraint of the Police was admirable.[114]

In fact the security forces did help in dealing with the results of the bombing. The RASC (Royal Army Service Corps) organized a shuttle of mobile water tanks on trucks to put out the fires caused by the blast. A bulldozer and other digging tackle were provided for clearing the debris and uncovering buried bodies. All available military ambulances were sent to the scene and the 1st HLI entered Sheikh Jarrach to ensure safe passage of traffic to the

Hadassah Hospital. However, after a police officer and two policemen were attacked 'All British troops and Police were ordered by their headquarters to withdraw from the area after angry crowds shouted to them to go'.[115]

The IZL and Lechi reacted with random attacks on British soldiers. An IZL unit present in the city centre, preparing to raid the stores of the Department of Public Works, wounded an Army RC Padre and killed his driver near the Jewish Agency buildings. Two RAF other ranks (ORs) were killed nearby. Altogether the IZL killed ten British soldiers on that day.[116]

The attacks continued on the following day (23rd February), while soldiers responded by firing on Jewish roadblocks and spraying with small arms fire Jewish buildings and positions in west Jerusalem and the Old City. Wishing to take advantage of the general chaos, Arab forces attacked Jewish neighbourhoods and vehicles. The HLI was instructed to establish a roadblock at the western entrance to Jerusalem on Jaffa Road and direct military traffic away from the centre, and Jaffa Road in particular. "Duffy" Ross of "A" Company, commander of the roadblock, reported that at about 16:00 hours an Army truck had hit a mine near his position (Figure 5.10).

Figure 5.10 Jerusalem. Bren carrier with crew from the 1st Battalion, the Highland Light Infantry.

Source: Yehuda Eisenstark; Courtesy of the I.D.F. Archive (file 0-490), Ministry of Defense, Israel.

His immediate search failed to produce the Jews responsible for the outrage, and when a sympathetic Jewish doctor offered to take the serious casualties into his nearby clinic [Wallach Hospital] "Duffy" Ross quite rightly accepted, as the men required immediate medical attention. Two men of the Suffolks were admitted to the Jewish clinic and were murdered in bed by I.Z.L. heroes who poured Sten bullets into them through the open window.[117]

It so happened that on the same day the Police evacuated the police station on Jaffa Road near the Machane Yehuda neighbourhood, and turned it over to the newly formed Jewish municipal police.[118] The HLI's Lightening Platoon sent to cover the evacuation reported: 'The Jews poured fire on the Police trucks, but the Lightening Platoon returned the fire, and did grand work in pulling the Police out of a nasty situation'.[119] After breaking for lunch, the Lightening Platoon returned to cover the transfer of stores choosing to drive through Mea Shearim so as to avoid Jaffa Road, 'where they would have been shot'. However,

> A Barrel Bomb, secreted in a road block in St. George's Road near Mea Shearim Police Station, had been set off, and had completely destroyed the 15 cwt. truck. This took place in a very nasty Jewish area which had given us a lot of trouble in the past. The Barrel Bomb was a favorite weapon of the gallant Jewish fighters. One of metal barrels in the Road Block was filled with explosive and iron bolts, and electrically detonated; another example of the underhand methods so common with the Jews.
>   The Jews were firing from the windows of houses on the wounded Jocks lying in the street, but the remainder of Lightening Platoon and the Police in Mea Shearim Police Station returned heavy fire, causing casualties and forced the Jews to withdraw.[120]

Six soldiers were killed and five wounded, one of whom later died of his injuries.

On the next day the firing continued. A soldier was killed and two officers, the wife of one of them and eight soldiers were injured in attacks on British vehicles. An armoured car was blown up by a mine on Jaffa Road while escorting a special crane brought from Beit Nabala in response to a request from the Jewish Agency.[121] Another vehicle was destroyed by an electrically detonated mine near the Jewish Sanhedria neighbourhood in north Jerusalem. The Army failed to force Jewish civilians to dismantle a roadblock in north-east Jerusalem wounding in the attempt a seventeen-year-old Jew.[122] At the same time, the Arabs attacked an Army position in Sheikh Jarrach as well as a no. 9 bus and an ambulance returning from Mt. Scopus.[123] On 22nd February, the Haganah commander of Jerusalem ordered the shooting of any British soldier who opens fire in

Jerusalem, and on 25th February the whole city outside the security zones was declared out of bounds for the Army.

Crawford of the HLI observed that 'the storm had broken, and the situation was now one of almost open warfare between the Jews and the Army'.[124] However, the Haganah did try to regain control over the Jewish forces. Also on 22nd February, the commander of Jerusalem ordered that arms carried by Jews (IZL and Lechi) who are not under orders of the Haganah should be confiscated.[125] And that no fire should be directed towards the security zones. On 25th February, an Haganah unit stopped the IZL from attacking the building of the British military court in Talbiye and confiscated their weapons.[126] Upon visiting the site of the bombing on 23rd February, Ben-Gurion noted in his diary that he could not ignore the fact that the IZL had in the past set the precedents for such actions.[127]

Contrary to Crawford's dramatic observation the storm did not in fact break. The Haganah's command succeeded in containing the frequency and ferocity of the clashes with the Army which, in turn, was eager to return to acceptable levels of violence by means such as avoidance of Jewish areas in west Jerusalem including Jaffa Road – the city's main east-west axis. The Haganah was much more worried about the increased effectiveness of the Arab attacks in general and on the convoys from the coast in particular cutting Jerusalem off from its main source of supplies. Crawford, on the other hand, maintained in retrospect that the main Jewish target remained the security forces. Every day, he wrote, 'a British soldier or constable was brutally murdered'.[128] His description of the soldiers' mood coincided with the more extreme manifestations of Jewish paranoia.

> The general feeling of the British troops was strongly in favor of the Arabs. They attempted to maintain their role of neutrality extremely well, but it would have been unnatural not to feel strongly and sometimes display their feelings towards one side or the other. They felt contempt and anger for cowardly, underhand methods of the Jews. For the Arabs, on the other hand one could not help feeling a certain liking an account of their childlike good humor. Moreover, though he might steal your kit or rifle, he would generally make some effort to keep a promise once given. It was not surprising, therefore, that the troops were on the whole in favour of the Arabs.[129]

Fortunately, for the cause of the status quo the next major Arab success (11th March), the bombing of the Jewish Agency, using a car of the American Consulate, was not attributed to the British.[130] The focus of the fighting shifted for a few weeks to the road and the situation in Jerusalem returned to tolerable. With most of west Jerusalem out of bounds, the Army tended to operate mainly from its fixed positions. The HLI forced to act when fired upon, 'were now allowed to use heavier weapons under extreme circumstances, and it proved to be an effective deterrent to Jew and Arab alike. Mr. Hugh Dunn ("B" Company), was the P.I.A.T. King, and his success with that weapon, and his keenness to use it, became legend in the Battalion'.[131]

During February and most of March, the Old City had remained relatively calm. In the Jewish Quarter, the Haganah had consolidated its authority over all military (including IZL and Lechi) and civilian (i.e., Weingarten) affairs. Defensive positions destroyed by the Army were rebuilt or abandoned.[132] The main Arab military efforts were directed elsewhere and the Army tried to further strengthen the Quarter's sense of security by constructing protective walls against Arab sniping.

The Haganah attributed changes in local Army-Jewish relations to the rotation of the HLI companies. "D" Company CO Major Davidson was considered friendly and helpful in stopping Arab sniping. According to "D"'s own account: 'Our job (and *what* a job) is keeping the Jews away from the Arabs and the Arabs away from the Jews, and, as usual the Jocks are doing their stuff in their own way with that British spirit which seems to have the knack of controlling everything'.[133]

The worst were the "Ritz Company" – "A" CO Captain Sherwood and especially the Company Sergeant Major "Dinger" Bell, and the Support Company CO Major Alec Brodie, who took up positions in the Quarter in mid-March. On 23rd March, a Jewish girl and a young man who were carrying a pistol and 'suspected of thug activity',[134] were apprehended and turned over to the Police after a severe beating. They were eventually released in west Jerusalem inside Zone B.[135] On 26th March, soldiers confiscated a periscope which was later returned by a sergeant without his commander's knowledge. A friendly junior officer, Lt. Howard, warned Weingarten of an impending search which he then conducted himself, with no results. He was replaced by Lt. Graham (previously commander of the mortar platoon which had been amalgamated with the anti-tank platoon) who was known for his hostility. Lt. Graham, with a large number of soldiers, conducted a violent and abusive search throughout the Quarter. Lt. Howard later explained that Graham had acted on his own initiative. To prevent escalation, the local Haganah command repeated its instruction to avoid friction with the Army.[136]

On Sunday, 28th March, the Support Company CO Major Alec Brodie received a report that Jews in the Quarter were training on a 2" mortar and decided to confiscate it. Accompanied by a corporal, Brodie surprised the Jews and seized one of the two mortars they were training with. When about to leave, after he fired in the air to summon reinforcements, Brodie was jumped by the Jews who were acting on an order by the Quarter's Haganah Commander – Moshe Rusnak – who was present nearby. One of the Jews grabbed the corporal's rifle, shot and killed him. The commander of the Haganah reserve unit, armed with a pistol, rushed to the site of the incident, shot and wounded Brodie in the shoulder. A group of soldiers, alerted by

Brodie's shot, arrived and opened automatic fire. The Jews withdrew under cover of the rifle they had seized from the corporal and alerted their nearest reserve units who closed in on the British troops.[137]

The ensuing battle was stopped at 13:00 hours when the wounded Major Brodie returned to the scene and offered to negotiate a cease-fire before "B" Company arrived as reinforcement and the fighting got completely out of hand. He agreed to Rusnak's demands that all soldiers withdraw from the Quarter and all recently confiscated weapons be returned. The Haganah would be allowed to bear arms openly within the Quarter and it would return the weapons taken from the soldiers.[138]

The Army's casualties in the fighting were one officer and one corporal killed, and eight soldiers wounded of whom, four died in hospital.[139] The Jews suffered one Haganah member killed and four wounded as well as four civilians wounded, one of whom later died.[140]

The Support Company left the Old City on 30th March and was replaced by Captain Faulkner's "B" Company. Rusnak accepted Faulkner's demand that his men refrain from carrying weapons openly, which would have created a problematic precedent. In return Faulkner promised to refrain from arms searches. According to the Haganah, some of the British soldiers had refused to take part in the fighting with the Jews and some provided the Haganah fighters with small arms ammunition and grenades.[141] Faulkner is reported to have warned the Haganah that next time there would be no cease-fire and advised that the Jews don't waste their force on squabbles with the Army.[142] Henceforth, fighting in the Old City returned to the routine of occasional exchanges of small arms fire.

Crawford of the HLI was greatly impressed at the time by the efforts made by the Quarter's Hospital and the head of its surgical unit Dr. Zvi Neumann on behalf of Lt. Alisdair Hillary, who had been badly wounded on 3rd April. Hillary had investigated with Captain Faulkner a report of Jewish tunnelling under the Reserve Position.[143] There had been some mining and counter-mining in the area and in the course of the search Hillary had detonated one of the mines. He was rushed to the Misgav Ladach Hospital in the Quarter and was immediately operated on. The 'whole Jewish staff did all they possibly could to save his life; their skill and untiring efforts were beyond praise'.[144] With the help of the Jewish Agency, an eye specialist was contacted who agreed to enter the Old City with a female assistant and treat Hillary.

Crawford accompanied the Lightening Platoon in smuggling the two into the Jewish Quarter under the eyes of the Arab militia. He was obviously much taken with the drama of the operation while his description reveals the severe self-imposed constraints of the Army's operation in Arab-controlled areas. Upon reaching an Arab roadblock,

> A silent figure would appear out of the shadows, rifle slung over his shoulder, and reluctantly withdrawing one hand from his greatcoat

pocket, signalled us to stop. Alan Grendon [C.O. of the platoon] and the I.O. [Crawford] leading the small column in the latter's Jeep, yelled the well-known password, "H.L.I.", and the Arab sentry, after a moment's peering at the vehicle, gave the usual reply, "O.K. Johnnie, Good-night." A Chorus of friendly insults echoes from the Jocks, and the Arab sentry, delighted at the camaraderie, would show his gleaming teeth in a wide grin and wave us on. This was the normal procedure whenever an H.L.I. truck went through an Arab Road Block.[145]

In this instance, at the Arab roadblock in Jaffa Gate,

> A too inquisitive sentry caused us a few anxious moments. In this case a bit of heavy-handed technique was the answer. Alan Grendon snapping "H.L.I. going into the Old City, hurry-up, George – get a move on – you know me, I.O. H.L.I. – hurry up!' either confused or convinced the Arab lazily dragged back the Dannert Wire and let us pass, muttering into his great coat collar, "O.K. Sir, O.K., O.K., come on, come on."
>
> Fifty yards further on we stopped [in the Armenian Quarter] under an archway, just clear of the Arab houses, and Alan Grendon and the I.O. looked at one another and heaved a sigh of relief.[146]

There was little anyone could do for Hillary and he died on 4th April.

The ultimate proof for the Jews of British perfidy was its failure to prevent the massacre of the Hadassah convoy on 13th April while making its way through Sheikh Jarrach to Mt. Scopus. Crawford's view of the Arabs as childlike and naughty was particularly inappropriate when applied to the inhabitants of Sheikh Jarrach.

> The Arabs were always friendly, but often had to be reprimanded. When they had fired either on Jews or on our Posts their excuse always was that newcomers to the area, generally Iraqis, had caused the trouble, being ignorant of the location of our positions. This was true, but their excuse for firing on the Jews, that the Jews had fired on them first of all, was not always so true. The inhabitants of Shaikh Jarrach, a wealthy residential district, were educated, intelligent, better class Arabs who were extremely friendly towards us and only too willing to co-operate with us.[147]

Despite the HLI's permanent positions and the Army's assurances that it would guarantee the safety of Jewish traffic to Mt. Scopus, all traffic was organized in convoys of armoured vehicles and coordinated with the Police who advised each convoy, through the commander of the Mea Shearim Station, on the safety of passage through Sheikh Jarrach. On 11th April, Brigadier Jones visited with Major Jack Churchill, newly appointed second in command of the 1st HLI, Mt. Scopus and expressed his confidence that the permanent presence of eighteen soldiers in Tony's Post[148] was sufficient to render superfluous Jewish armed convoy escorts, seen as a source of friction with local Arab forces.[149] Indeed, the latest convoys had made the two mile journey without incident.

The Hadassah convoy – two ambulances, two armoured buses, three trucks and two armoured cars, set off at 09:30 hours after receiving the assurances of the commander of the Mea Shearim Police Station that the road was clear. An ambush of about forty Arab volunteers led by a Syrian officer and a local Arab commander assembled in the Mufti's unfinished house opposite Tony's Post. They planted an electric mine in the road and waited.[150] At 09:40–09:45 hours, the convoy reached the site of the ambush. The mine was detonated between the lead armoured car and the ambulance following it, and created a large crater in the road. The armoured car was tossed by the explosion to the side of the road with its front in the crater. The ambulance, trying to reverse, was soon also stuck as were the two armoured buses, their drivers hit and their tyres punctured. The vehicles at the back of the convoy, another ambulance, the trucks and the second armoured car managed to turn around and return to safety.[151] The remaining armed escort held off the Arab attackers who were soon joined by a mass of armed Arabs from the nearby neighbourhoods.

Major Jack Churchill exemplified the unique breed of British eccentric and exceptional soldiers who flourish in wars but are often a menace to themselves peacetime.[152] On the morning of the 13th, he inspected a battalion parade in the barracks in St. Paul's German Hospice opposite the Damascus Gate, when he received a message from Tony's Post of the attack on the convoy. He left the parade, fetched his Dingo – a turretless small armoured car appropriated from the repair shop, and drove to Sheikh Jarrach. From the roof of Tony's Post, he observed the battle and the large number of Arabs on their way to join the fighting. He radioed on his own initiative 2nd Brigade HQ asking for an artillery observation officer and the use of two twenty-five pounders to stop the Arab attack but was turned down. He next requested two of the Life Guard's Staghounds armed with 37 mm guns and was told that they would be available as soon as they completed their immediate mission. At 10:00 hours, he was joined in Tony's Post by Crawford the IO, who 'from then on was almost constantly on the wireless set sending back Sitreps [situation reports], and passing messages for Major Churchill'.[153]

Powerless to stop the shooting, Churchill decided to try to rescue the passengers trapped in the buses. He instructed Battalion HQ to prepare a GMC armoured personnel carrier (APC), returned in his Dingo to the transport lines and collected the APC with a carrier as escort. Churchill then returned to the battlefield, positioned the carrier near a police armoured car, there to monitor the fighting, about fifty yards from the trapped vehicles, in a position from which to provide covering fire. Behind them, he left the APC. Churchill would later recount how he walked up to the convoy.

> As I walked along, swinging my blackthorn walking stick, I grinned like mad from side to side, as people are less likely to shoot at you if you smile at them. Of course, having come straight off a battalion parade, I was very dressed up – in glengarry, tunic, Sam Browne belt (but no claymore, worse luck!) kilt, hair sporran and red and white diced hose and white spats! This outfit in the middle of the battle together with my grinning at them, may have made the Arabs laugh because most of them have a sense of humor. Anyway they didn't shoot me![154]

Churchill hammered with his blackthorn on the door of the nearest bus, identified himself and offered to evacuate the passengers with the risk of exposure to Arab fire while leaving the bus. After debating their options among themselves, the passengers decided that they preferred to wait for the Haganah to rescue them. The same response came from the other bus. Meanwhile the carrier's Bren gunner had been badly wounded. Churchill ran back to his vehicles, sent the APC and the carrier back and returned to Tony's Post.[155]

At 11:30 hours, Tony's Post was reinforced by the Lightning Platoon. The Life Guards' Staghounds had also arrived but their one serviceable gun jammed after one shot.[156] Permission was then given to use 3" mortars placed in Robert's Post along Prophet Samuel street and fire was brought down on Arab positions near the convoy, and on the armed Arabs moving up Wadi Joz. At 13:00 hours, another half troop of the Life Guards arrived and provided additional fire. Finally at 15:00 hours, a platoon from "B" Company under the command of Captain Faulkenr made its way to Tony's Post and helped cover the evacuation of remaining passengers with the help of the Battalion Medical Doctor.[157]

By 1700 hours, all the survivors were evacuated and the firing died down. The Battalion CO Lt.-Col. Torquel Macleod arrived to supervise the clearing of the road, and by 08:00 hours the following morning it was opened to traffic.[158] The Battalion's casualties were two killed and three wounded. The Jewish casualties were seventy-eight dead and missing, shot and burnt alive in the buses or trying to escape, and twenty-four wounded.[159] Based on Arab sources, the Haganah estimated their loses at thirty killed and forty wounded.[160]

The Hadassah convoy is generally regarded in Israel as one of the worst disasters of the war. Israeli writers have mainly dealt with the Haganah's ineffective response which was largely due to its preoccupation with the arrival of the first large convoy following the Palmach's efforts to reopen the road to Jerusalem after the March setbacks. To most, British compliance or even active support of the Arabs was obvious.[161] Regardless of whether the reason for the Army's slow response was a conspiracy, collusion or simple ill will, it is clear that the Army had been reluctant to expose its soldiers to unnecessary risks by becoming directly and actively involved. Its concern to preserve a semblance of impartiality led to its insistence during the battle that it would act on the condition that Haganah forces kept their distance. This demand, in turn, served local Haganah commanders as an excuse for their failure to intervene and as proof of British complicity. The Army had hoped that its presence would serve as a deterrent but that clearly was not the case. A large Arab force had ambushed a Jewish convoy in front of an Army Post and kept attacking it within a short distance of both Battalion and Brigade HQs.

The Army's withdrawal from Safad, allowing the Haganah to occupy Tiberias and especially its redeployment in Haifa, convinced the Jewish leadership that the Army had become largely irrelevant and that its sole concerns were to minimize its loses and to carry out its withdrawal as smoothly as possible. General Macmillan had tried to extend the Army's new policy of early withdrawal from troublesome and non-essential areas to Jerusalem. General John T. Crocker, C. in C. Middle East Land Forces (and one of Montgomery's corps commanders in Normandy) agreed with him. However, the High Commissioner while fully aware of the difficulties the Army had been experiencing in Jerusalem refused to allow an early ending of the British presence there and thus of civilian rule in Palestine where the Army was to hold on for a few more weeks.[162] In any event, the Army had begun to move its headquarters to Haifa for the final phase of the evacuation, and withdrew troops and equipment from some of its Jerusalem installations thereby promoting rumours of an immanent evacuation.[163]

On 15th April, the Army evacuated the 2nd Air Support Signal Unit from the Augusta Victoria Hospital on the ridge connecting Mt. Scopus with Mount of Olives, overlooking the Old City. In August 1947, the Army had begun to move its Palestine HQ from the King David Hotel to Augusta Victoria.[164] The laying of the necessary communications infrastructure had been near completion when the UN resolution brought the work to a halt. Pioneers were now brought in to dismantle the installation and the Air Support Signal Unit secured the site while they worked. Their task completed and with the growing tension in north Jerusalem the Army decided to relocate its forces from Augusta Victoria to the Allenby Camp in south Jerusalem,[165] leaving in the site a garrison from the Jordanian Arab Army.[166] The move was misinterpreted by the Jewish local command as part of the anticipated early evacuation of Jerusalem which, it was assumed, would follow in a matter of days.[167]

The Haganah's limited troops in Jerusalem were tied down, with predominantly static and local responsibilities of defending Jewish neighbourhoods

and protecting traffic. The only forces close enough to deal with the consequences of an early evacuation were the 4th and 5th Palmach battalions
engaged in operations ("Nachshon" followed by "Harel") to open the road
to Jerusalem. Fearful of the possibility of local Arab forces occupying the
evacuated British security zones which were vital for the defence of west
Jerusalem, Shaltiel, commander of the Haganah in Jerusalem, exerted all
his influence at Haganah HQ and the national leadership to redirect the
Palmach to enter the city at the expense for the time being of its efforts along
the road.[168]

A stumbling block impeding co-operation between the Palmach and the
commander of the Harel Operation – Yitzhak Rabin – and the Haganah in
Jerusalem was the former's refusal to accept the latter's authority. As a com-
promise, the Haganah HQ appointed Yitzhak Sade, the first commander
of the Palmach, as commander of the joint forces in Operation "Yevusi":
The Harel battalions were ordered to redeploy and on 20th April the Palmach entered Jerusalem. But although the Army had been clearing out of
some installations such as the Syrian Orphanage and the Military Court, it
remained in most of its positions.

As an alternative to Yevusi's original mission Sadeh came up with a new
strategy. By occupying the ridges to the north, east and south of Jerusalem, the Arab neighbourhoods and the Old City could be isolated from the
Arab hinterland thereby shifting the demographic advantage in Jerusalem
in favour of the Jews. The first phase of the Yevusi operation was to be
the occupation of the northern ridge which overlooked the final stretch
of the road to the city and its northern neighbourhoods. By occupying
the villages of Beit Iksa and Nebi Samuel, the Palmach could extend its
territorial hold as far as the Jerusalem-Nablus road, cut Arab Jerusalem
off from the north and relieve the isolated Jewish villages of Neve Ya'akov
and Atarot.

The Palmach failed on the night of 22nd–23rd April to take Nebi Samuel
in a costly battle which ended with forty-four killed, and although another
unit managed to enter the village of Shuafat on the Jerusalem-Nablus road
it was ordered to withdraw.[169] The alternative which was still in line with
the intention of isolating Arab Jerusalem from the north as well as securing
the road to Mt. Scopus was the occupation of Sheikh Jarrach. Initial plans
made by the Jerusalem Haganah command to occupy Sheikh Jarrach and
demolish as many as its buildings as possible[170] were discussed with Jack
Churchill. The Haganah argued that since the civilian residents had already
left their houses which were occupied by local militias and volunteers, the
neighbourhood had become a war zone and its buildings military targets.
However, control of the road to Nablus through Sheikh Jarrach remained
a British priority and could not be compromised. Nevertheless, the commanders of Yevusi and the Palmach were confident that the Army had lost
its taste for fighting and would accept a fait-accompli.

Two companies of the Palmach's 5th Battalion attacked Sheikh Jarrach in the early hours of the morning of 25th April. One company ("B") occupied a number of buildings in the lower (southern) part of the neighbourhood and began demolishing them except that it had miscalculated the amount of explosives required and was unable to complete its mission. Having come under intensive and effective Army fire it chose to withdraw with one fighter-killed and twenty-five wounded.[171]

The second company ("A") seized an unfinished building ("Nashashibi House") in the upper part of Sheikh Jarrach overlooking the road north and the road to Mt. Scopus. The company fought off an Arab counter-attack and demolished a nearby building. Throughout the day, it continued to ex-change fire with Arab positions. According the Crawford;

> The Jews stated that they intended to hold their newly-won positions in order to keep the road open for the Hadassa convoys. The Arabs, on the other hand, declared that in order to keep open the Nablus road, they must, and would, drive the Jews from their positions.[172]

The Army, however, had no intention of leaving the matter to either side, thereby allowing the area to become an active battlefield. This, Brigadier Jones determined, 'could not under any circumstances be accepted because the road was vital to the British evacuation plan'.[173]

Throughout the 25th British and Jewish authorities negotiated the fate of the Palmach presence and the timing of its withdrawal to its original posi-tions.[174] Following the experience of Arab indifference to the presence of British troops during the attack on the Hadassah convoy, the HLI informed the local Arab command that

> they must neither interfere in our operations nor launch any attacks of their own. ...we had great difficulty in persuading the Arabs not to rush in there and then in an attempt to drive the Jews from Sheikh Jarrach. ... the Arabs when we told them of our intentions to expel the Jews were delighted, and promised not to interfere.[175]

Following discussions between the Army and the High Commissioner and negotiations with the Jewish Agency,[176] the Jewish leadership

> was informed that the Haganah must withdraw to their original posi-tions by 17:30 hrs or that they would be forcibly driven out. At the same time CO, HLI [Maclean] was given orders to prepare a plan of attack and certain additional sub-units and supporting arms were placed un-der his command.[177]

The 1st HLI was reinforced by "C" Company of the Warwickshires, a troop of Cromwell tanks, two troops of the Life Guards' armoured cars and a troop of twenty-five pounders. The Battalion's Support Company manned three outposts including Suffolk Post opposite the American Colony where the CO established his Battalion Tactical Headquarters with an Artillery Observation Post. The Regimental Aid Post was situated in the American Colony.[178]

Maclean's plan took into account the lack of field training of some of the troops. A speedy reaction and a speedy result were essential if a 'triangular contest' was to be avoided. The Warwickshires and the Life Guards were to secure the Tactical HQ and prevent Jewish reinforcement from reaching the Palmach assuming, erroneously, that it had arrived at Nashashibi House from the south. The infantry and tanks would attack from the south east.

During the day, a number of British officers approached Nashashibi House in an attempt to persuade its defenders to withdraw and thus avoid a confrontation with the Army. However, for various reasons, most of the unit's commanders were absent, leaving in charge an Non Commissioned Officer (NCO) who was given an unequivocal directive to stay put and to treat British threats as bluffs.[179]

The attack was carried out by HLI's "B" Company (Major Faulkner) supported by a troop[180] of tanks from 4th/7th Dragoon Guards and artillery. A composite HLI Company formed the reserve.[181] 'At 17:45 hrs, with the full approval of H.E. The High Commissioner, the troops moved into the attack'.[182] "B" Company mounted on the tanks drove as fast as they could along the edge of the built up area of Wadi Joz and through its olive groves, the only covered line of approach to upper Sheikh Jarrach, and took up positions covering both its target and the Hadassah Hospital should its defenders open fire in support of the Palmach. In addition, a searchlight which had been previously mounted on the roof of the Italian Hospice (and used in clearing the road after the attack on the Hadassah convoy) illuminated Nashashibi House blinding its defenders and facilitating the troops' orientation as darkness fall.

As soon as the tanks were detected, they came under fire from the Palmach. In response, the tanks opened fire with their guns and machine-guns, joined by the HLIs' Support Company from its various positions.

> From tac. H.Q., the whole show looked like a Searchlight Tattoo, with the "Palace" [Nashashibi House] gleaming white in the beam from the Italian Hospice, the 17-pdr. H.E. shells bursting in the interior with fiery red flashes and converging streams of tracers (some of them fired, it may be admitted, by the C.O., [Maclean] still in his church-going trews and spats) from the various covering positions all adding to the picture.
>
> The infantry advance was pressed with dash, and within 20 minutes the objective was in our hands at the cost of 1 man wounded to ourselves, 2 killed, 18 wounded and 37 prisoners to the Jews.[183]

The speed and the successful outcome of the attack were facilitated by the Palmach NCO left in charge of the House, who decided after the initial exchange of fire to withdraw. Most of the Palmach fighters made their way back to their lines the way they had come, that is, to the west. Contrary to Crawford's figures, only seventeen fighters who did not hear the order to retreat, were taken prisoner, two were killed one of whom was stabbed by a bayonet.[184] Most of those found in the House were wounded from the previous fighting. The Army wisely used mainly smoke and armour piercing shells which achieved the required shock without inflicting unnecessary loses and exacerbating the tension with the Haganah. The wounded were quickly transferred to the Hadassah Hospital and the prisoners were released in west Jerusalem. The Haganah agreed to keep out of Sheikh Jarrach with the Army's promise that the safety of the traffic to Mt. Scopus and Neve Ya'akov would be guaranteed, and that the Haganah would be alerted to the precise timing of the eventual evacuation.[185] In the Brigadier's view, the operation had been an unqualified success, in as much as 'until the final British evacuation SHEIK JARRACH remained a fairly quiet sector'.[186] This may be partly due to the relocation of the 1st HLI to the Allenby Barracks in south Jerusalem.

The battle of Sheikh Jarrach was meant to impress the Jewish side with the Army's resolve to use whatever means necessary to keep its evacuation routes safe and to re-establish its deterrence. With the Palmach still in Jerusalem, and with the realization of the futility of trying to occupy the ridges overlooking north Jerusalem, Yevusi HQ turned to strengthening the Haganah's hold on south Jerusalem by attacking the Arab neighbourhood of Qatamon. The 4th Palmach Battalion assaulted the monastery of St. Simon in the western edge of Qatamon, which had been used as a base by the Holy Jihad, under one of its veteran commanders – Ibrahim Abu Daya, and reinforced by Iraqi volunteers. After failing to secure the building on the night of the 27th April, the Palmach attacked the monastery again on the night of the 29th and defended it throughout the 30th against repeated counter-attacks. By the end of the day, the Arab lines facing the Monastery began to disintegrate following the appearance of an Haganah column in its rear, and its fighters withdrew into the neighbourhood. During the next day (1st May), the Jerusalem Haganah forces cleared Qatamon from its Arab defenders while the Palmach left Jerusalem and returned to its previous mission of opening the road.[187]

The 2nd Brigade had not been aware of the strategic concept which informed the Yevusi operations especially since it was based on the false premises of an early evacuation and an assumption of Army passivity. However, it was clear that the main benefit to the Haganah from occupying Qatamon would be 'to link up the circle' formed by the Jewish neighbourhoods in south Jerusalem thereby gaining control over the road south to Hebron and on to Beersheba.

While the fighting was confined to Qatamon the Army did not intervene. The HLI, now stationed in south Jerusalem sent two observers – Crawford and Allan Grendon – to follow the fighting.[188] During the first day of fighting after their initial elation at having, seemingly, trapped the Palmach in the monastery, the Arabs now 'badly shaken' clamoured for the Army's help.[189] The Brigadier's attempts to broker a truce were rejected by the triumphant Haganah[190] and the occupation of Qatamon was completed, at which point the Brigadier intervened.

> He was certain that the next Jewish move would be an attempt to move forward from QATAMON in order to link up with their settlement of MEQOR HAYIM to the EAST. Such action would have resulted in the ARABS from UPPER BAAQA launching a counter-attack and in the whole area becoming a battle ground. This could not be accepted as the main British evacuation route to the SOUTH via BETHLEHEM would be threatened thereby.
>
> Comdr 2 Inf Bde therefore sent for the representation of the Jewish Agency and informed him that any move by the JEWS further EAST would immediately involve them in a battle with British troops.[191]

To add to the credibility of his warning, a flight of four Spitfires made dry runs over Qatamon.[192]

In retrospect, Brigadier Jones was gratified by the Haganah acceding to his demand. The Arab militia in south Jerusalem was by then a spent force and the Haganah was careful to husband its strength in anticipation of a major operation to occupy the whole of west Jerusalem once the Army left. Brigadier Jones surmised that its compliance

> must very largely be attributed to the realization by the Jews that words could be followed by prompt action if the warning was disregarded.
> The lesson of SHEIKH JARRAH had been well taught.[193]

All that remained for him was to keep the lid on the fighting in Jerusalem as tight as possible and complete the preparations for the final evacuation.

Notes

1 Bruce Hoffman, *Anonymous Soldiers*, 378–381.
2 [Hebrew] *Al Hamishmar*, 6 February 1947.
3 *TNA* W.O. 261/513.
4 '2nd Battalion', *The Antelope*, May 1948, 11.
5 TNA W.O. 261/305 2nd Battalion The Royal Warwickshire Regiment for the Quarter ending 31 Mar. 48.
6 'General Sir Charles Jones,' *Times*, 6 January 1988. See also The *Independent* 30 May 2007 – "Splosh" 'on account of his allowing a bridge which he was building as a young sapper officer to disintegrate and fall into the water"

7 *TNA* W.O. 261/310 Quarterly Historical Report 1st Battalion The Suffolk Regiment Quarter ending 30 September 1947.

8 *TNA* W.O. 261/310 and *TNA* WO 261/311 Quarter ending 31 March 1948.

9 Ibid., and *The Suffolk Regimental Gazette* (Sept., Oct., 48), 15. In France, in 1940 Jones improvised defenses of 127th Infantry Brigade's HQ, 'from an anti-tank troop... Jones personally stopped two tanks in their tracks with well-aimed shots, from an anti-tank rifle,' *Times* (6 January 1988).

10 *The Suffolk Regimental Gazette* (November–December, 1947), 14–15.

11 Ibid. (May, June, 1948), 6.

12 Ibid.

13 '1st Battalion News (second Installment)', *The Suffolk Regimental Gazette* (May, June, 1948), 9.

14 Ibid., 11.

15 Ibid., 12.

16 '1st Battalion News,' *The Suffolk Regimental Gazette* (September, October, 1948), 10.

17 *The Suffolk Regimental Gazette* (May, June, 1948), 6.

18 Ibid.

19 Ibid., 9.

20 Imperial War Museum GB 554/41/407 recorded interview.

21 [Hebrew] Levy, 92–93.

22 Ibid., 94.

23 W.O. 261/311. Impatiently waiting permission to extricate the Jewish passengers Harper radioed:

> Am midways here and can't do anything. It appears that the Jews in the house are short of ammunition and the Arabs are putting on an attack and they cannot hold out much longer. Why have we been waiting here two hours when we could have got them out.

Transcript of the Army's radio traffic in the IDF Archive 10-446/1948.

24 Ibid., and Levy, 99. Levy, who was head of Haganah intelligence in Jerusalem mentions specifically negotiations with Lt.-Col. Harper, but mistakenly identified him as a staff officer of the 2nd Brigade.

25 [Hebrew] Yitzhak Kopf, *"Michmash" Battalion in the Jerusalem Battles in the War of Independence* (Jerusalem: Ammunition Hill, 2002), 122–124.

26 Ibid., 124. The CO of the Haganah company, Avraham "Abrasha" Tamir reached the rank of Major General in the IDF.

27 *The Suffolk Regimental Gazette* (May, June, 1948), 6, 9.

28 *The Suffolk Regimental Gazette* (September, October, 1948), 9.

29 Kopf, 124.

30 Marcus Cunliffe, *History of the Royal Warwickshire Regiment 1919–1955* (London: William Claws, 1956), 178–181.

31 '2nd Battalion,' *The Antelope* (May, 1948), 11. See also 24.

32 Ibid.

33 'The work of the Battalion,' *The Antelope* (May, 1948), 24.

34 Ibid.

35 Ibid.

36 Ibid.

37 W.O. 261/305.

38 *The Antelope* (May, 1948), 25.

39 W.O. 261/305.

40 Ibid. Photograph of the gun in Yemin Moshe in *The Gunner*, vol. 29, No. 12 (March, 1948), 297. The gun's position was behind Mishkenot Shananim, an alms house built by Montifiori just south of Yemin Moshe facing Mount Zion. The caption reads: 'A Peace-Preserver at Jerusalem.'

41 [Hebrew] Levy, 198, 200. [Hebrew] Itamar Radai, *A Tale of Two Cities: The Palestinian Arabs in Jerusalem and Jaffa, 1947–1948* (Tel Aviv: Dayan Center, Tel Aviv University, 2015), 65.

42 [Hebrew] Levy, 200; Radai, 39, 65.

43 W.O. 261/305, 'The work of the Battalion,' *The Antelope* (May, 1948), 25, '75th Field Battery, R.A. – Jerusalem (Formerly 29th Field Battery, R.A.),' *The Gunner*, vol. 30, No. 6 (September, 1948), 156.

44 W.O. 261/305, 'The work of the Battalion,' 25, Levy, 200.

45 W.O. 261/305, '2nd Battalion,' *The Antelope* (November, 1948), 102.

46 [Hebrew] Levy, 200–201.

47 *The Antelope* (November, 1948), 102.

48 W.O. 261/305.

49 See Lt. General Sir Brian Horrocks, 'The Highland Light Infantry A Special Introduction,' in L.B. Oatts, *The Highland Light Infantry (The 71st H.L.I. and 74th Highlanders)*, (London, Leo Cooper, 1969).

50 Lt. Col. L.B. Oatts, *Proud Heritage. The Story of the Highland Light Infantry, volume 4, 1919–1959* (Glasgow, London, Toronto; The House of Grant, 1963), 403.

51 '"A" Company Notes,' in *The Highland Light Infantry Chronicle*, vol. 43, No. 3 (July, 1947), 126.

52 '"C" Company Notes,' in ibid., 127.

53 'Anti-Tank Platoon Notes,' in ibid., 130.

54 '"C" Company Notes,' *The H.L.I. Chronicle*, vol. 43, No. 4 (October, 1947), 171.

55 *H.L.I. Chronicle*, vol. 43, No. 3 (July, 1947), 130.

56 *H.L.I. Chronicle*, vol. 43, No. 4 (October, 1947), 171.

57 'Notes from a Wilderness,' *H.L.I. Chronicle*, vol. 43, No. 4 (October, 1947), 172.

58 Captain J. Crawford [Battalion Intelligence Officer], 'The 71st in Jerusalem 1947–1948', a three part article published in *The H.L.I. Chronicle*, beginning vol. 44, No. 4 (October, 1948), 117. 'The 71st' was the Regiment's preferred historical name, changed in 1786.

59 'Signal Notes,' in *The H.L.I. Chronicle*, beginning vol. 44, No. 1 (January, 1948), 14.

60 'Intelligence Section Notes,' in ibid., 15.

61 '"A" Company Notes,' in ibid., 17.

62 'The 71st in Jerusalem' part 1, 118.

63 'H.Q. Company Notes,' *H.L.I. Chronicle*, beginning vol. 44, No. 1 (January, 1948), 14.

64 '"B" Company Notes, ibid., 17. According to Haganah reports during the evacuation of the Jewish population of the small isolated neighbourhood of Shimeon Ha'tsadiq near Sheik Jarach (21 January) the Army, ignoring police instructions, confiscated the Jewish defenders' weapons. The soldiers searched Jewish homes, destroyed property, confiscated valuables and then forced each of the evacuated inhabitants to sign a statement absolving the Army of any damage to private property. IDF Archive 22-446/1948, messages from and to Haganah intelligence in Jerusalem, 22 January 1948.

65 'The 71st in Jerusalem,' part 1, 119.

66 Ibid.

67 Ibid., [Hebrew] *Al-Hamishmar* (12 October 1947).

68 'The 71st in Jerusalem,' part 1, 119.

69 [Hebrew] *Al-Hamishmar* (14 November 1947); *Kol Ha'am* (14 November 1947); *Hamashkif* (14 November 1947); *Hazofe* (16 November 1947).

70 'The 71st in Jerusalem,' part 1, 120.

71 [Hebrew] Amos Eylon, *Jerusalem did not fall. Siege 1948* (Tel-Aviv: Tversky, 1948), 44–45.

72 '"D" Company Notes,' *H.L.I. Chronicle* (January, 1948), 19.
73 'The 71st in Jerusalem,' part 1, 120.
74 The definitive study of the Jewish Quarter in 1948 is [Hebrew] Moshe Ehrenvald, *Siege within Siege, The Jewish Quarter in the Old City of Jerusalem in the War of Independence* (Sde Boker: Ben Gurion Institute, 2004), 16–17.
75 *Statistical Abstract of Palestine 1944–1945* (Jerusalem: Government Printer, 1946), 22.
76 Ehrenvald, 34.
77 Ibid., 35–36.
78 Ibid., 37.
79 Ibid., 39.
80 'The 71st in Jerusalem,' part 1, 122.
81 Ibid.
82 Ibid., 122, also in Oatts, *Proud Heritage*, 405.
83 'The 71st in Jerusalem,' part 1, 122.
84 Ibid.
85 Ehrenvald, 40–47.
86 '"A" Company Notes,' *H.L.I. Chronicle* (April, 1948), 68.
87 'The 71st in Jerusalem,' part 1, 122.
88 [Hebrew] *Compilation the Civil Guard Corps in Jerusalem* (1947–1949) (Jerusalem: Published by Previous activists of the Civil Guard and the Haganah Organization, 1964), 54–55.
89 [Hebrew] *Davar*, 15 February and 17 February 1948.
90 'The 71st in Jerusalem,' part 1, 118.
91 [Hebrew] *Al-Hamishmar* (13 February 1948).
92 Ibid.
93 [Hebrew] Levy, 190, David Shaltiel, *Jerusalem '48* (Ministry of Defense, 1981), 86–87, Moshe Ehrenvald, *Siege within Siege, Mount Scopus in the War of Independence* (Jerusalem: Yad Izhak Ben-Zvi, 2010), 70–71.
94 *Palestine Post*, 17 March 1948.
95 'The 71st in Jerusalem,' part 1 *H.L.I. Chronicle.*
96 [Hebrew] *Davar* (15 February 1948).
97 [Hebrew] Ehrenvald, *Mt. Scopus*, 70–71.
98 *Palestine Post* (12 February 1948), The incident occurred on 7th February.
99 'The 71st in Jerusalem,' part 1, 121–122; [Hebrew] Levy, 190–192.
100 'The 71st in Jerusalem,' part 1, 122.
101 '"B" Company Notes,' in *H.L.I. Chronicle* (April, 1948), 69.
102 'Sergeants Mess' in ibid., 66.
103 [Hebrew] Levy, 328–329, *Davar* (2 February, 3 February 1948).
104 'The 71st in Jerusalem,' part 2; *The H.L.I. Chronicle*, vol. 45, No. 1 (January, 1949), 7.
105 [Hebrew] *Hamashkif* (4 March 1948).
106 'The 71st in Jerusalem,' part 2, 7.
107 Reference to Roy Farran's Police Special Squads which had been formed to fight Jewish terrorism. Farran was on trial for the abduction and murder of a young Lehi member. See David Cesarani, *Major Farran's Hat. The Untold Story of the Struggle to Establish the Jewish State* (Cambridge, MA: De Capo Press, 2009).
108 [Hebrew] *Davar* (19 February 1948); *Hamashkif* (19 February 1948).
109 The area was inexplicably described in the *H.L.I. Chronicle* as 'known to be the haunt of the worst type of Jewish thugs', 'The 71st in Jerusalem', part 2, 8.
110 *Palestine Post* (23 February 1948).
111 [Hebrew] Levy, 330.

112 'The 71st in Jerusalem,' part 2, 8.
113 [Hebrew] Levy, 330; *Al-Hamishmar* (22 March 1948).
114 'The 71st in Jerusalem,' part 2, 8.
115 *Palestine Post* (23 February 1948).
116 'The 71st in Jerusalem,' part 2, 8; [Hebrew] Levy, 330; Y. Ofir, *On the Walls* (Tel-Aviv: Jabotinsky Institute, [n.y.]), 38–39; Shaltiel, 88–89.
117 'The 71st in Jerusalem,' part 2, 9; *Paltstine Post* (23 February 1948). In fact, one soldier, Craftsman Birke, REME, attached to 1st Suffolk was killed. His escort Pte. Bennington, 1st Suffolk, was badly wounded but recovered, *The Suffold Regimental Gazette* (May, June, 1948), 6.
118 [Hebrew] *Hatzofe*, 16 February 1948.
119 'The 71st in Jerusalem,' part 2, 9.
120 Ibid. According to *Palestine Post*, 23 February 1948, Jewish casualties included a ten-year boy who was seriously wounded and his fifteen-year old brother.
121 *Palestine Post* (24 February 1948).
122 [Hebrew] *Davar* (24 February 1948).
123 Ibid.
124 'The 71st in Jerusalem,' part 2, 9.
125 [Hebrew] Shaltiel, 89; Levy, 330, 331.
126 [Hebrew] Levy, 330.
127 [Hebrew] *Ben-Gurion Diary*, 261.
128 'The 71st in Jerusalem,' part 2, 9.
129 Ibid.
130 [Hebrew] Levy, 201–203.
131 'The 71st in Jerusalem,' part 2, 10.
132 [Hebrew] Levy, 35–37.
133 '"D" Company Notes,' *The H.L.I. Chronicle*, vol. 44, No. 2 (April, 1948), 71.
134 'The 71st in Jerusalem,' part 2, 10.
135 [Hebrew] Levy, 38.
136 Ibid. the same instruction had been reissued in 7th March, Shaltiel, 101.
137 For a detailed account from the Jewish side, see [Hebrew] Aharon Liron (Altschuler), *Old Jerusalem in siege and in battle*, 4th ed. (Ministry of Defense, 1985), 104–107.
138 Ibid., 107; Levy, 38–39.
139 'The 71st in Jerusalem,' part 2, 11.
140 [Hebrew] Liron, 107.
141 [Hebrew] Levy, 39; Liron, 109.
142 [Hebrew] Liron, 113.
143 [Hebrew] Levy, 40; 'The 71st in Jerusalem,' part 2, 11.
144 'The 71st in Jerusalem,' part 2, 12.
145 Ibid.
146 Ibid.
147 Ibid, 10.
148 Home of Katy Antonius, widow of George Antonius, a prominent advocate of Palestine nationalism, and the mistress of General Evelyn Barker, the previous GOC of the Army in Palestine.
149 [Hebrew] Ehrenvald, *Mount Scopus*, 138.
150 Ibid., 144; Levy, 192; Rubinstein, *Kastel*, 321.
151 [Hebrew] Ehrenvald, 144–145.
152 His friend and biographer R. King-Clark summed up his memoir: 'We could do with more like Jack Churchill – my friend – but perhaps, not too many more!' R. King-Clark, *Jack Churchill 'Unlimited Boldness'* (Kuntsford, Cheshire: Fleur-de-Lys Publishing, 1997), 21. The same, incidentally, could be said of

King-Clark. See his *Free for a Blast* (London: Grenville Publishing Company, 1988).
153 'The 71st in Jerusalem,' part 2, 13.
154 King-Clark, 17. Churchill, while serving with No. 2 Commando in Italy, was in the habit of going into battle armed with a claymore.
155 Ibid, 18.
156 'The 71st in Jerusalem,' part 2, 14.
157 Ibid.
158 Ibid.
159 [Hebrew] Levy, 196.
160 Ibid., 197.
161 See [Hebrew] *Ben-Gurion Diary*, 360.
162 The debate on an early evacuation of Jerusalem has been documented in detail in [Hebrew] Yona Bandmann, *When will Britain withdraw from Jerusalem. The confrontation between the military commanders in the Middle East and the High Commissioner for Palestine* (Ministry of Defense, 2004), 57–60.
163 E.g. [Hebrew], *Davar* (1 April 1948).
164 TNA W.O. 261/269 SOHQ Pal.
165 [Hebrew] Kadish and Ahrenvald, *The Yevusi Battles*, 9.
166 There were three Jordanian regular infantry companies still in Palestine – in Haifa, Hebron and Jerusalem. Maan Abu Nowar, *The Jordanian-Israeli War 1948–1951 – A History of the Hashemite Kingdom of Jordan* (Reading: Ithaca Press, 2002), 73.
167 [Hebrew] Kadish and Ahrenvald, 10.
168 Ibid., 10–16.
169 [Hebrew] Ziv Angel, 'The Battle of Nebi Samuel', in ibid., 44, and Chapter 6, 57–60.
170 Initially, the systematic demolition of neighborhoods and villages in the Jerusalem area (beginning with the Qastel) was seen as a means of preventing their re-occupation by Arab forces taking advantage of Jewish manpower shortages, which precluded garrisoning most occupied built-up areas.
171 Kadish and Ehrenvald, 68–72.
172 'The 71st in Jerusalem,' part 3; *The H.L.I. Chronicle*, vol. 45, No. 2 (April, 1949), 42.
173 *TNA* W.O. WO 261/193 2 Inf Bde Quarterly Historical report for quarter ending 30 June, 48, Appendix "A" 'Notes of major clashes in the Sheikh Jarrach Qatamon districts of Jerusalem.'
174 Ibid.
175 'The 71st in Jerusalem,' part 3, 42.
176 [Hebrew] Motti Golani, *The Last Commissioner General Sir Alan Gordon Cunningham, 1945–1948* (Tel-Aviv: Am Oved, 2011), 275.
177 WO 261/193.
178 'The 71st in Jerusalem,' part 3, 42.
179 Kadish and Ehrenvald, 88–89.
180 4th Troop, "B" Squadron, under command of 2nd Brigade. See *4th/7th Royal Dragoon Guards Regimental Magazine* (December, 1948), 47.
181 'The 71st in Jerusalem,' part 3, 43.
182 WO 261/193.
183 'The 71st in Jerusalem,' part 3, 43; Following the Second World War the H.L.I. were allowed to re-adopt the kilt, hence the difference between the dress uniforms of Churchill (Kilt) and Maclean (trews).
184 Kadish and Ehrenvald, 89. Partly based on an interview with said NCO, Uri Amitai, 11 Aug. 2006 and his written testimony.

185 Ibid., 92–93.
186 W.O. 261/193.
187 Kadish and Ehrenvald, 144–169.
188 'The 71st in Jerusalem,' part 3, 45.
189 Ibid.
190 W.O. 261/193.
191 Ibid.
192 'The 71st in Jerusalem,' part 3, 45.
193 W.O. 261/193.

6 The Galilee and Haifa

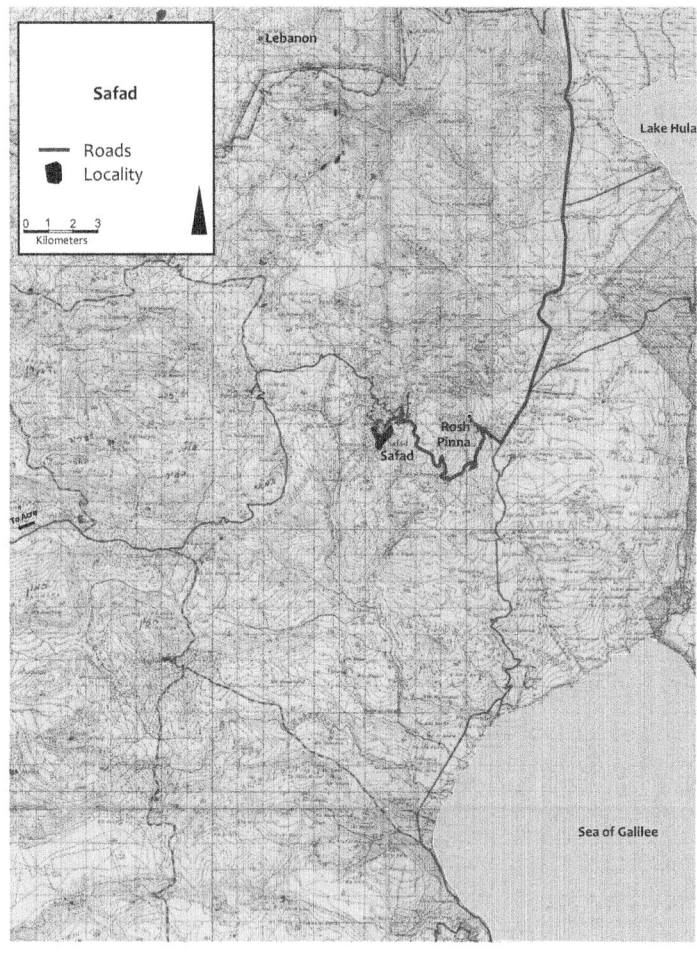

Map 6 Safad.
Source: Survey of Palestine maps 1947.

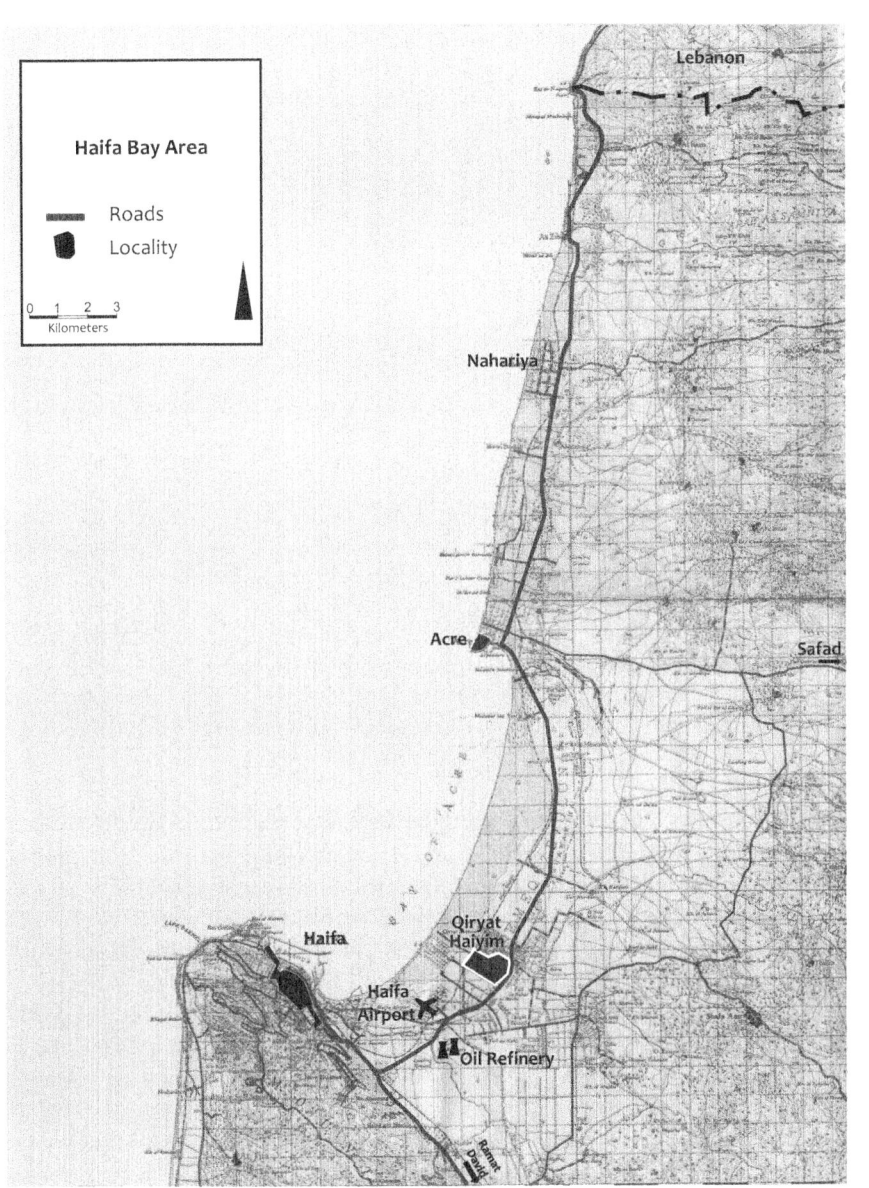

Map 7 Haifa area.
Source: Survey of Palestine maps 1947.

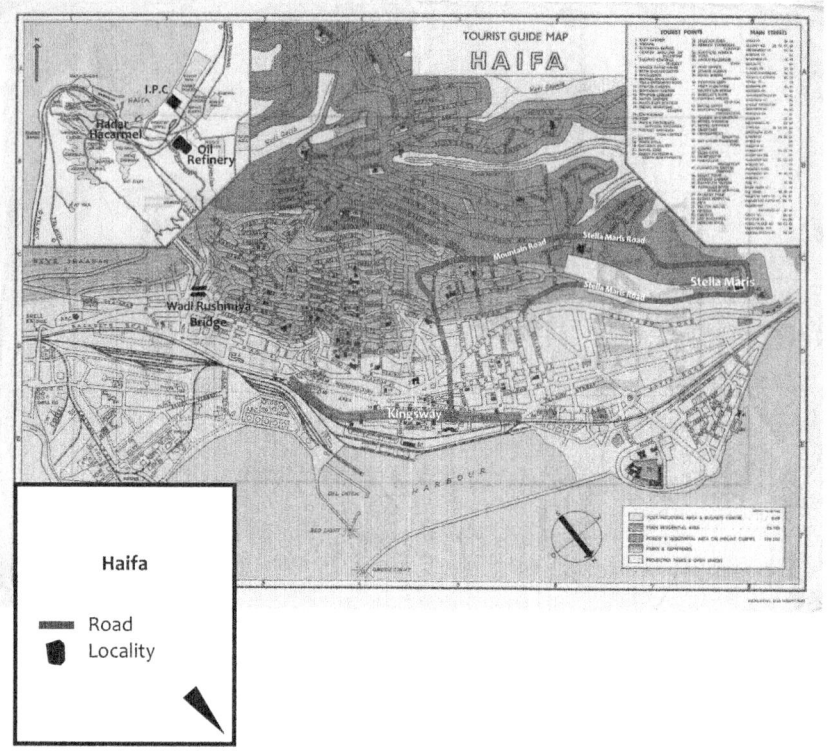

Map 8 Haifa.
Source: Tourist guide map Haifa (N.D.).

In the summer of 1947, the north of Palestine was considered the least troublesome, where 'Jews, Arabs and 1st parachute Brigade went about their respective activities. Instances in which Arabs caused trouble were still infrequent'.[1] The north consisted of two districts: Galilee with 2,790 square kilometres and a total population of 230,840 inhabitants and Haifa with 1,029 square kilometres and a population of 224,640.[2] In Haifa a majority of the inhabitants, by a small margin, were Jews – 66,000 compared to 35,940 Moslems and 26,570 Christians.[3] Some of the northern towns – Acre, Nazareth and Beisan – were Arab. Tiberias and Safad were mixed with a Jewish majority in Tiberias and on Arab majority in Safad.

Following the resumption of attempts to land illegal Jewish immigrants from post War Europe, Haifa became a centre of resistance to their deportation via the town's port to Cyprus. Their intercepted boats were brought to Haifa where their passengers were forcibly transferred to the "deportation ships" – troop ships that brought them to detention camps in Cyprus, where they remained until they could be included in a new quota of certificates for legal immigration. Resistance to deportation took the form of mass demonstrations and occasional attempts to sabotage the process. In comparison, the rest of the Galilee was reasonably peaceful and could be garrisoned by a small number of troops which, in the eastern Galilee included the predominantly Arab Transjordan Frontier Force (TJFF).

The eastern Galilee was the responsibility of the 1st Parachute Brigade with its HQ in Nazareth. But by the beginning of 1948, the 6th Airborne Division was gradually dissolved and its battalions returning to the United Kingdom or amalgamating. To replace the 1st Parachute Brigade, a special force was created (16th January) called CRAFORCE, commanded by the division's CRA (Commander Royal Artillery) Brigadier Cyril Harry ("Ted") Calqhounn, who had commanded an artillery battalion from Normandy until nearly the end of the war.[4] The force included the 17th/21st Lancers, 1st Para Battalion and the recently arrived 1st Irish Guards. Brigadier Calqhounn and a staff of six officers and sixty other ranks (ORs) set up Craforce HQ in the Lancers' camp in Tiberias.[5]

War came early to Craforce. On 9th January, two groups of some 300 Bedouins attacked from across the Syrian border the kibbutzim of Dan and Kfar Szold in the north-eastern Jordan Valley at the foot of the Golan escarpment. The reasons for the attack were local. There had been some tension between the Arab village of Al-Khisas, on the road to Dan and Kfar Szold, and its neighbouring kibbutzim. On 18th December, a wagon with two adults and a child from kibbutz Ma'ayan Baruch was attacked and the wagoner was killed. The same night a Palmach unit retaliated by raiding Khisas, contrary to the advice of the local Jewish 'Arabists', who thought it best to try and diffuse the situation rather than escalate it into a blood feud between the communities.[6] The local Palmach commanders insisted that the incident was a deliberate act of war with nationalist motives.[7] However, Khisas was under the patronage of the Emir Faour, sheikh of the Bedouin tribe of El Fadel and whose winter palace near the village was demolished in the Palmach raid.

In retaliation, 300 of Emir Faour's followers took up on 9th January positions on the Golan slopes 300 metres from, and overlooking, Kfar Szold and at 07:00 hours opened fire from within Syrian territory while most of the kibbutz members were having their breakfast in the communal dining hall.[8] The members quickly dispersed to their fixed positions and returned fire. By 08:30 hours, the kibbutz was ready to repel an attack. By then the Arab fire was reduced to sniping while the attackers remained stationary.

Since Christmas 1947, "C" Squadron of the Lancers reinforced by the troops from "A" Squadron (which had become a training squadron for the benefit of the new recruits) with staghound armoured cars and a troop of engineers from the 9th Airborne Squadron, Royal Engineers (RE), arrived in the Jewish village of Metula at the northernmost tip of the north-eastern border of Palestine.[9] Earlier in the autumn of 1947, there had been some concern that the Syrian Army intended to cross the border into Palestine (hence the presence of the Palmach in the northern kibbutzim). But by the end of the year, the situation along the border seemed to return to normal. 'The Commanding Officer [of the Lancers] …spent many long hours visiting the Arab and Jew notables, and found them, almost all, "about as straight as a screw piquet"'.[10]

News of the attack on Dan and Kfar Szold took some time to reach the Lancers.[11] Two troops, from "A" and "C" squadrons, were dispatched. Their initial progress was cautious and slow. The first troop

> Crossed the Jordan by a rickety bridge [probably west of Khisas] which only gave a couple of inches clearance either side of the bigger cars. On the far side of the river, the leading car going down the mud and rubble track came across a rough road-block, built of stones, some three feet high. The only answer appeared to be to charge it with one of the heavy cars, and while this effective, but mechanically disastrous manoeuvre was going on, the patrol was sniped at from the steep rocky hills across the Syrian frontier, and from an embankment closer by.[12]

It is not clear whether this was a premeditated attempt by the Arab attackers to isolate the area or a hasty improvisation by the local villagers, but in any event it did not impress the Lancers much. Although relatively newcomers to the northern Galilee, the practice was familiar, 'the casual "pot-shot" from either side was treated lightly, and generally ignored'.[13] Having reached a fork in the road, the commander left half the force by the junction and proceeded with the rest to investigate the situation in Dan. Dan had been attacked at around 07:15 hours by small arms fire from commanding positions on three sides of the kibbutz probably as a diversion to the main attack on Kfar Szold. Its members, better trained than those of Kfar Szold, quickly took up their positions and returned fire. The attackers tried to sabotage a remote water pipe which had been effectively mined. Following the mine's detonation, the attackers then tried to set fire to a storage shed but withdrew when fired on. The Arab attack finally ended with the arrival of the Lancers who fired, for good measure, a few shells into Syrian territory. The Lancers returned to the junction but some sporadic fire continued. The troop (from "C" Squadron), which had waited at the junction, was now sent to Dan and stopped the shooting with its own fire. 'So enthusiastic was the newly-arrived troop leader, that his first HE round had the additional task of removing the 'bung' and the end of his barrel before going to smite the enemy'.[14] The Lancers refused a request by the kibbutz settlers to cover a party, they wished to send to fix the damaged pipe and some irrigation ditches, although the requested assistance was provided on the next day.[15]

Having returned to the junction, the troop from Squadron "A" proceeded to Kfar Szold. The Lancers found a 'medium-sized village surrounded by a strong wooden fence and wire, with sandbagged emplacements on the perimeter, and a tall watch-tower [probably the water-tower with a manned position on top] in the center'.[16] According to the Israeli account, the Lancers were met by the kibbutz commander, who suggested that they continue south in the direction of kibbutz Shamir, located higher up on the slopes of the Golan. Along the road, near Khirbet as-Samman, they would reach a point level with the Arab positions and would be able to fire on them from their flank. The Lancers' commander chose instead to enter the kibbutz.[17]

'On entering the gates at about 9 a.m.[18] the troop came under heavy rifle and machine-gun fire which had been directed on to the village since earlier that morning'.[19] Following a hasty consultation, the Lancers' armoured cars were directed by the kibbutz commander to appropriate positions. The cars opened fire with their machine guns and two pounders, for which they were given retroactive permission.[20] A few flights of Spitfires at midday[21] added to the effect. Under the army's covering fire, some Jewish squads were sent up the slope but found the Arab positions deserted.[22]

> Crews dismounted and were fed and rested and entertained by the settlers until the evening. After appropriate courtesies, the crews headed for home, their only casualty the car that had charged the road-block.[23]

The incident reflected the transition from the pattern of "normal" intercommunal violence to open warfare. The circumstances were local and fairly commonplace, but now there were those who gave them a nationalist interpretation thereby endowing them with a grander significance. The local Jewish 'Arabists' had argued that the attack on the wagon and its passengers had nothing to do with the inhabitants of Khisas and that therefore they should not be held accountable. Neither were the settlers of Dan and Kfar Szold party to the raid on Khisas. The night raid as such, a swift surprise attack, culminating in the demolition of a few prominent buildings and the withdrawal of the attackers, was a common Haganah form of retaliation established during the latter part of the Arab Revolt of 1936–1939. The Arab response also followed the pattern of a traditional Fazaa (alarm) whereby one community mobilized its menfolk for an attack on another, which might involve the use of small arms, mainly individually owned rifles and pistols but little else. On the other hand, there was in the attack on Kfar Szold evidence of the use of machine-guns indicating the involvement of a central command with some means at its disposal. Furthermore, the timing of the attack apparently was set to form a diversion to the invasion from Lebanon of the 2nd Yarmouk Battalion of the Arab Liberation Army (ALA).[24]

The state of security in the north-east was further exacerbated by the departure of the TJFF prior to its disbandment.[25] The last active mounted cavalry regiment in the British Army (to which it was transferred in 1941), the TJFF was responsible for the integrity of the north-eastern border designated in October 1947 a sub-sector. At the time, it was placed under the command of the 6th Airborne Division, which had begun its own gradual disbandment with its shrinking in October from nine to six battalions.[26]

The TJFF's commander Colonel John 'Shan' Hackett had commanded the 4th Parachute Brigade in Arnhem. The UN Partition resolution sealed its fate, and early in 1948 it was being withdrawn from Palestine to Transjordan where it was disbanded at the end of February.[27] Some of its soldiers had by then deserted with their weapons and joined various local Arab militias. Others followed after they were discharged.

A major disruptive agent in the north was the ALA whose units had begun to infiltrate Palestine. The units of the ALA were usually organized according to country of origin, political affiliation and ethnicity. The largest formations were designated "battalion", the first of which, the 2nd Yarmouk, began entering Palestine on 8th January.[28] It consisted mainly of Syrian volunteers from Hama led by Adib Shishakli,[29] and a group of Palestinian fighters led by Abu Ibrahim El Za'ir ("the younger"), one of the leaders of the Arab Revolt. The battalion attacked on 20th January kibbutz Yehiam in the western Galilee.[30] The attackers displayed some tactical sophistication, one company attacked at dawn while another isolated the area. But the kibbutz was well prepared. It was defended by one hundred of its inhabitants, all armed, some of whom had served in the Palmach. In addition, it was reinforced by the Haganah and the Palmach. After opening fire, the Arabs tried to storm the kibbutz but were stopped by a wire obstacle and the defenders' fire, including a 2" mortar (The Arabs kept trying to close range under cover of a 60 mm mortar). Finally, by 11:45 hours the attackers began to withdraw. An hour later, a company of the 2nd Battalion Middlesex Regiment, stationed north of Acre, arrived and evacuated the dead and wounded defenders to the Jewish town of Nahariya.[31] In a separate incident, the Army rescued the passengers of a Jewish Settlements Police (JSP) armoured car who had abandoned their car when attacked in a Wadi, north of the kibbutz.[32]

The military-like attack failed, largely due to the attackers, poor performance and the strength of the defence. The Haganah had received prior warning, and in the early hours of the morning of the day of the attack, the kibbutz positions were manned, although the Palmach company sent to reinforce the kibbutz insisted on its morning run which was cut short when the Arabs opened fire. It was later alleged that the attack's failure was due to the poor performance of the Palestinian contingent led by Abu Ibrahim.[33] Abu Ibrahim and his men were next heard of in the lower Galilee where he set up camp in the village of Kafr Kanna.

The 2nd Middlesex, led by the CO, were called out again on the 21st following a garbled radio message. They were told that an attack that morning had already been repelled and were shown, as proof a body of an ALA fighter from the previous day.[34] Following his failure, Shishakli divided his battalion into a number of smaller formations and sent them to reinforce Arab towns and villages throughout the Galilee and in particular the towns of Safad and Acre.[35] Safad had 13,500 inhabitants of whom about 2,000 were Jews. Since the Arab massacre of 1929, the Jewish community had gone into demographic and economic decline. Its geographical distance from the centre of Jewish economic life and the limited local employment available resulted in the migration of the young with the remaining Jewish community confining itself to the Jewish Quarter. The community itself with 40% Sephardi Jews and 60% Eskenazi was divided, and its attitude towards Zionism and the Yishuv's leadership was at best ambivalent.[36]

In the beginning of 1948, "B" Company of the 2nd Middlesex was stationed in Safad under the command of the TJFF.[37] Safad had 'the reputation of a potential trouble spot' and many members of the company underwent there their baptism of fire and 'a first hand experience of Arab and Jewish strife'.[38] But those were still early days and the fighting in the town provided occasions for some crude hilarity – 'who will ever forget the senior N.C.O. who, when going for cover, came closer to the Arab sanitary arrangements than ever before?'[39] Otherwise, common concerns; the standard of accommodation – two requisitioned houses, preparations for the Christmas dinner, the Inter-Company Novices' Boxing championship (tied with "D" Company), Battalion Inter-Platoon Soccer Competition [ongoing] etc. But the situation in the Galilee was rapidly deteriorating and on 16th January "C" Company, 'with no few regrets' left the 'excitement and good living conditions' of Safad and rejoined the battalion, which had by then been given the tasks of the disbanding 3rd Parachute Brigade.[40]

The battalion was consequently made responsible for the Acre civil sub-district which consisted of the coastal plane from Haifa to the Lebanon border,[41] under the command of the 1st Parachute Brigade in Haifa. Safad now became the responsibility of the 1st Irish Guards as part of Craforce.

On the same day, as the attack on Yehiam, another ALA unit attacked kibbutz Tirat Zvi, near the Arab town of Beisan. The 1st Yarmouk Battalion of the ALA had crossed the Jordan on 20th January.[42] Rumours of an impending attack had reached the Haganah and the local Jewish settlements were on alert. The operation was preceded by a diversionary attack on the neighbouring kibbutz of Ein Ha'natziv of which the commander of Tirat Zvi was informed at 03:00 hours. By 03:30 hours, the alarm was sounded and at 03:57 hours the ALA opened fire. This continued until 05:00 hours stopped briefly and was renewed at 05:10 hours followed by a number of attempts to breach the kibbutz's defences from a number of directions, all of which failed. At 07:30 hours, the kibbutz was informed that the Army was ready to intervene. It arrived at 09:00 hours.[43]

The area south of the Sea of Galilee was the responsibility of the 1st (Guards) Parachute Battalion, which was to join the Guards as part of the general reorganization of the Airborne's battalions. Its H.Q. and "T" Company were in Samakh on the southern tip of the lake in an old TJFF camp, with "R" Company and elements of "S" Company stationed in the depot of the Palestine mounted police near Beisan.[44] The lateness of its intervention in a battle that took place seven kilometres away probably reflects the difficulties the Army experienced in obtaining intelligence on what was happening even in their immediate vicinity. Once alerted, "R" Company sent out a mobile patrol 'which succeeded in locating the Arab tactical headquarters and after a long parley the Arabs agreed to withdraw assisted by a short barrage of 3 inch mortar and machine-gun fire'.[45] During the next couple of days, a team from "R" Company found and removed from the battlefield the corpses of one Jew and forty-two Arabs.

Following its failure, the 1st Yarmouk left the Beisan Valley for its original destination in northern Samaria.[46] The 1st Para's CO John Nelson of the Grenadier Guards was convinced, however, that he had succeeded in pacifying the region by winning the Arabs' confidence.

> Two early opportunities presented themselves to demonstrate my good faith. In the first case the Arab had started the trouble by attacking a Jewish Kibbutz and appealed for help when they were counter-attacked. We duly came to their rescue and warned them to desist from this kind of enterprise in the future. A week later however an exact repetition occurred after which I again even more forcefully, pointed out the error of their ways. They explained at length that the first occasion was simply to test my integrity and the second to make a complete certainty of it![47]

Nelson sincerely maintained in retrospect that his firm but sympathetic policy carried the day.

> This friendship had two results. One was that peace in our area was almost entirely preserved. Jewish convoys to their outlying villages were no longer ambushed nor their Kibbutz raided. At the same time we managed to forestall any Jewish aggression on defenseless Arab farmsteads.
>
> The second intriguing result was my meeting and subsequent liaison with Fawzi Kauokji [Qawuqji].

The population of the Beisan sub-district (1944) was 25,590 of whom 7,000 were Jews, and 15,920 Moslems. The population of the town of Beisan was 5,180 Moslems and Christians, so the ratio of Jews to Arabs in the countryside was 7:10.5.[48] The overall density of the population (person per square kilometre) was 65.4, the lowest in the Galilee. The Jewish population of the sub-district, mainly in kibbutzim, was well organized, and security conscience. The trained and armed settlers were reinforced by the Haganah and the Palmach. Hence during the attack on Tirat Zvi there were seven armed platoons in nearby settlements some of which operated in the enemy's rear and some conducted a diversionary attack on Beisan.[49] Following the failure of the ALA's attack and its withdrawal from the area, the Haganah quickly gained the upper hand while waiting for the British Army to leave before occupying the Beisan Valley.

Whatever the reasons for the relative calm, the troops were content with their lot under conditions that hardly differed from service in similarly remote rural districts before 1948.

> By good diplomacy and prompt action it has been found possible to keep the area comparatively quiet. The Arab's code of hospitality is renowned throughout the world, and throughout history he has done his bargaining and all forms of business over a cup of coffee. By visiting the muktas [Mukhtars] of the local villages and drinking coffee accepting their invitations to a meal, we have won their confidence and they are prepared to listen to reason and obey our instructions. As our hosts helped us to handfuls of sheep and rice they have slowly told us their troubles (well punctuated with effusive compliments) and they have listened to and slowly digested the explanations of why they cannot have more rifles, why it is unwise to obstruct their Jewish neighbours, and so on. As a demonstration of impartiality, for every Arab lunch the Jewish settlements are visited for breakfast and tea and many problems have been thrashed out in their communal feeding sheds. It is felt that such diplomacy had prevented a great deal of trouble in the area.[50]

In order to enforce its polity of diplomatic peace-keeping, the battalion organized 'small mobile columns with 3-inch mortars and medium machine-guns', which were dispatched at any sign of impending violence to 'quell any disturbance, using the least possible force'. In addition, the battalion kept busy with the usual activities which included, weather permitting, bathing in the sea of Galilee and using 'the R.A.S.C. launch, which we acquired ostensibly for operational purposes', cross-country races, rugby, soccer and the Sergeants' Mess weekly whist drives.[51]

Qawuqji had arrived in Samaria on 4th March and set up his headquarters in the village of Jab'a north west of Nablus.[52] He was a curious instance of a military commander who had never won a battle, yet was widely known in the Arab world as a great military leader. Nelson, for one, was certain that 'No decision could be made on strategy until he arrived and no plans would be finalized without his approval'.[53] Consequently, he concluded from his dealings with the local Arabs that 'his influence would be greatly enhanced if it were known that I had actually talked to this super supremo'.[54] A meeting was arranged by the Arab District Officer of Beisan who, with Nelson, drove in a military Jeep to Qawagji's headquarters. After the usual exchange of pleasantries and two cups of coffee, Nelson explained the purpose of his visit.

> I did not wish to see the Arab cause ruined by military errors before the end of the British Mandate and I would be grateful if he would give me assurances that he would do nothing rash or aggressive with the army he had just brought with him... while he remained in my area.[55]

Nelson even promised Qawuqji that he would ensure that following the Army's evacuation weapons confiscated from the Jews would be made 'easily available' to the ALA.[56] By the time he departed, Nelson felt that 'we had established the basis of a friendship which was to prove very helpful in the future'.[57]

Nelson's command of the facts was at best tenuous. He thought Qawuqji was 'a Yugo-slav Moslem' whereas he was born in Tripoli, Lebanon and he had entered Palestine in March 1948 rather than in February. His headquarters were in Jab'a north-west of Nablus, not north east of Jenin. At the time, Qawuqji was trying to establish his authority as the supreme commander on behalf of the Arab league of the Arab forces in Samaria and the Galilee and to that end negotiated with both British and Jewish[58] representatives. He had no plans to initiate fighting in the Beisan area and his "friendship" with Nelson was not the reason for the district's relative calm.

The situation in Safad, on the other hand, was acknowledged as far more ominous. The local senior British officials – the District Police Commissioner Stacey Braham, the Assistant District Commissioner Sinclair and Brigadier Hackett CO of the TJFF thought that due to the paucity of the forces available there was little the Army could effectively do to ensure the pacification of the town and that it had best withdraw to the Teggart fort commanding its entrance.[59]

On 15th January, the 1st Battalion Irish Guards arrived in Rosh Pinna in the Jordan Valley, at the foot of the ridge on which Safad sits. The battalion settled in the evacuated TJFF camps (HQ) and in camp 280/281 about fifteen miles south with spectacular views of the Sea of Galilee to the south and of the snow covered Mt. Hermon to the north. A company took up positions in Safad.[60] Almost immediately the Guards began to take casualties. On the evening following their move, a Guardsman was killed by small arms fire. Shortly afterwards another Guardsman was killed when his carrier overturned. A third 'when his platoon was engaged by Arabs firing from the hills', and a fourth, a young officer, when his armoured car 'overturned on a hillside at night'.[61]

According to the CO's final report on the events which led to his unit's evacuation of Safad,

> By firm, fair, aggressive and immediate action, the troops soon made it clear that they were determined to keep law and order in the town. By hitting the Arabs hard, they were soon made to realize that to cross the path of the British troops was just not worth while.[62]
>
> The Operational Duties of the company were:
>
> 1   To keep main roads open to both Jewish and Arab traffic.
> 2   Provision of mobile troops to take immediate steps to quell disturbances in the area.

3   To keep law and order in Safad.
4   To remain neutral in dealing with both sides.[63]

The Irish Guards rotated their companies in Safad, every week, an indication of the perceived severity of local conditions.

It was their experience that

> The inhabitants take the political situation very seriously indeed. The "front line" is popular [among the troops] in spite of the fact that the work of mediation is difficult and often dangerous. Local clashes have been kept under control, major clashes prevented and all ranks have maintained an impartial attitude and carried out their tasks in a manner which has preserved a tolerable peace. Our efforts have earned the respect and a certain amount of trust from both sides.[64]

The Guards took up positions on top of the "Fort", the remains of a crusader fort in the centre of the town and its highest point, the municipal police station, a fortified building on the border between the Arab and Jewish quarters south of the "Fort", and in "Beit Shalva", a Jewish-owned stone building on the border between the quarters north of the "Fort". Additionally, the Army occupied the Tegart police fort at the entrance to Safad.[65] The troops soon developed a method for dealing with the frequent small arms exchanges between the quarters.

> When firing used to break out in the town, a Red Very light was always fired in the direction of the offending firer before British troops opened fire; thereby giving both sides the opportunity to cease fire before loss of life could be caused. The general aim was to persuade by consultation and firm action with 2-pdrs and P.I.A.T.s both sides, and especially the numerically weaker side – the Jews – to do nothing to antagonize the other.[66]

From February, units of the ALA infiltrating into the Galilee posed an additional threat to law and order, often attacking Jewish traffic.[67] On 4th February, 'a strong band' of ALA irregulars,

> Made the mistake, which unfortunately was not infrequent, of establishing an ambush for Jewish traffic (on this occasion between Tiberias and Rosh Pinna) and then engaging British vehicles in error. On the day in question, a ration truck of 17th/21st Lancers was fired at from a position overlooking the road and though one trooper was wounded the truck got through. One platoon from the Irish Guards, later reinforced by a second, was soon on the scene and an engagement ensued in which the main body of Arabs withdrew, covered by a small rearguard.[68]

The said rearguard consisting of six fighters, was eventually captured. The ALA men made an excellent impression on their captors. They were 'found to be first-class guerilla troops with a high morale, discipline, pride in themselves and faith in their cause... The were all Syrians and described themselves as soldiers of honour... well clothed, equipped and armed'. Their interrogators concluded that if they were representative of the ALA as a whole 'the Jews had a difficult time ahead'.[69]

In other incidents, a band crossing the Jordan was driven back by a platoon of Guardsmen from the battalion HQ. On 12th March, a group was discovered in the village of Qabba'a, north-east of Safad, consisting of 60–70 men 'armed with three different types of French rifles', and conducting themselves 'quite openly' in the village.[70]

The Jewish response to the added threat to its traffic was to protect its vehicles with armour platting and armed escorts and to retaliate by attacking Arab traffic thereby forcing the Army to augment its presence during daylight along the roads without seeming to prefer any of the sides by escorting their convoys.[71] Ever suspicious of the British intentions, the Jews refused to confine their use of the roads to prearranged routes and timetables, thereby reducing the Army's effectiveness in preventing attacks on traffic. A result was the occasional loss of Army vehicles. Thus on 10th March, three-ton Bedford lorry was held up by three Arabs who relieved the driver of his rifle. The truck was last observed on its way to the Syrian border.[72]

The Arabs of Safad received most of their supplies from the west, the Jews from the east via the Rosh Pinna-Safad road. The Haganah strategy was to attack Arab traffic on the road to Safad from the west forcing the Arabs to use the Rosh-Pinna-Safad road and as a result reduce their attacks on Jewish vehicles using the same road. The Army was party to the policy since its supplies were brought to Safad from Tiberias and Rosh Pinna. In order to secure the road, it had placed along it a standing patrol of two carriers, and one 3" mortar commanded by a senior Non Commissioned Officer (NCO) in a position which could be observed by all while they in turn would be able to detect the 'presence of illegally armed Arabs of Jewish Armed cars and to report at once to B.HQ' in Rosh Pinna'. 'Armoured cars' were defined as 'any veh [of whatever size] which has an armed body giving protection to people in the back'.[73] This precluded buses or trucks with armour plated driver cabins.

The first weeks of March were relatively calm, until on the 17th, an Arab ambush detonated an electric mine under a Jewish bus on the Rosh Pinna road, followed by two hand grenades. The timing of the detonation was slightly off. The mine exploded in front of the bus, creating a crater into which the bus fell. Fifteen passengers were hurt and the bus was towed by the Army to Rosh Pinna.[74] In retaliation, the 3rd Palmach Battalion, stationed on Mount Cna'an overlooking Safad, demolished bridges on the road to Safad from the west.[75]

The Arab response was another ambush along the Rosh Pinna road. The target was, again, a Jewish bus and the result was five passengers killed and four wounded. A Jewish force rushed to the site from Rosh Pinna as did a Police vehicle and an ambulance sent from Safad. According to the Guards' CO report, as soon as the Army arrived 'casualties were inflicted, and two Arabs were captured, one of whom was wounded'.[76] The others withdrew in the direction of the Arab village of Akbara, south of Safad. While driving down the hill to Rosh Pinna, the British vehicles were stopped by a Haganah roadblock and the two Arab prisoners were 'forcibly kidnapped'.[77] It turned out that the prisoners were of the Kadura clan, one of the largest and most powerful in Safad and whose members included the Mufti and the Mayor of the town.[78] They were quickly taken to kibbutz Mahanayim, north-west of Rosh Pinna.[79] While the Army was searching for them the prisoners were interrogated, using torture, tried by a "special field court", and sentenced to death by a firing squad.

The incident 'produced tremendous tension in the town, and a violent anti-British feeling. At this stage the A.D.C. [Assistant District Commissioner] Sinclair again strongly advised the evacuation of troops from the town'.[80]

In an attempt to pacify Safad's Arab community, the Army applied intense pressure on the local Haganah leadership to release the prisoners, including the confiscation of an armoured car seized at the entrance to the Haganah regional headquarters in kibbutz Ayelet Hashachar and the arrest of its six passengers, members of the Haganah, which the Army threatened would be taken to Haifa to stand trial. Eventually, the Haganah released one, badly tortured, prisoner. The other was shot and his body was found by a British patrol on the 24th with a note: 'Tried by a field court and found guilty'.[81]

> According to the Regimental History –
> To calm the situation the [Irish Guards'] Pipe Band was ordered to play to the Safadians; this had the desired effect and the tension eased, but it was a nervous moment for the Pipers as they marched down the no-man's-land of Safad wondering what might happen.[82]

The reasoning behind using the Pipers to ease the tension in Safad may have seemed obvious to the Guards, but it completely mystified the Jewish leadership. They eventually concluded that the Pipers' march accompanied by armed Guardsmen was a rouse designed to afford the commanders of the ALA, dressed up as British soldiers, a chance to reconnoitre the entrances to the Jewish quarter and its defence. Rumour even had it that Shishakli was one of the disguised Arabs.[83]

Eventually, the Army accepted that the problem was not tactical. Its methods were basically sound but as both sides were preparing for the final showdown once the Army left, they became 'confident of success and were unwilling to delay their efforts until after our evacuation'.[84] The initial plan, distributed by HQ 6th Airborne Division on 25th March 1948, was that the evacuation begin in mid-April starting with Metullah on the Lebanon border and the Tegart border fort of Nabi Yusha, followed on 1st May by Khalisa in the north and Semakh, south of the Sea of Galilee. By 14th May, the Army was to withdraw to Acre and the Police to Tiberias as part of the general evacuation of the country, to take place the next day (15th May).[85]

On 2nd April, general Stockwell, OC of 6th Airborne[86] who stayed on as commander of the forces in the north of Palestine, visited Safad, followed on 5th April by Brigadier J.C.C. Marriott of the 1st Guards Brigade which on 6th April replaced in Haifa the 1st Parachute Brigade. On the same day the IZL attacked the 12th Anti-Tank regiment RA in camp 80 near Karkur and Pardes Hanna.

The gunners were preparing for their imminent evacuation on 12th April to Tripolitania and were busy dismantling their self-propelled 17 pound (76.2 mm) anti-tank guns,[87] and preparing the M10s for shipping by removing the breech blocks and all movable auxiliary equipment (including their 0.5" anti-aircraft machine guns which could be used for close support).

> The soldiers working in the bright sunlight, clad only in their shorts and boots, went about their tasks with a zest born of anticipation of a more varied life among the fleshpots of Tripolitania. They rubbed away with their oily rags in the sinister shadow of the water tower.[88]

The water tower, an iconic feature of Jewish communities,[89] overlooked the camp from the north, in line with its main axis. It was generally felt that due to its position 'the life of the Regiment carried on as a goldfish swims in a bowl-for all to see'.[90]

> The water tower. The menace of its position had rot escaped the attention of the Commanding Officer. He had asked that it should be blown up, or at least that he should be allowed to exercise detailed supervision over those who visited it. ... neither of these measures were taken.[91]

The water tower had indeed served, at least in 1945–1946, as an Haganah observation post, monitoring movements of Army units during IS operations against the Jews.[92] But it is unclear whether it was manned in 1948 and by whom. In any event, it seems to have symbolized the menace posed by Jewish proximity to the camp. According to some British (but not Irgun Zvai Leumi (IZL) accounts,[93] it was used during the attack as a Bren position by the IZL.

An IZL force of some fifty fighters dressed in British Army uniforms and travelling in three Army trucks, followed by an armoured car, broke into the camp at about 07:00 hours, killing two sentries. Under the covering fire of the armoured car, the three trucks drove up to the three batteries' armouries and began loading their contents.[94] Meanwhile, the assault team, after killing the sentries, entered the guardroom, a small stone building about fifty yards from the main gate.

> Inside were four members of the guard, resting between their spells of duty. They were told to stand against the white-washed wall, facing it, and when they were in position they were all shot. None of them was more than twenty years of age.[95]

The CO Lt.-Col. Geoffrey H. Hildebrand, working in his office in the camp's centre, probably realized that if he could take out the raiders' armoured car his soldiers would stand a good chance of dealing with the rest. 'What is certain is that the Commanding Officer charged the armoured car with the idea of shooting the occupants with his pistol. They saw him coming and shot him. He died within a few hours from his wounds'.[96]

One of the battery commanders drove an unarmed and partly dismantled M10 onto the camp's main road with the intention of ramming the IZL armoured car and any of the trucks. On noticing its approach, the IZL quickly withdrew 'and almost in a matter of seconds the camp was cleared of the intruders'[97] who, after all, were there for the ammunition, not to do battle with the Army. In retaliation, the frustrated troops later used the M10s to plough up the orange grove opposite the camps.

The IZL did not attribute too much significance to the raid. Its purpose was to "confiscate" as many weapons as possible and the British soldiers killed were legitimate targets – enemy soldiers killed in battle. In Britain, however, the attack caused considerable shock. William Francis Hare, 5th Earl of Listowell, Minister of State for Colonial Affairs described it the next day (8th April) in the House of Lords as senseless murder,

> which added another tragedy to the long list of outrages perpetrated against our troops by members of the Jewish community... The most violence had been nurtured by the Jewish refusal to recognize it as an evil and to cooperate with the British authorities to eradicate it.[98] The Archbishop of York was even more strident. 'The late outrage, cold blooded and cruel, could only have been carried out by people who delighted in murder'.[99]

In the House, in response to a question, Creech Jones condemned the murder of British soldiers which served to underline the urgency of withdrawing from Palestine.[100] Churchill pointed out that the soldiers' safety was a concern.[101] Another question by Earl Winterton (Edward Turnour, 6th Earl Winterton and Baron Turnour) raised the matter of the Army's freedom of action. Winterton, who took great pride in his service in the Great War and had considered himself a guardian of the Army's interests, wondered if any of the defensive measures necessary required the approval of the High Commissioner.[102] A follow up question by Henderson Stewart (Liberal who had recently crossed over to the Conservatives) was whether the government thought that the Army's policy and powers in Palestine were sufficient to ensure the safety of the troops was answered in the affirmative.[103]

The issue was raised again on 13th April in a question by Winterton to Immanuel Shinwall, Secretary of State for War, as to whether he was prepared to 'give the fullest discretion to GOC Palestine and through him, to the unit commanders, to take whatever steps they think necessary to protect camps without reference to the Palestine Government, which is now in dissolution?'[104] Shinwall answered that such an order had already been issued a few days earlier.

The seriousness of the emerging incongruity between the official policy of preserving law and order throughout Palestine and the wish to safeguard the troops was at the time laid out in an article in the *Times* on the Army's policy in Palestine.

> The situation is artificial and requires for justification not only avoidance of civil war but also avoidance of heavy losses to the military forces. So far it has to a considerable extent fulfilled those conditions, but this last affair is a very ugly and disturbing one.[105]

As explained above upon becoming Chief of Imperial General Staff (CIGS), Field Marshall Montgomery observed that throughout the Empire the Army was often given assignments for which the means at its disposal were 'totally inadequate'.[106] He promised his generals, many of whom had served with him during the War, his complete 'support in facing up to unpleasant situations'.[107] Montgomery objected to the Labour Government's gradual divestment of Britain's global assets as it was doing in the Middle East. But once the policy had been determined, his main concern was the wellbeing of the Army and its morale as it had been during the European campaign.

Montgomery found an invaluable, if somewhat unexpected ally in Emmanuel 'Many' Shinwell, Secretary of State for War (since 7th October 1947), who he described as the best Secretary of State he had worked with.

> Shinwell had a quick and clear brain and his heart was in the right place; he could understand and decide quickly. Once he had satisfied himself that some line of action was essential, he would fight for it in the Cabinet and in Parliament. He and I became great friends.[108]

Shinwell, a Jew and one of the leaders of Red Clydeside, had lost his seat in the cabinet as Minister for Fuel and Power following the fuel crisis of the winter of 1947 which he had promised would not happen. Shinwell begrudged his dismissal, advocated by Cripps and Dalton, and was convinced that what with the history of Montgomery's stormy relations with previous Secretaries of State for War that his political enemies had set him up for another failure. At the time, he confessed, he had 'naturally resented' his appointment.[109] But to their mutual surprise Shinwell, his Parliamentary Secretary Col. Wig and Montgomery quickly formed an alliance against the rest of Westminster.

The causes on which Shinwell and Montgomery concentrated their efforts included the welfare and the wellbeing of the soldiers, the cuts, demanded by Dalton, in the Army's budget and Bevin's policy in Palestine. According to Shinwell's official biography, while not a devote Jew, the Holocaust had deepened his sympathy towards the Zionist demand for a national home for the Jews which was strengthened by his repulsion from Bevin's anti-Semitism.[110] Montgomery believed Palestine an important part of Britain's global strategy but by 1948 this view became irrelevant and it did not prevent him from joining forces against Bevin.

In Montgomery's view, the casualties sustained by the Army and the Police in Palestine were the result of the government's policy. As early as 1946, he stated categorically 'that if we were not prepared in maintain law and order [by fighting Jewish terrorism] in Palestine, it would be better to get out. I could not agree to a lot of young British lads being killed uselessly'.[111] His position remained unchanged throughout 1947 and he repeatedly reassured his commanders in the field that they had his backing in adjusting their missions to their means.

As late as early March 1948, General Stockwell still held that the preservation of law and order in the eastern Galilee served the preparations for the eventual evacuation.

> Arab-Jew conflict in the hinterland reflects directly on the Haifa area. By employing Craforce to maintain law and order in Eastern Galilee and to keep specified roads open for free running of all traffic in this area, I am enabled to hold the initiative in Haifa.[112]

By the end of March, General Macmillan had redefined the Army's priorities. The official policy now was to minimize friction between the Army and the warring communities even at the expense of law and order.

> Although the maintenance of law and order is a most important part of the Army's task, the main anxiety of the GOC at the present time is the lines of the Troops under his command.
>
> Punitive action against Arab or Jew must therefore wherever possible be avoided if it is likely to lead to a situation making the withdrawal of our forces costly or unnecessarily difficult. In particular, this applies to the area through which run the communications from Eastern Galilee and from Jerusalem.[113]

The change in priorities reflected a revaluation of the situation in Palestine – 'the most striking development is that both sides are now to all intents and purposes entirely disregarding the authority of the administration – and are preparing to face up to each other without any gloves on'.[114] At the time, the Haganah had begun offensive operations following the setbacks of March.

Meir Meiberg, the Haganah commander of Safad, dated the beginning of the Arab offensive against the Jewish quarter to 4th April when the Arabs demolished Beit Cohen, a three story building outside the Jewish quarter in the "Stalingrad" sector.[115] Although the building was not inhabited, nor was it a part of the Jewish quarter's defences, its destruction was seen as a new stage in the fighting.[116]

Arab attacks intensified in and around Safad in preparation of a final assault on the Jewish quarter. On the night of the 4th–5th April, an ALA platoon occupied hill 815.9 overlooking the small kibbutz of Ein Zeitim west of the town. On the 6th Lance Sergeant Tausey and Gurdsman Byrnes, escorting a water tank on its way back from a well near the Arab village of Farrdiya, west of Safad, were fired on and were wounded. The water tank was stopped 'and 3 men wearing European dress approached and relieved the driver, who was unhurt of his revolver and also the Bren and Sten of the escort.[117] Later 'Big' Byrnes, an old hand and a well liked Guardsman, died of his wounds.[118]

> Byrne was a typical old soldier, the type who never gets the credit he de-
> serves outside his own small community. It is the Byrnes of a battalion
> who are the sheet anchors, whose kit is always immaculate – for the sin-
> gle reason that over the years they have acquired a complete duplicate
> set – and whose turnout is always beyond reproach. Byrne had been a
> duty – Guardsman for seventeen years and wished to remain that way.
> 'Big' Byrne... was a huge man, six foot seven inches tall and broad with
> it, a fine heavy-weight boxer with fists like hams. He was a soft spoken
> County Wexford man, and his death was taken hard by the battalion.[119]

In the early hours of 7th April, the Palmach stormed and occupied hill 815.9. The Haganah left a permanent picket on it and on nearby hill 892.3, a prec-edent in the Galilee of what soon became a characteristic of the next phase of the war, that is, the permanent occupation of conquered territory in vio-lation of the territorial status quo.

On the previous day (6th April), an Arab force began an attack on kib-butz Lehavot Habashan in the Jordan Valley, east of the river. Craforce was informed on 7th April that the kibbutz had been under fire from Syrian territory for the past twenty-four hours.[120] The attacking force was reported to have consisted of the Bedouin followers of the Emir Faur, which had previously attacked Kfar Szold, and the ALA.[121] The kibbutz first came un-der fire on the morning of 6th April in a manner similar to the attack on Kfar Szold, that is, small arms fire from a safe distance and positions on the slopes of the Golan. However, some manoeuvring was attempted coupled with a coordinated destruction of bridges on the tributaries of the Jordan, in order to isolate the battlefield.

During the night of 6th–7th April, a faza'a was announced in the neighbouring Arab villages and on the morning of the 7th the defenders of Lehavot Habashan observed hundreds of villagers from the Lake Hula area joining the attackers, having taken up positions under the cover of darkness.[122] At 05:00 hours, on the 7th the firing was resumed. By then the system of mutual support between the local kibbutzim went into operation. A 3" mortar was used from the neighbouring kibbutz Shamir to disperse the Arab concentrations between the two settlements forcing the attackers to concentrate on the other, southern side of Lehavot Habashan.

The Army's arrival in Jeeps and armoured cars from 17th/21th Lancers was delayed by the damaged bridges and the difficulty in negotiation the muddy rough track from Shamir to Lehavot Habashan. Assisted by a light aircraft dispatched by Craforce HQ the troops took up positions about 200 yards north of the kibbutz and opened machine gun fire on the attackers positions but did not try to close in on them. Its 2" mortar bombs fell short of the Arabs, and close, to the kibbutz, positions.[123]

Concern that the Arabs, in their rear, might succeed in setting fire to and destroying the bridge, thereby blocking their way back and leaving them temporarily stranded, and with orders to avoid travelling at night, the Lancers withdrew at around 16:00 hours and returned to base.

Although the Arab attacks continued and the attackers were nearing the kibbutz positions, the defenders were not unduly worried knowing that the attacks would cease by nightfall and that Palmach help was on its way. The next morning (8th April) at 09:30 hours a well-armed Palmach force led by a company commander, of the 3rd Battalion (one of its platoons had been stationed in the kibbutz), outflanked the Arabs, attacked them and occupied their positions overlooking Lehavot Habashan, forcing them to withdraw gradually southwards.[124] A patrol from "C" Squadron of the Lancers, forced to make its final approach on foot arrived in Lehavot Habashan to discover that except for some sporadic fire the battle had ended. When they left at the end of the day, they observed that the 'Jews did not appear to be particularly worried'.

Growing Jewish confidence in their ability to deal directly with Arab forces including the ALA was also noticeable in Tiberias when on the 8th fighting erupted after a month's long ceasefire agreed upon by both communities.[125] The firing between Jewish and Arab positions in the old city on the shore of the Sea of Galilee, persisted the whole day and after a quiet night was resumed on the 9th forcing the Lancers to intervene. An appeal to the traditional leadership of both communities was of no avail and the Lancers opened fire with their armoured cars' two pounders on both sides, demanding that the shooting stop.[126]

On April 9th, Brigadier Calquhoun visited the Irish Guards in his northern sector and on the 11th CO 1st Irish Guards, Lt.-Col. Gordon-Watson met Safad's Arab Council.

And asked them if they considered that there was any possibility of arranging a truce under my conditions. They informed me that if the complete removal or surrender of the HAGANA was assured, they were perfectly prepared to guarantee the lives of and property of the Jewish residents, with whom they had lived quite happily for 70 years.[127]

I also met the Arab Commander-in-Chief Galilee [Shishakly, C.O. of 1st Yarmouk Battalion, A.L.A.], who told me quite frankly that he could not wait any longer for his attack in the EIN ZEITIM area and that his plan must include the cutting of the ROSH PINNA-SAFAD road.[128]

Doing so would isolate the Guards company from the rest of the battalion and hinder its evacuation, now that the road west had proven unsafe.

Meanwhile on the night of the 9th, the Arabs blew up a Jewish house and the Haganah retaliated on the 11th partly demolishing an Arab house.[129] It was observed that 'both sides were confident of success and were unwilling to delay their efforts until after our evacuation'.[130]

On the 12th, Gordon-Watson sent to General Stockwell his appreciation of the situation in Safad.

I appreciate that with 55 troops in two isolated billets in SAFAD town, and the possibility of all communication being cut, that I could not control or influence a battle between three of four thousand armed Arabs and some one thousand or so HAGANA.[131]

On the same day, Stockwell visited Safad met the Arab Council and the Arab Commander-in Chief Shishakli and asked them 'to maintain a moderate course' and to await the outcome of the UNO decision expected an 15th April concerning a general truce in Palestine. The Arabs' conditions were that the Jews withdraw from two of their positions – Mount Biriya to the north west of the town and the Technical School at the foot of the northern slope of the Citadel. The next day (13th April) Brigadier Calquhoun met the Jewish Council and instructed them that the Army would take over the Technical School and return it to them when evacuating the town. (No mention was made of Biriya which was beyond the Army's reach).[132]

The Army's appreciation of the odds was based primarily on the number of fighters on either side. The Jewish Council was advised that unless they agree to the Army's conditions it 'could not guarantee that there would not be a major battle in the town, which, with their numbers, they would not be able to stop. Nor would they be saved by the Army since, if its demands were rejected, it 'would have to "seriously consider" evacuating the town'.

They were also warned that the Arab terms eventually would be that the Arab Liberation Army would guarantee the lives and property of the Jews in SAFAD if the HAGANA completely withdrew. Under these conditions, the British Army would remain to enforce the peace.

According to Meiberg, the Jewish commander, these words came to the Council like a bolt from the blue. At once the masks were removed 'We knew it was impossible to accept any of his demands or suggestions'.[133]

On the same day (13th April) HQ North Sector, now officially responsible for northern Palestine, issued a modified Instruction for the withdrawal from the eastern Galilee, the 'result of recent developments, principally in the SAFAD area', which had made it 'necessary to revise the original plan considerably in order to prevent vital rd comns being cut'.[134] New plans were drawn should it became necessary to withdraw at short notice. The first phase would be the evacuation of Safad and the Khalisa Police Station, while assembling the 1st Irish Guards, "C" Squadron of the 17th/21st Lancers and Troop 1 AB Squadron RE in Rosh Pinna. At the opposite end of the Craforce sector Beisan would be evacuated and "B" Squadron of the Lancers together with Troop 1 Royal Horse Artillery under its command, move to Samakh. The wording of the Instruction conveyed a sense of urgency, in anticipation of sudden violent changes in the circumstances which were beyond the Army's control. 'Should it be necessary to put this plan into operation certain phases may have to be implemented at very short notice', allowing the Army to respond with maximum speed and flexibility.

The next day (14th April) the Jewish Council in Safad convened and at 15:00 hours informed the Army of its complete rejection of its offer.[135] Its answer had been dictated by the Haganah who, in this instance, chose to impose its position on the civilian leadership who was much less confident.[136] According to Meiberg, Gordon-Watson's response was angry and blunt. The Jews, he said, were suicidal and he would not be party to an inevitable massacre. He offered to arrange lorries with Red Cross flags for an evacuation of non-combatants under the Army's protection.[137] Next he passed the Jewish Council's reply to the Arab Council who, nevertheless, 'guaranteed that nothing would be done for three days, by which time the UNO decision would be known'.[138] According to Meiberg, the Guard's company commander Captain D.A. Lambert, revealed that the Army estimated that once all out fighting broke out the Jewish forces would last for two hours although Lambert himself thought that six hours was more realistic.[139]

Contrary to the Arab Council's reassurances, the Arab forces attacked during the night all along the "Stalingrad" sector, and after a three hours battle succeeded in demolishing a Jewish building (Beit Fruman), the third in ten days, just below the town's Police Station, where the Guards were now concentrated.[140] The fighting had come uncomfortably close to the troops. 'All the windows were broken, and troops and building were badly shaken'.[141] Following the fighting, the company commander pointed out to the local Jewish commander that the use of hand grenades by the Jewish defenders was endangering his soldiers and demanded that it stop, but to no avail.[142]

Gordon-Watson reported that on the morning of 15th April

very heavy fire broke out in the town, and some thousand Arabs appeared about to be making a major assault on the Jewish quarter. ... During the day a very large number of Arab reinforcements entered the town, these were a wild and most unruly element.[143]

A number of two pounder shells and the efforts of the District Super Intendent Barham and a member of the Arab Council succeeded in stopping the firing.

Braham's view was

That there were some three thousand armed Arabs in the town, and that under a plea of doing nothing, they were using the Army as a shield to complete their preparations... when they were ready to attack they would do so regardless of consequences to British lives... under these circumstances the Battalion would not get out of the town without heavy casualties, if they were able to get out at all by the one and only road.[144]

During the day (15th April) a soldier was killed and another wounded, and their weapons stolen by 'Safadian Arabs' in the village of Tabigha on the shore of the Sea of Galilee, and another soldier was badly wounded in Safad.[145]

Gordon-Watson in Rosh Pinna sent for Hilel Landsman of kibbutz Aye-let Hashachar, Head of the Upper Galilee Settlements Committee, and informed him 'that the British were evacuating Nebi Yusha and Khalsa Police stations, which was to occur simultaneously with the evacuation of Safad and would hand them over to the 'senior [i.e. Arab] policeman remaining'.[146]

I warned him that the Irish Guards had done everything possible to keep the peace in Safad town, and that all proposals for peace had been turned down. I warned him that there were several thousand of armed Arabs in Safad town, and several thousand more in the area North... it would not be possible for me to stop a battle of the magnitude expected with the troops at my disposal. ...I was not prepared to risk the lives of my soldiers any longer. ...I would be leaving Safad very shortly.[147]

His final offer was to declare Safad an 'Open City'. The Haganah leave the town and surrender their arms and since the ALA had promised that in that case 'they would respect the lives and property of the remaining resident Jews', the Army could then remain safely in town. Hopefully, by then 'the UNO decision might have made peace conditions possible'.

Gordon-Watson's suggestions fell on deaf ears and his faith in Arab promises resulted in the Haganah suspecting his motives. The British were by then completely distrusted. Safad, according to the Partition resolution, was to be part of the Jewish state and it was their responsibility to ensure that it would be so. The same afternoon (15th April) Landsman responded with a complete rejection of Gordon-Watson's proposals. Gordon-Watson then informed him that he could not guarantee anymore the lives of women and children and that he would be leaving Safad 'at short notice'.[148]

In a final effort to avert a massacre of Jewish civilians, Gordon-Watson made available four-three-ton lorries with Red Cross markings to evacuate, under a 24-hour truce, women and children. The trucks arrived at the town Police Station on 16th April at 14:00 hours, but their only passenger was, according to the Haganah version, one sick Jew.[149] The rest of Safad's Jews obeyed the Haganah's strict orders to stay put while the arrival of the trucks was interpreted as a clear indication of the imminent evacuation of the Army.

The situation in Safad continued to deteriorate. During the night of 15th–16th April, the Arabs attacked and demolished the Technical School, one of the main Jewish positions and their fire hit the Army's positions in Beit Shalva.[150] The next morning (16th April) Gordon-Watson visited his company in Safad. He found his soldiers 'very short of sleep; and with explosions nightly and double guards, they were very, very tired'.[151] With the situation in Tiberias coming to a head and the movement of troops and stores to Haifa already underway, no relief was available. All he had in reserve was a troop of armoured cars of the Lancers. It was obvious to him that the Arab fighters in Safad were out of control of either the local leadership or the ALA. Gordon-Watson met the Arab mayor, consulted with his company commander Captain D.A. Lambert and with the D.S.I. Barham and

> Decided quite definitely that I had done everything possible to stop a bloody battle, and that to remain any longer would postpone the evil day from day to day at great risk to my soldiers.
> I decided to withdraw that afternoon at 15:30 hours.[152]

By 15:25 hours, the town was clear of British troops and Police and the Arab offensive against the Jewish quarter had begun. The main government installations and Army positions outside the Jewish perimeter were either handed over to the Arabs or simply abandoned.

The reasons for the somewhat torturous process by which Gordon-Watson reached his decision on the timing of the final evacuation are to be found in the difficulty of his, as the senior officer in place, admitting that when all was said and done, he was unable to fulfil his mission of maintaining law and order until the official end of the Mandate, a mission which had not been officially rescinded by the High Commissioner. Furthermore, he was certain that by evacuating Safad he was condemning its Jewish population to be massacred. While the Government and the Army's high command were reluctant to admit publicly their failure, it was down to him to implement the change of policy thereby, he believed, sealing the fate of a whole community which hitherto he had protected. However, he need not have worried. The Arab offensive failed and Safad would be eventually

(11th May) occupied by the Haganah (mainly the 3rd Palmach battalion) while its Arab residents fled, an outcome unforeseen by the Army.

While the Arab attack on the Jewish quarter, on 16th April began, the Guards exiting the town came under fire from the Arabs rushing to occupy the Police fort at the entrance to Safad and from Arab reinforcements coming up the Rosh Pinna road. The incident provided the Guardsmen with a welcome excuse to let go with all weapons available. The ammunition expended in this minor and insignificant incident included eight rounds of a six pounder and a large quantity of SAA from light machine guns and rifles. Ten ALA fighters were reported killed and twenty wounded with no casualties to the Guards.[153]

Gordon-Watson signed his Report on the evacuation on 17th April with the assurance that 'Both sides know that I am available and have a great desire to arrange a truce as soon as they wish'. In a later note he added that the ALA, as feared, had blown up the road from Rosh Pinna in several places[154] thereby further reducing the Army's ability to intervene even if asked to.

While Gordon-Watson was trying to stabilize Safad, the situation in Tiberias was also slipping out of the Army's control. In Tiberias, the Jews enjoyed a clear and obvious advantage. In 1944 there were in Tiberias 4,500 Arabs and 6,000 Jews with (from 1928) a Jewish mayor.[155] Most of the Arab community resided in the old town on the shore of the Sea of Galilee whereas the Jewish community spread first south along the shore and then to the west up the slopes overlooking the old town. Only a small number of Jews remained in the walled town and by April they had left to safer quarters. The hinterland, on the other hand, was predominantly Arab, 22,450 to 13,100 Jews,[156] with two large Arab villages – Lubiya to the west on the main road to Nazareth with 2,350 residents[157] and Samakh on the southern shore of the lake with a population of 3,450.[158] However, the roads to Tiberias from all directions ran through Jewish-controlled areas leaving only the Sea as the old town's line of communication.

During the early stages of the Arab Revolt, the Arabs of Tiberias rioted. On a number of occasions, Jewish houses were bombed and set on fire and Jews were attacked and murdered. On 2nd October 1938, an Arab gang of about seventy fighters divided into two groups. One group attacked from the north-east the new Jewish neighbourhood of Kiryat Shmuel, murdered nineteen Jews, and withdrew westwards to Lubiya. Five Arab fighters were killed by a Jewish ambush, positioned to prevent an attack from the west. The other group attacked government and police instillations and set fire to Government House.

Following the attacks the Haganah sent to Tiberias new commanders to organize its defence and financed the construction of fortified positions. The British authorities, made aware of the threat to the Jewish neighbourhoods of an Arab attack from the outside, and powerless to provide adequate protection by its own means, allowed the presence of the JSP in the town and the registration of 200–300 special policemen. These would receive instruction in the use of small arms and basic tactics, and where to be mobilized in an emergency.[159] Consequently, most if not all of the Haganah members in Tiberias had received some military instruction and were licensed in an emergency to bear arms. By February 1948, the Haganah in Tiberias had 400 members, with two mobile squads on permanent alert and a platoon of local conscripts incorporated in the Golani Haganah Brigade as part of the 12th "Barak" Battalion which was responsible for the Jordan Valley and the upper Galilee to the west of Tiberias. Palmach units north of Tiberias (mainly platoons in kibbutzim) provided escorts for convoys to the upper eastern Galilee and were sent on occasional raids.[160] The Arabs of Tiberias were defended by about 500 fighters some of whom were incidental rein-forcements such as ex-policemen and ex-TJFF and about thirty Syrian vol-unteers with the ALA.[161] Relations between the two communities were good and so long as the traditional leadership was in control a truce was observed. The British armed presence was limited to the HQ of Craforce, the 17th/21st Lancers and the Police station.

With the outbreak of violence on 8th April, the Haganah decided to use the opportunity and tighten its hold on lower Tiberias thereby removing an obstacle created by the Arab positions along the wall to the free flow of Jewish traffic along the shore of the Sea of Galilee.[162] It was the Haganah's assessment that while the outburst of violence on 8th April that ended the cease fire, had been spontaneous, the Arabs were encouraged by the flight of the last Jewish inhabitants from the old city and believed that they could use the momentum to consolidate their control of the lower town and then renegotiate a cease fire 'as had been customary in Tiberias'.[163] As a counter-measure, soldiers of the 12th 'Barak' Battalion were sent into the old town to take up positions abandoned by local Jewish residents. The battle for Tiberias began.

While the local Arab force tried to isolate and thereby liquidate the Haganah positions in the old town, the Haganah embarked on a more am-bitious operation to isolate and demoralize the whole Arab old town, be-ginning with tightening its hold on the Arab hinterland. On 12th April, a platoon from 12th Battalion occupied a hill (Sheik Qaddum) overlooking the town and the road from the west. Another platoon completed the Jewish occupation of the western ridge above Tiberias including the small village of Nasir ad Din, destroyed its houses and killed some of its inhabitants (8–10 according to Palestinian sources). The rest fled thereby feeding Arab de-moralization. The two platoons then entered the old town and reinforced the Haganah positions there.[164] At the same time, under the cover of a di-versionary attack the Haganah succeeded in resupplying its positions in the old town from the sea.

Having removed the immediate threat to its positions in the old town the Haganah began its main assault on the Arab positions. The Army found itself powerless to stop the fighting 'owing to weakness in numbers'.[165] Lt.-Col. W.A.C. Anderson CO of the Lancers tried to stop the fighting by demanding that the Haganah evacuate its positions in the old town which, he believed, were the cause of the flare up.[166] The local commanders, whom he summoned, refused, so Anderson sent them an ultimatum to do so until 12:00 hours the next day (13th April) or else they will be shelled. Word of the ultimatum was passed on through political channels with the result that it was rescinded.[167] Once again the British command, including Anderson, met with the Haganah representatives who explained to them that the conflict between Jews and Arabs was really not their problem anymore. If they sought stability let both sides fight it out, thereby, they were confident, in three days, the fighting in Tiberias would end. The British command agreed not to intervene and the Haganah was given a green light to act. By 18th April, Tiberias was occupied and the Arab population was evacuated under British auspices to Nazareth and to Semakh. Thus four weeks before the formal end of the Mandate, the Haganah occupied a mixed town. The Army remained in its camps awaiting its final evacuation ten days later while the whole of the town of Tiberias came under Jewish rule.[168]

The security of the line of communication between Craforce and HQ Northern District in Haifa was the responsibility of the 3rd The King's Own Hussars' armoured cars. The regiment had been much depleted. Its "B" Squadrons had been dispatched to Germany and its "A" Squadron had been suspended (5th March). Its strength during the first quarter of 1948 was 29 officers and 434 ORs with an addition of 2 officers and 52 ORs under its command. Most of the Hussars were deployed in Haifa and in the Consolidated Oil Refineries north of the town. The rest – HQ and "C" Squadron including the remains of "A" Squadron – a total of six armoured car and one assault troop were stationed in the Ramat David airfield west of Nazareth. Their main duties were 'flag marches, uprooting illegal road blocks, escorts and patrols when incident have arisen that the Police have been incapable of dealing with'.[169] A common mission was removing under fire bodies of fighters from either side, for instance, on 17th March the bodies of the members of a Jewish patrol killed in 15th March in an ambush near kibbutz Beit Keshet in the lower Galilee. The initial incident ended well before the Army was informed of it. Seven Jewish settlers were killed following which fighters from both sides rushed to the scene resulting in exchanges of heavy small arms fire. The Arabs, situated along a ridge overlooking the area of the ambush, as well the kibbutz, prevented the extraction of the bodies for a couple of days. An armoured car troop and an assault troop commanded by Captain P.L. Stubbs tried with some policemen to reach the bodies but

> were themselves heavily engaged by the Arabs with several LMGs, who, it turned out the next day, thought them to be Haganah reinforcements. They returned fire with 0.30 Browning, 37mm and 3 inch shells in order to extricate one of their recce patrols.[170]

The eventual removal of the bodies was negotiated by local dignitaries whose authority over the fighting forces remained, in this instance, intact.

Apart from the Beit Keshet incident the area, as far as the Hussars were concerned, remained relatively peaceful,

> the quietest in Palestine, for the Jews are in many cases friendly and do not want trouble, while the Arabs are extremely friendly to us and have had orders not to start trouble till after the end of the mandate.[171]

It would seem that so long as they were not asked to help, the Hussars remained unaware of local violent incidents, raids, etc.

It was different when the Army could actually observe a battle taking place in plain sight.

> On the afternoon of April 4, as the Hussars looked across the plain of Esdraelon from their camp at Ramat David, they saw smoke drifting along the slope of Mount Carmel, and learned that the Arabs were attacking the Jewish settlement of Mishmar Ha'Emeq with guns and mortars, The regiments' orders were to avoid any risk of British casualties[172]

and to avoid travel at night. The next morning (5th April), three armoured cars, commanded by Captain Stubbs, were sent at first light to investigate. By then the firing had stopped.[173]

The Hussars' CO report of the fighting reveals a very sketchy understanding of the battle and its significance. A full ALA battalion – 'Kadisiya' consisting of Iraqi volunteers supported by four 75 mm field guns and a few armoured cars, was sent by Qawuqji to occupy and destroy kibbutz Mishmar Ha'Emeq in an attempt to assert his authority on the Arab forces in the north (and particularly in Haifa) and contrary to any understandings he may have had with the British. ALA fighters were sent ahead to take up positions in the Arab villages of Abu Shusha and Abu Zurayk north of the kibbutz thereby isolating it from its closest neighbours kibbutz Ha'Zorea and the town of Yokneam. The ALA planned to shell Mishmar Ha'Emeq from the north and the south and then attack and over-run it along the main road between Jenin in Samaria and Haifa, Qawuqji's main line of communications with the Arab forces in Haifa.[174] An Arab attack on the 4th failed to break through the kibbutz defences. At the time of Capt. Stubbs' arrival the Arab commanders were debating their next move.

Stubbs approached Mishmar Ha'Emeq from the south, the direction of the main Arab attack, encountering on the way two ALA roadblocks.

> A Syrian was in command and after being rather hostile at first became friendly but said he was not in command and could not do anything to stop the fighting. Capt. STUBBS contacted the District Officer who said he could arrange that the fighting would stop. He went away and came back later saying that there would be no more fighting. The night [5–6 April] was quiet.[175]

While the kibbutz was preparing for another attack, the Haganah was busy assembling a composite force from a number of its units, west of Mishmar Ha'Emeq. The Haganah plan was, once the ALA resumed its attack along the road, to counter-attack it from the high ground overlooking the road to the west. The truce the District Officer and Captain Stubbs thought they had arranged was no more than a lull in the fighting while both sides were preparing for its resumption.

During the night of 5th–6th April, the Haganah took up positions overlooking Mishmar Ha'Emeq from the south, west and north-west (including the Arab village of Abu Shusha). The Arab shelling was resumed the next day (6th April) at 16:30 hours and continued until about 22:00 hours. The rate of fire of the Arab artillery, Lt. Col. C. A. Peel The Hussars CO observed, 'was very slow and appeared to be extremely inaccurate'.[176] Early the next morning, Peel arrived at the kibbutz with armoured cars. He found the place peaceful despite being surrounded by the ALA and local militias. He met at 13:30 hours the Arab commander Colonel Mahdi Bey Saleh and told him that the firing must stop. Peel's efforts appear to have been an attempt to stop the battle and allow the situation to return to normal, contrary to the intentions of both sides.

> I told him that unless he withdrew his men the British Army would have to push them out, and that I was sure that he did not want to fight against the British any more than the British wanted to fire against either the Arabs or the Jews.[177]

Peel arranged an immediate meeting of representatives from the kibbutz with the Arab commander which took place in the village of al-Mans, further down the road to the south.[178] According to Peel's report, the ALA's demands were that the Jews do not 'carry out reprisal attacks against two neighbouring Arab villages' where it had taken up firing positions but was enable (or unwilling) to protect and to stop shooting at Arab vehicles travelling on the Jenin-Haifa road.[179] After a short discussion (forty-five minutes) at about 16:00 hours, the Jewish delegation agreed to the conditions and a twenty-four-hour truce was declared. A major provision was the evacuation of all the children and the women who wished to leave the kibbutz to the nearest Jewish settlement – Kfar Baruch, in Army vehicles. It was also agreed that negotiations would resume the next day (8th April). 'I then withdrew all troops at about 18:30 hours'.[180]

On the afternoon of the 8th, the Jewish side evaded the issue of a possible extension of the truce, but by nightfall both sides agreed to meet again the next morning and in the meantime, keep the peace. Peel recalled that the

> Jews remarked as I was going away that this would give each side more time to bring up reinforcements. I pointed out that that would be breaking the truce, but I had the impression that the Jews would still try and do so,[181]

as indeed both sides did.

On the same day (8th April), the Haganah had completed its preparations and during the night of 8–9 April a composite force, under the command of Yizchak Sade, began an attack on the ALA's southern flank and the village of Abu Shusha north of Mishmar Ha'Emeq.[182] Peel noted that the developing battle had moved away from the kibbutz. The Haganah attacked at night and defended its positions by day against Arab counter-attacks. There 'did not appear to be any fire directed into the settlement and none appeared to come from it'.[183]

The next (9th April) morning Peel returned to the area only to learn that the Haganah had attacked during the night contrary to the agreement he helped to negotiate. Further efforts in that direction seemed futile now that the Haganah went on the offensive. The ALA was keen to try to persuade the Army to put a stop to the fighting possibly fearing an imminent defeat. Peel:

> [I] told them that… they must stop the fighting in this area. I said that I realized that they were now involved in a battle and it might be difficult to extract themselves but that if all the firing had not stopped by tomorrow (10.4) I would have to take action with strong British forces to clear the whole area.[184]

Peel did try to contact the Jewish side but his jeep came under fire south of the kibbutz and he returned to camp where he wrote his report.

Meanwhile, the Hussars had received other assignments. On 9th April, a troop was to set up a road black (for five days) on the Hadera-Haifa road as part of punitive measures against the area's Jewish inhabitants following the IZL attack on camp 80. On the next day (10th April), all the regimental transport was used to move the 1st Parachute Battalion from Semakh to Haifa, accompanied by "C" Squadron. Escorts were also provided for the evacuation of the IPC (Iraqi Petroleum Company) installations to Lebanon leading to the final closure of the Consolidated Oil Refineries in Haifa on 13th April.[185]

While the Hussars were kept busy elsewhere, the battle of Mishmar Ha'Emeq reached its climax unobserved by the British Army. In 12th April, the ALA tried to renew its offensive but the Haganah counter-attacked from the flank while succeeding in opening the road to the kibbutz from the north. Two days later (14th April), the ALA disengaged and withdrew south back to Samaria.

In his report, Peel could not help express his sympathy for the ALA despite their being the aggressors and the eventual ruin of the local Arab villages they were meant to protect.

> Their discipline is good… They salute most punctually and then expect to shake hands. The guard at RA[H]Q [Rear Area Head Quarters] presented arms quite smartly when either – Mahdi Bey or I – came past

they are all extremely friendly and always greet one with a beaming smile. They look down on the locals almost as much as on the Jews. And appear to prefer us to anyone else in the country.[186]

The outcome of the battle proved most reassuring for the Haganah and the Jewish leadership. The ALAs command proved itself unprofessional and unskilled and their troops lacked stamina.[187] Despite their apparent material advantage, especially in field guns of which the Jews had none, they proved no match to the Haganah's improved tactical flexibility combining static and mobile defence in depth in the war's first deployment of battalion size forces in daytime pitched battle. The seemingly most ominous offensive Arab force in the country proved relatively lame and while the British Army was quite close by it had shown itself unwilling or unable to intervene in stopping the fighting or preventing the destruction of the Arab villages in the vicinity of Mishmar Ha'Emeq even when its honour was at stake. The Army, for its part, was not aware of the full extent and significance of the battle and when the truce it had negotiated was broken it simply withdrew back to its base and allowed the fighting to continue.

This pattern whereby the Army withdrew wherever the fighting endangered its troops and its interests were not threatened reached a dramatic climax in Haifa. The Jewish community in Haifa was roughly the same size as the Arab (both Moslems and Christians) and enjoyed a clear topographical advantage by settling on the upper slopes and the ridge of the Carmel whereas, as in Tiberias, the Arabs had concentrated in the lower town near the port. The government estimate for 1944 had in Haifa 35,940 Moslems, 26,570 Christians and 66,000 Jews. According to later figures, the population was constantly growing but the ratio between the communities remained with about a 51% majority of Jews.[188] In lower Haifa, the Arab Christians concentrated mainly in the west, the Moslems in the east. The Jews lived mainly in Hadar Ha'Carmel half way up the eastern slopes of Mt. Carmel and on the ridge in Achuza and Carmel Central. Haifa owed its rapid growth during the Mandate to the construction of the port (opened in 1933) financed by the government, which from its inception constituted a strategic deep water port serving imperial and regional needs. In the area north of the port, along the shore of the Bey of Acre, were situated Palestine's fuel processing facilities including the refineries which processed crude oil delivered by a pipeline from Iraq. The refineries were operated by Consolidated Refineries Ltd., which was owned jointly by the Anglo-Iranian Oil Company and Shell Oil. It began operation at the end of 1939 and with the demand created by the war its capacity by 1944 increased from one to four million tons annually which necessitated on additional supply of crude oil brought by tankers from Tripoli, Lebanon.[189] Full scale production required a workforce of about 2,100. Palestine was entirely dependent for oil on the Iraqi oil refined in Haifa. When operating at full capacity, more than three-fourths of refined fuel was exported.[190]

By the end of the war, the total water surface of the port was 279 acres, of which, 185 acres were deep water suitable for large ships. Installations included nine large transit sheds with road and rail access. Apart from handling cargo, the port could accommodate two large oil tankers in its oil dock. The port authority employed about 1,400, mostly casual workers, daily, of whom 200 were Jews. Additional workers were employed by private contractors. Ensuring the safety of the workers of the refineries and the oil industry as well as the port was vital for the operation of the Palestine economy.[191]

Another surge in Haifa's development came during the war when the town, its light industrial factories to the north and the camps to the south, became a major hub of military activity, including supply dumps and workshops for the allied armies, transit camps and recreational facilities of all sorts for the troops in Palestine and throughout the Middle East. The ever-growing demand for workers was fed by Jews from Europe (until and after the war) and Middle Eastern countries (including Jewish stevedores from Thessaloniki) and Arab unskilled labour from the rural hinterland and neighbouring countries.

The Jews of Haifa were mainly Zionists, with a large proportion of socialists, members of the General Labour Union (Ha'histadrut) whereas the unionization of the Arab unskilled workers was in its infancy. The Jewish workers were mainly employed in medium and large shops, living in newly constructed workers housing projects. They were known as a well-organized and disciplined community commonly referred to as "Red Haifa". Accordingly, Haifa had one of the largest and strongest Haganah branches, with its own local commanders and stockpiles of arms. Haifa's Arabs in comparison were disunited with rival local leaders vying with each other. The efforts of the exiled grand Mufti to unite the Arabs of Palestine under his authority had failed and as the political crisis intensified in the autumn of 1947 members of Haifa's more affluent families began leaving for neighbouring countries in anticipation of a breakdown in law and order.[192]

In the course of the reorganization of the Army's deployment in January 1947, the 6th Airborne Division took over from the 1st Infantry Division the Northern Sector of the Galilee and Haifa, with the 1st Parachute Brigade responsible for the Galilee, the 3rd Parachute Brigade for Haifa with the 3rd Hussars in Ramat David. Divisional Headquarters were in the Stella Maris monastery on the south-western ridge of Mt. Carmel. 'Haifa was regarded as a potential trouble spot, although it compared very favorable indeed in this respect with Tel Aviv'.[193]

As elsewhere in Palestine, the Partition Resolution changed the patterns of violence in Haifa, including mutual attacks on traffic and on each communities' neighbourhoods creating stretches of no-man's land consisting of abandoned and largely ruined building, terror attacks and road blocks.

In order to preserve the communities' morale and stop the civilians from leaving their homes, the armed militias on both sides maintained a highly visible presence to the dismay of the British authorities. From the Army's perspective,

> The Haganah all but came into the open... armed Haganah patrols and sub-units were frequently encountered by British forces, who took all possible steps to disarm them ...both Jewish and Arab leaders in Haifa were [frequently] commanded to attend the Divisional Commander's Orders. They were reprimanded with a severity which normally ensured the orderly behavior of themselves and their forces for at least several days.[194]

Whereas the traditional leaders of both communities were eager to preserve peaceful co-existence while preparing for the likelihood of a future armed conflict should the international community fail to sort things out, militants on both sides were busy trying to disrupt everyday life. On 3rd December, the IZL threw from a tender a homemade bombs on a large group of Arab labourers at the entrance to the Consolidated Oil Refiners. The act was described by the IZL as a 'counter-attack' against Arab terrorism.[195] Six Arabs were killed and about fifty wounded.[196] The Arabs at the entrance, joined by the Arab workers in the Refineries rioted and attacked their Jewish co-workers, thirty nine of whom were beaten to death. The Refineries were secured by Arab policemen under British command and an Arab Legion company, responsible for the power station and its equipment. During the riot, they were reinforced by troops from the 2nd/3rd Parachute Battalion, and the workers were evacuated in buses escorted by the armoured cars of "A" Squadron of the 3rd Hussars.[197]

The Jewish workers refused to return to work unless better security arrangements were made and the Arab Legion replaced.

> Consequently on 1 Jan 48 "C" Sqn [3rd Hussars] was sent to CRL [Consolidated Refineries Ltd.] to relieve the Arab Legion in an effort to restore confidence and to induce the workers to return. Their duties were mainly patrolling roads, escorting workers to and from (after work had started again) and "showing the flag" throughout the locality. Patrols were also carried out in Haifa, where sniping incidents were on the increase.[198]

The 3rd Hussars rotated its squadrons in Haifa weekly, operating, from 12th January, under the command of 66th Airborne Anti-Tank Regiment RA.

> They lived under canvas and fed mainly off Pacific Compo rations cooked over brew fires, until an ACC [Army Catering Corps] cook was sent out to them at the end of February. The rum ration was extremely welcome during the heavy rains.[199]

Once the workers returned to work and the Refineries resumed operation, the Squadrons' work in the area became fairly routine while attention shifted to Haifa town. There the situation was steadily worsening with frequent sniping between neighbourhoods and on traffic, and nightly raids. The Quarterly Report of the 3rd Hussars noted that

> As a result of several major incidents in which stolen British Army vehicles and uniforms have been used as disguise even Army vehicles are liable to be stopped and made to prove their identity and at night, especially in the Wadi Rushmiya area, any vehicle is liable to be shot at, but it is no longer the policy to search houses or vehicles unless firing had definitely been seen to come from them.[200]

Maurice Tugwell, then a young officer with the 6th Airborne, described in his suspense novel *Herzl Street* Wadi Rushmiya (Figure 6.1) as 'the most lethal place' in Haifa. The bridge over the Wadi carried the main road from the north to the large Jewish neighbourhood Hadar Ha'Carmel. The Arab neighbourhood on the western slopes of the Wadi – Ard el-Ghazzawi had originally housed the labourers from Gaza who built the bridge. Tugwell described it as 'a scruffy, unhygienic and generally wretched place, the only dwellings in it housed poor Arabs'. However, with the outbreak of hostilities, 'All at once this neglected and hitherto unloved wadi had acquired status. It was a killing ground'.[201] The Haganah began to operate in the area, its first retaliatory raid was the demolition of a three story building used by Arab fighters to attack traffic on the bridge and Jewish buildings in Hadar Ha'Carmel.[202] In an attempt to control the situation, the Paras established positions on either side of the bridge.[203]

Figure 6.1 Haifa. The Wadi Rushmiya bridge.
Source: Unknown photographer; Courtesy of the I.D.F. Archive (file 0-96202), Ministry of Defense, Israel.

By the end of 1947, most of the Arab civilian population left Wadi Rushmiya, many to the adjacent Halisa neighbourhood,[204] and Arab fighters from the local militia moved in. Tugwell,

> most days there was shooting. Occasionally a car or bus would be hit, and emerge on the far side carrying dead or wounded. The spectacle was observed by a platoon of paras on the northern side, who occupied a half-completed six story building we called Skeleton House. They had warned all civilians who would listen not to use this road, and not to expect to be saved by the Army if they got into trouble.[205]

The 3rd Hussars first Quarterly Report for 1948 stated with satisfaction that its three troops in Haifa, two in the Refineries area and one in town,

> Have done such good work in the way of house searches, removing illegal road blocks, rounding up snipers, impounding illegal armoured cars, supporting the Para battalions with 30 Browning and 37 mm [2 pounds] (These last were first used on 19 March to disperse Arab snipers), patrols etc. that Maj. Gen. Stockwell told us that we had won "the battle of HAIFA" for the division.[206]

One of the Army's main concerns in Haifa was the safe shipping of stores, this in addition to the continued operation of the Refineries and the safety of the Army's and ports' civilian workforce, and its daily passage to and from work.[207] Initially, the 2nd/3rd Parachute Battalion was made responsible for the town by means of placing platoons in stationary positions and running patrols. The 8th/9th Parachute Battalion was in charge of the various escorts. The two battalions rotated about every month. Most of the fighting took place at night and 'it was decided early on that no real harm could be done by night whether the troops intervened or not, provided that the movement of the contestants was restricted'.[208]

The creation of an array of static positions as the main means of dealing with snipers and heavier fire fights as well as forming bases for the operation of patrols, created its own problems.

> Their security was a matter of prime importance. They had to be of such a strength as to look after themselves for a period of a week or more without their garrisons becoming too weary from guards, O.P. [Observation Post] duties and patrols. They had to be secure against all forms of attack, particularly the forms concerned with large quantities of explosives... There had to be a sound administrative plan for feeding.[209]

The Jewish leadership, in general, and the Haganah in Haifa, in particular, were dismissive of the British declarations of neutrality.[210] Nor did the

Haganah suffer any compunctions in Haifa in using British uniforms to fool Arab roadblocks with the result that troops and Army vehicles were often attacked by Arabs who later explained that they were mistaken for Jews. On 22nd March, a three ton truck carrying 700 kilograms of explosives, led by a Jeep and followed by a tender, with Haganah fighters dressed up as para-troopers, drove into the Arab lower town. The explosion, destroyed a four story buildings and damaged others. It was excused as retaliation for the Arabs destroying on the previous day and by similar means the building of the Histadrut construction company Solel Boneh, near the port in which six Jews were killed and twenty-eight wounded, causing considerable elation on the Arab side and demoralization in the Jewish community. The bombing of the Arab building on the 22nd was done with equipment and explosives sent from Haganah headquarters in Tel Aviv following the demand by Moshe Carmel, the senior Haganah commander in Haifa, who suspected that the Arab bombing was coordinated with the Army.[211] Wilson, then Divisional G2(Intelligence) ignored in his account the Arab bombing on the 21st and was largely concerned with the fate of the Parachute Brigade HQ which had been sent to investigate. They were immediately seized by the enraged Arabs who were about to kill them, when some of the more responsible ones, succeeded in moving them into the Suq in an ambulance. After having been threatened again with immediate execution, the Jeep's passengers were handed over to the headquarters of the ALA in Haifa and after their iden-tity was confirmed by the Police, were released with 'profuse and genuine' apologies.[212]

The importance of Haifa to both sides resulted in a constant flow of arms, supplies and fighters which on the Arab side meant a growing influence of external forces and an intensification of the power struggles. In February Haifa's Arab National Committee appointed Lt. Mohammed al-Hammad al-Hunaitti of the Jordanian Arab Legion, as the commander of the Arab forces in Haifa.[213] He established a National Guard responsible for securing the Arab neighbourhoods and a company of 250 fighters as a mobile force. In doing so, he was helped by the garrison companies of the Jordanian Legion guarding government installations in Haifa, who provided weapons, ammu-nition and instructors. Al-Hunaitti took his orders from the Arab League in Damascus and was expected to consult with the local National Council before taking action with the result of constant friction with Arab Haifa's strong man Rashid al-Haj Ibrahim.[214]

On 17th March, on his way back from Damascus via Beirut, travelling in a convoy of five vehicles carrying arms and ammunition, Al Hunaitti was killed by a Haganah ambush and the cargo was destroyed.[215] The next day (18th May) Captain Amin Izz al-Din, a former Lebanese gendarme, was appointed Commander of the National Guards.[216] Ten days later (28th March), the ALA headquarters announced that Haifa was to form an inde-pendent military district under its direct command and appointed Shakib Wahab CO of the ALA's Druze battalion, as its commander.[217]

By then the Army felt that it was gradually losing control over the intensity and the geography of the fighting. In March, it still tried to establish its authority with the help of a form of flag marches by a composite troop including one Comet tank and two self-propelled Sexton guns from the 1st Regiment Royal Horse Artillery,[218] and the armoured cars of the 3rd Hussars.

> At varying intervals by day and night, mixed columns of tanks, armoured cars and infantry would patrol the streets... and if there was any cause to open fire on a Jewish or Arab post, there was a weight of fire power available which could take charge of all situations.[219]

The flag marches became armoured patrols. Wilson noted one consequence of the general escalation of fighting:

> In the last few months which the [6th Airborne] Division spent in Palestine, much of the sympathy which its members had felt inwardly towards the Arabs declined. The lawless elements had shown in this short period that they could carry out attacks very similar to those of the Jews, and many casualties were suffered at their hands.[220]

In a letter to his parents, dated 4th February, Wilson wrote: 'the Arabs have shown themselves to be second to none in the atrocity line'.[221]

A series of Arab setbacks, including the ALA's failure in Mishmar Ha'Emeq demoralized Haifa's Arabs, who began leaving their homes in growing numbers especially in contested areas between Arab and Jewish neighbourhoods. Abandoned buildings were quickly transformed into firing positions while adding to the Army's headaches. Stockwell's account of the events that led to his decision to evacuate most of Haifa began with an ALA offensive on '12 or 13 April', aimed at extending the Arab controlled territory.[222] The Army's efforts to restore some stability, especially on the night of 17th/18th April, met with only partial success and did not stop the firing on British troops.

On the 6th of April, the 1st Battalion the Coldstream Guards replaced the 2nd/3rd Parachute Battalion which had left Palestine. 'No one had any regrets at leaving the Holy Land. ...leaving the Jews and the Arabs to fight it out among themselves', recalled Major John Waddy of the 7th Parachute Battalion.

> We didn't hate the Jews: we were sorry for many of the immigrants, and especially the old people and the children, but we were annoyed at the impotence of their leaders in ruining the peace we had fought for. We felt that they were a lot of ungrateful shits.[223]

When handing over responsibility for Haifa Lt.-Col. Theo Birkbech CO 2nd/3rd Parachute Battalion presented Lt.-Col. John Chandos-Pole CO of the 1st Coldstrem Guards with his version of Kipling's If.

The Town Commander

If you can keep the Peace when all about you
   Are breaking it and blaming it on you.
If you can take a bomb and gently roll it.
   "Impartiality" first at Arab, then at Jew.
If you can go to sleep with a "not to worry"
   While the sounds of battle rage throughout the night
   Yours is the town and everything that's in
And you'll be a better man than I am Chandos-Pole.[224]

At first, the situation seemed to the Guardsmen to be under control, despite the continuous fire exchanges.

> Liaison with both sides played a very large part not only at 1st Guards Brigade and Battalion level, but also in the company areas and with each individual platoon commander. Both sides used to whine to British troops when firing started and say they had the worst of it, and both sides denied that they fired first. The Arab sense of humor was tremendous while the Jews had none. Both sides were prepared to try anything, but in almost every case the Jews were the more cunning.[225]

However, within a few days the situation was getting out of hand.

> Gradually liaison with the Jews and Arabs had less and less effect and shooting by night and sniping by day and the blowing up of houses by both sides became much more frequent. Stronger methods had to be used; houses of both sides were blown up, Piats were used more often, the Staghounds used their Brownings and 2-pounder guns, and the Comet was employed on a number of road blocks.[226]

As in Safad and Tiberias, the Army's commanders soon concluded that they had no practical means to stop the fighting. Stockwell had run out of reserves while the High Commissioner insisted on sticking to the official time table for the ending of the Mandate and the Army's evacuation of Haifa. With the safety of his soldiers at risk his one option was to shorten his front and his lines of communication and concentrate his troops as quickly as possible in their designated departure area, that is, Haifa. In doing so, a minimal security zone containing vital installations was defined, including besides the port the Army's headquarters on the Carmel, the airfield in Ramat David and the air strip north of Haifa town and most of the immediate coastal strip, including the camps and warehouses to the south and the workshops, the refineries and the military hospital to the north. The Army realized it had a moral obligation to prevent as best it could a massacre of civilians but not at any cost. It was, therefore, decided by the

Army's command that no further attempts to prevent fighting in the main town of Haifa would be made and that British troops would concentrate on securing the docks and their entrances, keeping all the routes into town open and maintain law and order only in these areas and in security zones east and west of the town containing major military installations.[227]

Meanwhile, the movement of troops in Haifa except in the vicinity of their camps was confined to daytime and ranks were ordered to carry personal arms and ammunition (fifty rounds of SAA for rifles) at all times[228] Stockwell's assessment, as described in his later report, was

> that my dispositions, made with all the forces at my disposal, were isolated and in themselves weak should any major assault be made by either side.[229]

When approaching both Arab and Jewish liaison officers requesting them to 'soften their tactics', they promised him that they 'were not taking any offensive action and only fired when they themselves were fired at,' and to abstain from any offensive action. 'It was obvious', Stockwell observed, 'that these statements were but vague and useless promises'.[230]

According to Philip Brutton, on the stuff of the Guards Brigade, General Stockwell, during a cocktail party in his headquarters on 17th April, made it known that his intention was to allow 'the Jews and Arabs to face one another in the central part of town'.[231]

On 19th April, General Macmillan conferred with Stockwell in Haifa and approved his plan for the redeployment of the Army in the town.[232] Later Stockwell met with Abba Khoushi, secretary of Haifa's Labour Council, and Harry Bailin, local representative of the Jewish Agency, who had tried in the past to persuade him to allow the Jews to occupy the town. They informed him that the Haganah intended to go on the offensive in order to remove the Arab threat to Hadar Ha'Carmel. Their intention, Stockwell surmised, was to try to gauge the British response to a Jewish move.[233]

Immediately afterwards Stockwell met with CO 1st Guards Brigade and his own 61(Ops) and produced a written appreciation of the situation. In it Stockwell defined his options considering both Haifa and the eastern Galilee as parts of one problem. The option of remaining in his positions in both was untenable in view of the expected cost. There was insufficient time to concentrate all the forces from eastern Galilee in Haifa to prevent the ultimate showdown between Arabs and Jews, while risking a destabilization of the Galilee. In his view, his only practical option was to redeploy.

> In my opinion it was vitally necessary to safeguard the British evacuation from Haifa and also to minimize in every way I could casualties to my forces, and still be in a position to exercise authority by negotiation and help to both communities in as great an area of the NORTHERN SECTOR as was possible with the forces at my disposal.[234]

By the 20th, the 1st Coldstream Guards were informed that

> It was decided by H.Q. NORTH PALESTINE, after information had been received concerning the future activities of both Jews and Arabs in HAIFA, that the troops of the 1st Bn. Coldstream Guards would be withdrawn from their controlling positions all over the town to a defensive line in the West of the town.
>
> A conference took place during the late afternoon with the full details of the evacuation of the positions in the town, which would take place as soon as it was ordered.[235]

The order to redeploy was issued by first light on 21st April.[236] At 04:30 hours, two companies of the Coldstream Guards withdrew from their positions in town and by 05:45 hours established a defensive line east of the port area along Kingsway road, the main downtown north-south axis, and up to the Carmel ridge and along it to the North Sector's headquarters. By 06:00 hours, the move had been completed.[237]

As for the rest of the Army in Haifa, the 40 Commando Royal Marines remained in the port with a few additional positions on Kingsway road guarding the gates to the docks, the 1st Battalion The Grenadier Guards remained in the east of the town where they protected the railway station, the approaches from the east, the Oil terminal including the Refineries, and the railway workshops. One company covered the cantonment area on Mt. Carmel. The Coldstream's Support Company with the Staghounds of the 3rd Hussars policed a zone along the coast.

The Coldstreams summed up the morning's events:

> The move of the two Coys in the early hours of the morning was completed entirely without incident and practically without a shot being fired. Much of this was due to the fact that both the Jews and Arabs were totally unaware of the withdrawal until well after it was under way and many failed to realize that the two Coys had left the control of the town until late into the morning.[238]

During the morning, General Stockwell met the representatives of both communities and informed them of the Army's new positions. After initial local efforts on both sides to occupy the vacated positions the shooting intensified during the afternoon as the Haganah launched Operation Scissors, to occupy Haifa initially prepared for when the Army withdraws from Palestine. After fierce fighting during the night 21st–22nd April Haifa, apart from the new British zone, was largely in Jewish hands.[239]

In his article 'The Fall of Haifa,' published in 1959 the Palestinian historian Walid Khalidi stated that 'there is evidence to indicate that the Zionists knew of the British withdrawl well ahead of the Arabs' and that a decisive factor in the Jewish victory was 'British-Zionist collusion or orchestration of effort'.[240] A sound conspiracy argument requires concrete documentary proof. Khalidi only has his interpretation of circumstantial evidence. 'What evidence is there for this British-Zionist collusion? The most significant is perhaps the conduct of the British civilian and military authorities particularly that of General Stockwell'.[241]

The only direct 'confirmation' of connivance is a claim made by Abba Khoushi, secretary of the Labour Council and one of the most powerful leaders of the towns' Jewish community, in 1958[242] and repeated as a fact (without a reference) in Dan Kurzman, *Genesis 1948*, in 1970.[243] Khoushi had been sent to the United States in October 1947 to raise money on behalf of the Histadrut and returned to a new reality on 5th February 1948.[244] Despite his own attempts and Ben Gurion's support, all security matters in Haifa were handled by Moshe Carmel (Zalitsky) of the Haganah.[245] Khoushi, who had been all powerful, found his position marginalized by the military. According to his own account he decided to approach Stockwell and convince him to turn Haifa over to the Jews.[246] Accompanied by Harry Beilin, representative of the Political Department of the Jewish Agency (but without a representative of the Haganah) Khoushi met Stockwell in his headquarters in the end of February and put to him his plan. A surprised Stockwell politely asked for time to think about it. When Khoushi asked when should he return for an answer he was told to come back in a month's time.[247]

At the end of March, Khoushi and Beilin returned and were told that while their plan was not unreasonable a final answer could not yet be given and that they might meet again in a fortnight, when Khoushi and Beilin were deferred for another week. Finally, on 20th April Stockwell, according to Khoushi, informed him that he was ready to adopt his suggested course of action,[248] by then the new lines of deployment had already been decided.

On 22nd April, while inspecting the newly occupied Arab neighbourhoods, Khoushi broke his leg and was taken to hospital where he was visited by Stockwell instead of meeting him as planned in his headquarters at 11:00 hours. It was a shame, Stockwell is supposed to have told him, that he would miss the negotiations on the surrender of Haifa's Arabs.[249]

None of the meetings mentioned by Khoushi were reported in Ben-Gurion's diary. Carmel in his memories of the war, published in 1949 confessed to having been taken completely by surprise by Stockwell's move.[250] According to Stockwell's biographer during the meeting with Khoushi and Beilin on the 19th, in which were present also Cyril Marriot, Political Adviser to GOC Palestine and Haifa's District Commissioner Alfred Nowl Law,[251] Khoushi threatened that the Jews would attack 'the area of Mt. Carmel,' and that he, Khoushi, had been sent from Tel Aviv to command the attack (which in any event is highly unlikely). Stockwell replied that the result of such an attack on an area which included his HQ 'could well result in direct combat with the British'.[252]

None of the British accounts of the meeting suggest even remotely collusion while Khoushi's account was clearly self-serving in claiming a major role in the events whereas in fact he was of minor importance. Khoushi further endowed his account with a story of a wager with Stockwell over a bottle of whiskey on the time it would take the Jews to occupy Haifa. Stockwell is said to have stated that even with the one and a half divisions at his disposal it could not be done in less than a week. Khoushi's estimate was 24–48 hours. Khoushi had Stockwell congratulating him in the hospital, on winning the bet.[253] The likelihood of a British Army General making a wager with a Jewish civic leader, who did not represent the Haganah, is slim. Apparently, a wager was made but it was with Mordechai Makleff, Carmel's deputy and a major in the British Army during the War.[254]

There is no reason to assume British – "Zionist" collusion. Stockwell's decision to redeploy, approved by GOC Palestine, was based on the reports and assessments of his commanders in the field. His choice of method to avoid loses while ensuring an undisturbed evacuation was in accordance with the polices adopted by other senior commanders in Palestine and in keeping with CIG's guide lines. The decisions to evacuate contested areas while in the last resort offering to transfer communities at risk to safety were seen as a reasonable option in a desperate situation. Stockwell's even-handedness, even if appreciated by the Jews, was not a sign of bias. His anti-Jewish ADC Captain Peter Cavendish was probably right in stating that Stockwell 'was concerned to treat everyone equally and if the situation [in Haifa] had been reversed he would have offered the same deal to the Arabs'.[255]

The 'deal' in question was Stockwell's attempt to persuade the remaining Arabs leaders in Haifa to face up to the Jewish victory, accede to the Haganah's terms of surrender and accept the Jewish offer to remain in their homes under Jewish rule, an option condemned by the Arab leadership abroad but occasionally accepted be local leaders who preferred Jewish rule to becoming refugees.[256] That however was not the case in Haifa.

The Jewish leadership in Haifa appealed on 21st April to the town's Arabs to remain in their homes.[257] During the night (21–22 April), the Haganah attacking down the hills from Hadar Ha'Carmel succeeded in breaking through the Arab defences in down town Haifa but were yet to meet up with the Palmach force which operated near the port. Meanwhile, the British Army sealed the town preventing the entry of Arab reinforcements but also removing an Haganah roadblock to the north to pre-empt a confrontation with the Arab Legion should its soldiers try to enter Haifa.[258] Throughout the night and the morning of 22nd April, while the battle was still in progress, the remaining Arab leaders repeatedly demanded an immediate British intervention to stop the fighting. Their request was reiterated during a meeting with General Stockwell in his headquarters in 10:00 hours.

Stockwell replied that he would intervene only to arrange a truce leaving the Arabs no alternative but to agree.[259]

Ya'akov Salomon, the Haganah liaison with Stockwell, was asked by Carmel in the early hours of 22nd April to draw up conditions for a truce. They included the complete surrender of all Arab forces, including foreign fighters, and weapons. The Arab population was to submit completely to the Haganah's authority and would be given its protection. Following an immediate curfew, the population would be allowed to return to its normal pursuits. Stockwell made some amendments 'which, broadly speaking, took certain demands out of the hands of the Haganah into the hands of the [civilian] authorities', and summoned the Jewish delegation. Following the Jewish approval of the amendments Stockwell arranged for a truce meeting in the Town Hall at 16:00 hours.[260]

The meeting was adjourned at 17:30 hours to allow the Arabs further consultations. These included a telephone call to Beirut, intercepted by Haganah intelligence, seeking instructions.[261] The meeting was resumed at 19:15 hours.

When the Arabs stated that they were not in a position to sign the truce, as they had no control over the Arab military elements in the town and that, in all sincerity, they could not fulfil the terms of the truce, even if they were to sign it. '...as alternative... the Arab population wished to evacuate HAIFA and... they would be grateful for military assistance'.[262] Stockwell's entreaties, backed by Salomon and Makleff, that the Arabs accept the Jewish terms and remain in Haifa, were to no avail, and a meeting of the Arab delegation with Stockwell to coordinate the evacuation was set for the next morning (23 April) at 11:00 hours.[263]

During the night battle (21–22 April) the companies of the Coldstream Guards remained bystanders. However, they gradually became involved in attempts to protect the increasing numbers of Arabs fleeing Haifa, well in advance of the negotiations. In the early hours of the morning appeals for help began to arrive, while the Haganah fighters,

> Were continually shooting down [from their higher positions] on all the Arabs who moved... This included completely indiscriminate and revolting machine gun fire, mortar fire and sniping on women and children sheltering in churches and attempting to get out of HAIFA through the gates into the docks. No. 3 Gate, the EAST GATE was the main gate through which they tried to get to the docks from where freighters were arranged to take the women and children to ACRE. The 40 RM.CDO. [Royal Marines Commando] who control the docks were unable to let many through at a time less the chaos should reign in the docks. They let the Arabs through in batches but there was considerable congestion outside the EAST GATE of hysterical and terrified Arab women and children and old people on whom the Jews opened up mercilessly with fire. Two officers of 40 RM.CDO. were seriously wounded whilst dealing with this tricky evacuation.

Staghounds of the 3rd Hussars spent much of the day endeavouring to quieten the shooting in the area but nothing but armoured vehicles were able to operate in front of the defensive ring round the center of town (Figure 6.2).[264]

The Staghounds also secured the passage of the Arab delegation to and from the truce negotiations. Later the Coldstream's CO Lt.-Col. Chandos – Pole was wounded by a Jewish sniper when escorting five ambulances in an attempt to evacuate some wounded Arabs.[265] The next day (23rd April), the battalion was reinforced by its no. 1 Company flown from England with the Second-in-Command Maj. B.E. Luard, who was promoted on arrival to Lt.-Colonel and appointed CO.[266]

40 Royal Marines Commando had arrived in late January 1948 from Malta and were made responsible for the security of the port including escorts for illegal Jewish immigrants (IJI) to internment camps in Cyprus.[267] Inside the port the Marines were faced with the Sisyphian task of trying to stem the constant pilfering from the port's warehouses. Now that the Coldstreamers had redeployed, the Marines manned all their previous positions near the port, where they soon came under Jewish fire. An officer from "B" Troop was wounded in the back from a burst of Bren fire.

> Reaction was rapid. Immediately a patrol of two N.C.O.s and two Marines went out to get the sniper. Working their way through a warren of buildings, with bullets whining overhead, they eventually succeeded in finding [the sniper] and killing him.[268]

Another Jewish sniper,

> whose accuracy had caused a traffic jam in Kingsway, was spotted firing from the windows of a house cased with armour plating. An armoured car squirted covering fire whilst a PIAT anti tank gun from "X" Troop was moved up into positon. To the delight of the weapon's crew, three rounds were enough to blow the sniper to bits, and his sheltering armour.[269]

These incidents were caused by Jewish fire on the entrance to the port, contrary to Haganah orders.[270] After two Marines' officers were wounded, one of them the Marines' doctor,

> Fire was returned and with the aid of the 37mm. gun of one of our Staghounds, quite a number of these snipers were silenced for good. A mortar position, which had landed several bombs near one of our dock-yard camps and had killed some Mauritian Pioneers in their camp, was also put out of action by the Staghound's gun.[271]

The accounts indicate that the Marines assumed that the fire came from the Haganah's positions. However, the Coldstreamers reported that on 23rd

April there were still a few 'desperate Arabs' who 'started up at intervals in the day' in a number of areas including the East Gate of the port.[272]

It was the Coldstreamers understanding that following the Arab-Jewish negotiations a truce was verbally agreed upon, according to which

> The Arabs should be allowed first to remove their dead, wounded, women and children, and then to leave Haifa themselves by boats organized from the docks and by convoys of trucks. All their arms would be taken from them by British Troops at the road blocks and these arms would be given over to the Jews after May 15th. Every facility was to be made for Palestinian Arabs to be shipped to Acre.[273]

A serious problem facing the Coldstreamers were Jews looting Arab property which began with house to house searches.[274] Soon the Haganah lost control. The Coldstream's sitrep for 27th April reported 'rumours of the Jewish Agency sending in further leaders [to take charge of the situation] were heard. Leaflets were dropped warning looters that they would be shot on sight'.[275] The general chaos, the desperation of the Arab population, and the temporary absence of effective authority were apparently too great a temptation for some of the British troops as well. The Coldstream Battalion's orders for 24th April warned:

> All ranks are reminded yet again that it is a Court Martial offense to take anything from any Arab or Jewish property or to receive any presents or bribes from a foreigner without the permission of an officer.[276]

Meanwhile, the Royal Marines with the help of the Hussars were trying to cope with the flow of frightened refugees.

> The Arabs camped outside the gate [of the port] near the main Arab quarter and were let into the port whenever boats, either WD [War Department]Z Craft or schooners were available.
>
> The people were in a bad state and were in most cases frightened to go back into town to collect their belongings; they were continually asking for escorts and trucks to help them get their things. Many others went by road and several times 40 Commando vehicles took part in the convoys taking people up to the Syrian [Lebanese?] frontier. Very few of these refugees had any food with them, and it fell to us to provide it, as well as provide any medical attention which was required.[277]

While the Haganah was allowed to occupy all of the town outside the British zone, the Army was at pains to assert its authority within the zone partly to ensure a safe evacuation and partly, perhaps, to save face and preserve the troops' moral. There had been a question of the appropriate authority on the Jewish side. On the 23rd Carmel proclaimed independent

Figure 6.2 Haifa. A British soldier and Arab refugees in the Port of Haifa.
Source: Fred Czasnik; Courtesy of the I.D.F. Archive (file 30-1), Ministry of Defense, Israel.

Jewish rule in Haifa. Ten days later, on 3rd May, the local civilian lead-ership declared the transfer of all authority to its hands.[278] Within the zone tension between the Army and the Jews remained. According to the Coldstreamers,

> After the Jewish success in the Center of Haifa the Haganah were inclined to be very "cocky", and to think they controlled the town. The Battalion was in reserve in Peninsular Barracks while the rifle compa-nies did turns of duty in the town. During May and the beginning of June [before and after the end of the Mandate] our main duties have been patrolling the outskirts and main routes of the town and removing and smashing the arms of Jews walking about in the security zones and areas where weapons were forbidden to them.
>
> Patrols and searches of suspected Haganah houses were somewhat in-tensified after 15th May, the end of the mandate, when the Jews around Haifa thought that they could then do what they liked all over Palestine, but they soon realized their mistake in Haifa.[279]

But despite the bravado, the Army's authority and hold on the area was fast diminishing as reflected in the Coldstream's Battalion Orders:

24th April – 'There will be no more sea bathing whatever except at the authorized bathing beach near the eastern bound of the camp [Peninsular Barracks]'.

27th April – 'All ranks are reminded that they may NOT walk out of the Barracks unless they are armed with a rifle and 50 rounds of S.A.A. And are in parties of four'.[280]

Once again regimental traditions took over in creating distractions, as reported by the Sergeants' Mess,

> No entertainment or social life outside barracks meant that members soon resolved to make up for this by intense Mess entertainment. Saturday nights now see all present, with C.S.M. Reid in charge of the "dogs." The fun is fast and furious, sometimes profitable and always hilarious, and on Tuesdays the weekly euchre drive is attended in force and is very popular.[281]

Despite the tough talk of the Coldstreamers, life in the zone according to Brutton, on Brigade's staff, was 'completely quite'.[282] 'General Stockwell and Brigadier George Johnson seem to have sufficient time to join the Yacht Club and attend a meeting'. At the Club, wrote Brutton, there was 'a certain air of dressing for dinner on the Titanic as the ship sank slowly and the band played on'. It had a library stocked with thrillers and a bar with good whiskey.[283] The two and a half months spent in the Haifa enclave by the 1st Guards Brigade and the units under its command 'are certainly the most relaxed and positively active of the two and a half years I spent in Palestine. Certainly Haganah must take its share of the credit' (Figure 6.3).

Brutton's colleague Andrew Gibson-Watt explained: in Haifa 'there were British and Jewish spheres of occupation. By consent, we were allowed into theirs, but they were not allowed into ours'. After the occupation of Haifa, the Jews immediately invested all their energies and attention first in occupying the western Galilee in preparation for an invasion of the Lebanese Army (which never came) and then in fighting the invading Arab armies

Figure 6.3 Haifa. Royal Marines NCOs and Haganah fighters at the entrance to the port.
Source: Fred Czasnik; Courtesy of the I.D.F. Archive (file 7-2), Ministry of Defense, Israel.

following the end of the Mandate and the declaration of Israeli independence. The Jews had no interest in the last units of the British Army who, in any event, were on their way out.[284] The Brigade's staff motored 'almost every afternoon' to the Atlit beach at the southern tip of their zone. 'The Brigadier was able to pursue his lepidoptery. We were able, after the day's work, to go to one of the Jewish night-clubs up on Mount Carmel, or out by launch to one of the watchful navel ships'.[285]

The wait eventually calmed the Coldstreamers. They 'were taking it in turn to do company duty in the town, which after the Arab defeat was considered safe except for the menace of rogue terrorism from either community',[286] and even that danger receded.[287] 'There was a cinema for all ranks, otherwise entertainment for the officers was largely restricted to dining in each others' messes'.[288]

The lessening of operational tension affected discipline. Coldstreamers were reminded: 'Sentries will remain standing at all times. Bren Magazine and PIAT Amn Boxes are NOT put into Posts to act as chairs'.[289]

Until 15th May, there remained the unpleasant but, by now, far less violent, duty to transfer illegal Jewish immigrants to Cyprus, for a stay, which would obviously be brief. Two illegal ships were intercepted and brought to Haifa. The first, San Michele, renamed Mishmar Ha'Emeq, left France on 14th April with 782 passengers including about 200 small children and babies and 100 pregnant women. Their instructions were to resort to passive resistance only and they were transferred on the 24th April to Cyprus with an escort of an officer and thirty Coldstreamers.[290] It was followed by the Tadorue ("Nachshon") which had set sail from France on the same day (14th April) with 550 passengers mainly members of various Zionist youth movements who were ordered to resist British boarding parties. The ship was intercepted on 26th April and brought to Haifa. Some resistance was indeed shown during the boarding, necessitating the use of water cannons and teargas, but the passengers gave little trouble to their escort, possibly because of the bad weather during the voyage to Cyprus'.[291]

All this while 'the army trucks were ferrying ordnance stores, destined to the Canal Zone, from the Atlit ordnance depot to the Haifa docks and the waiting ships'.[292] With the operational tension dropping to minimal, 'certain officers and NCOS, largely of the RAOC and other corps concerned principally with the technical matters, were tempted to set up shop and sell government property'.[293] Those caught, including a Lieutenant-Colonel, a Captain, and quite a number of Quartermaster Sergeants, were brought before Gibson-Watt, who found himself 'deep into court-martialling speculative RAOC personnel'.[294]

The country north of the bay of Haifa up to the Lebanese border was the responsibility of the 2nd Battalion Middlesex Regiment, the Die Hards, under the command of the 1st Guards Brigade in Haifa. The battalion had spent some time in Palestine shortly after the War, moved to Egypt's Canal Zone (Fayid) for a year, and returned to Palestine in March 1947. Despite having to forego the delights of the proximity of an ATS Camp for which the Die Hards were responsible, they welcomed the change of scenery with the qualification that 'the nefarious activities of a certain section of the Jewish community are definitely not so welcome'.[295] The effect of Spring in the coastal plain was immediate. "B" Company stationed in Tel Litvinsky, east of Tel Aviv, pronounced the place:

> Quite a pleasant spot – the weather ideal – the scent of orange and lemon blossoms in the air–wild flowers growing in profusion around the tents – numbers of goldfinches trilling their tremulous song – and last, but not least, the comfort of wireless in our tents... although difficulty is experienced in the evenings, due to the inevitable efforts of stray dogs who seem determined to make themselves heard.[296]

Soon the battalion was on the move again. First (minus a company sent to guard the Lydda train terminal) to Kfar Vitkin, by the sea, north of Netanya, where it partook in the search for the two kidnapped British sergeants – Operation Tiger. But not even the gruesome execution of the sergeants by the IZL and the mining of the site[297] succeeded in dampening the Die Hards' spirits. 'We have come to expect this sort of thing as a part of our routine, and all ranks accept it cheerfully in spite of somewhat trying conditions'. Indeed, "D" Company's account of its part in the operation is curiously devoid of the standard expressions of outrage.[298]

> [E]verybody seemed pleased with the change from camp routine. Considerable ingenuity was seen in the building of bivouacs on the cordon [of Netanya], and in the way in which all made themselves as comfortable as conditions permitted. One "bivvy"... was most fortunately situated by a large water tank which offered a refreshing dip at the close of the day. One post in particular had a very good field of view, and Cpl. Davies was always to be found keenly observing the Jews, especially the females!... Cpl. Champkin... spent his spare moments collecting large peculiar insects and reptiles. ...By the time the operation concluded some of us were reluctant to return to camp as we had found life so agreeable.[299]

Back in camp the companies were soon busy with sports including cricket, basketball, football, tennis, boxing and swimming in the sea. As elsewhere 'Facilities already in existence at the new location were negligible; the ground was in a deplorable condition, but it was not long before first-class basketball and cricket pitches had been built'.[300] Seventeen sports committees had been formed. 'Officers were appointed in charge of each game, or activity and the system of champion company was reinstituted'.[301]

During the autumn of 1947, the Die Hards trained in Transjordan with the 3rd Brigade and a detachment under the 2nd Brigade in their wartime role of Medium Machine Gun (Vickers) crews and later as demonstrators of the operation of MMGs to the battalions of the 3rd Brigade.[302]

From Transjordan the battalion returned to Karkur, near Pardes Hana, and by the end of 1947 gradually concentrated in camp 253, near the Arab village of Sumeiriya, north of Acre, 'a troublesome Arab town',[303] on the road to the Jewish town of Nahariya. The battalion was to complete its delayed conversion from Machine Guns back to an Infantry Battalion,[304] which entailed forming a new Support Company with machine guns from the other companies and a mortar platoon, and the reorganization of companies "A" and "C". Company "D" was made responsible for Acre and its prison, "B" Company had been temporarily sent to Safad. The rest 'had an illegal ship to deal with,'[305] as well as numerous road blocks, convoy escorts, flag marches and the relief of Jewish settlements under attack. On 20th January, a company was sent to the help of kibbutz Yehiam, which was attacked by the ALA and local Arabs. The company arrived after the attackers withdrew and returned with six wounded from the kibbutz who were brought to Nahariya.[306] From 18th January to 27th February, "C" Company was sent to occupy 'a very pleasant and compact hill camp' vacated by the TJFF near kibbutz Eilon, on the Lebanese border, where guard duty was light 'and the change of countryside is much appreciated, those people with the Battalion in Palestine will know how tired one becomes of the same view through the "wire".'[307] Similarly, "D" Company in Acre inhabited a small camp 'ideally situated on the seashore, and with spring-like weather... bathing and fishing are the order of the day.'[308] Before long "D" company suffered its first fatal casualty in a prison riot with the result that the number of sentries were increased. But once the prison windows were blocked the additional sentries were removed and life went back to normal.

The Die Hards' magazine summarized the Battalion's last three months in Palestine as 'a period of great activity and considerable interest'.[309] Unlike many other battalions who felt that by withdrawing from contested areas ahead of schedule and by leaving behind them chaos rather than the law and order they were initially committed to preserving, they had failed in their mission, the 2nd Middlesex felt that although the security situation had reduced the effectiveness of their efforts it had also 'given us the satisfaction of having a worthwhile job of work to do in maintaining order'.[310] Their sum operational activities included

> five flag marches, three operations to end fighting between Jews and Arabs, demolition of two blockhouses, three turn-outs in support of the prison authorities at Acre, and regaining possession of the GOC's car, which had been held up at an Arab road block. In addition the Battalion has provided a very great number of road block parties, as well as routine daily protection of essential military and civilian convoys.[311]

Although the 'Security restrictions have hampered recreation', they did not prevent the Die Hards From competing in various sports. It had 'reached the final of the 6th Airborne Divisional Inter-Unit Boxing, provided two winners in the divisional Individual Boxing Championships and one in the Palestine Command Championships, and came second in the Divisional Cross-Country Running Championship', meanwhile the constant fighting proved extremely inconvenient.

> Jewish detonation of an Arab explosives convoy wrecked the power-lines, depriving us of electricity, and thus also of running water and camps cinema shows, for over a month. In addition C.S.E [Combined Services Entertainment] shows have ceased. What it meant to the Battalion to have the Band here can therefore be imagined.[312]

When HQ Company had planned a sporting rifle meeting, in turned out that 'unfortunately the local Arabs looted the ranges the night before'.

The western Galilee had its share of dramatic events. On 17th March, the Haganah ambushed and destroyed at the northern entrance to Kiryat Motzkin the aforementioned Arab munitions convey killing the Arab commander of Haifa el-Haniti.[313] The Arabs retaliated with a series of local, un-coordinated attacks in Haifa.

The demolition of the ammunition carrying trucks dislodged an electric transformer thereby cutting the power supply to the western Galilee north of Kiryat Motzkin including the 2nd Middlesex's camp. The next morning (18th March) two teams of the Palestine Electric Company with an escort of two carriers of the Royal Horse Artillery, stationed near Acre, went to fix the line. One team remained in Kiryat Motzkin and the other, four technicians in an armoured tender, and the two carriers, one in front and one behind, with ten Gunners, proceeded towards Acre to mend a cable in the RAF camp which had been damaged a few days earlier.[314] While passing near the Moslem cemetery east of Acre an Arab ambush detonated a mine under the leading carrier and then attacked and killed the four technicians and five gunners. The remaining five made their escape north in their carrier while firing on their assailants.[315]

There followed a series of attacks, mainly on vehicles by Jews and Arabs throughout the Acre sub-district which involved the 2nd Middlesex in a number of minor operations aimed at restoring the peace. These included, on Good Friday, the recovery of the GOC's car by the carrier section, after it had been abandoned when fired upon by Arabs and then taken by the Jews. 'Fortunately the GOC was not travelling in the car at that time'.[316] The electric cables were only mended in late April by Jewish technicians covered by the Die Hards.

> As a result of their efforts we enjoyed the luxury of electric light and pumped water again for 24 hours until our neighbours, a Railway

Operating Squadron R.E., sheared through the cables once more when evacuating a railway engine by road on a transporter.[317]

Towards the end of March the Jewish side suffered one of its worst defeats in a series of bloody setbacks when a convoy to kibbutz Yehiam was attacked and destroyed on 27th March. After the aforementioned road attacks the local Arab and Jewish leadership agreed (23th March) to reopen the main road in western Galilee to each other's traffic. On the 26th, a Jewish convoy from Nahariya reached the three kibbutzim along the Lebanese border. At the time reports were received by the Haganah of the intention of the locally stationed ALA battalion and militias from the Arab villages to attack Jewish convoys. The ALA's command resented the truce agreed upon without its consent whereas the peaceful journey of the convoy on the 26th created on the Jewish side, a false sense of security. The convoy was attacked near the cemetery of the Arab village of al-Kabri. Forty-seven of its ninety passengers were killed and its vehicles destroyed.[318]

Ordinarily by this stage, the Haganah was reluctant to ask for the Army's help but in the absence of a close enough reserve and in view of the seriousness of the convoy's plight the 2nd Middlesex in Sumeiriya were called. The inlying platoon and the carrier section left immediately followed by the rest of the battalion.

> Movement was necessarily slow owing to considerable Arab and Jewish firing, and by the time the Battalion had reached the scene of the ambush darkness had fallen. Owing to standing orders from Brigade H.Q. prohibiting operations by night, the Battalion had to withdraw back to camp under-cover of the carriers.[319]

Later that evening the RHA Sextons, in support of the 2nd Middlesex fired twelve rounds of HE twenty-five pounders on the village of Kabri.[320]

The next morning (28th March) the inlying platoon and the carrier section returned to the battlefield. A truce had been arranged allowing a party of Palestine Police to tow to Nahariya the burnt vehicles and to collect the mutilated bodies of the Jews killed, 'a most unpleasant and depressing task'.[321] Yet the regimental account remained relatively casual. The inlying platoon consisted of the Regimental Band. Consequently 'one of our almost regular Sunday morning classical concerts had to be cancelled as... we were called out to clear up the mess after an Arab-Jewish battle the previous day'.[322]

While its shrinking establishment meant an increase in the operational load on its soldiers, the 2nd Middlesex maintained a laid back attitude towards events which was helped by a minimal number of casualties, and made possible by maintaining cordial relations with all parties (the Druze villages to the east remained neutral). It offered to help a kibbutz to evacuate its children,[323] and its response to exchanges of fire was not excessive, and was even-handed (including the demolition of a Jewish position near kibbutz Evron for firing on Arab traffic).[324] Nor was it over ambitions in its attempts to pacify the area. In the more remote Arab villages along the Lebanese border the war between Jews and Arabs appeared to be no more than a rumour. Whenever a patrol sent by "C" Company from the Eilon camp,

> visited an Arab village the complete patrol would be invited indoors to coffee or food. At first (when we were uneducated in these matters) sentries would be placed on vehicles, but the Arabs explained that wireless sets and vehicles were their responsibility while members of the patrol were their guests, and we soon came to appreciate their deep social code. At other times W.D. property was fair game and much sought after.[325]

Indeed the Die Hards appear to have possessed a rare ability to enjoy themselves, whatever the circumstances. Ordered to block the road to Acre after the incident of 18th March, soldiers from "D" Company 'digging in across the road, spent five days very happily roughing it and returned to camp extremely sunburnt and in the best of spirits'.[326] A few days later (21.3) the Haganah blew up a railway bridge outside Acre and derailed the train. 'The latter became a source of much amusement, as nobody could be found near the scene of the wreckage and no authority seemed interested in it least of all the railway company – and it became known as "'D' Company's train".[327]

A fly in the ointment were the news of the 2nd Battalion's impending dissolution and its amalgamation with the 1st Battalion. The very prospect 'aroused horror and consternation, especially among the regulars'.[328]

During the battle of Haifa (21–22 April), "B" Company on detachment since 1st March was defence company of HQ of the 1st Guards Brigade where it enjoyed 'a grandstand view of the fireworks in the city below,'[329] Two platoons guarded the railway shops and the oil refineries but fortunately 'only had to open fire once'. "D" Company was sent to stop an Haganah attack on Acre on the night of 25–26 April. A company of the 21st Battalion, Carmeli Brigade, supported by 3" mortars deployed south of Acre and occupied "Napoleon's Hill" overlooking the town from the east. A Palmach unit advanced in armoured cars from the east as far as the Moslem cemetery and the first line of houses, demolishing on its way the headquarters of the local National Guard.[330] "D" Company prevented by Army orders from operating at night, waited in slit trenches until morning. At 05:00 hours, the 1st RHA shelled Napoleon's Hill while the inlying platoons from camp 253 and from "D" Company led, in carriers, the rest of the battalion in an attack on the Haganah lines which were quickly abandoned.[331]

Some of the shells fired by the Haganah mortars landed in Acre prison enabling most of the prisoners to break out. The remaining Jewish prisoners, characterized as 'criminal lunatics' were transported by the Die Hards to the Jewish authorities in nearby Kiryat Chaim thereby ending the Battalion's responsibility for the prison's security.[332]

As a result of the battle of Haifa the town of Acre was swamped by Arab refugees, overwhelming the local authorities and Acre's antiquated infra-structure. Typhus soon broke out with the result that fifty-five men of "D" Company and members of the Palestine Police were admitted to the British Military Hospital a few miles away, near the air strip north of Haifa, where two of the soldiers died. The rest of "D" Company was quarantined in a camp next to the hospital with the remaining British policemen. The remainder of the battalion joined in camp 253 by a troop of Sextons secured columns of Arab refugees on their way to Lebanon. The last of these passed on 3rd May after which the ALA destroyed the Na'aman bridge[333] presumably to prevent the complete abandonment of Acre. Thus, with the main coastal road cut, 'the Battalion's continued presence north of Acre was now no longer necessary or desirable' and on 6th May it moved to the Haifa air strip and reinforced the Guards.[334] Meanwhile, the Royal Engineers replaced the destroyed bridge with a Bailey bridge which was used during the Army's withdrawal.[335]

As might be expected the final withdrawal from camp 253 provided its surrealistic moments.

> The Arabs near Camp 253, with their uncanny instinct for loot, gathered like voltures in the surrounding area, waiting for the final withdrawl; a difference of opinion between representatives of two local villages as to who should take possession caused a sharp exchange of shots, which eventually died down when those responsible discovered that the guns of the 1st RHA were trained in their direction and that the Arab Liberation Army in any case proposed to disposes both contesting parties. The Army's [ALA] representative (who, it proved, had won two British decorations as a Warrant Officer in H.M. Forces during the 1939–1945 War) finally took over the camp from Lt.-Col. A.D. Henderson, with such formality that "long rolls" and an Arab Garrison Engineer and Barrack Officer were almost expected to appear at any moment.[336]

The question of the identity of the new authorities confronted the 2nd Battalion's CO Lt.-Col. Henderson in another manner when informed in the Haifa airstrip.

> that a party of Jews had arrived with the intention of declaring the airfield to be under joint British-Jewish control, and of hoisting their flag, the Star of David. A quick turn out of every available man and the manning of 4 M.M.G.s which the Battalion had been able to retain convinced the Jews that any such attempt might prove unwise, and they withdrew leaving their spokesman to be taken by the C.O. to H.Q. Palestine (by then located in Haifa) for discussion of the position of the civilian airlines on the airfield. H.Q. Palestine subsequently permitted the flag to be hoisted.[337]

Furthermore, it was agreed in a meeting with General Stockwell (29 April) that the airfield would be open to Jewish civilian flights and that an Haganah liaison officer be appointed to co-ordinate its use.[338]

On 13–14 May, the Haganah Carmeli Brigade occupied the coastal road from Haifa north to the border and occupied the adjacent Arab villages. On the 16th, following the formal end of the Mandate it attacked Acre and on the 17th the town surrendered. The Haganah, about to became Israel's Defense Force (IDF), now occupied the whole coast of western Galilee as far as the Lebanon border.

Also on the 16th a few miles away the 2nd Middlesex celebrated Albuhera Day in Haifa's airfield,

> The band played at Reveille and a team of Corporals, L/Corporals and Privates defeated the Officers, Warrant Officers and Sergeants at Cricket during the morning. The Sergeants' Mess was entertained by the officers… before lunch, and during the afternoon all ranks thoroughly enjoyed an excellent fun fair… members of the Signal Platoon ran a most successful electric roulette wheel [other teams] operated a dice den, …[a] greasy pole… throwing a cricket ball on a chip flint wicket [which made] googly bowlers of most of us, …a spectacular financial coup somewhat disguised as a dog race,

etc. In the evening the dance band visited "D" Company still in nearby quarantine, a film was screened for all the rest and the Officers were entertained by the Warrant Officers and Sergeants in the Sergeants' Mess.[339]

Notes

1   Major R.D. Wilson, *Cardon and Search with 6th Airforce Division in Palestine* (Aldershot: Gale and Polden, 1949), 143.
2   *Statistical Abstract of Palestine 1944–1945*, 23.
3   Ibid., 22.
4   *Times*, 19 June 1946.
5   *The White Lancer and the Vedette*, vol. 30, May 1948, 4.
6   See [Hebrew] Ezra Danin, *Zioni bechol tnai, part 1* (Jerusalm: Kidoom, 1987), 220–221.
7   [Hebrew] Itamar Radai, *The Third Battalion the 'Galilee Battalion' of the Yiftach Palmach Brigade* (Mikve Israel: Yehuda Dekel Library, 2014), 39–40.
8   [Hebrew] 'The attack on Kfar Szold', in Binyamin Etzioni (ed.), *Ilan Vashelach. The battles of the Golani Brigade* (Ma'arachot, n.d.), 78. The book is one of the brigades' histories published by the IDF after the war.
9   Blake, *A History*, 243. At the time "B" Squadron was running railway patrols.
10   *The White Lancer and Vedette*, May 1948, 4.
11   According to the account in Etzioni, 79, the call from the kibbutzim for assistance was relayed through kibbutz Kfar Giladi near Metula.
12   Blake, *A History*, 243–244.
13   Ibid., 244.
14   Ibid.

15 [Hebrew] Report by the commander of Dan, 12 January 1948, in *Kibbutz Dan in the War of Independence 1947–1948* (Kibbutz Dan, 1978), 60–62.

16 Blake, *A History*, 244.

17 Etzioni, 79.

18 10:30 hours according to the Israeli account.

19 Blake, *A History*, 244.

20 Ibid. See also Major R. Stacle, 'A Parachutist in Palestine', in *Household Magazine*, Spring 1948, 10. Major Stacle had been sent with a Platoon and 3" mortars to the Lancers' HQ in Metula. He described the scenes in Kfar Szold: 'like a race meeting.'

21 *Palestine Post*, 11 January 1948.

22 Etzioni, 79.

23 Blake, *A History*, 244

24 [Hebrew] Avraham Sela, 'The Arab Liberation Army', 215; Yoav Gelber, *Palestine 1948*, 125.

25 Wilson, *Cordon and Search*, 148.

26 Ibid., 152.

27 Roy Fullick, *Shan Hackett The Pursuit of Exactitude* (Barnsley: Leo Cooper, 2003), 168–169.

28 Sela, 214.

29 Ibid. After the war, Shishakli led a successful coup in Syria and became Prime Minister, 1952 and President, 1953 until deposed in 1954.

30 For a detailed account of the battle as seen by the defenders, see [Hebrew] David Coren, *The Western Galilee in the War of Independence* (Ministry of Defence, 1988), 44–49.

31 Coren, 45–48, National Army Museum 1999-11-190-23 Dept. APFS, 2nd Bn. Middlesex Regiment War Diary 1 January 1948 – 31 March 1948, entry for 28th January. Yechiam was identified as Kefar Jiddin, Jiddin being the ruins of a crusader fort which was part of the kibbutz. In the British 1:100,000 map the place in marked Khirbet Jiddin.

32 Coren, 48–49.

33 Sela, 216.

34 Coren, 49.

35 Sela, 218.

36 [Hebrew] Shmaryahu Ben Pazi, *Community at War. The Jews of Safad in the years 1947–1948* (Jerusalem: Ariel, 2006), 13. [Hebrew] Mustafa Abbasi, *Arabs and Jews in a Mixed City* (Jerusalem: Yad Izhak Ben-Zvi, 2015), 65–67. Abbasi estimated the population in April 1948 as 10,950 Arabs and 1,900 Jews.

37 '"B" Company', in *The Die-Hards*, vol. 8, No. 5 (March, 1948), 152.

38 Ibid.

39 Ibid., 152–153.

40 Wilson, 152, '2nd Battalion the Middlesex Regiment [D.C.O.] [Duke of Cambridge's Own] "B" Company' in *The Die Hards*, vol. 8, No. 5, March 1948, and No. 8, September 1948. The battalion was reinforced by 1st Regiment Horse Artillery and 52nd Observation Regiment R.A.

41 2nd Middlesex War Diary, 17 January 1948.

42 *Ben Gurion Diary*, vol. 1, 187n5.

43 Etzioni, 80–81.

44 '1st (Guards) Parachute Battalion', *Household Magazine*, Spring 1948, 41.

45 Ibid., 42.

46 Gelber, 55.

47 John Nelson, *Always a Grenadier*, printed ms., 62.

48 *Statistical Abstract 1944–1945*, 22–23.

49 [Hebrew] Zrubavel Gilad (ed.), *The Palmach book vol. 2* (Hakkibutz Hameuchad, c. 1953), 129.
50 *The Household Magazine*, Spring 1948, 42.
51 Ibid.
52 Gelber, 54.
53 Nelson, 63.
54 Ibid.
55 Ibid.
56 Ibid., 64.
57 Ibid.
58 [Hebrew] Elchanan Oren, 'The campaign in the approaches to Haifa April, 1948', in *Ma'arachot*, 1976, 54–60, 251–252.
59 King's College, London, Liddel, Hart Centre, Stockwell Papers 6/12/5 Lt. Col. D.M.L. Gordon Watson, 'Rosh Pinna, 17 April 1948.
60 T.N.A. W.O. 261/301 Quarterly Historical Report of 1st Battalion Irish Guards, Quarter ending 31 March 1948, signed 16 April.
61 '1st battalion Irish Guards', *The Household Magazine*, Spring 1948, 38.
62 'Report and the events.'
63 W.O. 261/301.
64 *The Household Magazine*, Spring 1948, 38.
65 [Hebrew] Yehezkel Hameiri, *Safad in the Independence War 2nd ed.* (Ministry of Defense, 1989), 15.
66 'Report on the events.'
67 Sela, 215.
68 Wilson, 146.
69 Ibid.
70 W.O. 216/301.
71 [Hebrew] Hameiri, 31–32.
72 W.O. 261/301.
73 Ibid.
74 [Hebrew] Alon Kadish, *The British Army's Evacuation of Safad* (Jerusalem: Ariel, 2006), 89–90, published with Shmaryahu Ben-Pazi, 'Community at war'.
75 Ibid., 90.
76 'Report on the events'.
77 Ibid.
78 Abbasi, 52–55.
79 Kadish, 91.
80 'Report on the events'.
81 Kadish, 91–92.
82 Peter Verney, *The Micks The Story of the Irish Guards* (London: Peter Davies, 1970), 172. Also 'Report of the events', A photograph of the event in *Irish Guards The First Hundred Years 1900–2000* (Staplehurst: Spellmount Publishers, 2000), 124.
83 Kadish, 92–93.
84 *The Household Magazine*, Summer 1948, 81.
85 T.N.A. W.O. 275/19 6 ABDIV OP INTR No. 7, 25 March 1948.
86 On the 2nd April the 6th Airborne Headquarters closed down.
87 Mounted on M-10 tank destroyers, replacing their original 3" (76mm) guns.
88 Colonel G.S. Hatch, 'Terrorist Raid', in Major Maurice Tugwell (ed.), *The Unquiet Peace: Stories from the Post-War Army* (London: Allan Wingate, 1957), 48.
89 It is on the coat of arms of numerous towns including Karkur and, today, Pardes Hanah-Karkur.

90 Hatch, 50. See also statement by Peter G. Upton (2001), a former gunner in 12th Anti-Tank, in R.A. Archive, Woolwich, URG 25.
91 Hatch, 49–50.
92 [Hebrew] Dov B. Ben-Meir, *Brushing the Cows' Teeth. Youth in an Agricultural School in Eretz Yisrael* (Alpha Communications, 1999), 262–264.
93 See in R.A. Archive UR6 25 statements by Upton and Leonard Wykes.
94 Hatch, 51–54. See also statement by Arthur Creech Jones, Secretary of State for the Colonies in the Commons 8 April 1948. *Porliamentary Debates (Hausard) Fifth series*, vol. 449, and *House of Commons Official Report, seventh volume of session 1947–1948*, London: HMSO, 1948, 358–359. *Times*, 7 April 1948. T.N.A. W.O. 261/574 Fortnightly Intelligence Newsletter no. 65 issued by HQ British Troops in Palestine, April 48 and no. 66, 21 April 48.
   [Hebrew] Joseph Evron, *Gidi: The Jewish Insurgency against the British in Palestine* (Ministry of Defense, 2001), 296–301. Lazar, *Jaffa*, 107–111, Niv. 139–140.
95 Hatch, 53.
96 Ibid.
97 Hatch, 57. Upton.
98 *Times*, 8 April 1948.
99 Ibid.
100 *Paliamentory Debates*, 358–359.
101 Ibid, 360.
102 Ibid. See Kenneth Rose's biographical article in Lord Blake and C.S. Nicholls, (eds.) *The Dictionary of National Biography 1971–1980* (Oxford: Oxford University Press, 1986), 1024–1026.
103 *Parliamentary Debates*, 361.
104 Ibid., 772.
105 *Times*, 10 April 1948.
106 Montgomery, 385.
107 Ibid., 384.
108 Montgomery, 385.
109 Many Shinwell, *Lead with the Left: My First Ninety Six Years* (London: Cassell, 1981), 142. See also Hugh Dalton, *High Tide and After Memoirs 1945–1960* (London: Frederick Muller Ltd, 1962), 246, and Peter Slowe, *Many Shinwell: An Authorized Biography* (London and Boulder, CO: Pluto Press, 1993), 237.
110 Slowe, 244–246.
111 Montgomety, 419.
112 Stockwell papers, 6/19, Stockwell to H.Q. Palestine. Subject: withdrawl from Palestine, 1 March 1948.
113 Stockwell papers, 6/1/44, Brigadier Kirkman (Chief of Staff, H.Q. Palestine) to Commander 1 Inf. Dir. GABDIV, 2 Inf. Bde., Subject: Internal Security, 29 March 1948.
114 T.N.A. W.O. 261/1574 Fortnightly Intelligence Newsletter No. 66, issued by H.Q. British troops in Palestine, for the period 2359 hrs 7 April – 2359 hrs 19 April 1948.
115 A common Jewish practice in 1948 was to glorify positions, sectors, roads and even whole communities by naming them after heroic battles and operations in World War Two. Extreme examples are the "Burma Road" (about six kilometers) and "Negbagrad", a kibbutz of about 375 residents.
116 [Hebrew] Meir Meivar-Meiberg, *Beleagured and Liberated, The Full Story of Safad Under Siege in 1948* (Tel Aviv: Milo, 1989), 220–221. Wilson 232 dated the change to 2nd April when the Army was asked to intervene in stopping the exchanges of fire between the quarters.

117 T.N.A. W.O. 261/301 Quarterly Historical Report 1st Bn I G quarter ending 20 June 1948, Appendix A.
118 Verney, 173.
119 Ibid.
120 T.N.A. W.O. 275/54 6 AB Div Log of Events February – May 48,070920 and Sitrep 071920.
121 *Palestine Post*, 8 April 1948, [Hebrew] *Al Hamishmar*, 6 April 1948.
122 [Hebrew] Chaim Kahana, 'Lehavot Habashan in the Fire of Attacks', *The Book of Hashomer Hatzair vol.3* (Merchavia: Sifriyat Hapoalim, 1964), 259–260.
123 Kahana, 260 and W.O. 275/54.
124 Kahana, 261–262, Radai, *The Third Battalion*, 49.
125 [Hebrew] Shalev, 'Tiberias was the first to be liberated', *Davar*, 3 May 1948, Moshe Zacharin, *The Forty Day Campaign to Free Tiberias* (Ministy of Defense, 1993), 28–30.
126 [Hebrew] IDF Archive 1951/128,18 Zeev Optocski (Haganah commander of Tiberias) to Golani (local Haganah brigade) report of events, 10 April 1948.
127 Omitting the massacre of Safad's Jews in 1929.
128 Report on the events.
129 Meiberg, 224–225, Gordon-Watson, in his report, mistook the Jewish attack on the 11th for an Arab one.
130 *The Household Magazine*, Summer 1948, 81.
131 Report on the events.
132 Ibid.
133 Meiberg, 233.
134 T.N.A. W.O. 275/19 H.Q. North Sector to H.Q. Craforce, 13 April 1948.
135 Report on the events.
136 For the mood within the Jewish Community, see Dan Kurtzman, *Genesis 1948 The First Arab-Israeli War* (New York and Cleveland: The World Publishing Company, 1970), 162.
137 Meiber, 234.
138 Report on the events.
139 Meiber, 235.
140 Ibid., 236–237, and Report of the events.
141 Report of the events.
142 Meiber, 237.
143 Report of the events.
144 Ibid.
145 Ibid.
146 Ibid.
147 Ibid.
148 Ibid.
149 Meiber, 250–251. According to Gordon-Watson's report, 'one dead Jew, two old men and one woman'.
150 Ibid., 141–142.
151 Report of the events.
152 Ibid.
153 Ibid., and WO 261/301 Diary 16 April.
154 Report of the events.
155 *Statistical Abstract 1944–1945*, 22.
156 Ibid.
157 Khalidi, *All that remains*, 526–527.
158 Ibid., 537
159 [Hebrew] Nachum Av, *The Struggle for Tiberias* (Ministry of Defense, 1991), 22–31; Gershon Rivlin (ed.), *La'esh ve'Lamagen*, 3rd ed. (Ministry of Defense, 1964), 178–179.

160 Av, 61–63.

161 Ibid., 62.

162 [Hebrew] Yitzchak Shusterman, 'Stages in the battles of the town', in Etzioni, *Ilan va'shelach*, 107.

163 IDF Archive 1951/128, 18 Barak (Intelligence) to Brigade Intelligence Officer, 'Why did the Arabs leave Tiberias', April 1948.

164 Ibid and Etzioni, 107.

165 Wilson, 197.

166 *Forty Days*, 36–37.

167 Ibid., 37–38.

168 Ibid., 40–42.

169 T.N.A. W.O. 261/223 Quarterly Historical Report of The Third The King's Own Hussars for the Quarter ending 31 March 1948.

170 W.O. 261/223.

171 Ibid.

172 Hector Bolito, *The Galloping Third: The Story of the 3rd The King's Own Hussars* (London: John Murray, 1963), 309.

173 W.O. 261/223 Lt.Col. C.A. Peel C.O. of 3rd the King's Own Hussars, 'Report on the Negotiations over the Mishmar Ha'Emeq fighting.'

174 An analysis of the battle in [Hebrew] Elchanan Oren, 'The campaign in the outskirts of Haifa, April 1948', in *Ma'arachot*, 251–252, October 1976, 54–60.

175 W.O. 261/223 'Report'.

176 Ibid.

177 Ibid.

178 [Hebrew] Amiram Ezov, *Mishmar Ha'Emeq Will Stand* (Or Yehuda: 'Kinneret Zmora-Bitan, Dvir, 2013), 135–139.

179 A somewhat different version of the details according to the memories of one of the Jewish representatives in ibid.

180 W.O. 261/223 'Report'.

181 Ibid.

182 Oren, 59.

183 W.O. 261/223 'Report'.

184 Ibid.

185 W.O. 261/223 Quarterly Report.

186 Ibid., 'Report'.

187 Ben Gurion *Diary*, vol. 1, 356, entry for 19 April. Sade reporting on the battle.

188 *Statistical Abstract 1944–1945*, 22, and [Hebrew] *Bemivchan Hakravot 1948–1949* (*Davar* yearbook), 394. The main study of Arab Haifa in 1948 is [Hebrew] Tamir Goren, *The Fall of Arab Haifa in 1948* (Sde Boker: the Ben-Gurion Research Institute, The Ministry of Defense, and the Haganah Historical Archives, 2006).

189 Benjamin Shwadran, *The Middle East, Oil and Great Powers* (New York: Prager, 1955), 410–411.

190 Ibid., 413.

191 *A Survey of Palestine vol. 2* [1946] (Washington, DC: Institute for Palestinian Studies, 1991), 856–857.

192 Goren, 47.

193 Wilson, 97.

194 Ibid., 156. For an early example see [Hebrew] Zadok Eshel, *Ma'arachot Ha'haganah Be'Chaifa* (Ministry of Defense, 1978), 301–302.

195 [Hebrew] David Niv, *In Open War (1947–1948) The Irgun Zvai Leumi Part Six* (Tel Aviv: Klausner Institute, 1980), 19.

196 [Hebrew] David Coren, *The Refineries' Massacre and Security in Places of Mixed Employment in Haifa – 1948* (Ramat Efal: The Center for the Study of the History of the Haganah, 1988), 17.

197 Wilson, 157–158, T.N.A. W.O. 261/223 Quarterly Report.
198 W.O. 261/223.
199 Ibid. Composite Rations were a pack of a day's rations for six men.
200 Ibid.
201 Maurice Tugwell, *Herzl Street* (Princeton, NJ: X libris, 1997), 68.
202 Goren, 64. For a detailed chronicle of events during December 1947, see Coren, 7–11.
203 Wilson, 172.
204 Goren, 191.
205 Tugwell, 68.
206 W.O. 261/223.
207 Wilson, 168.
208 Ibid., 170.
209 Ibid., 172.
210 For instance, Haifa's Haganah commander in [Hebrew] Moshe Carmel, *Ma'ara-chot Ha'zafon*, 2nd ed. (IDF and Ha'kibbutz Hameuchad, 1949), 16–17.
211 Carmel, 28–32. Also Eshel, 340–341. Carmel was designated Commander of Haifa's Haganah Brigade – "Carmeli".
212 Wilson, 173–174. Carmel in his account mentioned the Jeep's plight but only because the Haganah first mistook it for its own, delayed on its way back to the Jewish lines.
213 Goren, 104, Maan Abu Nowar, *The Jordanian-Israeli War*, 41–42.
214 Goren, 115.
215 Goren, 120, Eshel, 338–339.
216 Abu Nowar, 43.
217 Goren, 123–124.
218 T.N.A. W.O. 261/226 1st Regt R.H. Artillery for quarter ending 31 March 1948, and '1st Regiment, Royal Horse Artillery-Fayid', in *The Gunner*, vol. 30, No. 6 (September, 1948), 157. The troop remained in Haifa until April.
219 Wilson, 176.
220 Ibid., 176–177.
221 Wilson, *Tempting the Fates*, 146.
222 T.N.A. WO 275/118 (also Stockwell papers 6/13) 'Report by CO North Sector Major General H.C. Stockwell... Leading up to and after the Arab-Jewish clashes in Haifa on 21/22 April 1948' signed 24 April 1948.
223 Max Arthur, *Men of the Red Barret Airborne Forces 1940–1990* (London: Warner Books, 1992), 442.
224 [Hebrew] Ya'akov Salomon, *In My Own Way* (Jerusalem: Edanim Publishers, 1980), photograph between pages 304 and 305.
225 'Coldstream Guards 1st Battalion', in *Household Brigade Magazine*, Summer 1948, 77. Also T.N.A. W.O. 201/297 Quarterly Historical Report 1st Bn. Cold-stream Guards for the quarter ending 30st June 1948.
226 Ibid.
227 Ibid.
228 Wellington Barracks London, Coldstream Guards Archive, Battalion Orders No. 66 [17th] April 1948, No. 78 [19th] April 1948
229 W.O. 275/118 Report by GOC.
230 Ibid.
231 Philip Brutton, *A Captin's Mandate Palestine 1946–1948* (London: Lee Cooper, 1996), 136. See also Wilson, *Cordon and Search*, 191.
232 Salomon, 124.
233 W.O. 275/118 Report by GOC.
234 Ibid.
235 T.N.A. W.O. 201/297 Battalion Sitrep No. 15.

236 W.O. 275/118 Report by GOC.
237 Ibid., and W.O. 201/297.
238 W.O. 201/297 Sitrep 211630.
239 An official detailed Jewish account of the battle in Eshel, *Ma'arachot*.
240 Walid Khalidi, 'The Fall of Haifa', in *Middle East Forum*, vol. 35, No. 10 (December, 1959), 25, 26.
241 Ibid., 26.
242 [Hebrew] Khaviv Can'an, *Betset Habritim* (Tel Aviv, Gadish Books, 1958), ch. 6.
243 Dan Kurtzman, *Genesis 1948 the First Arab-Israeli War* (New York and Cleveland: The World Publishing Company, 1970), 152–153. See also J.P. Riley, *The Life and Campaigns of General Hughie Stokwell*, 178.
244 [Hebrew] Zadok Eshel, *Aba Khoushi – Man of Haifa* (Ministry of Defense, 2002), 103, 105.
245 Ibid., 107. See also Ben Gurion *Diary*, vol. 1, 371, entry for 26 April 1948.
246 Cna'an, 126.
247 Ibid., 177.
248 Ibid.
249 Ibid., 128.
250 Carmel, 85–86.
251 Law, while serving as a Captain on the staff of the first High Commissioner married in 1921 Minna Weitzmann M.D., sister of Chaim Weitzmann. She died in 1925. Law's second wife, Minna's niece, died in 1931.
252 Riley, 178.
253 Cna'an, 128.
254 Brutton, 137 [Hebrew] Amos Goren, *Mordechai Makleff* (Tel Aviv: Am Oved, 2002), 86.
255 Riley, 173.
256 See Hillel Cohen, *Army of Shadows Palestinian Collaboration with Zionism, 1917–1948* (Oakland: University of California Press, 2008).
257 Goren, 135–136; Salomon, 127–131; Brutton, 138.
258 [Hebrew] Zadok Eshel, *Carmeli Brigade in the War of Independence* (Ministry of Defense, 1973), 148–149, Haj Muhamad Nimr el Khatib, Min Athar el Nakba (translated from Arabic) in *Be'eyney Ha'Oyev* (IDF, 1954), 23.
259 Riley, 181, Goren, 207–208, W.O. 275/118 Report by GOC.
260 Report by GOC.
261 Goren, 217–219.
262 Report by GOC.
263 Ibid., and Goren, 221.
264 W.O. 201/297 Battalion Sitrep No. 16.
265 W.O. 261/223 Quarterly Report 30 June.
266 Richard Crichton, *The Coldstream Guards 1946–1970* (The Coldstream Guards, 1972), 19.
267 T.N.A. W.O. 275/11 C. in C. Med to COMPAL 15 January 1948.
268 V.A.J.H., 'Last Days in Palestine Commandos' role in the Withdrawl', in *the Globe and Laurel* vol. LVI, No. 8 (August 1948), 232. According to an earlier account in *The Globe and Laurel*, No. 7, July 1948, two Jewish snipers were traced and killed.
269 'Last Days in Palestina.'
270 Eshel, *Ma'arachot*, 365. Mortar fire was also directed at the Arab market.
271 *The Globe and Laurel*, July 1948, 217, W.O. 261/223 Quarterly Report of the 3rd The King's Own Hussars for quarter ending 30 June 1948.
272 W.O. 201/297.
273 W.O. 201/297 Battalion Sitrep No. 17, 24th April, 1630 hours.

274 Ibid. Eshel, *Ma'arachot*, 378, some of the looters were Arabs.

275 W.O. 201/297 Sitrep No. 18, 27 April 1948.

276 Coldstream Archive, Battalion Orders to June 1948, No. 83 [24th] April 1948.

277 *The Globe and Laurel*, July 1948, 217. According to the Coldstreams Sitrep 18, the transfer of refugees was with 42 craft and 24 3 ton lorries, to Acre.

278 Eshel, *Ma'arachot*, 379, 384.

279 'Coldstream Guards', in *The Household Brigade Magazine*, Summer 1948, 77.

280 Battalion orders Nos. 83 and 86.

281 *The Household Magazine*, Summer 1948, 78. See also in ibid. 'Grenadier Guards', 74.

282 Brutton, 138.

283 Ibid., 138.

284 Gibson-Watt, 238.

285 Ibid., 239.

286 Brutton, 149.

287 Coldsteam Battalion Orders No. 98 [12] May, 1948 'Information has now been received that STERN and IZL are not likely to be active in this area. Walking out in IN BOUNDS Areas now in pairs.'

288 Brutton, 149.

289 Battalion orders No. 104 [19] May, 1948.

290 W.O. 201/297 Sitrep No. 18, 25th April. [Hebrew] Reuben Aharoni, *Leaning Masts. Ships of Jewish Illegal Immigration and Arms, after World War II* (edited by Efi Meltzer for the Center for the History of the defense force, the Haganah, 1997), 124–125, 202.

291 W.O. 201/297 Strep No. 19 27th April, and Aharoni, 126–127.

292 Gibson-Watt, 239.

293 Brutton, 142.

294 Gibson-Watt, 218, 238.

295 2nd Battalion News', *The Die Hards: The Journal of the Middlesex Regiment*, Inglis Barracks, Mill Hill, London, vol. VIII, No. 2 (June, 1947), 45.

296 Ibid., 47.

297 For a detailed account, see Bruce Hoffman, 453–457.

298 *The Die Hards*, No. 3, September 1947, 87.

299 Ibid., No. 4, December 1947, 87.

300 Ibid., No. 3, 91.

301 Ibid.

302 Ibid., No. 4, 15.

303 Ibid., No. 5, 1948, 151.

304 NAM 1999-11-190-23 Dept. APES, '2nd Bn the Middlesex Rgt (DCO) Trg. Directive No. 1'.

305 An Italian sail boat Archimidis (renamed Haumot Hameuchadot – "the U.N"), with 537 immigrants beached near Nahariya on 1st January 1948 and its passengers dispersed before the Army had time to apprehend them.

306 NAM 1999-11-190-33 Dept. APFs War Diary 1–2 January, *The Die Hards* No. 5, March 1948, 151–152.

307 *Die Hards*, No. 5, 153.

308 Ibid., 154.

309 Ibid., No. 6, June 1948, No. 7, September 1948, 186.

310 Ibid.

311 Ibid., 187.

312 Ibid.

313 For accounts of the ambush, see Eshel, *Ma'arachot*, 338–339, and [Hebrew] Josef Argaman, *Pale was the Night* (Tel Aviv: Miskal, 2003), 82–84.

314 [Hebrew] *Hamashkif*, 19 March 1948.
315 Ibid., and T.N.A. W.O. 261/226 1st regiment Royal House Artillery, Quarter ending 31 March 1948, *the Die Hards* nos. 6 and 7, 188.
316 *The Die Hards* nos. 6 and 7, 188.
317 Ibid., 214.
318 [Hebrew] Eshel, *Chativat Carmeli*, 86–93, [Hebrew] Immanuel Hareuveni, *Shayeret Yechiam* 2nd ed. (Ministry of Defense, 1990).
319 *The Die Hards* nos. 6 and 7, 188, Eshel, *Carmeli*, 90.
320 WO 261/226, NAM War Diary, 27 March.
321 *The Die Hards* nos. 6 and 7, 188, Eshel, *Carmeli*, 91, NAM War Diary, 28 March.
322 *The Die Hards* nos. 6 and 7, 191.
323 Coren, 91, 94, 108.
324 Coren, 72. NAM War Diary 19 March.
325 *The Die Hards* nos. 6 and 7, 189.
326 Ibid., 190.
327 Ibid.
328 Ibid., 188.
329 Ibid.
330 Eshel, *Carmeli*, 176.
331 *The Die Hards* nos. 6 and 7, 214, Eshel, *Carmeli*, 176. It was later alleged by the Jews that the chairman of the Acre National Committee had bought from the Army a ten minutes barrage delivered by 1 RHA. This is highly unlikely in view of the launching of a full attack by the 2nd Middlesex.
332 *The Die Hards* nos. 6 and 7, 214.
333 Ibid., Eshel, *Carmeli*, 177.
334 *The Die Hards* nos. 6 and 7, 214.
335 Eshel, *Carmeli*, 177.
336 *The Die Hards* nos. 6 and 7, 216.
337 Ibid.
338 Ben Gurion *Diary*, vol. 1, entry for 1st May 1948, 381.
339 *The Die Hards* nos. 6 and 7, 216.

7 Jaffa[1]

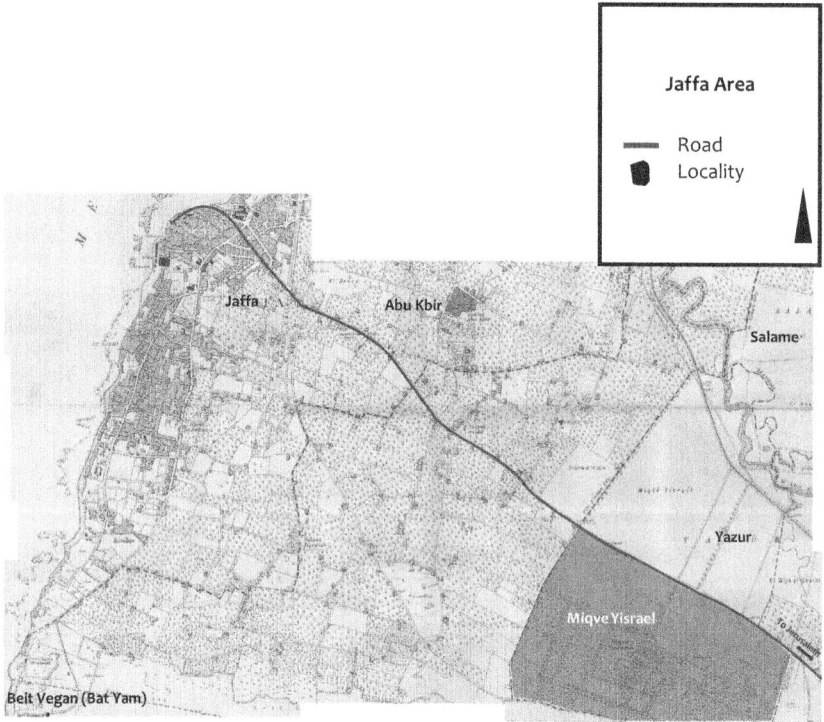

Map 9 Jaffa area.
Source: Survey of Palestine maps 1930, Govmap.gov.il.

After centuries of stagnation, Jaffa developed during the nineteenth century into the second (after Jerusalem) largest town in Palestine, with an estimated population on the eve of the First World War of 40,000–50,000,[2] and the country's main port.[3] In the years following the British occupation and the establishment of the Mandate, the increase in Jewish immigration resulted in the rapid development of the Jewish town of Tel Aviv, north of

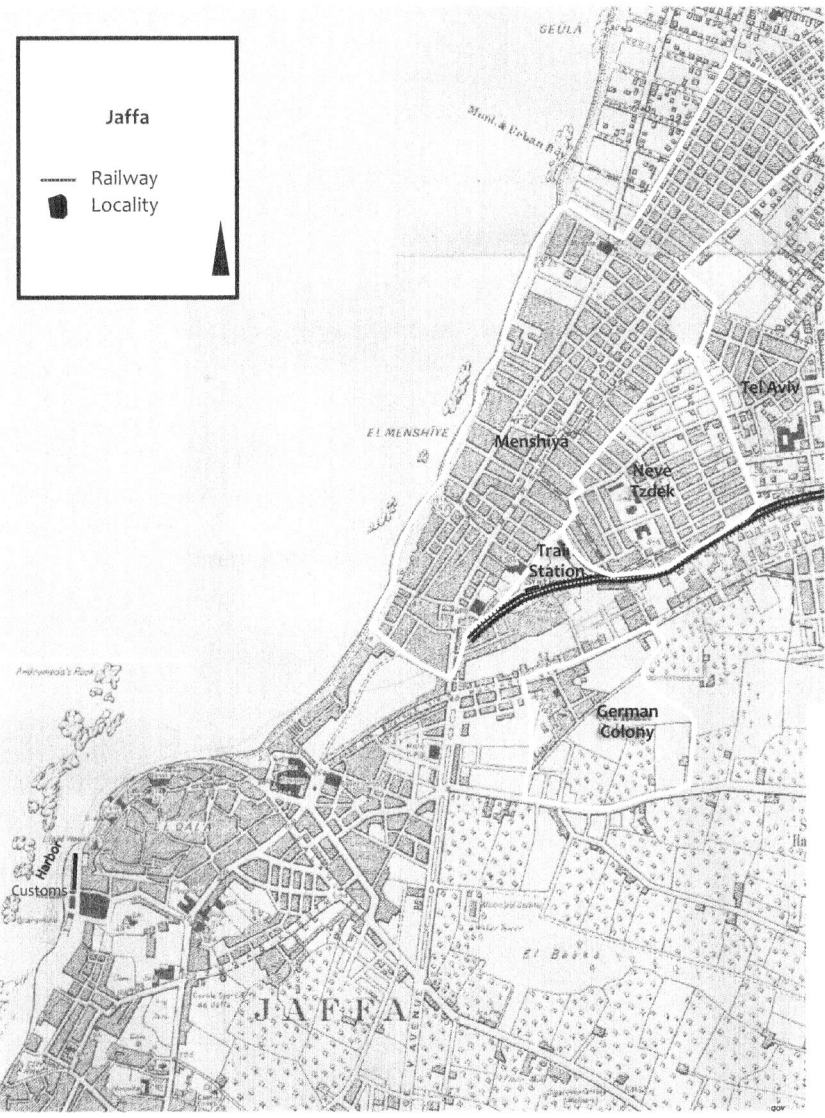

Map 10 Jaffa.
Source: Survey of Palestine maps 1930, Govmap.gov.il.

Jaffa, which soon became the country's largest city and the centre of the Jewish community (the "Yishuv") with, by the end of the Mandate, 183,000 inhabitants out of a total Jewish population of 609,000.[4]

Jaffa, at the time, continued to develop but at a slower rate, with, in 1947, a population of 104,000 of whom 30,000 were Jews and 54,000 (53%) Moslem

Arabs.[5] Thus by 1947, Jaffa's population was smaller than Tel Aviv's and more heterogeneous. A large proportion of its Arab residents consisted of migrant workers who congregated in the northern and eastern neighbourhoods, adjacent to Tel Aviv's poorest neighbourhoods. During the same period, the Jewish urban communities that became the towns of Bat Yam and Holon developed to the south and south-east of Jaffa confining its spatial development to the east where large Arab villages formed the town's hinterland.

According to the Partition Plan, Jaffa was to be part of the Arab state despite its being largely surrounded by Jewish communities.[6] At the time of the UN debate on partition, Haganah headquarters (HQ) in Tel Aviv had already been fully mobilized, expecting a repetition of previous patterns of violence between Jaffa and Tel Aviv. Three hundred and eighteen of its members manned positions mostly in the southern neighbourhoods facing Jaffa.[7] During the next few days, intelligence reaching the Haganah indicated that the Arabs were preparing a major attack. It was eventually launched from the village of Salama, on the Hatikva and Beit Ya'akov neighbourhoods in southern Tel Aviv on the night of 8th December with diversionary attacks further west.[8] The attack began at 19:00 hours along a front of one kilometre with intense small arms fire and a frontal orderly assault on Haganah positions. The defenders were forced to withdraw into the neighbourhoods, while some of the attackers began looting the outlying houses. The attack was blocked by a second line of prepared positions and then repulsed by a counter-attack by the Haganah's front's reserves.[9] By 22:00 hours the battle was over.

The nearest British unit was the 1st Battalion The King's Own Scottish Borderers (KOSB). With the change of mission, following the partition resolution, from fighting Jewish terrorism to keeping the peace between Jews and Arabs, the Borderers noted that following the three day's Arab general strike in the beginning of December, the 'attitude of the Jews towards both military and police personnel completely changed'.[10]

The situation deteriorated rapidly.

> To begin with, the Arabs contented themselves with stoning Jewish vehicles and beating up the occupants caught. As the tempo increased, Jews and Arabs caught and killed anyone of the opposing side, who exposed themselves to holdups, and then full scale armed attacks on each other's villages began.[11]

The Arab attack on the Hatikva and Beit Ya'akov neighbourhoods led to the Battalion's 'first large scale action... in keeping the peace'.[12] On 10th December, two companies were sent to restore order in the area – "A" Company, and a section of carriers to Salama, and "C" Company, a section of carriers and the force's headquarters to Hatikva. "A" Company remained in Salama for five days, 'keeping the peace, doing patrol, guards, and incidentally eating oranges by the hundred. It is not known how many orange groves the Company cleared, but we certainly made a gap in some Arab's citrus sales'.[13]

As soon as the Salama-Hatikva front seemed to calm down, the battalion was sent to guard the Jaffa Police HQ – "Jaffoon", with responsibility for the town and enforcing the curfew in Abu Kabir – its eastern outskirts. The Borderers noted that

> A "front" was opened up on the border and a "no man's land" soon developed. Movement in the burnt out part of the town became nil and any civilian (and at times troops) who did stray there was promptly dealt with by either Arab or Jewish snipers.[14]

The Army's mission evolved from keeping the peace to ensuring that both sides kept to their positions across no man's land, mainly by enforcing a curfew between 17:00 and 06:00 hours, and by means 'of continual patrolling, arresting the curfew breakers and the mopping up of snipers' posts'.[15] By 24th December, the Borderers were added the responsibility for Manshiya – the westernmost neighbourhood between Jaffa and Tel Aviv, thereby necessitating the commitment of the whole battalion. Jaffa and the road east would remain a battalion size mission until the end of the Mandate, with HQ situated in Jaffoon.

But these were early days, and the 3rd Brigade was able to arrange to relieve the Irish and English battalions for Christmas and the Scots for Hogmanay. On Christmas, the Borders took up in addition to their usual positions those of the 3rd Battalion.

The Coldstream Guards (who were about to leave Palestine, replaced by the 1st Battalion), 'but with the prospect of being relived for New Year all ranks remained remarkably cheerful and, except for the frequent sight of non-military revelers, Christmas Day passed by almost unnoticed'.[16] Nor were they disappointed. New Year's Eve, celebrated in the Battalion's camp in Lydda, which 'was exactly as it should be'.[17]

There followed a few weeks with most of the battalion in Jaffa and part of it in Lydda. In 28th January, the Borderers replaced the 1st Battalion The Argyll and Sutherland Highlanders, left the 3rd Brigade and became the Sarafand Garrison. The Argylls joined in the 3rd Brigade and the 2nd Battalion The Royal Lincolnshire Regiment and the 2nd Royal Irish Fusiliers, expecting 'a welcome change to the eternal guards of Sarafand'.[18] During one of its periods in Jaffa, it reported that a

> good standard of morale has been most noticeable in recent operations and in spite of the long hours of duty demanded almost all ranks prefer the tasks they are now carrying out to those rather more static and uninteresting guard duties to which previously they had been restricted.[19]

The Argylls moved on 3rd February into the Lydda Domestic Camp, while "B", "D" and part of "S" companies were sent in pouring rain to Manshiya. There, one company guarded Jaffoon while the other patrolled Manshiya, rotating every week,

> The work was hard, but by no means dull, and consisted of frequent foot and carrier patrols. The area itself might well be taken for a town through which the tide of war has passed. The houses are derelict and the streets deserted. The only people to be seen are the Haganah and the Arab defenders, all of whom are well armed.

A week later, when "D" Company left Jaffoon and changed places with "B" Company, its excitement was palpable.

> The change of routine is in accordance with everyone's desire and there is a sense of excitement on these patrols. Action can be anticipated and, in fact on more than one occasion there have been minor incidents. While the general policy is that of keeping the peace, both opposing sides occasionally make mistakes about our identity which sometimes result in the exchange of fire. It is heartening to know that our patrols do appear to prevent general outbreak of trouble and that their purpose is being fulfilled.[20]

One of the main advantages of taking up more active missions was the return to soldiering in platoons. The change, after four months of garrison duties, required some readjustments. Following the move,

> Platoons were quickly reformed, and Orderly Sergeants and such people were chased at once to the duties of Section Commanders. Ammunition, shovels and weapons were checked. In fact, extremely warlike and enthusiastic preparations were carried out for a real "do".[21]

Once in Manshiya 'Platoon organization and spirit, somewhat lacking in our previous commitments, went up 100 per cent'.[22] The rest of the battalion remaining in Lydda had to make do with guard duty in the battalion camp and the airport while providing an immediate action platoon. 'We... are very disappointed not be forming a part of the operational detachment on the Jaffa-Tel Aviv boundary'.[23]

Adding to the misery of those who remained in Lydda was the camp itself, adjacent to the train station in the western part of the town, which was a 'sea of mud',

> a great come-down from Sarafand [a small distance away] The huts are inclined to fall apart and are very chilly, as there is no form of heating in them. The ground develops into a particularly sticky form of mud at

the least provocation. However… we are duly thankful that we do not need to use tents.[24]

On 19th February, the battalions of the 3rd Brigade rotated their assignments, and the 2nd Battalion The Royal Lincolnshire Regiment moved to Jaffa with three infantry companies ("B", "C" and "D") and a platoon of carriers.[25] Veterans[26] of Jaffa, in particular, the Lincolnshires, were far less excited when they took up their positions. For instance, the company in Jaffoon was less impressed than the Argylls by the sounds of nightly battles and the danger of stray bullets.

> We soon learnt to ignore the nightly 'battles' taking place in the Manshiya and Abu Kabir areas of Jaffa. A/CSM [Acting Company Sergeant Major] Smith gives us to understand that he personally has had many hair-breadth escapes from sudden and violent death whilst walking from the Sgt's Mess to the Orderly Room – or should we say from the Orderly Room to the Sgt's Mess?[27]

Similarly, their return to curfew enforcing in Manshiya was regarded as less than exhilarating – 'a difficult and unenviable task in the center of one of the most troublesome areas of Palestine'.[28]

The 2nd Lincolnshires rotated after a fortnight and were replaced by the 2nd Battalion The Royal Irish Fusiliers. The mission kept evolving. The Manshiya company moved into the railway workshops, north of the cantonment, on the edge of their zone of operations. The company in the cantonment now also manned a roadblock on the Ramle-Jaffa road and guarded the Jaffa Post Office in town. The carriers provided an additional patrol to the port during the day and escorts for daily transports of railway workers to Lydda. When required, the battalion also enforced curfews in Abu Kabir.[29]

The establishments of the battalions were constantly diminishing. During the quarter ending 31st March 1948, the 1st Argylls were reduced from 41 officers and 906 other ranks (ORs) to 34 officers and 784 ORs. The Fusiliers were reduced during the same period to 34 officers and 831 ORs. Meanwhile the number of assignments kept growing in accordance with occasional fluctuations in the intensity of the fighting. However, 'very little fire from either Jews or Arabs had been directed against the troops', whereas 'a sniper battle between Jews and Arabs went on almost every day and night with varying intensity'. On many nights, the soldiers in the railway workshops and the cantonment, 'got little or no sleep due to the increased tempo of the Small Arms, Mortar and grenade battle[s] which went on. No grenades or Mortar bombs fell into the security zone'.[30] Occasionally, when a British soldier was seriously wounded or killed, the Army usually destroyed the building, Jewish or Arab, from which the shots were fired.[31]

Thanks to the presence of British troops, the front between Jaffa and Tel Aviv remained stationary although the firing intensified. The Irgun Zvai

Leumi (IZL) tried from the outset to take an active part in the defence of southern Tel Aviv where it had many supporters, and eventually got the local Haganah command to accede to the erection of six IZL positions manned by its fighters, and to conduct the occasional raid on an Arab position.[32]

At first, the IZL continued attacking British targets under the pretext of ensuring that they indeed leave Palestine and were not tempted to remain to help the Arabs prevent the establishment of a Jewish state. During April 1948, it was becoming clear that the Haganah was gaining the upper hand while the Army was on its way out. The IZL became increasingly worried that while the Haganah would soon be facing the major challenges of occupying and defending the territory of the new Jewish state while forming its official army, the IZL would become insignificant thereby undermining its chances of becoming a relevant political force in the new state. The IZL wished to negotiate an agreement with the leadership of the Yishuv whereby it would be allowed to amalgamate with the Haganah while preserving its organic units and thereby remaining an identifiable participant in the national effort.

In March 1948, the Haganah high command distributed Plan D ("Dalet"), fleshed out in February and based on a scenario derived from the Governments' official policy of preserving law and order, and maintaining the territorial status quo between Jews and Arabs until the actual termination of the Mandate.[33] The implication was that the Haganah would have to act swiftly and decisively as soon as the British Army left, to occupy and then defend the territory of the Jewish state against a likely invasion of the regular Arab armies. Speed and concentration of effort were of essence. This was not the time to get bogged down by urban warfare. Arab towns should be encircled and isolated, their population's morale broken and their essential services immobilized.[34] The unanticipated withdrawal of British troops from some of the mixed towns, on the one hand, and the firm British reaction to the Haganah attempt to attack Acre, on the other, meant that the plans for Jaffa remained unchanged. The city would be surrounded and isolated but not attacked,[35] although the Tel Aviv Haganah command made plans for the eventual occupation when and if it became feasible militarily and politically.[36]

At the end of 1947, the IZL began to consider Jaffa as a possible target but no concrete operational plans were made for an attack.[37] At the time, it lacked the military capability and experience to undertake such an operation. The IZL did little, during the following months in that direction except for gathering intelligence.[38] Actual planning began only on 22nd April with a meeting convened by Menachem Begin, the IZL commander, who ordered an attack within forty-eight hours.[39] The IZL's confidence in its ability to take on a well-defended Arab city was largely based on its recent acquisition of large quantities of ammunition and explosives.[40] Its field commanders were informed of the attack on the 23rd, and the fighters began to assemble on the next day.

Begin's attempts to justify the attack on Jaffa on military grounds – the sniping on Tel Aviv and the danger of it providing a bridgehead for an

Egyptian amphibious landing, are unconvincing. Tel Aviv had learnt to live with the snipping and could withstand the few remaining weeks of the Mandate, and the Egyptian Army did not have the capability to mount a serious amphibious landing. Begin's actual reason was to demonstrate to the leaders of the Yishuv that the military potential of the IZL should not and could not be ignored and that it should be allowed to join the future army while keeping its units intact. An agreement along those lines had been reached on 12th April, but Ben-Gurion and other labour leaders raised various objections. An IZL attack on a scale comparable to the Haganah's recent dramatic operation in Haifa would force the last objectors to concede while, judging by events in Haifa, the British Army would remain passive.[41]

Following the Arab debacle in Haifa and the flight of most of its inhabitants, the British Foreign Office was inundated with telegrams from its legations in Arab capitals conveying protests and accusations by Arab leaders of the British betrayal of Palestine's Arabs. The Army was accused of having done nothing to stop the killing of Arab civilians while preventing Arab reinforcements from coming to their aid. Furthermore, General Stockwell had forced Haifa's Arab headers to accept the Jews' terms of surrender.[42] Britain's closest ally in the region King Abdullah of Jordan appealed to the High Commissioner to prevent the Jews from accomplishing in Jerusalem and Jaffa what they had in Haifa. If Britain was unable to keep its promise of preserving stability in Palestine until the end of the Mandate, warned the General Secretary of the Arab League, the Arab states would be forced to intervene presently with their own armies.[43] The Army itself was concerned that the intensification of the anti-British sentiment among Palestine's Arabs might threaten the course of the evacuation and that British's overall position in the Middle East might suffer.

With the news of the Haganah's success in Haifa, the Foreign Office received reports of a massacre of the city's Arabs. The general hysteria of the Arab accounts of the fate of the population were reflected in Ernest Bevin's outburst at a meeting on 23rd April in Number 10 in which Montgomery stated categorically that on the basis of the Army's reports.

> The whole affair was grossly exaggerated, and at no time had the situation got out of hand. Ernie then blew up, and concluded his outburst by saying that he had been "let down by the Army." I got very angry and said that he would have to withdraw the insult.[44]

Montgomery was relentless in his feuds. On 12th May, after the Army had "redeemed" itself in defending Jaffa from a Jewish attack, at a meeting with A.V. Alexander, the Minister of Defense, the latter tried to belittle the significance of Bevin's charge. Montgomery, by his own account,

> went right off the deep end I said that the Army had not forgotten Mr. Bevin's previous statement that he staked his political reputation on

the successful solution of the Palestine problem. He had consistently refused to listen to the Army's views, he had been led down the garden path by the Colonial Secretary and the High Commissioner, he had made a proper mess of the whole business, and that now he was trying to make the Army the scapegoat. I was not going to put up with this.[45]

One result of these altercations was a sense in the Army and the Mandate government that their reputation was at stake and a determination that the story of Haifa must not be allowed to recur. Jaffa must be kept Arab even if only for a few more weeks until the withdrawal after which it was bound to be occupied by the Jews. The reality of the threat to Jaffa was brought home by the IZL's attack on Manshiya.

On 22nd April, the Royal Irish Fusiliers had two companies, "A" and "C" in Jaffa, under the command of Major G.J. Hamilton, where they had relieved Companies "B" and "D". A recently added mission was a guard on the Law Courts at the edge of Manshiya, near the train station, in order to prevent the Arabs from occupying the building and using it for sniping in the direction of the Jewish Neve Tzedek neighbourhood to the east.[46] While the IZL attack did not start until 25th April, the Fusiliers noted an intensification of the nightly exchanges. On the night of the 22nd, 'the mortaring of Jaffa by the Jews was much heavier than usual, and it became clear that this was part of a definite softening up process preparatory to an attack of Jaffa, with the port as the main objective'.[47]

The next day (23rd April), in anticipation of an attack, the Fusiliers redeployed. They withdrew from the railway workshops 'the main administrative installations and offices' reducing their presence there to 'a compact platoon post', in an attempt to minimize the danger of a mortar or even a frontal attack.[48]

> In actual fact, sniping on the section posts and the cookhouse started almost immediately... In addition to the change in layout, all posts were strengthened and the layout of the zone reorganized to withstand mortaring and sniping. Up to this time any sort of attack from either side had been considered quite out of the question and the fortification of the perimeter was meagre.[49]

It may be assumed that the Arab side took note and made their own preparations for a possible attack.

The first major IZL attempt to break through the Arab line came on the morning of 25th April at 07:00 hours. The IZL succeeded in assembling what for it was an unprecedented force of some five companies, about 400 fighters with two additional auxiliary companies about 240 strong.[50] They were armed with a prodigious quantity of weapons and ammunition including four armoured cars, two Piats and two 3" mortars (without sights) with twenty tons of bombs stolen from the train, near Binyamina, and two tons of explosives.[51] Formidable as the force was in terms of the fighting in April 1948, the IZL fighters had received little if any regular military training in operating as units, their commanders barely knew each other and their tactical skills in general and urban combat in particular were slight. The plan for the first stage of the battle was to isolate Manshiya from the rest of Jaffa by attacking from Neve Zedek westwards to the sea and cutting Manshiya off from the town. The next stage would be to clear and occupy Manshiya as far as Tel Aviv to the north and attack the centre of Jaffa to the south.

For two days, the IZL attacks failed to break through the Arab defences, manned in depth by about 300 well-organized fighters in well-placed positions able to provide mutual fire support. During the battle, the IZL mortars, unable to provide close accurate support, shelled the town centre causing general panic among the civilian population many of whom tried to leave with whatever they could carry, by sea or land.[52] Despite the IZL's lack of military success, the operation's political goals had been achieved, and after two days of fighting, Begin was summoned to the Haganah HQ for some last-minute discussions and the signing of an agreement which inter alia sanctioned the ongoing attack. Begin at this point was prepared to abandon the operation, but his field commanders insisted on their being allowed to continue until victory. The force was withdrawn, reorganized, its tactics revised, based on the lessons learnt in the two days of fighting, and on the afternoon of the 27th, the attack was resumed.

Fighting continued throughout the night and on the morning of the 28th at 07:00 hours, the IZL finally succeeded in breaking through the Arab line to the seashore. A force moved north to complete the occupation of Manshiya while another force began advancing south into Jaffa. On the same day (28th April), the Haganah began its own operation, Chametz, aimed at completing the encirclement of Jaffa by occupying the large villages to its east.[53] From the Fusiliers point of view,

> During these three days... the platoon in the railway workshops, which was changed every two days from "A" Company, was under constant fire from snipers. One corner of the workshops, known as "Casualty Corner", overlooked the main railway yards, which afforded an excellent line of advance for the IZL attack on the Manshieh Police Station, which was one of the main objectives. It was evident that the Jews strongly objected to our presence so near to them. Sniping was very accurate and three of our four wounded were actually shot while observing though embrasures in the sandbag emplacement at "Casual Corner" from a distance of from 200 to 300 yards.[54]

Up to then, and apart from attempts to silence snipers, the troops were under orders to take no action.

After the first day of the attack, the force in Jaffoon, fearing an IZL attack on their positions, was reinforced by two Cromwell tanks from the

4th/7th Royal Dragoon Guards ("B" Squadron, 2nd Troop) and a troop of two armoured cars from the Life Guards.

> During the afternoon the combined troops made a "flag march" through Jaffa, observed with great enthusiasm by the inhabitants, who were panic-stricken by the mortaring and by the reports of sweeping Jewish successes. One tank, with Daimlers [armoured cars with 2 pdr guns], went to the southern end of Jaffa to the Gold Star factory [the Cabir brewery] from which vantage point the Jews had been sniping the occasional Arab in Jaffa. The [tank's] 75 mm was not used except to fire over the building.[55]

Following the IZL's final breakthrough to the shore and the beginning of its push south into Jaffa, there was a real danger that the troops in the railway yards and Jaffoon would find themselves outflanked from the west and isolated from the town while it was being occupied. The remaining tanks of the 2nd Troop of the Dragoons were dispatched from Sarafand with two platoons of the Lincolnshires for protection, and arrived in Jaffoon at 13:30 hours. They

> Went straight out to the only forward position outside the compound. The crews of the two original tanks, who had had very little sleep for the past three nights, and yet no action, were furious at this cavalier treatment. Very soon they could hear, from the inside of the compound, the report of 75's and chater of besas [machine guns]. A dense cloud of smoke lay over the railway yard, where an Irgun sniper aboard a rail wagon had finally been paid off with 75 H.E. [High Explosive shell]... Targets were numerous: road blocks, M.G. posts and snipers all came in for rough treatment.[56]

Twice within a matter of days, British troops clashed with Jewish forces: first with the Palmach in Jerusalem (25th April) and now with the IZL in Jaffa. In both cases, Jewish commanders mistakenly assumed that after Haifa the British Army in Palestine would not fight to maintain the status quo, even where it declared that it had a particular interest.

> The tank "Ajax" nosed round a corner to find itself face-to-face with a Jewish 15 cwt. armoured truck. Just after the truck had been blown apart, the tank commander... was himself hit. He subsequently died of these wounds.
>
> Another tank was brought to replace "Ajax." By dusk we really felt that the IZL had had a bad shaking from the tanks. Next morning the two forward tanks went off the mark at sunrise, the house containing the worst sniper was wrecked, another vehicle believed to be an armoured bus, was knocked out and various road-blocks, snipers, etc., were obliterated.[57]

In addition to the tanks and armoured cars, the 3rd Brigade reinforced the Jaffa garrison (28th April) with "B" Company of the Argyll and Sutherlands. The Company, which was due to take over from the Fusiliers on the 30th, was quickly organized and dispatched. On its arrival in the afternoon of the 28th, it joined a composite force commanded by Major G.J. Hamilton of the Fusiliers, who at 14:30 hours received orders to stop the Jews' attack.[58] Some 200 Arab irregulars still manned positions in Manshiya facing the IZL. Hamilton arranged his forces in a front of about 300 yards beginning at the north-western corner of the cantonment and ending on the seashore. They started off from the area of the Law Courts,

> From here the tanks worked down the narrow streets and into the railway yards, engaging the Jewish barricade, with their 75mm. guns. This was carried out with great boldness, infantry support being quite out of the question due to the very heavy small arms fire coming down the street.[59]

"B" Company of the Argylls was sent to take over a portion of the line in a densely built area 'with houses huddled close together'.[60] Within about an hour, by 15:30 hours, the IZL's advance south into Jaffa was stopped, 'and, indeed, had been sent shuddering back about 200 yards into Manshiya, much to the relief of the [Fusiliers'] platoon in the workshops, who had been playing a most active part in the battle'.[61]

Due to its sketchy understanding of the complexity of the Jewish intentions, the differences between the Haganah's strategy and the IZL's, etc., the Army assumed a coordinated Jewish offensive, expecting follow-up attacks from the east-on-Tel-a-Rish and from the south on Jabaliya in an overall effort to occupy Jaffa, thus realizing its worst fear.[62] In fact, the IZL's attack had forced the Haganah's hand, and fearing a general breakdown of the situation in the Tel Aviv southern front and their own loss of face, brought forward their operation ("Chametz") for the encirclement of Jaffa.

Part of the Haganah's operation was a battalion-size attack by the Givati Brigade on Tel-a-Rish, a village overlooking the eastern approach to Jaffa, a key component in the town's eastern line of defences. Situated on a small hill, it provided an important observation post on the Jewish agricultural school of Mikve Israel and the urban community of Holon, south east of Jaffa. The Arab positions included a central, two-story pillbox and a well-designed and -constructed system of defensive positions in depth, armed with some automatic weapons and light mortars.[63] Tel-a-Rish was stormed and occupied by Givati in the early hours of the 28th. But a counter-attack by the ALA reinforcement sent to Jaffa and commanded by Michel Issa, a veteran of the TJFF, forced an overconfident Jewish force to withdraw, with heavy loses. Michel Issa and his fighters then proceeded into Jaffa had joined the fighting in Manshiya.[64]

Certain that the next move by the Haganah would be an attack from Bat-Yam, south of Jaffa, four Spitfires were sent from the Ramat David Royal

Air Force (RAF) station, in the north, to attack the Jewish position in the brewery on the Bat-Yam Jaffa border. According to the station's Operations Record Book, 'Jewish forces were in possession but they vacated the building after [Spitfire] attacks with machine guns and 20 mm cannon'.[65] It was the RAF's understanding that had it not provided air support to the Army's effort of 'clearing Jews from outskirts [of] Jaffa area', it 'would definitely involve heavier casualties'.[66] The RAF was well satisfied with the results of this first (and only) use of aircraft firepower in 'the present disturbances'.[67] AOC (Air Officer Commanding) Air Commodore W.L. Dawson wrote: 'police and civil reports state all four aircraft hit target. Jewish advance stopped largely as result air action and Arab moral in that area has rocketed'.[68] The next day dummy runs were made with Tempests on loan from Iraq.[69] By the time Dawson compiled his final report on the role of the RAF in the evacuation of Palestine, the Spitfires action in Jaffa had assumed heroic proportions.

Dawson proclaimed the brewery a vital position,

> Its capture was an essential part of the land operation, but would obviously be expensive in casualties. At the urgent request of G.O.C. I agreed to take on this objective from the air. The actual damage inflicted on the building was admittedly small and largely confined to doors, windows, window frames, etc., but the attack was entirely effective in that the post was immediately evacuated and was occupied by our forces without resistance... this small operation is a good example of the use of minimum force and the saving of British casualties by air action.[70]

Except that the Spitfires appear to have attacked the wrong building and to have prevented an offensive which was never intended the Jewish record of events mentions an air attack on an apartment block in Holon and on a fortified position on the road to Mikve Israel, nowhere near the Bat Yam-Jaffa border and the Cabir brewery. As far as the Haganah was concerned, the source of the official report on Jerusalem Radio of an attack on an important Jewish position which served as a base for an attack from Bat Yam on Jaffa was a mystery.[71]

At 17:30 hours of 28th April, Lt.-Colonel Neilson CO of the 1st Battalion The Argyll and Sutherland Regiment, was called to the 3rd Brigade HQ and ordered to move the rest of his Battalion, less "A" and "C" Companies, into Jaffa early the next morning (29th April). The Argylls arrived at around 07:00 hours to find the Jaffa they knew transformed.

> Previously the streets had teemed with people; now they were deserted, and all the shop shutters were down. The difference was very striking, and the hurriedly built sandbag emplacements and road blocks emphasized the fact that war really had come to Jaffa.[72]

"D" Company was sent to Manshiya to complete the manning of the front line, taking over from "B" Company. Battalion HQ was housed in Police HQ in the cantonment with "S" Company as mobile reserve. However, to their disgust 'the whole affair... fizzled out too soon'.[73] Apparently, the mortar crews of "S" Company felt especially aggrieved. Having gone to the trouble of drawing the mortars out of stores and preparing them for action, they were not permitted to fire them.[74]

On the morning of 29th April, the Army resumed its attack on the IZL positions, supported by a troop of twenty-five pounders of the 41st Field Regiment Royal Artillery (RA), 'which successfully engaged known Jewish strong points behind their F.D.L.s [Forward Defense Line], especially the 3 inch mortar positions'.[75] Typically, having after months of frustrating routine internal security duties, been allowed to fire their guns, the gunners let go with eighty (or possibly ninety) shells 'and were credited by the Jews with 80-60 [actually 17][76] dead IZL. We were satisfied'.[77] By 12:00 hours the Jews asked for a truce.

By then the British forces in Jaffa consisted of Companies "B", "D" and "S" of the Argylls, two companies ("B" joined on the 29th) of the Fusiliers, a weak company (two platoons) of the Lincolnshires, one troop of tanks from the 4th/7th Dragoon Guards and, in support, a Battery of the 41st Field Regiment R.A. a RAF Squadron and two Royal Navy (RN) destroyers, which lay off shore.[78] Later, on the 30th Companies "A" and "C" of the Argylls completed the battalion in Jaffa after a company of the 2nd Battalion, The King's Regiment was flown in from Cyprus to take up their positions in and around Lydda,[79] while the rest of the King's battalion sailed to Haifa, and reached Lydda by road.

In Manshiya after the IZL attack and the Army's counter-attacks,

> There was hardly a building which did not show signs of the fighting and many were completely demolished. The streets forward of the ["D"] company positions were filled high with debris and the majority were impassible except on foot. The Jaffoon cantonment itself was hardly touched... although the electric light and water services worked now on a rather hit or miss principle.[80]

Although the Haganah had asked for a truce, the situation on both sides remained, for a while, fluid. In the British line,

> the forward companies were somewhat nonplussed by those members of the Arab irregulars who floated around the positions. They were a happy-go-lucky lot, and worked on the assumption that the Battalion posts were for the use of all friendly armies and it was some time before they were persuaded that they were not open to all comers. They blazed away quite happily at Jewish positions both real and imaginary, and

wanted the Battalion to attack, offering to guide it through Manshiya. The offer was not accepted.[81]

On the Jewish side, the problem was controlling the IZL fighters. The Haganah was informed on the 28th of the agreement with the IZL and that all IZL positions were under command of the local Haganah front commander. At the same time, the Haganah was instructed to avoid any confrontations with the IZL.[82] In reality so long as IZL fighters were present, friction remained. During the night of 30th at about 01:00 hours,

> The Jews occupied a school building about 30 yards in front of "B" Company's right-hand platoon... opening heavy fire on it. An attempt to lay a charge against the house occupied by the Platoon was feared, but this did not materialize, although it was probably the object of the attack as that particular house dominated a large proportion of Manshiya.
> Fire was opened with all available weapons but it was not until two armoured cars... intervened that the Jews were forced to withdraw.[83]

When the IZL offensive had begun, William Fuller, Lydda District Commissioner, warned the Mayor of Tel Aviv that should the attack result in the occupation of a part of Jaffa the Army would be forced to intervene.[84] As the battle continued, Fuller added the threat to bomb and shell Tel Aviv. The Army, acting on orders which came from the High Commissioner, blocked with little difficulty the IZL's attempt to advance south into Jaffa. At the time, Bevin's concern was that Jaffa remains Arab thereby demonstrating Britain's determination to defend Palestine's Arabs.[85] In fact, the Army had already done as much and the Jewish Agency announced that the Jews had no intention of occupying Jaffa or disrupting its inhabitants' lives. The IZL forces in the field were reluctant to accept these restrictions but, with mounting political pressure on its leadership and military pressure on its positions, they finally acceded to a cease-fire (29th April) and truce discussions began.[86]

Fuller convened representatives of both sides on the afternoon of the 29th and again the next morning (30th April) at 09:30 hours at which Amos Ben-Gurion (son of David Ben-Gurion), the liaison officer of the Jewish Agency to the Police and the Army in central Palestine, accepted in essence the British demands. General Murray CO 1st Division agreed, later the same morning, to recognize the status quo including the Jewish occupation of Manshiya provided that the IZL leave the area and its positions were turned over to the Haganah. Accordingly, Murray issued on 30th April 'Orders... for Jaffa' which he signed as 'Military Commander Lydda District'. The Orders defined the line to be manned by the Army by 12:00 hours 1st May with the provision that 'no armed person of either side will be allowed to cross this line and any armed person approaching it will be shot or captured'. 'Any fighting with small arms or mortars by either side will be punished severely by the Army only' and 'Any infringement... by either side will result in the full weight of the Army being used without further warning'. The Orders would remain in force until the end of the Mandate.[87]

The line consisted of 'frontier control posts... on all the roads leading from Jaffa to Tel Aviv' and from Neve Zedek to the sea. 'For every British post there was to be a Jewish one 10 to 20 yards away'.[88] The British field commanders were sceptical whether the Haganah could or would 'clear all IZL and Stern [none of whom were involved] gangsters from the area'. Therefore, it was with extreme caution that on 13:45 hours on 1st May soldiers of the two front companies of the Argylls,

> Moved forward, searching all houses for booby traps and IZL and Stern Gangsters. Others remained in their positions, ready to give covering fire to the forward parties if it proved necessary, while the remainder faced into Jaffa to prevent any Arabs following up. The advance was covered by tanks, and a reconnaissance party, under the Commanding Officer, moved forward in the carriers immediately behind the leading troops.[89]

Progress was slow due to the debris blocking the roads. But the main street north was quickly cleared for the tanks passing through the Jewish positions while the rest of the operation was carried out on foot. Some of the troops expected, or perhaps hoped for, the worst. Lance Corporal Agnew of "D" Company took no chances.

> He was observed advancing with a cut-throat razor in his stocking, a couple of grenades in his belt, a sten gun nursed in his arms and its bandolier across his chest, a pointed knuckle duster in his right fist, and ferocious scowl on his face. In addition, in his shirt was the tattered regimental flag of the 8th Battalion which flew at Cassino, and of which this N.C.O. is the proud possessor. It was as well that the Jew did not start anything – others were equally well prepared.[90]

The Argylls need not have worried. 'The whole operation went off without incident, and sites for the posts of both sides were selected in conjunction with the local Haganah representatives. They were occupied immediately' (Figure 7.1).[91] Meanwhile a company of Fusiliers took over the positions vacated in the rear in order to establish a line facing Jaffa to prevent armed Arabs from trying to advance northwards, a threat which quickly became academic. Internal Arab squabbles led to the withdrawal of Arab forces from Jaffa, many joining the masses of refugees leaving by road to Ramle and the south, under the auspices of the Army. The emptying of Jaffa solved a possible difficulty were the final withdrawal to take place with

Figure 7.1 Jaffa. Soldiers of the 1st Battalion The Argyll and Sutherland Highlanders Regiment constructing a position in the deserted Arab neighbourhood of Manshiya.
Source: Fred Czasnik; Courtesy of the I.D.F. Archive (file 2-8-12), Ministry of Defense, Israel.

both sides in positions facing each other – 'it might well have proved a most
tricky operation'.[92]

Thus ended the IZL offensive. Along the Manshiya line, both sides
quickly established a peaceful and even friendly routine for the two remaining weeks of the Mandate. The Argylls passed their days

> In routine guard duties interspersed with anti-looting patrols. Only at
> night was there any firing worth mentioning, but no serious incidents
> developed... relations with the Haganah who manned the opposite
> posts were correct if not friendly; no attempt was made at concealment
> by either side, and free movement was possible everywhere.[93]

The force along the line was gradually reduced to the 1st Argyll and Sutherland Battalion with one company of Fusiliers and a troop of four Comet
tanks from the 4th Royal Tank Regiment under command, sent to Palestine
to help cover the final evacuation.[94] 'The thought of leaving Palestine for
good was now uppermost in the minds of most'.[95] The troops were busy
making life as comfortable and enjoyable as possible. "D" Company, coming from guard duty in the Beit Nabala Stores Dump, demonstrated the
acquisitive skills of nomadic units.

> It became quite pleasant. Each platoon found itself billets that remained
> standing amid the general destruction. Every man had his own bed,
> mattress, and silk coverlets, and every other man had his Primus stove

[pressurized burner]. Looting was not on, the utmost practical use was made of every article available to make life comfortable.[96]

An "operational" pass time was initiated by one of the junior officers, who

> Put the Hanhagah[sic] on tenterhooks with his imaginary mine field, which he placed on the beach and surrounded with wire under the cover of dark. There was a full supporting cast, and the historionic abilities of Sergt. Martin were a vital factor in this operation, his orders and cautions on the disposal of the mines being most convincing. Or so we gathered from the Jews the next day.[97]

Indeed, an intelligence report of the Tel Aviv Haganah Brigade (Kiryati) reported the laying of a mine field on the beach intended to prevent Arab infiltration to the north.[98]

News of the battle and its aftermath attracted a large numbers of visitors whose opportunities for sightseeing trips and exchanges of military hospitality had been greatly reduced. "D" Company's platoons vied with each other in producing cups of tea for frontline visitors. Ten Platoon seems to have excelled in serving visitors with sausages, eggs and chips. They even kept their own hens 'which thereafter travelled with it'.[99] The Company exchanged places after six days with "C" Company in Jaffoon, and was back after another five days. The stream of visitors proved unabated, including 'numerous representatives of the Press' and GOC Palestine Lieut.-General G.H.A. Macmillan, Colonel of the Regiment.[100]

Similarly, "A" Company brought from its fortnight in Manshiya the memory of 'a kind of "Stalingrad" existence' among the ruins.

> We managed to make ourselves fairly comfortable on the whole, and certainly fed well on local pigeons and hens. The chief trouble was the smell from the various dead things buried in the ruins. This was overcome to a certain extent by liberal use of Chanel No. 5 "liberated" from a destroyed store. Wives and girl-friends of "A" Company please note that Chanel No. 5 has lost its use for us.[101]

Finally, "C" Company marked its time in Manshiya by several surprising incidents:

> the surprise on the face of the Company Commander and C.S.M. when a party of glamorous nursing sisters was disgorged from a bevy of staff cars in the middle of the Company area, the even greater surprise registered when they announced that they had come to see the front line, a visit they had been promised by the Brigadier, the surprise on the face of the Company Commander's dog when it bumped a trip wire and put

up a magnesium flare; and, finally, the surprise of 7 Platoon when they discovered how much furniture and rubbish can be stored in one house, which surprise was heightened considerably when they were told it was to be their billet and would be cleared and cleaned forthwith.[102]

Part of the Army's deployment in Jaffa for the last remaining weeks of the Mandate was to provide on 4th May a small mobile force stationed just east of the town, entrusted with keeping the road to Sarafand open thereby securing the exodus of Jaffa's inhabitants. Should the Jews renew their attack, the force would form a mobile reserve for an immediate response. Christened FISHFORCE and commanded by Major J.G. Fisher, it was made up of "D" Company and two platoons from "C" Company of the Fusiliers, with two sections of carriers, the four Comet tanks from the 4th RTR with a troop of four twenty-five pounders from the 41st Field Regiment RA stationed in Sarafand on immediate call. Fishforce occupied a large Arab house in Abu Kebir, just outside Jaffa, near the junction of the Jaffa–Sarafand and the Tel Aviv road. During the April battles, the Haganah had occupied Abu Kebir. It was now agreed that it would withdraw from the road and allow the Army to take up posts along it. In addition, a platoon with a M10 mounted 17 pounder from "U" Battery of the 12th Anti-Tank Regiment was placed in nearby Tel-a-Rish 'as a guarantee to the Jews that the village would not by occupied by Arab snipers'.[103] The A/T Battery commander, though, was less than happy with the arrangement, feeling 'that mere infantry could [not] be relied upon to look after and guard his gun properly'.[104]

Fishforce was organized as two patrols of one platoon each, with two carriers and two tanks. The tanks camped overnight in Sarafand and every morning came out to join the carriers. One patrol remained in Abu Kabir as reserve while the other patrolled the road that eventually would serve for the evacuation.[105] On the evening of the force's first day, it was called out to Jaffa Port where the Arabs were looting the warehouses. The CO, who went ahead, learnt that the Police had the situation under control but were waiting to be relieved. 'The Arabs were in turmoil and every corner, including the Customs office, was occupied by families of Arab refugees. The stench was indescribable'. The troop's main mission, it transpired, was to protect the flour from looting.

> On the second night the sentries were attacked by a crowd of about 100 unarmed Arabs, who succeeded in breaking open one door, but fire was opened and six Arabs were killed and several wounded and the situation was restored without any casualties in the platoon. Lt. Matthew's boxer dog, Billy, must be mentioned. He was put into a warehouse and cleared it on his own in a matter of minutes, several Arabs were severely bitten!

After three days, the flower was removed and distributed and the problem solved.[106] No other incidents were reported.

Arab Jaffa became a ghost town. According to an eye witness, the American-Jewish reporter I.F. Stone,

> A few armed leftovers of the Arab forces, some Iraqi deserters, Chetniks, and a handful of Nazis still remained behind foraging in the empty town, lurking in the smelly little alleys and behind the drawn shutters of forlorn houses. Iron shutters were down in front of the shops. The only sign of business activity was an aged Arab offering a few radishes and cucumbers for sale on the pavement outside the French hospital. ... "All the Jews have to do," said a British sergeant, "is fire one 25 pounder and these Arabs bale out."[107]

Although the British political leadership had gone out of its way to ensure that Jaffa remain Arab, most of its residents chose to leave before the evacuation[108] mainly by the road east secured by the Army. Attempts to declare Jaffa an open city, thereby hopefully keeping it out of future fighting, proved futile since the city's emergency committee would not endorse such a request, and Tel Aviv's leaders would not discuss it.[109] The last members of Jaffa's Arab elite left, many to Aman, as did the staff of the local hospitals, one of which, Dajani, moved to Ramle. The various foreign fighters left as well after looting shops and homes. Water supply was erratic and petrol ran out.[110] The town was gradually and systematically looted by civilians, IZL and Haganah units.[111] Jaffa quickly became a near empty shell. There was no real community left and just as the Army was about to leave the last remaining civic leaders surrendered (13th May) to the Haganah.

Notes

1 On Jaffa, in the first half of the 20th century, see [Hebrew] Tamir Goren, *Rise and Fall: The Urban Development of Jaffa and Its Place in Jewish-Arab Strife in Palestine 1917–1947* (Jerusalem: Yad Izhak Ben-Zvi, 2016), Itamar Radai, *A Tale of Two Cities: The Palestinian Arabs in Jerusalem and Jaffa, 1947–1948* (Tel Aviv-Yafo: Tel Aviv University, 2015), Arnon Golan, Jacov Peleg, Alon Kadish, Yona Bandmann, *The Jaffa Battles, 1948* (Sde Boker: The Ben-Gurion Research Institute, Ben-Gurion University of the Negev, 2017).
2 Of whom 61.4% were Moslems, 18.6% Christians and 20% Jews.
3 Golan et al., 19–20, 23.
4 Ibid., 26.
5 Ibid., 27.
6 Ibid., 46.
7 [Hebrew] Joseph Olitzki, *Me'meoraot Lemilchama* [From Disturbances to War] (Haganah H.Q. in Tel Aviv and I.D.F. Cultural Service, 1951), 71.
8 '2nd Battalion Notes. Our Duties in Palestine', in *The "Faugh-a-Ballagh" The Regimental Gazette of The Royal Irish Fusiliers*, vol. 37, No. 164 (July, 1948), 292; Olitzki, 132.
9 Olitzki, 132–135. IDF Archive, Tel Hashomer, Circular 11 December 1947, 1–3/1948.
10 T.N.A. W.O. 261/322, Report 10 October–31 December 1947.

11 '1st Battalion,' *The Borderers' Chronicle*, June 48, 38.

12 Ibid.

13 Ibid., March 48, 9.

14 Ibid.

15 Ibid., June 1948, 38.

16 Ibid.

17 Ibid., March 48, 8.

18 '1st Battalion, Battalion Notes', *The Thin Red Line: The Regimental Magazine of the Argyll and Sutherland Highlanders (Priness Louise's)*, vol. 2, No. 3 (May, 1948), 57.

19 T.N.A. W.O. 261/322, and *The Thin Red Line*, June 1948, 39.

20 *The Thin Red Line*, May 1948, 61.

21 Ibid., 59.

22 Ibid.

23 Ibid., 58.

24 Ibid.

25 Lincolnshire Record Office, Lincoln, REGI/Bix5/794, and *The Royal Lincolnshire Regiment Monthly News Letter*, No. 11, February 1948, 5.

26 The C.O. Lt.-Col. S.A. Cooke had served with Wingate in Burma.

27 *News Letter*, No. 11, 7.

28 Ibid., 8.

29 T.N.A. W.O. 261/381 and W.O. 261/381.

30 W.O. 261/381.

31 For instance, *The "Faugh-a-Ballagh" [clear the way] The Regimental Gazette of the Royal Irish Fusiliers*, vol. 37, No. 164 (July, 1948), 292.

32 Golan, Chapter 2.

33 On the development of Plan Dalet, see [Hebrew] Shoshana Shitftel (ed.), *Plan "D": The First Strategic Plan in the Independence War* (Ministry of Defense and IDF Archive, 2008).

34 For Jaffa in particular, see ibid., 322.

35 Golan, 88–89.

36 Ibid., 94.

37 Ibid., 95–97. See also Menachem Begin, *The Revolt,* revised edition [first published in Hebrew in 1957] (London: W.H. Allen, 1979), ch. 29 'The Conquest of Jaffa.'

38 Evron, *Gidi*, 311.

39 Golan, 97.

40 Including from its raid on Camp 80 and the ammunition train near Binyamina on 18th April.

41 Golan, 98–100.

42 Ibid., 163.

43 Ibid., 164.

44 Montgomery, *Memoirs*, 425.

45 Ibid.

46 'The Jewish Attack on Jaffa,' *The Faugih-a-Ballagh*, July 1948, 292.

47 Ibid.

48 Ibid., 294.

49 Ibid.

50 Golan, 106.

51 A detailed IZL account in [Hebrew] Chaim Lazar (Litani), *The Conquest of Jaffa* (Tel Aviv: Shelach, 1951), 122.

52 Golan, 113–119, *The Faugh-a-Ballagh*, 294.

53 Golan, 120–123.

54 *The Faugh-a-Ballagh*, 294.

55 Jaffa – Tel Aviv Battle', in *4th/7th Royal Dragoon Guards Regimental Magazine*, December 1948, 49.

56 Ibid., 50.

57 Ibid.

58 *The Faugh-a-Ballagh*, 295.

59 Ibid.

60 'Jaffa and the Evacuation. The Last Days of the 1st Battalion in Palestine', in *The Thin Red Line*, vol. 2, No. 3 (September, 1948), 78.

61 *The Faugh-a-Ballagh*, 295.

62 See T.N.A. W.O. 261/381 'Appendix "A" Jaffa Commitments,' in Quarterly Historical Report of the 2Bn The Royal Irish Fusiliers for the quarter ending 31 March 1948.

63 Golan, 126–127.

64 Ibid., 129–130. See also Seth J. Franzman and Jeran Culibrk, 'Strange Bed fellows: The Bosnians and Yugoslav Volunteers in the 1948 War in Israel/Palestine', in *Istorij'a*, 20. veka. 1/2009, 197.

65 T.N.A. AIR 28/659 Operations Record Book, RAF Station Ramat David, 28 April 1948.

66 T.N.A. AIR 24/1912 Appendix "E" Air Headquarters Operations Record Book for the month of April 1948, The HQRAF MWD/ME.

67 T.N.A. AIR 24/1912 Operations Record Book Air H.Q. Levant 28 April 1948.

68 Similarly, T.N.A. W.O. 261/574 H.Q. Pal. G (Air) Branch Historical Record, 1 April–30 June 1948, 'though no great damage was done, it undoubtedly showed the Jews that we were prepared to use aircraft in an offensive role. In the present instance, it caused them to withdraw from the area'. See also Brian Cull, Shlomo Aloni with David Nicolle, *Spitfires over Israel* (London: Grub Street, n.y.), 110.

69 T.N.A. AIR 24/1912 App. AOL 368, 28 April 1948 and App. F, AOL 362, 29 April.

70 T.N.A. AIR 23/8350 'Report on the Evacuation of the Royal Air Force from Palestine by Air Vice Marshall W. L. Dawson, C.B., C.B.E. Air Officer Commanding Levant,' 10.

71 [Hebrew] Joseph Olitzki, *Mul ir oyenet. Sefer Ha"haganah" al Bat-Yam* (Bat Yam: Irgun Chavrei Hahaganah beBat Yam, 1984), 151.

72 *The Thin Red Line*, 78.

73 Ibid., 97

74 Ibid., 105.

75 *The Faugh-a-Ballagh*, 295.

76 Lazar, 259–301.

77 'Last Days in Palestine. The Record of the 41st Field Regiment', in *The Gunner*, vol. 30, No. 5 (August, 1948), 127. See also John Donovon (ed.), *'A Very Fine Commander': The Memoirs of General Sir Horatius Murray* (Barnsley, South Yorkshire: Pen and Sword, 2010), 219.

78 *The Thin Red Line*, 78.

79 Ibid., 81, 'Exodus 1948,' *The Kingsman – The Journal of The King's Regiment*, No. 26 (July, 1948), 13.

80 *The Thin Red Line*, 78.

81 Ibid.

82 Instruction signed 'Hillel' (Galili) 28 April 1948, Tel Hashomer, IDF Archive, 321/1948, 1. See also Lazar, 217–219.

83 *The Thin Red Line*, 81.

84 Golan, 151–152.

85 Ibid., 153.
86 Ibid., 156–157.
87 T.N.A. W.O. 261/574 Appendix "A".
88 *The Thin Red Line*, 78.
89 Ibid.
90 Ibid., 102.
91 Ibid., 81.
92 Ibid.
93 Ibid.
94 Major Kenneth Macksey, *The Tanks History of the Royal Tank Regiment, 1945–1975* (London, Melbourne: Arms and Armour Press, 1979), 45–46. T.N.A. W.O. 261/579 Quarterly Historical Report for the 4th Royal Tank Regiment Quarter ending 30 June 48. The troop of the 4th RTR relieved the troop of the 4th/7th.
95 *The Thin Red Line*, 82.
96 Ibid., 102.
97 Ibid.
98 Efal, Yad Tabenkin Archive, section 15, Avraham Eilon, container 3, file 1, document 23 'The Army of Jaffa – TA Border,' 4 May 1948.
99 *The Thin Red Line*, 103.
100 Ibid.
101 Ibid., 98.
102 Ibid., 100.
103 *The Faugh-a-Ballagh*, 295, T.N.A. W.O. 261/381, '"U" Battery on Road Patrol', in *The Gunner*, Oct. 1948. The Q.M.S. [Battery Quarter Master Sergeant] while visiting the M10 was able to "liberate" a number of 'useful articles from the deserted city'.
104 *The Faugh-a-Ballagh*, 295.
105 Ibid.
106 Ibid., 295–296.
107 I.F. Stone, *This is Israel* (New York: Boni and Gaer, 1948), 28.
108 Golan, 178–179.
109 Ibid., 179.
110 Olitzky, *Memeoraot*, 406; Radai, 236–242.
111 For the latter see IDF archive 321/1948, 52, Kiryati to "Nachman" [Senya Sirkin, senior commander in the Tel Aviv Haganah], 13 May 1948.

8 The course of the evacuation

The Army's final report 'The Withdrawal from Palestine 1 April–30 June 48' issued by Headquarters Palestine and Transjordan[1] described its later stages as 'conducted as an operation of war with the support of the Royal Navy and the Royal Air Force'. While forced to adapt to the escalating war between Jews and Arabs, the Army increasingly concentrated on the manner and timing of the evacuation, while gradually abandoning its original mission of fully maintaining law and order throughout Palestine, for the sake of securing a quick and clean evacuation when ordered to do so.

The report characterized the first (of three) phases of the withdrawal, 1st–30st April, as 'adjustment and "clearing the decks".' In accordance with earlier plans, the Army initially shed unnecessary units but these plans hadn't accounted for the increase in the Army's missions. In changing the policy, the number of units under command remained higher than planned and most of them were actively engaged in a manner which was likely to complicate their extraction. An example of the effect of changing circumstances of the Army's establishment was Southforce in El Bureij, near the Egyptian border.

> It had not been the original intention to retain troops in the SOUTH Sector once the area had been evacuated by 61 Lorried Infantry Brigade on 28 February; but this in fact became necessary in order to keep open the road and rail communications to RAFAH and the SOUTH for the evacuation of troops and material.[2]

Soon it became apparent that the blanket was too short and that moving troops around to fill in an increasing number of operational gaps in the Army's map of deployment failed to stabilize the situation. In some areas, diluting the Army's presence entailed considerable risk. An example is the central sector where on 6th April the 1st Guards Brigade was moved to Haifa to replace the 1st Parachute Brigade which was leaving Palestine. 'It marked the first occasion on which troops were of necessity "thin on the ground" in a Jewish area notorious for its anti-British activities'.[3] A solution was to bring in as a short-term measure reinforcements from outside

Palestine who, travelling light, would be easier to evacuate. These included on 15th April a troop of tanks from 4th/7th Dragoon Guards, who were sent to Jerusalem, 'The city had not seen tanks as part of its Garrison for a considerable period'[4] and therefore, their appearance would, hopefully, constitute a deterrent well beyond its size. This at a time in which the Army's reluctance to endanger its troops or its lines of communication could result in what the civil authority considered a dereliction of its duty.

The frustration of the High Commissioner was unmistakable in his description in a private letter to the Colonial Secretary of the Army's reaction to the Jewish massacre in Deir Yassin (8th April) west of Jerusalem, a case in which 'our authority has progressively weakened to a greater extent than that in what even I had foreseen'. Following the village's occupation by the Irgun Zvai Leumi (IZL),

> I wanted the soldiers to attack it, if necessary with all the power they can produce and turn out the Jews. But I am told that they are not in a position to do so, or indeed do anything which may provoke conflict with either side as their troops are already fully committed.[5]

Deir Yassin was not within the Jerusalem security zones and its position was of no significance to the Army. The Army's response was very different when positions along the evacuation routes were endangered, as in Sheik Jarrach.

Reinforcements and the improvisation of special task forces often proved insufficient. The creation of Rail-force to secure the evacuation of Army stores by land to Egypt and to protect the trains and their workers failed to stop attacks on the rolling stock, their contents or the lines, by both Jewish dissident groups and Arab looters operating 'in many cases with the connivance of Arab railway staffs'.[6] Consequently, whereas on 29th January, the General Manager of Palestine Railways, A.F. Kirby stated that the Railways (and Ports) would remain in full operation after 15th May until the final evacuation of all British troops, the trains in fact gradually came to a complete halt on 27th April.[7] As a result, a large amount of military stores could not be evacuated due to the limited (and costly) shipping available through Haifa and was left to be stolen, sold (often illegally) or disabled and abandoned. Thus, the 1st Airborne Field Squadron, Royal Engineers was responsible for stripping condemned fighting vehicles, throwing them into Wadi Falah (Beit Oren) and setting them alight with flame thrower liquid by remote control, some to be later salvaged and refitted or cannibalized by the Israeli Army.[8]

Violence spread geographical beyond the "traditional" trouble spots such as the mixed towns and Jewish traffic on roads running through Arab-controlled territory. The result was a greater dispersion of units left largely on their own to cope as best they could. Troops were hit sporadically, with a few dramatic incidents such as the IZL attack on camp 80, a situation which became politically intolerable in Britain. With dwindling resources and no promise of sufficient reinforcements, the Army, in keeping with the Chief of Imperial General Staff (CIGS)'s general policy, began to downsize its local commitments without always consulting with higher authorities.

At first, the Army was prepared, indeed the troops were keen to become actively involved in forcefully stopping local battles and impressing on both communities its might and its determination to preserve law and order by whatever means. Curiously, the Army was slow to accept that flag marches and fire demonstrations became a source of entertainment for the locals (and the troops) and in general a waste of time, petrol and engine hours. They appear to have been such a regular feature of imperial policing that in some regions they were still used while abandoned as ineffective elsewhere. Local commanders increasingly sought to avoid notoriously dangerous roads seeking safer alternatives both for themselves and for civilian traffic. This was noticeable early on in the southern sector and in the centre where the Army was forced to admit that despite the government's undertaking it could not guarantee the safety of all roads at all times. Where no alternative was available as in the Latrun-Jerusalem stretch of the main road, the Army stopped using it for its own purposes, and directed its traffic to other, safer if less convenient roads, changing its evacuation plan accordingly and allowing Arabs and Jews to fight it out with minimal interference. Similarly, in Safad, the Army stopped using the Acre-Safad road following Arab attacks on its vehicles, thereby allowing the Jews to attack and occupy positions west of the town, isolating it from its western Arab hinterland.

Without realizing it, these local changes in policy and deployment had a dramatic effect on the course of the Arab-Israeli War. In the south, the diminishing presence of the Army along the main arteries apart from the main coastal road and the Beersheba-Gaza, Beersheba-Ujja roads, designated evacuation routes to Egypt, resulted in the Haganah readily assuming responsibility for the security of the Jewish convoys and the teams mending the water lines while gradually gaining control of the open stretches east of Gaza and around Beersheba. The main Arab-armed presence in the area were the Bedouins, who initiated most of the early confrontations but whose flocks were extremely vulnerable to Jewish retaliation and whose motivation was largely profit. When threatened, they moved to safer regions or else reached an agreement with their Jewish neighbours.[9] The Egyptian invasion in May changed the balance of power in the south and Israel had to fight long and hard to regain its hold on it.

The Army's decision to stop using the Latrun-Jerusalem road had more dramatic and far-reaching consequences. Once the Army stopped intervening forcefully in breaking up Arab ambushes against Jewish convoys, added to which was the considerable improvement in Arab tactical skills, due the completion of training of the main Arab militia, the Jihad-el-Mukades and the arrival of Iraqi Army volunteers as part of the Arab Liberation Army, Jewish traffic came to a standstill. With the dependence of Jewish Jerusalem on supplies from Tel Aviv and the coast, and the breakdown of the convoy system, the Haganah was forced to go on the offensive a month and a half before it had initially planned to. Israeli historiography marks the resultant Nachshon Operation as a turning point in the course of the war both in the size of the force assembled (a brigade) and the mission which was to clear the road and thereby occupy the ridges and villages along it rather than just push through another convoy. Henceforth, the British policy of maintaining the spatial status quo was virtually abandoned. Arabs (Mishmar Ha'Emek) and Jews (Jerusalem, the eastern Galilee) went on the offensive with the objective of occupying and destroying enemy communities while the Army at most offered to broker a local truce for the evacuation of non-combatants and removal of bodies and wounded but little else. Hence it came as a surprise to some of the Jewish forces when late in April the Army reacted forcefully in Jerusalem (Sheikh Jarrach) and Jaffa to stop Jewish forces from occupying Arab areas.

While events along the Latrun-Jerusalem road had little impact on the Army and the evacuation plan, developments in the Galilee were seen as far more significant. In the words of the final Withdrawl Report: 'On 16 April the step back towards Haifa began in the NORTH EAST with 1 Irish Guards evacuating Safad'.[10] The issue here was not the control of a stretch of road but the fate of a mixed town in which the Army was responsible for keeping the two communities apart and preventing what appeared to be a certain massacre of the Jews by the Arabs should they be allowed to gain the upper hand and act freely. After lengthy deliberations and with the High Commissioner powerless to offer an alternative, the Army withdrew its one company from Safad certain that the refusal of the small Jewish community to evacuate under British auspices would result in its massacre.

Once the principle of withdrawing from contested towns and areas was acceded and the precedent established, the eastern Galilee was gradually evacuated well before the end of the Mandate. Following Safad, the Army allowed the Haganah's occupation of Tiberias (18th April). The Jewish superiority in the eastern Galilee and the Beisan Valley created the stability which allowed the gradual concentration of the Craforce units in Rosh Pinna, Tiberias and Zemach, and their later move without incident to Haifa. Another result of the change in policy was that most of the Arabs of the northern Jordan Valley (to be joined in 11th May by the Arabs of Safad) became refugees before the end of the Mandate.

In the 'Withdrawl' Report, the outcome of the battle of Haifa was described as 'the first major Jewish victory over the Arabs and its effects on the political situation and the morale of the opposing sides was far reaching'. But this was not the main concern of General Stockwell, CO. North Sector. He

> had appreciated that he must always keep in view the primary object of the evacuation of troops and material through Haifa with the minimum

interference and loss of British lives. To this it was essential for Haifa to remain quiet. He did not consider he had sufficient troops available to join issue with both sides, which would almost certainly result in prolonged, bitter and costly fighting. He therefore redeployed his forces in Haifa to protect British interests and lines of communication and essential civilian installations and services. The City did in fact remain completely quiet from that time until evacuation.[11]

From his point of view, all other consequences were, in relation, of minor concern. Hence, by implication, the Army's surprise, when vehemently criticized for having allowed a major political and diplomatic crisis, reflected in Bevin's outburst of having been 'let down by the Army', eliciting Montgomery's furious response.

The unhurried pace of the final withdrawal from the eastern Galilee followed by the rest of the Galilee with the stability resulting from the occupation of the evacuated areas by the Haganah was later reflected in the low priority given to the Galilee by Ben-Gurion and the Haganah HQ (but not by Moshe Carmel) following the battle of Haifa, based on the evaluation that the area was relatively well prepared to withstand an external attack. Meanwhile, the Army units assembling in Haifa settled into a peaceful routine while awaiting their turn to leave.

Similarly, following the encirclement of Jaffa and the departure of most of its inhabitants, the evacuation of the 3rd Brigade proved uneventful, although logistically complicated by the wide dispersal of some of its subunits. For the Argyll and Sutherlands concentrated in Jaffa the move was straightforward. The evacuation orders were issued on 13th May and included the remaining civil administration and the police.[12] During the day, all non-essential troops were sent to Lydda Camp, leaving only combat soldiers and their commanders. Early on D-day, "B" and "D" Companies withdrew from the line. "A" Company was replaced in the cantonment by "C" Company and "B" Company of the Irish Fusiliers. Next came the last companies in Jaffa. "D" Company took over the positions in Lydda airport from the King's Regiment while "B" Company and the Fusiliers with the tanks left Jaffa. The Haganah had been informed in advance of the moves. 'They made no attempt to interfere-rather naturally, as Jaffa was now being left wide open to them – and did not even advance at once, although before the withdrawl was complete they were following up as close as they dared'.[13] Finally, the civil administration, the Police, the tanks and Fishforce left, 'and the Jaffa force was thereby dissolved'.

Various last minute assignments north of Lydda were to secure the traffic from Jerusalem through Beit Ur on its way to Haifa. It was felt that the road 'lay unpleasantly close to Tel Aviv and was therefore particularly vulnerable to Jewish interference'. Additionally, it was believed that the Lydda airport, once evacuated, 'was likely to be the scene of a battle between Arab and Jew', nearby petrol storage tanks might be set on fire and 'the resulting blaze would have attracted both sides, with the usual results' endangering the northbound traffic. But none of these fears materialized and the night of 14th–15th May proved 'surprisingly quiet... considering the situation and the possibilities'.[14]

The rest of the Argylls were put to work packing and loading their vehicles 'to and beyond capacity', possibly a reflection of the prodigious amount of equipment they had accumulated in their various stations in Palestine. Their move to the Egyptian border at Rafah was conducted as a tactical operation of an all-arms column designated NEILFORCE. It 'was fervently hoped that there would be no interference. Even given a completely peaceful run, there were grave doubts as to whether some of the vehicles could ever get to the other end'.[15]

At 06:30 hours on 15th May, the column began to move. It took half an hour just to leave camp, which was immediately occupied by an unimpressive looking Arab force. 'They did not look capable of with-holding the smallest attack'. The column halted in Qastina, where the battalion had been stationed in early 1947. The camp, they noted, 'had been reduced to heaps of rubble; not a roof remained, and the roads were overgrown with weeds'. Here they waited until 14:00 hours when the last of the other columns passed them. They were joined by the 3rd Hussars coming under command, forming the Army's rear guard.

The 3rd Hussars had left Ramat David on 30th April following the battle of Haifa. It settled in the deserted camp 21 east of Netanya and kept the coastal road secure for the passage of the Army's Headquarters from Jerusalem to Haifa in advance of the main withdrawal. Two troops were detached for assignments elsewhere, initially in Jaffa and Jerusalem and then in Sarafand, patrolling the roads in the area of Latrun, Masmiya, Ramle and Lydda through which major evacuation columns would pass.[16] The end of the Mandate was palpable. 'The people in the countryside were preparing for war, and some semblance of order prevailed only in the main towns and over connecting roads'.[17] Typically, their record of their trip to the border (Operation Scuttle) noted their old camps, some taken over by the Haganah, others, nearer the border, by the invading Egyptian army. Thus Aqir airbase, 'where many... had done their parachute training, and must have brought back many memories, not all of them pleasant'. Near Aqir they witnessed two Egyptian Spitfires strafing a Jewish Dakota.[18]

Further down the road, the adjutant noted,

> At Gaza we passed the Egyptian Army, halted, facing north, waiting to attack the Jews. The officers were celebrating the 'capture' of the entirely Arab town of Gaza, ...we saw enough tanks, guns and soldiers to realize that the Egyptians had the power to cut straight through Palestine. All they lacked was the leadership, organization and discipline – these the Jews had, and it was enough.[19]

"C" Squadron's first impression of the Egyptian Army was of 'a very smart Anti-Aircraft Battery, but soon enough only a mile or so behind we saw the usual sight of one "wog" taxi pulling two others with a fat officer, sitting in the back'.[20] The Argyll and Sutherlands, passing, just south of Gaza, an Egyptian Army column, reacted in the time-honoured manner of passing 'somewhat caustic comments, but the Egyptians, mistaking their remarks for those of well-wishing, smiled and cheered as the battalion passed'.[21]

The Egyptian Air Force's bombing and strafing ahead of the invading column included a British Army camp just south of Gaza town. Fear of a repeat attack the next morning resulted in the 1st Division countermanding the instruction not to travel by night for fear of mines, by ordering not to stop but complete the move to the border that same day, 'mines or no mines'. 'As darkness fell the Battalion was played over the Palestine border by the pipers'.[22]

With the Jewish occupation of Haifa and the stabilization of the situation in Jaffa, there remained, as a major concern, the evacuation of Jerusalem. The Army wanted to leave early and move the seat of government to Haifa. Lt.-General Macmillan wrote shortly after the evacuation that Jerusalem,

> was militarily unsound position to hold or to evacuate at the last possible moment, but it was politically essential to remain there since the Government functions were centralized in it and the Government could not have carried on from elsewhere.[23]

Similarly, the High Commissioner wrote to the Colonial Secretary on 12th April that 'the soldiers' suggestion' of an early move to Haifa was

> From our angle a most unattractive proposition. To abandon Jerusalem to become a battlefield, and then to go on sitting in Haifa unable to function, would to my mind be even more damaging to British prestige than all that is happening so far.'[24]

In order to ensure a clean last minute extraction of the 2nd Brigade's troops, some late reinforcements were brought to Jerusalem including 42 Royal Marines Commando which arrived from Malta by sea in Haifa on 2nd May and drove the next morning to Jerusalem. The order to move to Palestine on 28th April at 12:30 hours 'by the fastest possible means' came as a surprise.[25] By 23:00 hours, the 42 Commando had boarded the H.M.L.S.T. (Landing Ship Tanks) *Striker*. Meanwhile, 45 Commando were flown in from Benghazi, in two batches, to Ramat David to form a reserve for the 1st Guards Brigade in Haifa, but it soon became apparent that the situation there was well in hand and they returned on 12th May. In Jerusalem, 42 Commandos under command of the 1st Guards Parachute Battalions came up from Latrun and took up the position previously held by Highland Light Infantry (HLI) in Sheikh Jarrach overlooking the northern evacuation route to the Beit-Ur-Latrun road and to Qalandiya airport.

Having spent the previous three months desert training in Tripolitania, the Commandos reaction to the scenery on the way from Haifa was typical.

> How green the country was, even to the tops of the hills! Here were tall grasses and flowers of the field, and hollyhocks growing wild. It was twice like England, once in this greenness to which we had grown unaccustomed, and once from the familiarity of having from our earliest days – though often unconsciously, perhaps – applied the great images of the Bible to our own hills and sheep and goats.
>
> Throughout the whole journey we saw far less of the Jews than we did of the Arabs. We never had time to understand either much beyond the things which immediately affected us; and our impartiality was not strained.[26]

After settling into their positions in north Jerusalem, the Commandos soon realized that while Jews and Arabs were busy shooting at each other mainly during darkness, they had little interest in their presence there. 'And so we stayed, at the ready, until after a week one wondered just what sort of strain had been put on Units that had been in Palestine for a year or more'.[27]

Lt.-Col. John Nelson commanding officer (CO) 1st Para, now in the positions commanding the northern entrance to Jerusalem took great pride in his diplomatic skills displayed in the Beisan Valley and his friendship with "Fawzi" (Fauzi Al-Qawuqji) which he was certain had ensured local Arab co-operation, not realizing that Qawuqji was an outsider in these parts, representing external interests. Qawuqji had moved south to the Jerusalem sector, following his failure in Mishmar Ha'Emek in an attempt to fill the void in the Arab command created by the death of Abd al-Qadir al-Hussayni. By way of advertising his presence and his might, Qawuqji positioned his old 75 mm French field guns on the ridge of Nebi Samuel and began to shell Jerusalem somewhat in the manner of the IZL in Jaffa. Nelson advised him to stop. 'He gave his promise, we had a cup of coffee and I was able to report to the G.O.C. that this sort of thing would not happen again. It did not'.[28] Indeed, Qawuqji gave up on Jerusalem and moved west but for reasons other than Nelson's advice.

At the time, Nelson came to the conclusion that the only way to stop the shooting north of Jerusalem 'would be to eliminate the Jewish forces in the Hadassar [Hadasah Hospital]'. With the 1st Battalion Paras (Airborne) and 42nd Commando (Royal Marines),[29] a move that could only serve to re-ignite the fighting in Jerusalem and endanger the evacuation. 'It was a great relief,' one of the Commando's observed, 'when the whole thing was called off because we were pulling out'.[30] Still the Commandos expected that they might well have to withdraw under fire, not realizing that the preparations they had observed on both sides were solely for the forthcoming confrontation. In the event,

> The High Commissioner's column passed through us up the road, and in half an hour we had followed him, and the British power had left Jerusalem. We saw him fly off from Qualandia [Qalandia], and then started our drive back to Haifa.[31]

The column to Haifa included the 1st Paras, the Commandos, some Royal Air Force (RAF) staff and some police, covered by the tanks of "B" Squadron, 4th/7th Dragoons under command of Nelson. His account again reflecting his bias:

> I had hoped to drive entirely through Arab country [presumably through Nablus] which although involving a longer and more mountainous route would, I was confident, afford us complete safety from ambush or attack. My Arab friends had declared that after 30 years as their guests in Palestine they would never molest us while we were leaving.[32]

But he was ordered to travel through Jewish-occupied areas so as to ensure that the column reached Haifa by daylight. 'No fighting took place that day in Palestine and all Jewish Kibbutzim flew the Red flag alongside that of the star of David'.[33]

The main body of the 2nd Brigade travelled south via Hebron and Beersheba. The dispersal of the battalions in Jerusalem helped in that evacuation meant organizing separate convoys each in its own zone. The southernmost, the 1st Suffolk had taken over on 26th April the positions of HLI close to the northern wall of the Old City, "C" Zone, the Jewish Quarter in the Old City and the convoys hauling potash from the Dead Sea[34] (but without Sheikh Jarach). The Jocks were moved out of harm's way and the sensitive road north, to the southern "A" Zone near the contested neighbourhood of Katamon. The Suffolk's reported on their ten days in and near the Old City in their usual tone of cheerful detachment.

> Romantic names such as Greek Convent, Dung Gate (less romantic) and the Hole in the Wall, became household words. Company Headquarters was fully established in the Jaffa Gate Police Station and, through narrow twisting streets groups of "A" Company would find their way – first with wonder, but soon with the confidence of knowledge – heavily laden with "Compo" and the prospect of steak and kidney pie.[35]

Their main task was to try with diplomacy by day and Bren gun fire by night, to stop the firing while the Mandate Government tried to establish a truce in Jerusalem.

The Suffolks were resigned to their much diminished influence on the state of security in Jerusalem. This had its advantages. 'The tempo of Arab Jew violence has risen to a pitch where interest in British personnel declined, except as a source of arms, and was concentrated on the enemy'.[36]

Evacuation began on the evening of 13th May with "A" Company leaving the Old City at 17:00 hours. At 05:00 hours, the next morning (14th May) it occupied the Italian Hospice on the road to Sheikh Jarach from which it covered the withdrawal of 85 Field Battery R.A. and remaining in position until the High Commissioner drove by on his way to Qalandia. The Suffolks then withdrew south through the areas held by the 2nd Warwickshires and the 1st HLI, took up positions covering the road to Bethlehem and after all the remaining units of the Brigade passed them, including most of their own battalion joined the end of the column.[37]

The sense of relief on leaving Jerusalem was heightened in the 2nd Warwickshires, who, suffering from a severe manpower shortage, were warned by 'a reliable source that the Stern Gang had made a thorough reconnaissance of the Zone, and intended to raid our armouries'.[38]

> This meant that by night all guards on the perimeter wire were strengthened, and extra guards had to be found for B[attalion] H.Q. As well as an Inlying Picquet Platoon had to be kept ready at a moment's notice to go to any part of the zone, should the Stern Gang attack. However, this never happened.[39]

In addition, it was feared that at the moment of the evacuation both sides would endeavour to capture the main buildings in the security zone in central Jerusalem with little regard for the safety of any British troops caught in the middle. The Brigadier anticipating the problem arranged for the battalion commanders of the Suffolks and Warwickshires to meet with representatives and local commanders of the Haganah to arrange a quiet transfer of the zones to take place while the troops were still there (Figures 8.1 and 8.2).[40]

On the evening of the 13th, 'The last of the kit was loaded onto the transport, and Companies took up their final positions for the withdrawl'.[41] The same evening officials of the Jewish Agency

> gave a small party to a few members of each Company, in appreciation, they said, of the fine example and gentlemanly way in which the 2nd Battalion, The Royal Warwickshire Regiment, had conducted itself during its tour in Jerusalem. This party was given in the Unit Canteen.

At 10:00 hours, the next morning they began their evacuation.[42]

Figure 8.1 Jerusalem. Folding coils of Dannert wire on Jaffa street, facing the Generali Building, in front of Zone C, where most government offices were located, 14 May 1948.

Source: Yehuda Eisenstark; Courtesy of the I.D.F. Archive (file 0-232), Ministry of Defense, Israel.

Figure 8.2 Jerusalem. British soldiers leaving Zone C while Haganah fighters prepare to take over.

Source: Yehuda Eisenstark; Courtesy of the I.D.F. Archive (file 0-279), Ministry of Defense, Israel.

A similar story in which the initiative was the Army's was published by the *Palestine Post* on the day of the evacuation (14th May), under the title 'Bidding Farewell.'

> Three Army officers, telephoned the Jewish Agency offices one night this week, saying they wanted to bid farewell. They were asked to come up to the Agency offices, where they were received by a Jewish representative who took them with a Haganah escort – to the Eden Hotel [outside the security zone] for a farewell drink. After many hand shakes and expressions of good will, the officers were escorted back to Zone B gates.[43]

On the other hand, a Jewish farewell gesture to the HLI Jocks was received in a different, if typical, manner. It consisted of,

> A case marked "Whiskey", a present to "A" Company by some Jews when they saw the men vacating posts. This was treated with the greatest suspicion and thoroughly "frisked" by the Pioneers before being opened. It was the "real Mckay" – Canadian version.[44]

The HLI left Jerusalem in tactical formation in 13:00 hours, the last battalion, it recorded proudly, to cross the municipal boundary[45] (Suffolk's "A" Company's account not withstanding). 'The Holy City was thus abandoned after thirty years of British occupation, and left for infidels to squabble over and bathe in blood'.[46] In a characteristically sour note, the historian of the Regiment summed up its experience in Palestine.

> The task of maintaining law and order in Palestine after the [world] war was, without doubt, the most unpleasant and thankless duty upon which the 71st had ever been engaged. It is asking a great deal of soldiers, to expect them to keep their tempers and refrain from reprisals for months on end among a hostile population, when their comrades are being brutally cut down in the exercise of their duty. The Metropolitan Police have a world-wide reputation for imperturability and forbearance under the most trying circumstances; but murder one or two of them, and see what happens! The courage and discipline shown by the 71st during their long months in Palestine was indeed remarkable to a high degree especially when it is remembered that the majority were young recruits from Glasgow, with but a year of service. The whole circumstances of the surrender of the Mandate – of a trust, that is, freely undertaken after the Holy Land had been gloriously delivered from the oppression of the Turk, was in any case shameful and depressing, offering no shadow of a cause in the furtherance of which men will willingly give their lives.[47]

On a different note, Brigadier Jones wrote in his quarterly report that in spite of the hardships his troops had endured in Jerusalem, 'Turnout and the paying of compliments were of a very high standard... When the Brigade evacuated to EGYPT this standard suffered a definite setback temporally [sic]'.[48]

At 08:00 hours on 14th May, a Guard of Honour drawn up from "B" Company of the HLI was mounted at Government House for the High Commissioner Sir Alan Cunningham, who, for his last day in Palestine, donned his General's uniform. At 08:15 hours, after inspecting the Guard, Cunningham left on his way to Qalandia airport.[49] Along the route, he inspected another Guard of Honour with the ninety-nine years old colours of the 1st Battalion The Suffolk Regiment drawn up in front of Damascus Gate.[50] Upon leaving the boundaries of the city, the 40 Commandos mounted another Guard.[51]

Air Officer Commanding (AOC) Palestine, W.L. Dawson had been given on D minus 1 complete control of Qalandia.[52] A convoy of senior government officials arrived at 07:30 hours. At 08:30 hours, the High Commissioner arrived at the airport with General Officer Commanding (GOC) MacMillan, who was to fly with him to Haifa and then remain in the enclave after the formal end of the Mandate, responsible for the British interests in Palestine until the last troops left.[53] Cunningham inspected yet another Guard of Honour, this one of the RAF Regiment, and departed to Haifa in a twin engine Anson piloted by Dawson. A second Anson followed with MacMillan and his staff, a third with baggage, two Dakotas with Civil officials, two light Taylorcraft Austers for liaison with the ground columns and finally two single engine Proctors, used for communication, in reserve. Dawson's SASO (Senior Air Staff Officer) Wing Commander R.H. Whitehouse was given the honour of the last RAF pilot to fly out of Qalandia.[54] During Cunningham's last hour in Jerusalem, four Spitfires circled over the city and Qalandia and later covered his flight to Haifa along with three Lancaster heavy bombers.

On arriving in Haifa airport, the Spitfires 'did a perfectly timed fly-past' as Cunningham was driven to the port,[55] where he inspected his last Guard of Honour for the day comprised of soldiers from King's Company, the 1st Battalion The Grenadier Guards, 40 Commando Royal Marines and the Pipes of the Irish Guards.

Before a company, which included British officials, 'press representatives from all over the world, and tough, fierce-looking Guards R.S.M., and to the sound of clicking cameras and martial music provided by the picturesque Irish Guards pipers in their saffron kilts, the combined Units gave a performance which can best be described as superb'.[56]

Finally, the High Commissioner embarked on Vice-Admiral Troubridge's barge and accompanied by a seventeen-gun salute from the cruiser H.M.S. *Euryalus* and a flypast of a dozen Spitfires from the Aircraft Carrier H.M.S. *Ocean*, left the shores of Palestine first to the *Euryalus*, and at one minute before midnight to *Ocean*, just outside Palestine's territorial waters. Thus the British Mandate reached its official end.

While an event of paramount political significance, the whole affair was entirely dominated by military ceremony and pageantry down to the High Commissioner's uniform. Each branch of the armed forces was carefully assigned a role that would ensure its visibility in the proceeding. 'It would be interesting to know' wrote a Royal Marine acutely aware the uniqueness of the occasion, 'how many times in the history of the Corps a combined Guard of Honour has been provided from the Brigade of Guards and the Royal Marines'.[57]

As most of the Army evacuated Palestine, there remained the 1st Guards Brigade with RAF and RN contingents in the Haifa enclave to ensure the shipment of the maximum quantity of the remaining stores before leaving at the end of June (Figures 8.3 and 8.4). A sense of those last days is provided by Robin McGavel Graves, later CO 45 Commando.

> Having a farewell drink with someone from 6th Airborne Division, I was offered a couple of Deerhound [Stagheund] armoured cars and two ex-Palestine Police armoured cars. As these were in excess of their G 1098 scale [Standard issue] they could not take them with them. A bottle of whiskey clinched the deal and I felt very proud of my new possessions... after explaining what super mobile pill-boxes they would be and how useful in supporting our vehicle patrols they would prove, we were allowed to keep our armour. Sadly before we left... we had to set fire to them.[58]

Figure 8.3 Haifa. A Staghound armoured car embarking on a landing ship tanks (LSTs).

Source: Fred Czasnik; Courtesy of the I.D.F. Archive (file 20-5), Ministry of Defense, Israel.

Figure 8.4 Haifa. Troops embarking on a LST.
Source: Fred Czasnik; Courtesy of the I.D.F. Archive (file 37-31), Ministry of Defense, Israel.

The last major operational incident involving the British Army while in the Haifa enclave were three consecutive Spitfire attacks by the Royal Egyptian Air Force (REAF) on the RAF station in Ramat David on the morning of 22nd May. In the absence of a warning system, the first attack came as a complete surprise. Two Egyptian Spitfires bombed and strafed at about 06:10 hours destroying two RAF Spitfires on the ground and damaging eight other. The station commander Wing Commander Victor F. Streatfield, assuming that the attackers were Israeli, immediately sent two of his Spitfires to fly over Israeli airfields in search of recently landed aircraft, and destroy them. They flew as far as Aqir where they met with heavy and accurate anti-aircraft fire.[59] Another pair of fighters was sent to form a standing patrol over the field.

At 07:45 hours, three more Egyptian aircraft attacked the (empty) main hangar and hit an unserviceable Spitfire. Two of the attackers were shot down by the patrol and the third was hit by ground fire and landed in Israeli territory. A third attack by two Spitfires occurred on 09:15 hours. Three Dakotas sent to evacuate personnel and equipment came in to land. One received a direct hit and was destroyed, one was severely damaged, its pilot and navigator killed and three airmen injured. The third was also seriously damaged. Both attackers were shot down by the patrol.[60] There were no further attacks and after a twenty four hour delay the evacuation of Ramat David was resumed.

The last troops in Palestine left on 29th and 30th June. Both the 1st Guards Brigade and 40 Commando (under command) were able to claim to have been the last units out.[61] A small commando detachment formed the GOC's bodyguard. MacMillan insisted that he be the very last soldier to leave forcing a midshipman detailed to cast off the launch to board ahead of him.[62]

Two weeks earlier, on 15th June, the 1st Battalion Irish Guards embarked on H.T. Empire Test on their way to Tripoli. The voyage,

> In spite of foreboding to the contrary, proved from the comfort side to be up to the standard of a Mediterranean cruise, and the weather could not have been improved upon.
>
> Entertainment on the voyage consisted of tombola, cinema etc., and the big event was an Inter-Company Tug-of-War, which was won by No. 3 Company. This was followed by a pull between a Battalion scratch team and the ship's crew, which was fairly easily won by the Battalion.
>
> Fortunately for the honour of the Battalion, an event between our officers and the ship's officers did not take place.[63]

Soldiering was back to normal.

Notes

1 T.N.A. W.O. 261/574.
2 Ibid.
3 Ibid.
4 Ibid.
5 NAM 8303-104/26, General Sir Alan Cunningham to Colonial Secretary, 12 April 1948.
6 W.O. 261/574.
7 Israel State Archive 4959/52-n, Palestine General Managers' Office Haifa, 29 January 1948.
8 'Death Valley – in Palestine', *Soldier*, vol. 4, No. 6 (August, 1948). See [Hebrew] Amiad Brezner, *Origins of the Israeli Armourd Corps* (Ma'arachot: Ministry of Defense, 1995), 57, 68, 182, 235.
9 See [Hebrew] Hanina Porat, *Jewish Mukhtars in the Negev: The Story of the Mukhtars of Jewish Settlements: Their Relationship with the British Mandatory Government and Their Bedouin Neighours 1908–1948* (Mikve Israel: Yehuda Dekel Library, 2015).
10 T.N.A. W.O. 261/574 'The Withdrawl'.
11 Ibid.
12 *The Faugh-a-Ballagh*, July 1948, 296.
13 *The Thin Red Line*, vol. 2, No. 3, September 1948, 82.
14 Ibid.
15 Ibid.
16 T.N.A. W.O. 261/223 Quarterly Historical Report of the 3rd The King's Own Hussars For Quarter Ending 30 June 1948.
17 Bolito, *The Galloping Third*, 309–310.
18 *3rd the King's Own Hussars Regimental Journal*, vol. 3, No. 3 (January, 1949), 83. According to the IAF official history, a bombing run of Egyptian Dakotas caused no damage. [Hebrew] Maj. Avi Cohen, *The History of Israeli Air Force in the War for Independence October 1947–July 1948* (Ministry of Defense, 2004), 134.
19 Captain John Melhuish in Bolitho, *The Galloping Third*, 310.
20 *3rd Hussars Journal*, 83–84. See Rameses [Major C.S. Jarvis] *Oriental Spotlight* [1937] (London: John Murray, 1944), 87: 'Seniority in the Egyptian Army "is entirely by weight."
21 *The Thin Red Line*, 83.

22 Ibid., 82–83.
23 Lt.-General G.A.A. Macmillan, 'The Evacuation of Palestine', *Journal of Royal United Services Institute*, November 1948, 609.
24 NAM 8303-104/26 Cunningham to Colonial Secretary, 12 April 1948.
25 'Last Days in Palestine Commando's role in the withdrawl', in *The Globe and Laurel*, vol. 56, No. 8 (August 1948), 232.
26 P. Le. S. Harris, 'Journey to Jerusalem', in *The Globe and Laurel*, vol. 56, No. 10 (October, 1948), 302–303.
27 Ibid., 303.
28 Nelson, *Always a Grenadier*, 67. See also [Hebrew] Rubinstein, *Kastel*, 303.
29 Robin McGarel Groves in Robin Neillands, *By Sea and Land: The Story of the Royal Marine Commandos*, [1987] (Barnsley, S. Yorkshire: Pen and Sword Military Classics, 2004), 235–236. Also 'Last Days in Palestine,' 33.
30 Neillands, 236.
31 'Journey to Jerusalem', 303.
32 Nelson, 67.
33 Ibid.
34 T.N.A. W.O. 261/311 1st Suffolk Regiment Quarterly Historical Report for Quarter ending 30 June 1948.
35 *The Suffolk Regiment Gazette*, September, October 1948, 12.
36 W.O. 261/311.
37 Ibid.
38 *The Antelope*, November 1948, 107.
39 Ibid.
40 The report of the Haganah liaison officer is printed in full in [Hebrew] Motti Golani, *The Last Commissioner General Sir Alan Gordon Cunningham 1945–1948* (Tel Aviv: Am Oved, 2011), 307–308.
41 *The Antelope*, November 1948, 102.
42 Ibid.
43 *Palestine Post*, 14 May 1948.
44 *The Highland Light Infantry Chronicle*, vol. 45, No. 2 (April, 1949), 45.
45 Ibid.
46 Lt.-Col. L.B. Oatts, *Proud Heritage: The Story of the Highland Light Infantry, Volume Four 1919–1959* (Glasgow, London, Toronto: The House of Grant, 1963), 406. At the time, Oatts commanded the Regimental Training Center in Glasgow.
47 Ibid., 406–407.
48 T.N.A. W.O. 261/193 Quarterly Historical report H.Q. 2 Infantry Brigade for the Quarter ending 30 June 1948.
49 *The Highland Light Infantry Chronicle*, April 1949, 45. See also July 1948, 90.
50 W.O. 261/311, and *The Sufforlk Regiment Magazine*, September, October, 1948, 12 and photograph on p. 11.
51 *The Globe and Laurel*, August 1948, 233.
52 T.N.A. AIR 23/8350, 16.
53 *The Babe*, 135.
54 AIR 23/8350, 17, and *Spitfires over Israel*, 123.
55 AIR 23/8350, 17,
56 'Last Days in Palestine', *The Globe and Laurel*, August 1948, 233.
57 Ibid.
58 Neillands, 239.
59 *Spitfires over Israel*, 139–140, AIR 23/8350, 19, W.O. 261/574. H.Q. Pal 'G' Branch.
60 AIR 23/8350, 20, WO 201/574.
61 Lindsay, *Once a Grenadier*, 29; Neillands, 240.
62 *The Babe*, 135.
63 'Irish Guards,' in *The Household Brigade Magazine*, Summer 1948, 82.

9 Some final observations and conclusions

In the annals of Britain's minor, post–Second World War campaigns largely associated with the global process of decolonialization, the withdrawal from Palestine is merely one of several small, frustrating affairs. 'It had not been a glamorous nor a glorious campaign… The Army was well out of it. Nevertheless, despite appallingly complex circumstances, the regiments acquitted themselves well'.[1] The Army's casualties during, roughly, its last year in Palestine (1 June 1947–30 June 1948) were 13 officers and 161 other ranks (ORs) killed and 37 officers and 382 ORs wounded,[2] numbers far from negligible but minute compared to the campaigns of the World War. They are also less than those of the more dramatic campaign in Malaya and on a scale similar to Cyprus and Aden.[3]

By the time of the UN General Assembly's decision (181) to adapt the partition recommendation of its Special Committee on Palestine (UNSCOP), the Army was well on its way to returning to its pre-war traditional role of policing the Empire while preparing for a major confrontation with the emerging Soviet threat. This allowed the battalions that survived the post-war cuts to revert to the old Army's regimental traditions which proved, as in the past, of great help in isolating the soldiers from the worst features of the escalating inter-communal fighting in Palestine which quickly got out of hand. Most of the battalions in Palestine were constantly on the move from one frustrating assignment to another while trying to cope with the continuous erosion of its authority and effectiveness and the rise in the threats to the safety of the troops. They were saved from demoralization by a constant preoccupation with the planning and execution of largely self-generating activities including a large variety of sports, the arrangement of matches and competitions, hunting, preparing for parades, and various ceremonial and social affairs, training fresh reinforcements and adapting battalions to changes in their roles. Not least were various improvised and inane projects, testimony of soldiers' propensity to invest time and effort in displays of great silliness, such as during regimental commemoration days which often took the form of carnivals involving prodigious eating, drinking and controlled mayhem, sightseeing trips to sites associated by the Bible, forays into the desert, etc. All these were reported in great detail and with enthusiasm in the regimental journals side-by-side with reports of operational activities or other similarly momentous occasions. The nomadic nature of many of the Palestine battalions and their companies, constantly on the move from one part of the country to another, added to the introverted nature of regimental life. Wherever and whenever a unit or subunit found itself in a new location dealing with new problems, it immediately busied itself with a large variety of activities largely unrelated to the operational challenges of the worsening situation in Palestine.

These introverted activities provided an important psychological shield which protected units from the mental anguish which might have otherwise affected them, the result of dealing with the worst consequences of the escalating violence and their failure to contain it, such as the recovery of mutilated bodies from scenes of fighting. The battalions' quarterly reports, supported by the reports of brigade, division and general headquarters, repeatedly record the troops' high morale, especially when actively involved in some operational mission requiring movement or shooting, regardless of its purpose or effectiveness. This was often the case when units or subunits switched from routine static duties to patrols, retaliations, prevention, deterrence, etc. An example are the flag marches which had little if any deterring effect but provided the troops (and the locals) much amusement and a chance to tour parts of the country and observe its inhabitants. Accordingly, units leaving Palestine to more peaceful but boring posts such as the Canal Zone in Egypt experienced a drop in morale, usually manifested in a rise in the volume of daily sick parades or in deteriorating discipline.

On the subject of discipline and morale, the occasional instance of excessive use of fire power should not be interpreted as overreaction due to panic. It is a common response of soldiers, especially young ones, who were normally restricted in the use of their weapons, to let go, when allowed, with all they had regardless of whether the volume of fire was justified operationally or proportionate. Combat soldiers like to use their arms especially when they are normally not allowed to. In such instances, troops normally take not-so-secret pride in having expanded prodigious amounts of ammunition regardless of the actual need.

At the end of the day, the battalions leaving Palestine, some to other posts, some to be disbanded or amalgamated, were not greatly traumatized by their experience. More likely, they regarded in time their tour of duty there as unpleasant and frustrating with memory largely coloured by later events including the impression of the eventual victory of Israeli arms, and the evolving problem of the Arab refugees. This combined with their initial notions of the country and their mission. Common romantic associations were the Bible stories and the popular romantic image of T.E. Lawrence and the Arab revolt of the First World War, which had little to do with Palestine. Many had arrived in Palestine with some sympathy for the Jews following the Second World War and the pressing problem of relocation which with the Jews proved more complex than simply returning dislocated people to their places of origin. At the same time, they were often seen as interlopers who forced themselves on the country and its Arab inhabitants against their will.

42 Royal Marine Commando was unexpectedly sent to Haifa (Figure 9.2) where it arrived on 2nd May. It drove directly to Jerusalem (Figure 9.1), where it took up positions north of the city. It returned to Haifa along the same route eleven days later. An account of their trip reflects how little the current situation, with the final showdown near at hand, affected their basic and simplistic romantic view of Palestine and its population.

> At Ramleh we were in an Arab town. The main street was crowded. The children shouted and waved as we passed, but all others, looked on in silence. Every man carried a rifle and a heavy leather bandolier studded with working in metal. Five, dressed in white flowing robes, passed us in a jeep, and afterwards one, his rifle across his back, trotted his horse away from the road across broken country.[4]

This was pure romance. Ramle at this stage of the war was of no military significance (it would be occupied by the Israel Defence Force [IDF] on 11–12 July) but the playful children, the anachronistically armed men, the

Figure 9.1 Arab Palestine Jerusalem's Old City, David Street.

Figure 9.2 Arab Palestine. Downtown (Arab) Haifa and the Port as seen from Hadar HaCarmel.

appearance of five riders in a jeep dressed in white robes and finally one armed horse rider trotting away from the convoy is sheer drama.

> Further north across the coastal plain the Jews make an appearance as an antithesis to the romantic Arab and the Land of the Bible he inhabits.
>
> In the plain we ran through Jewish country to our Journey's end. Here men and women worked in the fields in shorts and brightly cellulosed American
>
> trucks fetched and carried for the farms. This was as much of the stake and difference between Jew and Arab as we saw. In the hills – those same hills perhaps, on which Enoch the Dreamer[5] walked with God – the Arabs lived for the most part as they had lived since the days when the New Testament was being lived, in their grey-stoned square-housed, citadel like villages, close to the land, sufficient to themselves, right and – in the best sense that can be given to the word-picturesque. To the plain the Jews had brought development and all the ugliness and seeming impropriety all the gain of modern farming, where the smell of cement was stronger that the smell of earth. This was what we have come to call "progress". And value it as we may, it is a force not to be denied, hard to be withstood (Figures 9.3–9.5).[6]

On the whole, the troops arrived, and remained, ignorant of the shifting nature and complexities of the Arab-Jewish struggle for Palestine, fuelled by the very un-British passions of nationalism. During their last months in Palestine, their instinctive sympathy for the Arabs was somewhat, but not

Figure 9.3 Jewish Palestine. Kubbutz Ein Harod, Jesreel Valley (Plain of Esdraelon), founded 1921.

Figure 9.4 Jewish Palestine. Downtown Tel Aviv, Cinema Mograbi (opened 1930).

entirely, eroded when the troops were faced with Arab violence. A common attitude was 'a plague on both your houses'.[7]

Throughout the Mandate, the Army was largely dependent for its local intelligence on the Police and civil administration especially when the Army was employed in support of these agencies. However, following the UN resolution, the Police rapidly became ineffective due to the mass desertions of its Arab personnel, who usually left with their arms, and the civil

Figure 9.5 Jewish Palestine. Downtown Tel Aviv, Herzl street (built 1909).

administration was similarly disintegrating. The troops were often operating blind for lack of reliable intelligence on local inter-communal relations, the balance of power within the communities, alliances and ancient feuds, etc. Consequently, company and battalion officers often sought to compensate by establishing on their own initiative contacts with the leaders (presumed or real) of the communities in their zones of responsibility. The problem was that occasionally they got it wrong, lacking any training in the collection and analysis of information and easily taken in by appearances. This was often the case with the Arab Liberation Army (ALA) which impressed, at first sight, many officers who came into contact with it, whereas by the end of the Mandate it had failed to fulfil its mission of protecting Palestine's Arabs, often causing more harm than good. An extreme example was Lt.-Colonel John Nelson CO 1st Guards Para Battalion who was convinced that he had established a firm understanding and friendship with the ALA Commander Qawuqji. Contrary to his convictions, Nelson had no noticeable influence on Qawuqji's decisions while the later allowed Nelson's illusion of actual friendly co-operation between them. (Nelson, like many other commanders, when writing their memoirs years later never bothered to verify their memories by means of later scholarship and stuck to their initial impressions.)

The confusion, it should be noted, was often mutual, certainly on the Jewish side. Jewish interlocutors often misinterpreted British attitudes and intentions, assuming, as a rule, that the British were pro-Arab and anti-Jewish except for particular "righteous" individuals. For example, Nachum Av, one of the leaders of the Jewish community in Tiberias (Figure 9.6) described in a memoir Lt.-Colonel W.A.C. Anderson CO 17th/21st Lancers as 'Colonel' Anderson CO of a battalion of parachutists, a sworn Arab sympathizer, who often tended to take their side.[8] British soldiers were often identified by Jews as the notoriously aggressive parachutists of the 6th Airborne Division, the "Kalaniyot" (anemones) regardless of their actual unit or the colour of their headgear. Any action taken by the Army which was not perceived as supportive of the Jews was automatically branded as a typical manifestation of anti-Jewish sentiment. According to Av's own account, Anderson took an active part in negotiating the evacuation of the Arabs of Tiberias (Figure 9.6) in an effort to prevent a massacre and in the transfer of the town's civil administration to the Jews.[9] Another local Jewish leader, Moshe Zachar, described in his own memoir how following the Haganah's occupation of Tiberias, he invited as a gesture of good will, Anderson to a friendly meeting with the local Haganah commander. Anderson in this account 'excelled in demonstrating superiority towards us, and regarded himself as defender of the Arabs'. When asked for the reasons for his hostility, Anderson denied any such sentiment although he was aware that the Jews considered him hostile.[10] He was often invited by the Arabs to their quarters as their guest but he was fed up with their coffee, while at the same time he was never invited by the Jews. Zachar admitted that it had never occurred to them to do so assuming he would refuse.[11]

Ignorance of the policies of the Army and of its reasons for its actions in certain incidents coupled with well-ingrained suppositions of the general British attitude towards each side were reflected in Israeli historiography which paid the subject little attention, or else relied heavily on the intelligence on the Army collected by the Haganah. A common intelligence fallacy was to interpret British action on the basis of presupposed intentions. The superficiality of Jewish analysis of Army policy is evident in the false confidence that led to the "battle" of Sheikh Jarrach, the result of the

Figure 9.6 Arab Palestine, Downtown (Arab) Tiberias and the Sea of Galilee.

mistaken assumption that the conduct of the Army in Haifa indicated a general unwillingness to fight regardless of its stated policy of preventing any potential threat to the designated routes of evacuation. The same mistake was made by the Irgun Zvai Leumi (IZL) in its attack on Manshiya, whereas the government had given its guarantee that Jaffa would remain Arab as long as it was still in authority. On the issue of British military decision making, Israeli and Arab historians assumed a common rationale and, in the absence of documentary proof, similar evaluations were based on what to them seemed self-evident.

Historical analysis based on the assumption of common interests is evident in attempts to explain the Arab setback in Haifa as an outcome of a conspiracy between the Army and the Jews, both of whom were the clear beneficiaries at the Arabs' expense. A feature of the retrospective misconstruction of the Army's decision in changing its policy in Haifa is its spatial dimension. Israeli and Arab accounts of the battle of Haifa confine the geographical boundaries of their versions of the course of events to the town. For the Army and more particularly General Stockwell, the geographical area of the change was the northern district from Hadera to the Lebanese border. The decision to withdraw from the main positions in Haifa to a narrow enclosure with the port at its centre was the final stage in a series of events which included the IZL's attack on camp 80, the withdrawal from Safad and the Jewish occupation of Tiberias. Having decided to prefer the safety of the troops to the maintenance of territorial integrity of either communities, there was no point in holding on to positions in the eastern Galilee that endangered soldiers' lives and were not essential for the security of the final evacuation. Unaware of the relevance of the sequence of events outside Haifa that led to the evacuation of positions in it has rendered the change in policy incomprehensible and fuelled the conspiracy theory of British-Jewish collusion.

The accusation of collusion is part of the moralistic debate on the identity of the perpetrators of the Palestinian Arabs' disaster – the "Nakba", and hence those responsible for its rectification. As far as the Army was concerned, the voluntary or forced removal of citizens from war zones was a common feature of modern warfare wherever fighting took place in inhabited areas. It became a "problem" by dint of a political decision not to allow the return of the refugees to their homes once the fighting had ended. Decisions aimed at rendering the removal of population, threatened by fighting, permanent or to initiate demographic changes following the political outcome of the war often were part of an effort to establish ethnically homogenous nation-states, legitimized by the principle of self-determination and the quest for regional stability.[12] The flight of the civilian population of villages and towns, Arabs and Jews, was not only accepted by the Army as an anticipated feature of the fighting but was also encouraged as a way to avoid massacres and pacify contested areas. Thus, the Army offered to arrange and protect the transfer of the Jews from Safad and the Arabs from

Tiberias. In Haifa, they accepted the Jewish appeals to the town's Arabs to remain under their rule as sincere, but did not try to prevent their leaving. Instead, they did their utmost to secure their departure at the risk to British soldiers' lives. In Jaffa, the Army prevented the Jewish occupation of the town fully aware that their protection of Jaffa's Arabs would be removed within a fortnight. Here too the Army did not try to stop the population from leaving while protecting their exit. On the whole, it seems that the Army was largely indifferent to the flight of civilians which, in time, became the defining experience of the Palestinian national movement. They were far more concerned with stabilizing the situation both to ensure a smooth evacuation and to prevent massacres which would force them to return. Oddly enough the believers on the Jewish side in British-Arab collusion to prevent the creation of a Jewish state[13] assumed that the intentional creation of instability ("tohubohu") was a British tactic to ensure that it would be asked to return as protector of the country.

Battalion and detached company commanders often enjoyed, especially during the first months of fighting, considerable freedom in their choice of means for dealing with local circumstances. They were mostly veterans of the fighting in the Second World War with plenty of combat experience sometimes in the same role (having been reduced in rank after the war) and were not much impressed by the threats from local militias, Jewish or Arab. Means were adopted to local needs in keeping with the policies laid down by Brigade and Division. The different temperament and evaluation of battalion commanders with the frequent movement of units often resulted in changes in tactics and policies which tended to confuse local Jewish commanders and consequently Israeli historians when attempting to define Army policy on the basis of its actions as in the case of arms searches and confiscations.

When allowed, the Army fought well. Many of the soldiers were young, inexperienced and partly trained. But the battalions still had a core of older, veteran soldiers and Non Commissioned Officers (NCOs) and every opportunity was used to improve the training of the new recruits. The main problem, however, were not the occasional short battles, but the oppressive grind of keeping law and order. Here the most important qualities were discipline, a stiff upper lip and forbearance, a combination of detachment and restraint. Fortunately, these qualities were quite common in the Palestine battalions, especially in those possessing a tradition of self-conscious decorum, such as the Foot Guards, qualities reflected in their appearance and general demeanour. The worst were the Jocks of the 1st Highland Light Infantry (HLI) in Jerusalem who went out of their way to foment violence and pick fights with Jews. It was the only unit in Palestine whose own chronicle, official history and operational record bear distinctive traces of anti-Semitism.[14] In between those two extremes some units were more laid back and quietist than others, but on the whole the Army did its best in coping with a frustrating mission under difficult circumstances and emerged from the experience largely unscathed and much relieved to be rid of it.

At the same time, not quite aware of the overall consequences of its actions, the Army caused a major change in the time table and manner of the actual end of the Mandate. Its early regional evacuations and increasing passivity resulted in a series of decisive confrontations between Jews and Arabs weeks ahead of the formal end of the Mandate. The resultant Jewish victories allowed the Declaration of the State of Israel (14th May) within borders which the, by now, experienced and nearly fully formed, Haganah army was able to defend against the invasion by Arab regular armies rather than have to simultaneously occupy the area and defend it as initially envisioned. By then the Palestinian Arab militias were no longer a major military force.[15]

Notes

1 Michael Dewar, *Brush Fire Wars Minor Campaigns of the British Army since 1945* [1984] (London: Robert Hale, 1990), 26.
2 T.N.A. W.O. 261/549 Quarterly Historical Record General Staff G (Plans and Operations) GHG MELF March–December, 1948.
3 Dewar, *Brush Fire Wars*, Appendix E, 198.
4 P. Le S. Harris, 'Journey to Jerusalem', in *The Globe and Laurel*, vol. 56, No. 10 (October, 1948), 302–303.
5 A curious reference to the prophecy of Enoch, 'the seventh from Adam' in The General Epistle of Jude: 14–16 in which the Lord on judgement day, with ten thousand of his saints will 'convince all that are ungodly among them of all their ungodly deeds which they have ungodly committed, and of all their hard speeches which ungodly sinners have spoken against him'.
6 'Journey to Jerusalem', 304.
7 Shakespeare, *Romeo and Juliet*, Act 3, Scene 1. See for instance, the reaction of the normally pro-Arab Dare Wilson in a letter to his parents dated 4th February 1948, Major General Dare Wilson, *Tempting the Fates: A Memoir of Service in the Second World War Palestine, Korea, Kenya and Aden* (Barnsley, South Yorkshire: Pen & Sword, 2006), 146.
8 [Hebrew] Nachum Av, *The Struggle for Tiberias* (Ministry of Defense, 1991), 62–63.
9 Ibid., 207.
10 [Hebrew] *The Forty Day Campaign to Free Tiberias* (Ministry of Defense, 1993), 46–47.
11 Ibid.
12 See Norman Rose, *A Senseless Squalid War Voices from Palestine 1890s–1948* (London: Pimlico, 2010), 214.
13 For instance, Ben-Gurion in a speech from 6 February 1948 in [Hebrew] Meir Avizohar and Avi Bareli (editors), *Now or Never Proceeding of Mapai (The Labour Party of Eretz-Israel) in the closing year of the British Mandate Introductions and Documents* (Beit Berl: Ayanot, 1989), 307–310.
14 A similar propensity for violence and expressions of anti-Jewish bias can be found in some units of the 6th Airborne Division during the preceding period when the main threat was Jewish terrorism.
15 The figures in this chapter are all commercial postcards depicting their purchasers' versions of the views of Palestine.

Appendix A
British military journals

The Antelope (The Royal Warwicksire Regiment).
The Annals of the King's Royal Rifle Corps.
The Borderers' Chronicle (The King's Own Scottish Borderers).
The Die Hards. The Journal of the Middlesex Regiment.
The "Faugh-a-Ballagh". The Regimental Gazette of the Royal Irish Fusiliers.
4th/7th Royal Dragoon Guards Regimental Magazine.
1st Battalion the Irish Guards *Newsletter.*
The Globe and Laurel (Royal Marines).
The Gunner.
The Household Brigade Magazine.
Journal of the Royal United Services Institute.
The Kingsman – The Journal of the King's Regiment.
The King's Royal Rifle Corps Chronicle.
The Roussillon Gazette Journal of the Royal Sussex Regiment.
The Royal Engineers Journal.
2nd Battalion. The Royal Lincolnshire Regiment *Monthly News Letter.*
Soldier. The British Army Magazine.
The Suffolk Regimental Gazette.
The Tank.
The Thin red Line. Regimental Journal of the Argyll and Sutherland Highlanders.
3rd The King's Own Hussars Journal
The White Lancer and the Vedette (17th/21st Lancers).

Appendix B
British military archives

Argyll and Sutherland Highlanders Archive, Stirling Castle, Scotland.
Coldstream Guards Archive, Wellington Barracks, London.
Imperial War Museum, London.
Irish Guards Archive, Wellington Barracks, London.
King's Own Scottish Borderers Regiment Archive, Berwick-upon-Tweed.
Liddell Hart Centre, King's College, London.
The Middlesex Regiment, The National Army Museum.
Royal Artillery Archive, Woolwich.
Royal Engineers Archive, Gillingham.
Royal Irish Fusiliers Archive, Armagh.
Royal Lincolnshire Regiment, Lincolnshire County Archives, Lincolnshire.
17th/21st Lancers Archive, Lancer House, Grantham.
The Tank Museum, Bovington, Warham.
The National Archive (TNA).

Index

Note: Page numbers followed by "n" refer to notes.